A Systems Perspective of Parenting

The Individual, the Family, and the Social Network

Thomas W. Roberts

Appalachian State University

Brooks/Cole Publishing Company
Pacific Grove, California

I(T)P ™
The trademark ITP is used under license.

Brooks/Cole Publishing Company
A Division of Wadsworth, Inc.

© 1994 by Wadsworth, Inc., Belmont, California 94002. All rights reserved. No part of this book may be reproduced, stored in a retrieval system, or transcribed, in any form or by any means—electronic, mechanical, photocopying, recording, or otherwise—without the prior written permission of the publisher, Brooks/Cole Publishing Company, Pacific Grove, California 93950, a division of Wadsworth, Inc.

Printed in the United States of America
10 9 8 7 6 5 4 3 2 1

Library of Congress Cataloging-in-Publication Data

Roberts, Thomas W.
    A systems perspective of parenting : the individual, the family, and the social network / Thomas W. Roberts.
        p. cm.
    Includes bibliographical references and index.
    ISBN 0-534-15546-4
    1. Parenting. 2. System theory. I. Title.
HQ755.8.R615 1994
306.874—dc20
                                              93-41870
                                            CIP

Sponsoring Editor: Vicki Knight
Editorial Associate: Lauri Banks Ataide
Production Coordinator: Fiorella Ljunggren
Production: Greg Hubit Bookworks
Manuscript Editor: Margaret Moore
Permissions Editor: Elaine Jones
Interior Design: Wendy Calmenson
Cover Design: Sharon L. Kinghan
Cover Photo: Tib/West, David Hamilton
Art and Photo Coordinator: Greg Hubit
Interior Illustration: Susan Benoit
Typesetting: ColorType, Inc.
Cover Printing: Color Dot Graphics, Inc.
Printing and Binding: Arcata Graphics/Fairfield
(Credits continue on p. 402.)

For Spencer and Kara

Brief Contents

Contents

■ **Chapter 7   Parenting the School-Age Child
from 6 to 12 Years Old**   **206**

■ **Chapter 12   A Systems Perspective of Family Violence**   **370**

In the past decade, the systems paradigm has become the dominant approach in marriage and family therapy. Numerous texts are available that describe the systems approach to therapy for many dysfunctions traditionally viewed as caused by, and residing in, the individual. However, although the systems paradigm has been acknowledged for therapeutic interventions, broader applications of it to subjects such as parent/child relations and the understanding of normal family behavior, have not been developed. In fact, to date there is not a single text available on parenting from a systems perspective, although several recent books contain chapters on parenting from a systems perspective.

The purpose of this book is to develop a systems model of parenting in the normal family—that is, a model that applies to the normal family life cycle rather than to clinical or dysfunctional families. This model, referred to as the systems/dialectical model, views the total ecosystem affecting the behavior of humans as composed of three autonomous and interdependent subsystems—the individual, the family, and the social network—and considers child behavior problems as the outcome of the interaction of these subsystems. It is a model that integrates individual developmental psychology, family life-cycle development, dialectical psychology, and systems theory. Besides this model, other systemic approaches describing social behavior through the interdependence of subsystems are important topics of discussion in this text.

The need for a textbook on parenting from the family systems perspective is illustrated by the number of recent research articles emphasizing the importance of family dynamics in the parent/child relationship. The family unit has been redefined as a unit of co-developing persons embedded in a larger context. This redefinition of the family is correlated with the proliferation of parent-education programs, which emphasize the importance of the participation of all family members for successful change.

Audience

This textbook is designed for university courses on parenting and other family-relations courses at both the undergraduate and the graduate level. The book can be used in such interdisciplinary fields as psychology, counseling, child development, and sociology.

Organization of the Book

Chapter 1 presents a systems perspective of parenting and clarifies the issues related to parenting from both a theoretical and a practical standpoint. Chapter 2 develops a model for child development based on systems concepts. Chapter 3 critiques common parent-education theories and briefly describes how a parent-education program may be implemented from a systems perspective. Chapters 4 through 8 discuss the systems/dialectical model of parenting through the family life cycle. More specifically, Chapter 4 includes such issues as the marital relationship, the decision to have a child, and fatherhood and motherhood. Chapter 5 discusses toddlerhood, focusing on self-help skills, self-control, language development, play, and parent/child interaction. The chapter also discusses the unique use of play as a means of guiding and directing the child's behavior. Chapter 6 addresses the development of self-esteem, morality, and parent/child relationships and introduces the use of storytelling as a disciplinary technique. Chapter 7 discusses intellectual development, developmental tasks, school as a system, social development, and parent/child relationships. Early and late adolescence are discussed in Chapter 8; two of the topics highlighted here are differentiation from the family of origin and problematic adolescent behavior. Chapter 9 focuses on parenting in the single-parent family and the remarried family. Chapter 10 reviews literature on parenting from different cultural perspectives. Chapter 11 applies the systems/dialectical model to the task of parenting the exceptional child. In the final chapter, the model addresses the issue of family violence.

Each chapter begins with the presentation of a current myth about parenting that is generally accepted as correct but has largely negative consequences. The content of the chapter is designed to correct the myth by replacing it with a more adaptive proposition about parenting, which is stated at the end of the chapter. Following the myth is a set of true/false questions that test the students' knowledge before reading the chapter. Toward the end of each chapter is a "Family Portrait" section, which is a case example based on the chapter content, followed by a compare/contrast discussion of ways to resolve the family's problems according to a systems/dialectical model and other approaches. Answers to the true/false questions, a list of key concepts, and study questions appear at the end of each chapter.

Acknowledgments

Many people have contributed to the writing of this book. First, I would like to thank Mark Francisco, sales representative for Brooks/Cole, who asked me in a casual conversation if I had an idea for a book. At the time I was teaching a survey course in parent/child relations at Western Kentucky University and was unable to find a suitable text that covered systems concepts. Two friends and colleagues, Dr. Delbert Hayden and Louella Fong, encouraged me to develop the systems approach to parenting and shared their ideas on systemic parenting. This led to my writing an article that was published in *Family Science Review* with the help of then-editor Geoffrey Leigh. The article, which became the prototype for this book, was critically answered by Gary W. Peterson in the same edition of *Family Science Review,* and I responded to Peterson's article in the next edition of the journal. This debate on the systems perspective of parenting helped me think through and develop my position.

I would like to offer special thanks to Vicki Knight, Managing Editor at Brooks/Cole, and the entire Brooks/Cole staff for their patience and thoughtful suggestions. I also wish to thank Cathy Lewis of Western Kentucky University for her assistance in preparing some of the manuscript and to Glenda Hubbard of Appalachian State University for her editorial suggestions on parts of the manuscript. In addition, I wish to acknowledge the following professionals who read and made extensive comments on the manuscript: Debra L. Berke of the University of Delaware, Linda Dannison of Western Michigan University, Jackie Gray of the University of North Carolina at Greensboro, Mary S. Link of Miami University, Philip Newman, Bernita Quoss of the University of Wyoming, and James Slavik of Eastern Illinois University.

It would be remiss if I failed to mention family and friends whose support made it possible for me to have the time I needed to research and write this book. Most especially, I wish to thank my wife, Karen, who sacrificed some of her own interests in order to fill in for me in parenting our two children, Spencer and Kara, during the writing of this book.

Thomas W. Roberts

Chapter 1

A Systems Perspective of Parenting

Parenting Myth ■ Parenting myths are unfounded beliefs about parenting that large numbers of people share. Each chapter begins with a common unfounded belief about parenting. In the course of the chapter, a more informed view of parenting is presented. Each chapter concludes with a more adequate statement or proposition about parenting that reflects the material covered in the preceding discussion.

Misbehavior in children represents an internal process. Attempts to bring about change should focus on the child's noncompliant behavior rather than on the child's interaction with others.

Test Your Knowledge ■ The following questions are designed to test your knowledge before reading the material in this chapter. The answers appear at the end of the chapter.

1 First-order change and second-order change are essentially the same, except that first-order change must come before second-order change. True or false?

2 Circular causality refers to a reciprocal process without a specific beginning or end. True or false?

3 Family homeostasis implies that stable families are functional. True or false?

4 A systems perspective of parenting considers the context in which the behavior occurs as important as the behavior itself. True or false?

5 From a systems perspective, a child's misbehavior may be related to the child's being above the parent in the family hierarchy. True or false?

6 Family rules are usually known to and acknowledged by all family members. True or false?

Over the past several decades a paradigm shift has occurred in the conceptualization and treatment of family problems. *Paradigm* refers to a set of beliefs or presuppositions that explain reality and determine both the issues worthy of scientific investigation and the methods appropriate for researching those issues (Becvar & Becvar, 1988). When a paradigm answers most of the questions posed by reality, it is described as *normal science* (Kuhn, 1970). During periods of crisis, when the paradigm fails to provide satisfactory answers to questions posed through scientific investigation, a **paradigm shift** occurs. This period of uncertainty regarding an established paradigm is referred to as *extraordinary science* (Kuhn, 1970). This period of extraordinary science is replaced by a new paradigm, which in turn leads to a period of normal science. In time the new paradigm will be subjected to inquiries and fail to provide adequate answers, therefore giving way to another period of extraordinary science in a paradigm shift to a new paradigm.

Before the 1940s the dominant paradigm both in human development and in therapy focused on individual, or intrapsychic, causes. The early part of the 1990s was dominated by Freud's (1955, 1959) theory, which focused on the emotional problems that develop within the individual as a result of unresolved conflicts from childhood. Although these early family conflicts were viewed as having tremendous impact on a person's adult behavior, the dynamics of the family were never considered important in the therapeutic process. Essentially, Freud saw an individual's early family relationships as the cause of problems in adult life.

Viewing the individual as a misfit within his/her family or social environment, **intrapsychic therapists** attempted to change the person's response to others. The goal of therapy was to help the individual become more functional in daily activities and interpersonal relationships. Not only did most therapists using this model fail to achieve this goal, but for a significant period of time, they separated the patient from his/her social environment through extended hospitalizations. Hospitalized patients returning home to family relationships frequently needed to be rehospitalized, only to improve in the hospital and deteriorate again after discharge.

Beginning in the 1940s a number of influential family therapists have maintained that the formation and maintenance of behavior patterns by family members have reciprocal effects on all members (Ackerman, 1966; Bateson, 1974; Bell, 1961; Bowen, 1978; Haley, 1973, 1976; Jackson, 1959; Lidz & Lidz, 1949; S. Minuchin, 1974, 1984; Satir, 1964, 1972; Whitaker, 1975; Wynne, 1970). The paradigm shift in therapy has focused less on individual dynamics: the individual is not seen as emotionally or mentally ill; rather, he/she is believed to have an implicit and operative function for the entire family. A more inclusive view is taken of the formation and maintenance of problems. Individual problems are considered to be the product of **recursive,** or recurring, **feedback loops** including both the family and the larger society. As a result of this paradigm shift, the therapist includes both the nuclear and the extended family members in therapy sessions. In fact, some systems therapists insist on the presence of these extended-family members even if they must travel a great distance to attend therapy sessions (Napier & Whitaker, 1978).

During this same period of time, theories of human development began to shift toward an interactional, or contextual, approach (Belsky, 1984; Bronfenbrenner,

1979; Ford, 1987; Lerner, 1988; Nesselroade & von Eye, 1985) (see Chapter 2). In an interactional, or contextual, approach to development, the focus shifts from the psychological level to the multilevel dimensions of development. The developing child is understood from his/her interaction with parents, siblings, and the family's cultural ties. The individual not only is shaped by this interaction but also shapes the environment so that both change.

The contextual approach most often has been associated with a life-span perspective of development (Lerner & Kauffman, 1985). A life-span view of development suggests that life stages, such as childhood and adulthood, must be studied as interactive parts of a process rather than as separate entities. Development is viewed across the total life span and across different generations as they move through time. And culture, instead of being considered a mere backdrop for development, is seen as a dynamic force that develops and changes along with the individual.

Whereas the paradigm shift in marriage and family therapy and human development theories has moved toward a normal science stance, no family systems perspective has been developed for other family issues. These areas are primarily concerned with normal family development such as parenting, the development of intimacy and love, and attachment behavior. Parenting models still tend to see the child's behavior—rather than the context in which the child is embedded—as problematic (see Chapter 3).

Perhaps a major reason why a systems approach has not been applied to parenting lies in the root of the systems approach. Systems theory provides a broad or general orientation, but does not give specific answers. Unfortunately, one test of modern theories has been the criterion that it be specifically applied in a kind of "cookbook" manner, particularly in parenting. To date, not a single textbook is available on parenting from a systems perspective.

The purpose of this book is to develop a model for parenting from a systems perspective. This model is intended to be broad enough, yet specifically applied to parent/child relations, to encompass the various disciplines related to parenting, including developmental psychology, child development, sociology, and family science. Although these disciplines represent various paradigms, a systems, or interactional, perspective frequently appears in the literature of each discipline. This book consolidates and integrates these concepts under a systems paradigm.

The systems perspective in this book reflects the generic development of general systems theory applied to the family. The writings of Ludwig von Bertalanffy (1952, 1968a, 1968b) are important in the early application of systems theory to parenting. His writings are sometimes ignored by family theorists when applying systems theory to families. In writing this book, I was tempted to simply review the application of systems concepts by family therapists and then apply it to normal family development and parenting. While to some extent that was done, an integration of the aforementioned disciplines was considered most important.

A number of premises are important in applying a systems perspective to parenting. First, the application of systems concepts in parenting must include **individual development**. The contribution the individual makes to the present situation is rarely developed in a systems paradigm. Individual differences noted in the child development literature generally have not been addressed in parenting models. Child development literature over the past several decades indicates that children differ from birth on a number of variables, including temperament, level of activity, and responsiveness to surroundings (Korner et al., 1985; Thomas & Chess, 1977). These individual characteristics operate in a circular or reciprocal manner: family members interact with each other and the social context. This resultant interactional focus means that the total social network must be considered when discussing individual behavior.

Second, although the family is the primary social unit in understanding the behaviors of its members, the larger social network, including school and peer relationships, must be considered. The peer network and school network play a large part in the interactional pattern of the family by increasing the number of interactive variables. Further, the family's place in society—its cultural ties with the larger society—may significantly impact the interactional patterns within the family. Ignoring the larger social network may give more importance to the family unit than it deserves. For example, a bad relationship with a teacher may contribute more to a particular child's school performance than the home environment.

Third, as emphasized by Bertalanffy (1968a), individuals live in a symbolic world that includes more than the present context. Among these symbols are language, art, religion, and even history. Bertalanffy viewed this symbolic system as a major contribution to normal and abnormal behavior. For Bertalanffy, problematic behavior resulted in a breakdown in the symbolic system. For example, misbehavior in a child may reflect a family system in which current symbols no longer meaningfully represent experiences. While the child does not cognitively understand this circumstance, the misbehavior may be a way to grapple with the family's loss of meaningful symbols.

Humans live in a world of symbolic reality rather than objective reality according to Bertalanffy (1968a). **Objective reality** refers to facts and events, whereas **symbolic reality** refers to one's subjective experience of the world through symbols that stand for real objects. Although stress may be related to emotional illness, the more plausible explanation for such illness according to Bertalanffy is that symbols in modern societies are no longer meaningful. The loss of shared meaningful symbols impedes the individual from participation in the common human experience.

Fourth, the individual lives in two worlds simultaneously, the symbolic just mentioned, and the biological. The biological aspects of human nature for the most part have been ignored in the family systems literature. Parenting models have generally neglected biological or physiological explorations and considerations in explaining the causes of problems within families. Consequently, the physical or biological contributions have been explained in other terms. Recently, a new emphasis has emerged that not only recognizes the contributions of biology but also suggests the need to incorporate this dimension in systems thought (Doherty, 1990). This new approach, referred to as the **bio-psychosocial model,** emphasizes the role biological or physiological factors may play in certain marital or family problems and, concomitantly, the role these problem interactions may play in individual physical disorders. The inclusion of biological factors of behavior in parenting would focus on certain genetic characteristics some children possess that affect parenting. Such biological or genetic differences continue through a person's lifetime and are important corollaries to interaction.

■ Principles of Family Systems Theory

This section of the chapter presents the basic principles of **general systems theory** as applied to family interaction. It is followed by a section that relates systems theory specifically to parenting. The final section discusses a case that illustrates the concepts presented in the chapter.

Wholeness

According to Bertalanffy (1968a), a *system* is "complexes of elements standing in interaction," which means that in all human organizations there is an underlying pattern or structure. The characteristic of **wholeness** in a system is defined as an integrated entity that is more than the sum of its independent parts. Because the various parts of the system are interdependent and have a repeatable pattern, to separate them into parts would undermine the functional capacity of the system. One cannot understand a family by simply describing individual members. All families are tied together in ways that render individual explanations for behavior unintelligible.

Two individuals in a relationship must consider not only their individual characteristics but also the relationship itself (Becvar & Becvar, 1988). Complexity in the system is increased as children are added to the system and the larger social network. For example, when a child is added to the family, a natural triangle may form. The mother may be closer to the infant in the early months, and, consequently, the father may feel left out. The father's feeling left out and depressed, however, is a family circumstance that involves the mother and the infant.

This systems analysis of parent/child relationships in terms of the whole rather than the sum of the parts means that a change in any one member will effect change in the other members. For example, the father probably will have to do more child care and work around the house when the mother returns to work.

Family Rules

A family is a social group organized or governed by a repeatable set of rules (Jackson, 1965a). **Family rules** clarify and regulate family interactions and may be derived from a particular culture or passed down from one generation to the next. They are referred to as normative because they define closeness and distance between members, regulate how families allocate resources, and determine the division of power within the family (Burr, Day, & Bahr, 1993).

■ *To understand individual behavior in this family, the interdependence of family members must be analyzed.*

For Jackson (1965a), rules determine not only present interaction but also future interaction within the family. Soon after marrying, the couple establishes guidelines for their communication that determine how they will interact over time. Jackson's term for marital interaction, quid pro quo, suggests that the marital relationship is based on an equal exchange of something for something.

After the couple has children, family interactions become more complex. Jackson (1965b) described this developing pattern as a redundancy principle because the observation of families suggests that instead of using a wide range of options in responding to one another, family members tend to use the same options over and over again. A particular family therefore does not use all the alternatives in communicating that are open to them. In order to understand a particular family, one must understand and analyze the rules governing that family's interaction patterns. Family health or family dysfunction are related to the redundant interactional patterns. These family rules are ultimately governed by family meta-rules, "which typically take the form of unstated family directives offering principles for interpreting rules, as well as family rules for changing rules" (Goldenberg & Goldenberg, 1991).

The redundancy pattern of rules, defined as non-normative rules, refers to rules that govern communication between family members over a period of time (Burr et al., 1993). Although members may not be aware of the particular patterns that recur, every interaction is governed by them. For example, the morning routine of getting children off to school takes a particular sequence. In the Johnson family, the mother arises first and puts the coffee pot on, then she calls her husband, who rolls out of bed for ten minutes of exercise. At the completion of his exercise, the father takes a shower and rouses their 6-year-old son. The family then eats breakfast together, and father and son finish dressing. The mother takes her shower while the father drives the son to school and continues on to work. While no one in the family is aware of the rule governing getting to work and school in the mornings, it serves to maintain order and stability.

In parenting, when an individual expects that certain roles be performed, a set of rules accompany those expectations. For example, a father may see himself as a disciplinarian, while a mother sees herself as a nurturer. When these roles are rigid and do not vary, both spouses may be disappointed in the other's behavior. The wife may criticize the husband for not being as nurturing, while the husband may criticize the wife for not providing discipline.

Rigid family rules complement the development of relationship roles in families. Family roles appear to have a complementary mechanism whereby one member behaves in one way while another member may develop behavior in an opposite or complementary manner. This complementary mechanism may operate between a couple in such a way as to demand cooperation from both, though neither would recognize or admit their collaboration (Scarf, 1987). For example, when Bill and Mary married they played opposite roles in the relationship. Because he was away from home during the week, Mary took the caretaker role and Bill took the role of disciplinarian. Although initially this arrangement was helpful in creating a structure for and maintaining continuity in role behavior, over time it created problems for Bill and Mary in that neither was satisfied with the other's performance. In complementary parenting, each parent becomes overresponsible in a particular area. Both parents are set up to displease and ultimately fail. Bill as the overresponsive disciplinarian accuses Mary of not doing her job, but she makes sure he does not succeed by criticizing his performance or by aligning with their child against him.

This pattern, once established, is hard to modify (Osborne, 1989). Each parent attempts to change by doing more of the same, but the net result is to further intensify and solidify their pattern. This dividing of competencies into complementary behavior is like disowning certain traits and projecting them on to the other parent. For example, Mary does not want to discipline but has difficulty accepting the discipline Bill hands out to their child. Her rejection of his discipline is actually the disowning of a part of herself.

Family Boundaries

Family boundaries are the physical and emotional barriers that distinguish individuals and families and regulate the amount of contact occurring among them (see Figure 1.1). Physical boundaries may include a family member's favorite chair or a room that others do not use. Emotional boundaries regulate the amount of closeness and distance within the family through creating a subsystem of family members that includes some members and excludes other members. (S. Minuchin, 1974). The formation and maintenance of subsystems within the family are necessary in order for

Rigid boundary   Clear boundary   Diffuse boundary

Figure 1.1 ■ Family boundaries.   (From S. Minuchin, *Families and family therapy.* Cambridge, MA: Harvard University Press, 1974.)

adequate relationships to develop. The three subsystems in the family are the spousal, the parental, and the sibling (S. Minuchin, 1974). The spousal subsystem refers to the marital bond between the husband and wife; the parental subsystem refers to their duties and responsibilities as parents. The sibling subsystem refers to the relationship among siblings.

Montgomery and Fewer (1988) have challenged the concept of boundaries in a critique of systems theory. They view the concept of boundary as being imprecise and having many different meanings in the literature. As a result, they recommend substituting the term *relative openness* for the term *boundary* because they believe relative openness is not contaminated by different meanings and refers specifically to the degree of permeability, or openness, in the system. While Montgomery and Fewer make helpful and interesting insights about systems theory, the term *boundary* has been retained in this book. To substitute relative openness for boundary does not clarify the family experience being labeled. It seems that the concept of relative openness could itself refer to a variety of family experiences. This book uses the concept of boundary to refer specifically to elements that form unity and separateness among individuals and regulate the amount of interpersonal contact.

The three types of boundaries depicted in Figure 1.1 represent different ways of relating among family members. Clear boundaries are physical, mental, or emotional barriers that allow for adaptation and change. Rigid boundaries restrict adaptation and change. Diffuse boundaries allow for too much change and adaptation.

The issue of family boundaries is primarily one of togetherness versus separateness. Every family must address how close or distant members are because this configuration determines how members interact and how much interaction is allowed outside the family. Families that forego extrafamilial involvement for close contact among members may be characterized as closed where much of one's life is controlled by the family. The part of a person's life not controlled by the family would be seen as threatening to other family members. This overemphasis on togetherness creates "fusion," which results from a person not being able to separate from the family emotional system. A person who is most unable to differentiate will be most susceptible to emotional problems (Bowen, 1978).

The opposite end from togetherness is the separateness of individuals from one another (Osborne, 1989). Family members separated from one another are generally "emotionally cut off" but not truly differentiated (Bowen, 1978). Separateness is usually attempted by distance, or avoiding the presence of others. As long as the distance is maintained, one can boast of not being controlled or manipulated by significant others. The painful truth of lack of emotional differentiation is felt, however, as soon as one must come into close contact with the other person or persons. Relationships characterized by distance are as fused as those reactive, overinvolved relationships.

Family Hierarchy

Families have an organized structure within which their members assume roles and carry out responsibilities. From a systems perspective, normal families are viewed as being organized **hierarchically,** regulated by the generations (Haley, 1976). The implication for parenting is that families are not democratic in the sense that power is equal across generations. Parents are in the executive position of leadership in the family, and children are in a subordinate position. Although complete equality of power between parents is very difficult to achieve, a sharing of parental power keeps both parents involved with children.

In the leadership role, parents make decisions affecting the safety and security of all members. They must monitor activities that members are involved in to determine the potential for danger. For example, when a family is planning to take a trip in a snowstorm, children may not consider or even understand the danger involved. Taking blankets, flashlights, candles, a rope, and some food may never enter the mind of a child. In such situations, parents must assume the leadership role without deferring to or asking the advice of a child.

Some other types of daily behavior, such as TV watching, doing homework, eating meals, and going to bed, usually are regulated by the parents. While these parental decisions should not be rigid and unyielding, parents must at least have veto power in order to ensure consistent patterns of behavior. The amount of parental involvement in these decisions may vary relative to the age and maturity level of the child.

There are, of course, other types of decisions that can be made by the family as a group or left to children to make. For example, family activities or vacations, a child's preference for toys, and the celebration of certain holidays should be decided upon through the family interaction process. Relationships with extended kin and friends usually are seen as individual decisions, except where parents perceive that those relationships would be harmful.

Three types of family hierarchy are shown in Figure 1.2a. In the authoritative style of parenting, both parents have fairly equal authority. Healthy families appear to share roles, however, and the parents may change roles with the children "as if" the children were in an executive position in the family (Whitaker & Keith, 1981). For example, the father may say to the 5-year-old son, "You be the dad and set the table, and I'll be the kid and complain." This play, or "as if" dimension, in family relations allows for flexibility in family relationships. In authoritarian parenting, the child is not allowed to give input into decision making—the parents always set the rules. On the other hand, laissez-faire parents, who let children decide for themselves, take too

(a) Styles

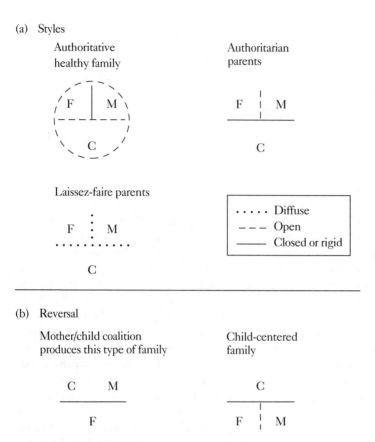

Figure 1.2 ■ **Family hierarchy.**

little control because they fear they will lose compliance from the child. The end result of parents failing to take the executive position and not maintaining a firm but warm boundary between themselves and their child or children is a confused family hierarchy in which children may misbehave in order to force the establishment of parenting authority. A vicious circle can develop and be perpetuated in that the more the parents resist taking the authoritative position—which is a balance between the authoritarian and lassiez-faire positions—the more the child persists in misbehavior.

A breakdown in the hierarchy occurs when a parent forms a cross-generational coalition with a child (S. Minuchin, 1974). In a cross-generational coalition, one parent is closer to a child or children than is the other parent. The child in this situation becomes confused about his/her proper role in the family. Likewise, the excluded parent has questions about his/her place in the family becoming, perhaps, accustomed to the peripheral position. Neither parent is able to discipline a child in a preferred position with one of the parents. The distant parent is neutralized by the close parent, and the close parent fails to set limits unless the child freely acquiesces.

Finally, as shown in Figure 1.2b, some families have a complete reversal where the child is in charge of the family. In these families, frequently referred to as child-centered families (Bowen, 1978), the child controls relationships in the family. The child, while enjoying his/her position in the hierarchy, is really looking for parental structure. One can assume that children with chronic misbehavior problems are members of families with hierarchical imbalances.

Family Homeostasis

The concept of **homeostasis**, a hallmark of general systems theory, assumes that a system attempts to maintain stability in the midst of frequent internal and external changes to the system. A system exchanges information with the environment through a continuous feedback loop, which is the evaluation of feedback by family members that leads to attempts to change the family in ways that will change the feedback. The homeostatic process, dynamic and ever changing, attempts to keep information from the environment in check without causing great distress within the system. For example, the fact that the father's job may be phased out in the next few months may create an increase in stress within the family that upsets the family's sense of well-being, or balance. Family members may express this increase of stress through an inability to discuss issues rationally or an increase in the father's con-sumption of alcohol. When the family is able to discuss issues rationally again or the father reduces his alcohol intake, the family can be said to return to normal, or homeostasis.

In parenting behavior, homeostatic balance is sought when a parent intervenes to stop two children from fighting over the same toy. Parental intervention aims to re-store equilibrium in the system. The misbehavior of the child, resulting from the interactional pattern in the family rather than the child's independent behavior, may represent an escalation in the feedback loop, signaling a need for a return to equilibrium.

In the past, family researchers tended to describe the homeostatic model as simi-lar to the thermostat on the home heating and cooling system. In order to maintain the temperature at a certain level, the thermostat must alternately cause the heat or cooling to be activated. When applied to the family, this model meant that family members behaved in ways that maintained balance in the same way the thermostat operated to maintain temperature. When stress reached a certain level of intensity, family members attempted to return things to the previous level of homeostasis, or steady state.

This thermostatic view of homeostasis in the family has been challenged by a number of family researchers (Dell, 1982; Hoffman, 1981; Montgomery & Fewer, 1988). Dell believes that the concept of homeostasis implies that one part of the sys-tem has a function for the system that was caused by something outside the system. For example, to say that a child's misbehavior stabilizes a family and keeps it in a steady state as the concept of homeostasis does, tends to imply dualism in that the child has properties or traits which do not depend on the child's familial context. In place of homeostasis, Dell substitutes the concept of coherence, or "fit," suggesting that all behavior within the family occurs as a consequence of the interactions among members. According to this view, a true systemic view of the family, therefore, must demonstrate circular causality rather than see one part of the system responsible for other parts (Hoffman, 1981).

This criticism of the traditional view of the family as a homeostatic system has been referred to as the "new epistemology." Epistemology refers to how we know something. The proponents of the new epistemology believe strongly in a circular paradigm of causality. They suggest that increasing stress until new solutions and a homeostatic balance can be found would benefit families who are experiencing instability. Consequently, the family is always forming new homeostatic levels rather than reinstating a previous stability.

The preceding criticisms of homeostasis seem more window dressing than real. Salvador Minuchin (1974), who bases his theory on homeostasis, for example, develops his model of change in exactly the manner referred to by the new epistemologists; namely, stress demands a new level of homeostasis and reorganization at a different level than before. Moreover, the argument advancing the need to replace the term *homeostasis* with *coherence* is like throwing the baby out with the bath water. Homeostasis has been applied to a number of child development theories (Piaget, 1926) as well as adult development through the life cycle (Carter & McGoldrick, 1989).

Using the term *coherence* in place of *homeostasis* may also be problematic. Coherence (Dell, 1982) implies a structural determinism: the structure determines the outcome of how one family member responds to another family member. A member of a system behaves according to the context and can respond only from its repertoire of behaviors. According to Dell, the response of a person to a particular event is coherent in that the response "fits," or is consistent with, the behavior repertoire of that person in that context. This type of argument—that a person behaves in a certain way because that is the way he/she is—is a tautology. To say that a person's behavior fits the context says nothing about the dynamic process or interactional components of the behavior. Furthermore, it would be difficult to explain the experience of novelty or spontaneous behavior from the concept of coherence.

The position taken in this book, as will be discussed in greater detail in Chapter 2, is the development of the concept of homeostasis/morphogenesis as the basic paradigm for child development and adult development through the family life cycle. This homeostasis/morphogenesis model includes individual biological aspects, family interactional patterns, and the larger social context. An individual's behavior within the family is a complex intertwining of these various aspects of the total **social network** through its homeostatic and morphogenic functions. As such, the context for one individual may vary with the context of another within the same family. The misbehavior of a child in this perspective would be much more complex than simply focusing on the parent/child dyad. The entire social network must be analyzed and understood as it contributes to the child's behavior.

Family Communication and Feedback Loops

A systems perspective recognizes the importance of communication and the processing of information through feedback loops (Watzlawick, Beavin, & Jackson, 1967). With a family system, communication occurs continuously through both verbal and nonverbal interactions. Feedback loops refer to the mechanism by which these interactions occur and are maintained. Feedback is the mechanism by which a family maintains its homeostasis while monitoring the system and making adjustments (Goldenberg & Goldenberg, 1991).

Such daily activities as brushing teeth, going to bed, and watching TV are monitored through feedback loops that occur routinely. As long as these automatic activities occur as usual, not much attention is drawn to them. Some feedback, however, may signal that something new has been introduced into the system. This new feedback may cause the system to expand toward new and adaptive behavior or toward chaotic behavior.

There are generally two types of feedback, negative and positive. Negative feedback tends to dampen the input and reduce the potential for change, thus returning to an equilibrium. Positive feedback amplifies the original input and leads to more rapid change in the system (Constantine, 1986). Negative feedback is not necessarily more desirable than positive feedback. These two feedback loops simply serve two necessary functions for the family: one loop functions to maintain equilibrium, and the other loop functions to facilitate change. How a family uses these two types of feedback may depend more on the "degree of calibration"—that is, how much deviation the family would allow (Goldenberg & Goldenberg, 1991, p. 43). For example, in responding to the misbehavior of a child, the parents' degree of calibration may determine both when to intervene and how much intervention to do.

The main function of feedback loops in the family system is to act as a self-corrective mechanism (Becvar & Becvar, 1988). These feedback loops keep the system stable but able to change. Although the function of feedback loops is self-corrective, the system is never static; rather, it maintains itself by being able to change and adapt as needed. The constant flow from the environment and back again is never conducive to sameness, even though homeostasis may be maintained (see Figure 1.3).

The reality of this constant process of change and adaptability is evident as the family moves through their life cycle and makes adaptations as needed (Becvar & Becvar, 1988). For example, parents who persist in using parenting strategies for adolescents that were useful for preschool children will discover rebellious and uncooperative children. New parenting strategies are needed at different stages of the family life cycle. Positive feedback operates during time of adaptation to change and maintains the system in times of little overt change.

Family Morphogenesis

While homeostasis has been applied to family dynamics as previously noted, an equally important concept, morphogenesis, has received little attention in the literature. **Morphogenesis** refers to changes that take place within systems. Functional

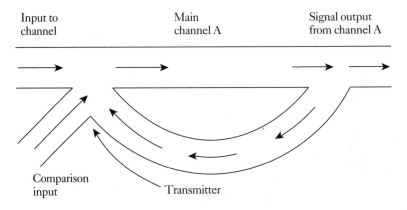

| Input to channel | Main channel A | Signal output from channel A |

Comparison input   Transmitter

Negative input recirculates as additional input and acts as a control or correcting activity of the input from channel A.

Figure 1.3 ■ Communication loop. (From J. G. Miller, *Living systems.* New York: McGraw-Hill, 1978, p. 36.)

systems are characterized by both stability and change. A system, therefore, cannot be characterized as representing either a steady state or constant change, but as operating within a constant dynamic tension between stability and change (Becvar & Becvar, 1988).

When a family is experiencing a new situation, such as transition from one life stage to another, the control function that allows the family to respond appropriately is referred to as morphogenesis. Periods of transitions in the family life cycle particularly must be met with appropriate morphogenetic or change responses. Other unexpected changes in the family, such as illness or financial difficulties, may also demand a reorganization of the family structure. This balance in morphogenesis and **morphostasis,** or homeostasis, is viewed as dynamic in that the process is in constant flux.

■ Issues Related to Systems Theory

Systems theory provides a unique way of understanding family dynamics. The preceding principles challenge cause-and-effect explanations for family interaction, including parent/child relations. Below is a discussion of issues raised by applying a systems paradigm to family interaction and parenting.

Circular Causality

Linear thinking has been a dominant theme in our society. The old paradigm of individual and family process was based on a linear, or one-way, view of reality. According

■ *A linear view of parent/child relations assumes that the child is bad and the child's misbehavior must be corrected by the parent.*

to the concept of **linear causality,** anything can be understood if the chain of events is known and it is possible to predict what is likely to happen in the future because outcomes tend to recur from similar causes. Causality in a system is viewed as circular rather than linear.

The new systems paradigm posits a recursive, or circular, view of causation in that X and Y are both antecedents to one another. In the old paradigm, X would cause Y in a unidirectional model of cause and effect. As depicted in Figure 1.4, circular causality does not reside at a beginning point or an ending point but rather is seen at the interface between individuals or systems (Bateson, 1970).

In a family system, the concept of **circular causality** means that outcomes result from indeterminant aspects of family living. The behavior of any family member is related to the behavior of other family members. This complexity is increased when one considers the larger social systems in which the family is embedded. Being able to predict the outcome of any event is difficult given the complexity of the recursive nature of interactions (Becvar & Becvar, 1988).

In parent/child relations, theorists simplify this complexity by focusing on one side of the interactional process. Most often they focus on the child's behavior first of all as needing changing, and on the parent's role in changing the child's behavior. This

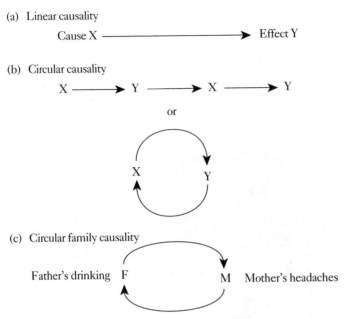

Father's drinking and mother's headaches are mutually causal.

Figure 1.4 ■ Linear causality and circular causality.

way of viewing the parent/child relationship is at the very heart of a linear system that fails to explain the overall process of interaction. The ecosystem—the community or environment surrounding a family unit—would be fragmented by reducing the interaction to a cause-and-effect formula. A child's misbehavior is much more complex than the simple view that it results from poor parenting techniques. For example, misbehavior in the child represents a total ecosystem that includes relationships with extended kin, friends, and parents. All of these relationships are embedded within a particular social and cultural setting.

Viewing parent/child interactions as circular causality forces a revision in the way parents and parent educators address some parenting problems. The following is an example of the need to consider the entire context of an event rather than look at the event as a cause-and-effect situation.

> Mrs. Smith was a foster parent who was participating in a program for difficult to place foster children. She was an extremely successful single parent whose own children were away at college despite the financial poverty that characterized their neighborhood. Moreover, the neighborhood children regarded Mrs. Smith with great affection and spent many hours playing at her home. Her foster child, James, had experienced considerable abuse and neglect from his chemically dependent mother. One day, while watching Saturday morning wrestling on television, James "accidentally" broke a glass ashtray. Following the recommendations of the behavioral parent training that she had received, Mrs. Smith had James clean up the ashtray and sent him to his room for fifteen minutes. Thirty

minutes later, James accidentally knocked over and broke a table lamp. This time, Mrs. Smith sent James to his room for forty-five minutes. Shortly thereafter, James went into Mrs. Smith's bedroom and started to jump up and down on the bed while punching holes in the ceiling with a broom handle. Mrs. Smith ran into the room and proceeded to physically assault James (Henggeler & Borduin, 1990, p. 14).

This example does not justify child abuse as the authors point out. It does suggest, however, that there is much more occurring in this example than merely a foster mother abusing her foster child. It suggests that Mrs. Smith's behavior "fit" the ecosystem, or the larger social network. The recursiveness of the behavior involved suggests that no one is at fault and that a change in the system might be appropriate to improve the situation.

In family interactional patterns, circular causality refers to the complex pattern of interaction where there is no discernible cause. Rather, there is a complex interactional loop that does not have a distinct beginning or end. In parent/child interactions, it is more important to view the overall sequence of interaction rather than to see the parent or child contributing to the interaction unequally.

The parent/child relationship is reciprocal in that both parent and child are responsible for the outcome. The parent is not seen as more important than the child in forming, shaping, or maintaining the interaction or its outcome. Parent-education models must be concerned with the interactional sequence and not a one-sided part of the interaction.

A circular concept of causality, in contrast to a linear concept, means that families must be viewed as open evolving systems in which free choices are possible regardless of circumstances. The freedom to choose may have limitations, but the pathway is not determined. Past choices, however, may to some degree provide a parameter for present and future choices. For example, if a couple delays the choice of having a child past the childbearing years, future choices regarding childbearing will be limited. Other choices, such as career development and location of residence, may predispose but not cause families to select certain outcomes.

Equifinality

In terms of cause and effect, "equifinality" means that many causes may lead to the same outcome or that one cause may lead to many outcomes (Bavelas & Segal, 1982). Applied to parenting, equifinality means that the misbehavior of a child may reflect a number of interrelated causes, none of which may be the causes ascribed to the behavior. For example, 4-year-old Johnny may be considered a "bad" boy by his baby sitter because he will not play with his baby sister. His not playing with his sister may be predicated on a number of interrelated events that his baby sitter ignores; for instance, his baby sister does not "play" in the same way he expects her to, she cries easily, or she cannot stay on task long enough for Johnny.

Another aspect of equifinality is that the same parenting behavior may lead to different outcomes. For example, parents who are too strict may have children who are aggressive or resentful and children who are withdrawn. Parents who are very bonded to their children may get as an outcome both children who overachieve and those who underachieve.

The other family scenario related to equifinality is that the same outcome may be related to different parenting behaviors. For example, the emergence of a family problem may occur at an expected family life-cycle stage or during an unexpected series of events. A child who has a temper tantrum in the grocery store may reflect either a too rigid or a too lenient parenting style.

Family Triangles

The dyadic relationship, consisting of two persons, is considered unstable because of the tendency to bring in a third party (Bowen, 1976). The instability in the dyadic relationship results from the inevitable tension and stress experienced by the two persons. When a third person is introduced into the relationship to reduce the stress level and return the situation to normal, the outcome results in no overall change in the primary dyad and some of the tension is expressed through the third party and one of the two primary persons in the dyad.

The family is predisposed to form **triangles,** such as when a child intrudes on the primary dyad of mother and father. When tension reaches a certain level between parents, one parent may form a close bond with a child or children as a way of reducing the tension with the other parent. Parents who are split in this way by a child find that neither the distant parent nor the parent close to the child is effective in parenting. The distant parent, typically the father, is reduced in status by the mother/child alliance, and the mother's alliance with the child renders her ineffective in controlling the child's behavior.

Triangles that occur frequently in family interactions may or may not be dysfunctional (Friedman, 1985). Dysfunctional triangles tend to be intense or rigid and, consequently, reduce the ability of family members to change or to resolve a conflict. They hamper the growth and development of individual family members because the energy needed to resolve the primary conflict is diverted into other areas. When parents are split by a child, the tension in that dyad increases and the child is set up for misbehavior (see Figure 1.5).

Triangles are not limited to three persons but may include many people in a three-sided system (Nichols, 1984). For example, a family triangle may consist of a father at point A with a mother at a distant point B who is close to several children at point C. This basic three-sided triangle is found often, particularly when there is extrafamilial involvement, such as school. Often the teacher or peers at school form the third angle of the triangle. Solving the problems created by these triangles may be extremely difficult because of the lack of opportunity to get all parties together.

At least four different outcomes have been associated with triangles (Kerr & Bowen, 1988). First, a relatively close twosome can be triangulated by the introduction of a third party. As will be discussed later in a section on transition to parenthood, the birth of a child can be a traumatic experience for a couple, as the shift needed in roles from spouse to co-parent can be extremely difficult. Second, a close twosome can be destabilized by the removal of a third party. The classic example relevant here

(a)   The family is a natural triangle.

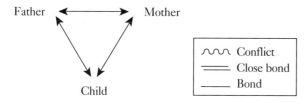

(b)   Conflict in the primary relation between parents with the child being triangulated into the relationship by the mother.

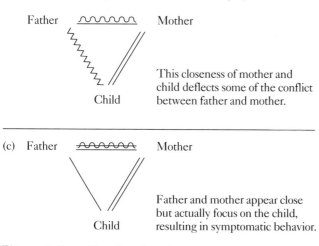

This closeness of mother and child deflects some of the conflict between father and mother.

(c)   Father   Mother

Father and mother appear close but actually focus on the child, resulting in symptomatic behavior.

Figure 1.5 ■ Family triangles.   (Based on theory of M. Bowen, *Family therapy in clinical practice.* New York: Aronson.)

is the couple married for 25 years who become unstable after a child leaves home. The couple no longer have an adequate definition of their relationship. Third, a distant couple may become more stable after the addition of a third party. An unhappy couple actually become happier and more stable after the birth of a child. Finally, a quarreling twosome can be restabilized by the removal of a third party. For example, the child refuses to be the confidant of either or both parents when conflict emerges. This removal of the child from the middle point between the parents means they must find a new and, hopefully, more adaptive way of relating to each other.

Individuality

While individuals are a part of larger systems such as families and extrafamilial systems, individual emotions and cognitions also play an important role in human behavior (L'Abate, 1985). Individual cognitive development plays a major role in how that person interacts with other family members.

While developmental psychology until recently has focused on individual development without considering the context in which that development has taken place, family systems theory has neglected individual dynamics (P. Minuchin, 1985). Although developmental psychology and family science share the belief that the family is very important in understanding human behavior, these two disciplines have not always shared methods or insights about how problems develop and persist. From a systems perspective, the individual contributes to the system that regulates his/her behavior. According to this viewpoint, the individual is best observed in his/her own environment rather than in a clinical setting.

Perhaps a major limitation of systems theory has been the selection of the family as the unit of focus. This selection is an arbitrary decision because there is actually little distinction between discussing the behavior of an individual, the behavior of an individual within a family, and the behavior of an individual from the standpoint of society. The family and society are inextricably linked.

A basic assumption in this book is that simply focusing on the family rather than the individual does not provide much in the long run. The individual, family, and larger social context must be viewed as three distinct but interdependent systems that are structurally unique. Establishing three unique and interdependent systems as the unit of focus prevents such conclusions as Dell's statement that individuals cannot display independent behavior without creating dualism.

The Family System and the Larger Social Network

The isolation of the family from the larger social network noted in the literature by family researchers has resulted in placing too much importance on family relationships. With a current 50% divorce rate and about 25% of households being considered nonfamily (National Center for Health Statistics, 1987), it is apparent that the family is not the all-encompassing system affecting individual behavior. It is extremely difficult to separate the family and the individual from their society and culture (Boulding, 1975). According to Bertalanffy (1968a), language, art, and religion are important symbols that help determine human behavior. These cultural symbols may be more important in analyzing the functional and dysfunctional behavior of family members than in analyzing individual behavior.

Bronfenbrenner (1979) developed a model for describing the family in the context of the larger environment and labeled it the human ecological system. The first level of this system is the **microsystem,** or the interactional relationship within the family. The second level, the **mesosystem,** refers to the interactions among various systems such as the family, workplace, school, peer group, and neighborhood. The third level is the **ecosystem,** or the major institutions of society. The fourth level, the **macrosystem,** generally corresponds to Bertalanffy's (1968a) system of symbols, in that behavior is highly influenced by unrecognized cultural values and expectations. According to an ecosystem view, the behavior of a family member must be considered on a number of levels in order to be fully understood.

There tends to be stress throughout all four levels that results from a poor "eco-logical fit" between the family's level of functioning and other levels. A pronounced lack of fit for the family indicates problems. Families with members who have prob-lems, including parent/child problems, have poor ecological fits across the various levels.

First-Order and Second-Order Parenting

An interesting distinction of a systems perspective is the concept of how individuals and systems change. In most theories, change occurs when an individual begins to behave differently as a result of greater insight or working through previous problems in individual or interpersonal behavior. Similarly, **first-order change** is the systems label for individual or systems change that requires the person to try something new (Watzlawick, Weakland, & Fisch, 1974). **First-order parenting** occurs when the par-ent guides or directs the child in appropriate behavior. The parent is the agent of change for the child, much as the therapist is the agent of change for a patient. The parent "stands outside the dynamic"—that is, observes the child's behavior—and attempts to perform "cures" by "reinforcing" or "punishing" certain behavior (Patter-son, 1977; Patterson & Gullion, 1968). For example, the inappropriate involvement of extended kin can compromise parenting effectiveness. If a grandmother takes care of an infant while the mother works, she also may take on more of the parental role than the mother wishes. The grandmother may make unwanted suggestions about any-thing from what baby food to buy to when to use diaper-rash powder. A first-order change would involve the mother finding another child-care situation and taking the child for short visits to the grandmother's house.

A **second-order change** refers to a change in the structure of the system. **Second-order parenting** refers to parenting whereby the structure of the parent/child relation must be changed. For example, when a child has a temper tantrum in a grocery store because the parent won't buy her candy, the parent uses second-order parenting by looking at everything involved in the tantrum, not just attempting to stop the tan-trum. The parent may be perpetuating the child's behavior by clearly stating expected behavior. Second-order parenting also involves the parent looking at his/her own behavior and at any pertinent variables rather than simply focusing on changing the child's behavior as would be done in first-order parenting.

The concept of second-order parenting introduces a third dimension of parenting in addition to nurturance and control—namely, the interactive or ecological dimen-sion (see Chapter 3). Parents are also part of the process rather than standing outside of it as the other approaches to parenting tend to suggest. Being part of the process, parents must change as well as their children. This change is most often second-order because the structure of the system is altered.

Table 1.1 compares first-order and second-order parenting. Most parenting of behavioral disorders appears to necessitate second-order rather than first-order methods. Because most parent-education models are concerned with first-order

Table 1.1 ■ Comparing First-Order and Second-Order Parenting

First-order parenting is appropriate when:
- The child's misbehavior is mild or the child simply needs direction. These are the misbehaviors that often get mentioned in "how to parent" approaches to parenting. For example, the child dawdles in the morning and makes the family late for school and work, or the child refuses to come to the dinner table need only to be addressed by the parent from a first-order approach. The parent simply takes control by setting a consequence for the child for this minor misbehavior.
- Open communication would help the parent and the child resolve the difficulty. Attempting to come to an agreement or compromise of a fairly clear issue would constitute a first-order change.

Second-order parenting is appropriate when major change must occur in the structure of the child's ecosystem. For example, when a child's school performance decreases from an "A" average to below passing, a second-order change may be considered the most appropriate parenting response. The poor school grades would be seen as reflecting the child's ecosystem. A thorough discussion with the child and parents might be necessary to determine the appropriate solution. To simply focus on the child's school problems by making suggestions about how to improve school performance without understanding other issues would be seen as an ineffective first-order method. Perhaps the problem with school grades started when the family moved to a new community, or the parents "fell out of love" and began to argue most of the time.

methods, the complex structure of the ecosystem is not altered. Prognosis for lasting change would be poor for a problem that responds better to second-order than first-order methods.

■ The Contribution of a Systems Perspective of Parenting

A systems perspective makes many contributions to parenting. The present section of this chapter is not an exhaustive rendition of these contributions, but rather a summary of the more relevant ones.

The major contribution of a systems perspective to parenting is the addition of a third dimension to parenting, the interactional dimension, by placing the misbehavior of the child within an interactional context. As stated earlier, other approaches to parenting focus on the control and/or nurturant functions of parenting. The interactional context of the systems perspective reduces the tendency to focus on the child's misbehavior while the behavior of parents and siblings goes unnoticed. When this interaction among family members is ignored, a number of possible out-

Table 1.2 ■ The Contribution of Systems Concepts to Parenting

- Places the behavior of the child within an interactional context
- Focuses on circular causality
- Emphasizes second-order parenting
- Is concerned about normal family development
- Does not blame the parent or the child
- Considers the child's total ecosystem
- Does not offer a "how to" approach
- Believes in a wide range of parenting behaviors
- Emphasizes the uniqueness of each child

comes follow. First, a child is generally labeled as "bad" in the sense that the child's problem behavior is seen as coming from inside the child. In this case, an Adlerian would focus on attempting to find the child's mistaken goal, and a behaviorist would try to determine how the misbehavior was being reinforced. Second, according to other parenting models, the parent's response to the child is observer, or helper, or reinforcer of behavior. These models ignore the dynamic aspect of interaction between parent and child as emphasized by systems theory.

Since the family is a rule-governed system, a child's misbehavior cannot be changed unless the whole system is involved. Physically separating the problem child from the family, or explaining the child's behavior without referring to other family members' behavior, reduces the chances for change. Typically, parents and siblings maintain problem behavior in a child by using a means of alleviating the problem behavior that actually serves to perpetuate it. For example, when a mother gives in to her child's temper tantrum as a possible solution, the problem is now more difficult than ever. In this regard, the solution has become the problem in the sense that giving in to the temper tantrum would become the focus for change (Amatea, 1989).

A systems parenting model assumes that causation results from the circular patterns of interaction and can be changed only when those patterns are the focus of change. Second-order parenting refers to the effort to change these underlying patterns through a change in the system itself. Parents, as part of the interaction pattern, must accept responsibility for contributing to the problem. Parents also will be aware that they must change as well as their child. Second-order change will alter the homeostatic balance in the family, resulting in a new steady state.

Many problems arise in families as a result of normal transitions and changes. The failure of an individual to meet these transitions creatively can result in inability to change and dysfunction. Healthy individuals and families are able to meet challenges openly and creatively. Although the family has been seen as the major player in transition, extrafamilial relationships, stresses, and changes play a major role in individual behavior within the family (see Chapter 11).

Table 1.2 summarizes the contributions of systems concepts to parenting.

Family Portrait ▪▪▪▪▪▪▪▪▪▪

T he Smith family consists of the father, Bill, and Mary, the mother, both 35, and Skip, age 4. The Smiths, married 10 years, both hold professional-level jobs. Skip has developed normally but from birth has seemed temperamental and difficult at times to control. As an infant, his sleeping patterns were irregular. As he developed, he seemed more difficult to control in that he was constantly into things. His language development is extensive for a 4-year-old, in both his vocabulary and his understanding of words. His parents are not particularly concerned about his language development and temperamental behavior.

Until he was about 3 years old, Skip stayed at home with a baby sitter. Both parents had flexibility in their schedules and needed a sitter for only about 20 hours a week. Then Skip began attending a day-care center. The first month was a nightmare. Although he never cried, he clung to his father's arm in the car during the ride to the day-care center in the mornings. Teachers reported that he did not talk or interact with other children for the first two weeks. When he is picked up in the afternoon, he frequently appears angry, hits his father, and yells when asked about his day. The day-care teachers have discussed the possibility of referring Skip to a child psychologist for evaluation. The Smiths are considering taking him out of day care and finding a sitter.

To complicate matters more, his mother has been promoted on her job and is less flexible in her schedule. In fact, she is now spending much less time with Skip than before. Some weeks she is out of town several nights.

Bill spends most of his time in the evening taking care of Skip. This closer bond with his father is evident when Skip needs consoling. If he hurts himself or just wants to be picked up, he always goes to his father first. He even refuses offers by his mother to console him and cries until his father takes him. At times, Bill resents his wife for this situation. While he supports her career, her absence from the home and Skip's anger and resentment toward his mother make Bill believe that she should wait to advance in her job until Skip is older.

Although the Smiths have a supportive marriage, Skip's behavior problems and Mary's less flexible schedule have increased stress. When Mary comes home from a trip, Bill is ready to turn Skip over to her and take a break from parenting for a while. But Mary is tired from her trip and wants to be left alone and given the opportunity to unwind. In addition, Mary is often agitated from her trip and needs Bill to listen to her talk about the problems she had on the trip. His burden of having to continue the sole parenting role after his wife returns does not predispose him to be supportive of his wife. After a few initial negative exchanges between Bill and Mary, the rest of the evening is spent mainly in silence.

Bill's parents, who live nearby, have frequent contact with Skip, but Bill and Mary have never asked them to baby sit. The elder Smiths put some pressure on Bill to have Skip spend more time with them. They also have given Bill more support because they believe that a mother's place is in the home.

Compare and Contrast

Various models of parenting would approach the Smith family from different perspectives. The models with more application and development in the literature will be discussed and compared with a systems perspective. These models are: Parent Effectiveness Training (PET) (Gordon, 1975), Adlerian Parenting (Dreikurs & Soltz, 1964), and Behavior Modification (Patterson & Gullion, 1968). Systematic Training for Effective Parenting (STEP) (Dinkmeyer & McKay, 1976), an Adlerian model that has received much attention in the research literature, is a workshop format based on the work of Dreikurs. For this reason, it will be referred to interchangeably with Dreikurs.

First, PET would identify the problem in the Smith family as a parent/child problem. The family situation as just described would not be considered important in discussing strategies for change in Skip's behavior. The father would be encouraged to evoke both passive and active listening. For example, when the father asked about the child's day and the child responded by yelling, the father might simply respond by saying, "I see" or "Tell me more about it" (Gordon, 1975). The father also could use active listening to encourage Skip to express these negative feelings about attending day care. The thrust of PET is toward the parent creating an atmosphere of acceptance and respect, which opens resources within the child to solve the problem.

The STEP model would focus on Skip's "misbehavior" of yelling and hitting the father when he was picked up from day care. How Bill reacted to this behavior would indicate the goal of Skip's misbehavior. Bill's reaction generally was to become more solicitous of Skip followed by becoming increasingly frustrated and irritable. According to this model, a probable cause of Skip's misbehavior is that he wants attention (Dinkmeyer & McKay, 1976). Bill would want to be kind but firm with Skip about hitting. He would communicate that he understood and accepted Skip's feelings of being left out. He might discuss other possible actions with Skip. He would not want to label Skip's behavior negatively and would need to control his negative reaction to Skip's hitting. A logical consequence might be for the father to go to another room until Skip can interact without hitting.

Adlerians also would make suggestions to Mary about how to handle Skip on her return from a trip. She could announce that she needed an hour to unpack and relax before spending time with Skip. If Skip did not comply with this request, a logical consequence might be that she would not be able to play with him in an hour.

Behaviorists would view the Smith family in a very narrow sense. First, the desired behavior to change is Skip's hitting and yelling at his father when he is picked up from day care. Bill would need to keep track of how frequently the behavior was occurring. He should reward Skip for appropriate behavior and punish the hitting. A family specialist would develop a contingency schedule for the Smiths to apply for a given period of time. (A contingency schedule is a plan by which the child is rewarded for behaving as expected.)

Generally from a behavioral perspective, one problem is tackled at a time. After there was some improvement in Skip's behavior when his father picked him up from day care, his behavior with his mother would be addressed. Skip would be rewarded when he did not hit his mother upon her return home from a trip. His failure to comply would result in his being placed in time-out, or separation from other family members.

In contrast to the preceding models, a systems perspective begins with the family background and relationship patterns. One of the most significant factors, generally ignored by the other approaches, is the transition from Skip being taken care of at home to being in day care. He is going through an adjustment period to a new and different lifestyle setting. In addition, his mother is away from home several nights a week. Skip is feeling somewhat abandoned and unimportant.

The major failing in understanding this case from the perspective of PET is that Skip is not able to discuss his feelings about abandonment or lack of time with his mother. Attempting to discover who is causing the problem would only focus attention on Skip. The net effect would be a rather insensitive response to Skip's aggressive behavior.

The behavioral model offers few ideas for improving Skip's behavior. In fact, his hitting and yelling at his father would be the major issue. The family situation of the mother's change of job would not be considered an important part of the issue. The closer bond with the father and the underlying marital tension also would not be addressed from a behavioral perspective.

A systems perspective recognizes the family change as the underlying factor. The Smiths might need to shift to second-order parenting, consisting of a change in the system itself. This would involve the mother being especially responsive to Skip and spending extra time with him. For example, although Mary might be tired from her trip, 30 minutes spent with Bill and Skip when she returned might set up a completely different sequence of events. Skip may be able to express his missing her when away in appropriate ways rather than through the usual anger.

The father might use his closeness to Skip to comment on the disappointment Skip might be feeling , because he does not have his own baby sitter anymore. In addition, the parents might invite one of the children in Skip's class to the house for a few hours to help Skip form some bonding with another child.

Bill might express his feelings more openly to Mary about her being out of town overnight. He could show her some support and affection when she returns from a trip rather than the usual anger and withdrawn behavior. Bill's hidden anger may have acted to cue Skip to be aggressive toward his mother.

The involvement of Bill's parents also would need to be addressed. In one sense they are triangulating into the family by influencing Bill through inappropriately expressing their opinion of Mary's career advancement. Although Bill does not actively solicit their involvement, he nonetheless allows it to happen. As long as he allows his parents to intrude in this manner, he will not takes steps to reduce the tension with Mary.

The grandparents' view may also represent an internal conflict that Bill has about Mary's career advancement. For example, while he wants to be supportive, his cultural expectation is that she take the lead in child rearing. On the one hand, Bill wants to show support for his wife's career plans partly because he truly believes that women should have the right to pursue career opportunities that interest them. He is torn between wanting to show support and feeling overburdened with child-care and home responsibilities.

In sum, a systems perspective would view Skip's misbehavior from the standpoint of family structure and interaction. Change would need to occur in the way Bill and Mary handle Skip's behavior problems. The life-cycle transitions of Skip's adjusting to going to a day-care center and his mother's increased employment commitment away from home would be the focus of alleviating Skip's misbehavior.

■■■■■■■■■■■

Parenting Proposition

Misbehavior in children is perpetuated by the structure of the interactional patterns in the child's ecosystem. When change occurs in the child, a concomitant change occurs in the child's ecosystem.

Answers to "Test Your Knowledge"

1. F   4. T
2. T   5. T
3. F   6. F

Key Concepts

paradigm shift
intrapsychic
recursive feedback loops
individual development
objective reality
symbolic reality
bio-psychosocial model
general systems theory
wholeness
family rules
family boundaries
family hierarchy
family homeostasis
social network

family morphogenesis
family morphostasis
linear causality
circular causality
family communication
family triangles
microsystem
mesosystem
ecosystem
macrosystem
first-order change
first-order parenting
second-order change
second-order parenting

Study Questions

1 Discuss the paradigm shift that has occurred in the conceptualization of emotional problems. What are the basic tenets of the new paradigm?

2 Discuss four considerations in applying a systems theory to parenting.

3 Compare and contrast linear and circular causality.

4 Discuss Bronfrenbrenner's dimensions of his concept ecosystem. How are these concepts important to parenting?

5 Compare and contrast first- and second-order change.

6 What is second-order parenting? Give three examples of second-order parenting.

7 Discuss the following concepts of systems theory: wholeness, family boundaries, family hierarchy, family homeostasis. Give at least two examples of how these concepts can be applied to parenting.

8 Discuss the following concepts of systems theory: family morphostasis/ morphogenesis, family rules. Give at least two examples of how these concepts can be applied to parenting.

9 Discuss the following concepts of systems theory: family triangles, recursive feedback loops. Give at least two examples of how these concepts can be applied to parenting.

10 How does a systems perspective differ from other parenting strategies in dealing with misbehavior in children?

References

Ackerman, N. W. (1966). *Treating the troubled family.* New York: Basic Books.

Amatea, E. S. (1989). *Brief strategic intervention for school behavior problems.* San Francisco: Jossey-Bass.

Bateson, G. (1970). An open letter to Anatol Rappoport. *ETC: A Review of General Systems Theory, XXVII* (3), 359–363.

Bateson, G. (1974). Double bind. In S. Brand (Ed.), *II Cybernetics frontiers* (pp. 9–33). New York: Random House.

Bavelas, J. B., & Segal, L. (1982). Family systems theory: Background and implications. *Journal of Communications, 32,* 99–107.

Becvar, D. S., & Becvar, R. J. (1988). *Family therapy: A systemic integration.* Boston: Allyn & Bacon.

Bell, J. E. (1961). *Family group therapy* (Public Health Monograph No. 64). Washington, DC: U.S. Government Printing Office.

Belsky, J. (1984). The determinants of parenting: A process model. *Child Development, 55,* 83–96.

Bertalanffy, L. von (1952). *Robots, men, and minds.* New York: Braziller.

Bertalanffy, L. von (1968a). *General systems therapy: Foundation, development, applications.* New York: Braziller.

Bertalanffy, L. von (1968b). General systems theory: A critical review. In W. Buckley (Ed.), *Modern systems research for the behavioral scientist* (pp. 11–30). Chicago: Aldine.

Boulding, K. E. (1975). General systems theory: The skeleton of science. In B. D. Ruben & J. Y. Kim (Eds.), *General systems theory and human communication.* Rochelle Park, NJ: Hayden Book Company.

Bowen, M. (1976). Theory and practice of psychotherapy. In P. J. Guerin (Ed.), *Family therapy: Theory and practice* (pp. 42–90). New York: Gardner Press.

Bowen, M. (1978). *Family therapy in clinical practice.* New York: Aronson.

Bronfenbrenner, U. (1979). *The ecology of human development.* Cambridge, MA: Harvard University Press.

Burr, W. R., Day, R. D., & Bahr, K. S. (1993). *Family science.* Pacific Grove, CA: Brooks/Cole.

Carter, E. A., & McGoldrick, M. (Eds.). (1989). *The changing family life cycle: A framework for family therapy* (2nd ed.). New York: Harvard University Press.

Constantine, L. L. (1986). *Family paradigms: The practice of theory in family therapy.* New York: Guilford Press.

Dell, P. F. (1982). Beyond homeostasis: Toward a concept of coherence. *Family Process, 21,* 21–42.

Dinkmeyer, D., Sr., & McKay, G. (1976). *Parent's handbook* (A part of the complete STEP Program). Circle Pines, MN: American Guidance Service.

Doherty, W. J. (1990, October). *Family therapy and family medicine: A new partnership.* Paper presented at the 48th annual meeting of the American Association for Marriage and Family Therapy (AAMFT), Washington, DC.

Dreikurs, R., & Soltz, V. (1964). *Children: The challenge.* New York: Hawthorn.

Ford, D. H. (1987). *Humans as self-constructing living systems: A developmental perspective on personality and behavior.* Hillsdale, NJ: Erlbaum.

Freud, S. (1955). Analysis of a phobia in a five-year-old boy (1909). *The standard edition of the complete psychological works of Sigmund Freud* (Vol. 10). London: Hogarth.

Freud, S. (1959). Fragments of an analysis of a case of hysteria (1905). *Collected papers* (Vol. 10). New York: Basic Books.

Friedman, E. H. (1985). *Generation to generation.* New York: Guilford Press.

Goldenberg, H., & Goldenberg, I. (1990). *Counseling today's families.* Pacific Grove, CA: Brooks/Cole.

Goldenberg, I., & Goldenberg, H. (1985). *Family therapy: An overview* (2nd ed.). Pacific Grove, CA: Brooks/Cole.

Goldenberg, I., & Goldenberg, H. (1991). *Family therapy: An overview* (3rd ed.). Pacific Grove, CA: Brooks/Cole.

Gordon, T. (1975). *P.E.T.: Parent effectiveness training.* New York: New American Library.

Haley, J. (1973). *Uncommon therapy: The psychiatric techniques of Milton H. Erickson, M.D.* New York: Norton.

Haley, J. (1976). *Problem-solving therapy.* San Francisco: Jossey-Bass.

Hammer, T. J., & Turner, P. H. (1990). *Parenting in contemporary society* (2nd ed.). Englewood Cliffs, NJ: Prentice-Hall.

Henggeler, S., & Borduin, C. (1990). *Family therapy and beyond.* Pacific Grove, CA: Brooks/Cole.

Hoffman, L. (1981). *Foundations of family therapy.* New York: Basic Books.

Jackson, D. D. (1959). Family interaction, family homeostasis, and some implications for conjoint family therapy. In J. Masserman (Ed.), *Individual and family dynamics.* New York: Grune & Stratton.

Jackson, D. D. (1965a). Family rules: Marital grid pro quo. *Archives of General Psychiatry, 12,* 589–594.

Jackson, D. D. (1965b). The study of the family. *Family Process, 4,* 1–20.

Kerr, M. E., & Bowen, M. (1988). *Family evaluation: An approach based on Bowen theory.* New York: Norton.

Korner, A. F., Zeanah, C. H., Linden, J., Berkowitz, R. I., Kraemer, H. C., & Agras, W. S. (1985). The relationship between neonatal and later activity and temperament. *Child Development, 56,* 38–42.

Kuhn, T. (1970). *The structure of scientific revolution.* Chicago: University of Chicago Press.

L'Abate, L. (1985). The status and future of family psychology and therapy. In L. L'Abate (Ed.), *The handbook of family psychology and therapy* (Vol. 2, pp. 1417–1435). Pacific Grove, CA: Brooks/Cole.

Lerner, R. M. (1988). Personality and development: A life-span perspective. In E. M. Hetherington, R. M. Lerner, & M. Perlmutter (Eds.), *Child development in life-span perspective* (pp. 21–46). Hillsdale, NJ: Erlbaum.

Lerner, R. M., & Kauffman, M. B. (1985). The concept of development in contextualism. *Developmental Review, 5,* 309–333.

Lidz, R., & Lidz, T. (1949). The family environment of schizophrenic patients. *American Journal of Psychiatry, 106,* 332–345.

Miller, J. G. (1978). *Living systems.* New York: McGraw-Hill.

Minuchin, P. (1985). Families and individual development: Provocation from the field of family therapy. *Child Development, 56,* 289–302.

Minuchin, S. (1974). *Families and family therapy.* Cambridge, MA: Harvard University Press.

Minuchin, S. (1984). *Family kaleidoscope.* Cambridge, MA: Harvard University Press.

Montgomery, J., & Fewer, W. (1988). *Family systems and beyond.* New York: Human Science Press.

Napier, A. Y., & Whitaker, C. A. (1978). *The family crucible.* New York: Harper & Row.

National Center for Health Statistics (1987). Births, marriages, divorces, and deaths for 1987. *Monthly Vital Statistics Report.* Washington, DC: U.S. Government Printing Office.

Nesselroade, J. R., & von Eye, A. (Eds.). (1985). *Individual development and social change: Explanatory analysis.* New York: Academic Press.

Nichols, M. (1984). *Family therapy: Concepts and methods.* New York: Gardner Press.

Osborne, P. (1989). *Parenting for the 90s.* Intercourse, PA: Good Books.

Patterson, G. R. (1977). *Living with children* (rev. ed.). Champaign, IL: Research Press.

Patterson, G. R., & Gullion, M. (1968). *Living with children.* Champaign, IL: Research Press.

Piaget, J. (1926). *The language and thought of the child.* New York: Harcourt Brace.

Satir, V. M. (1964). *Conjoint family therapy.* Palo Alto, CA: Science and Behavior Books.

Satir, V. M. (1972). *Peoplemaking.* Palo Alto, CA: Science and Behavior Books.

Scarf, M. (1987). *Intimate partners: Patterns in love and marriage.* New York: Random House.

Thomas, A., & Chess, S. (1977). *Temperament and development.* New York: Brunner/Mazel.

Watzlawick, P., Beavin, J., & Jackson, D. D. (1967). *Pragmatics of human communication.* New York: Norton.

Watzlawick, P., Weakland, J., & Fisch, R. (1974). *Change: Principles of problem formation and problem resolution.* New York: Norton.

Whitaker, C. A. (1975). Psychotherapy of the absurd: With a special emphasis on the psychotherapy of aggression. *Family Process, 14,* 1–16.

Whitaker, C. A., & Keith, D. V. (1981). Symbolic-experiential family therapy. In A. S. Gurman & D. P. Kniskern (Eds.), *Handbook of family therapy.* New York: Brunner/Mazel.

Wynne, L. C. (1970). Communication disorder and the quest for relatedness in families of schizophrenics. *American Journal of Psychoanalysis, 30,* 100–114.

Chapter 2

Human Development and Parenting

Parenting Myth ■ Development can be defined as progressive changes in the way an organism interacts with the environment (Baer, 1970).

Test Your Knowledge ■ The following questions are designed to test your knowledge before reading the material in this chapter. Answers appear at the end of the chapter.

1 There is indisputable evidence that men and women differ in moral judgment. True or false?

2 Jean Piaget's model of cognitive development can be called an equilibrium model. True or false?

3 Arrested socialization refers to the parents' failure to socialize the child. True or false?

4 Cross-cultural research supports Piaget's stage of formal operations. True or false?

5 A systems/dialectical model of development is a unidirectional model. True or false?

6 A dialectical process implies a continuous process with the past. True or false?

T heories of **child development** attempt to explain how the individual changes physically, mentally, and emotionally throughout the life course. These changes are typically described as orderly and structured and also can be described as a process of **maturation,** or the development from the least to the most complex. For example, physical development can be explained in terms of advancing from a primitive to a more complex series and ordering of processes.

Closely associated with the concept of maturation is the concept of **learning,** or the persistence of changes into a repeatable pattern of expression. Development has been viewed as an intermingling of these two concepts. For example, many experiences demand a certain level of physical maturation but also must be coupled with learning, typically viewed as practice in the specific experience (Shaffer, 1989).

Theories of child development differ in how they conceptualize the role of maturation and learning. Some pay more attention to maturation and biological factors, whereas others focus more on learning. Generally, there is concern for how the individual develops across the life cycle, although there is a tendency to compartmentalize this development rather than focus on the overall process itself (Shaffer, 1989).

Over the past several decades, an increasing trend in developmental psychology has been to view the individual in a multilevel framework, which includes psychological, biological, and environmental dimensions (Lerner, 1989). Viewing human development from a life-span perspective has emphasized the historical context of development. Human development in any one period of history tends to represent to some degree events specific to that period. For example, the effects of the Depression on the development of children during that period have been clearly demonstrated (Elder, Liker, & Cross, 1984). As a consequence of inconsistent or erratic parenting during the Depression, many children failed to enter adulthood prepared for the demands of a career and responsible living.

The emphasis on life-span development also has suggested that development could take multiple directions, or to be considered "plastic." Throughout life some people enhance their developmental outcomes while other people decrease them. Across the life span, many factors contribute to the developmental changes experienced by individuals. These changes at any period of development are viewed as interrelated with changes at other periods of development.

The purpose of this chapter is to summarize briefly those theories that might be consistent with a systems perspective of child development. This summary takes the form of structuring the theories into the three interlocking systems of individual, family, and social network. A framework for developing a systems model incorporating these theories will be discussed. Finally, specific application of this model will be applied to conduct disorder.

Applied specifically to parenting, this chapter focuses on the multidimensional aspects of behavioral problems in children. Based on recent research, these problems are associated with individual, family, and extrafamilial factors. Transitions or changes in the individual, the family, and the extrafamilial network account for much of the dynamic process associated with human behavior. Specific changes in the child related to age and intellectual ability provide a map of expected behaviors. This cognitive development in the child is further enhanced by moral attitudes and the ability to respond to the desires of others.

Concomitant with individual development over time is the developmental process of the family unit. This family context also is evolving in a larger social context including the extended family and extrafamilial components, such as school and work settings. This view of individuals and families evolving together through time forms the basic concept in understanding all human behavior, including parenting. In merging the developmental concept with systems theory, this chapter presents a **process model of parenting** referred to as the systems/dialectical model. This process model challenges **unidirectional parenting models,** which view the parent as an agent of socialization and the child as the object of socialization.

■ The Individual

Individual **cognitive development** refers to all the age-related changes or transitions in perception, memory, intellectual reasoning, judgment, and decision making (Perlmutter, 1988). Memory, keeping track of people, past events, and happenings, combined with intellectual skills, allow the individual to understand and put in perspective meaningful experiences and relationships.

Cognitive Development

The cognitive development theory of Jean Piaget (1954) is consistent with a systems paradigm because it describes the child's intellectual development as a holistic construct; that is, cognition is greater than the sum of its parts. At any given age, children use different reasoning abilities in performing tasks (Flavell, 1982). From Piaget's point of view, humans are considered active creators of knowledge. Inherent in this view of cognition are the biological constraints in defining both cognition and the nature of cognitive development (Perlmutter, 1988). Intelligence develops systematically through a stimulating and supporting environment.

Piaget's (1950) view of intelligence as being in **equilibrium**—that is, balanced steady position—implies that the child actively encounter the environment and must make adjustments in order to cope with new and different experiences. Disequilibrium occurs when the child does not completely understand and accept new information. The struggle to understand, master, or incorporate new experiences assumes a continuous process of interaction between the individual and the environment.

Experiences are explained and organized into certain structures or patterns referred to as **schemata.** Schemata in the infant are the result of repeated exposure to certain events. For example, when an infant shows preference for a parent over a stranger, she is reflecting a particular schema, or organization of experience. This continuous process of understanding the world through schemata is referred to as **adaptation** (Piaget, 1952). In adapting to new experiences, individuals create their own knowledge.

According to Piaget (1954), in creating their own knowledge children integrate new experience through the process of **assimilation.** For example, when an infant sucks on a new toy presented by the mother, he is using the existing schema of knowing the world through sensations of sucking and movements to "know" the new object. On the other hand, if the child's existing schema does not allow for knowledge of the new experience, he must use another type of behavior called **accommodation.** For example, if the child attempts to put a tennis ball in his mouth to suck, another sensorimotor behavior would have to be used, such as banging or throwing, to acquire information about the object to develop a schema. Learning by accommodation is a much more powerful means of learning than learning by verbal instruction. Optimal learning is enhanced by familiar but challenging situations.

Piaget's (1954) stages of cognitive development are consistent with a systems perspective in that he was more interested in how children arrived at decisions than in the decisions themselves. As such he was not interested in explaining the differences in competency levels of different children, nor was he interested in explaining why some children lack interest in a subject such as math and other children excel in math. His main focus was on how new structures developed for cognitive activity, not in explaining individual differences. He addressed this process of the developing structure of cognition through four distinct stages: sensorimotor, preoperational, concrete operations, and formal operations.

The first stage in Piaget's sequence of cognitive development is the sensorimotor stage. The infant learns through the inborn ability to act on external objects, having no internal awareness of him/herself (Piaget, 1954). This stage, lasting from birth to approximately 2 years of age, culminates in the coordination of movement with internal awareness, a sense of self-identity, a rudimentary concept of causality, and the belief in object permanence, the belief that objects continue to exist after they have been moved out of sight.

The second stage, preoperational, from age 2 until age 5 or 6, is dominated by egocentric and illogical thinking. Learning to think symbolically, however, through the use of language is the primary achievement during the preoperational stage. Play takes on a more imaginative expression during this stage as children act out various roles. The egocentrism of the previous stage decreases to some degree as the child recognizes that others may not share his/her viewpoint.

During the third stage, concrete operations, which corresponds primarily to the elementary school years, the child learns to think more logically, begins to see the connection between events, and has a more logical view of causality. While the child is more logical in thought in this stage, he/she continues to be less egocentric as well. Gradually, the child begins to see that parents have different beliefs and perspectives about events that may be as viable as his/her own.

The final stage is referred to as the formal operations stage. In this stage, roughly the period of adolescence, adultlike rational processing occurs. The adolescent tries to reason about hypothetical as well as concrete occurrences, which is generally referred to in adulthood as rational ability. The formal operations thinker is able to weigh alternative positions before making a decision and can consider the consequences of one's own and others' behavior.

Although the formal operations stage may have certain advantages over previous stages, adolescents may experience more egocentrism than their grade-school counterparts (Elkind, 1981). They frequently act as if others are aware of their thoughts and concerns and tend to exaggerate their feelings and deny that others may have similar feelings. Adolescents tend to believe that no one could possibly know how they feel.

Moral Development

In addition to focusing on the development of the rational process, some researchers have paid attention to the development of moral attitudes and behaviors (Gilligan, 1977, 1982; Kohlberg, 1969). Consistent with a systems perspective, Kohlberg's (1969) three stages of **moral development** are based on the construct of "structured wholes," or organized systems of thought. Generally the stages, each consisting of two substages, occur as an invariant advancing sequence. This sequence is hierarchically significant in that moral reasoning at the highest level incorporates and exceeds thinking at the lower level. Children, particularly preschoolers, do not share the same moral attitudes about behavior as their parents. The earliest level of moral development is referred to as the premoral level. The child's general way of responding at this level is to maximize reward and minimize punishment with little concern for the rights or feelings of others. This premoral attitude corresponds with the cognitive egocentric level.

During the elementary school years prior to the onset of adolescence, children shift from the premoral to a legalistic point of view, referred to as the conventional level (Kohlberg, 1969). In this stage, the child conforms to laws and guidelines for behavior ordered by parents, teachers, and other authorities. There is little or no internalizing of moral behavior, except to follow the dictates of those perceived to be more knowledgeable. For example, a child may stay in his seat during study hall because that is the rule, not because failing to do so would be disruptive to other students.

The highest level of moral development is the principled level. By the onset of adolescence, some children are capable of principled reasoning, or making moral judgments based on a set of internal standards about justice. As adolescents move from early to late adolescence, their ability to reason shifts from conventional to a more complex understanding of the responsibility for behavior. By late adolescence and early adulthood, there is a shift to the more advanced level of moral reasoning (Kohlberg, 1969).

There has been some concern that **gender differences** were ignored in the development of these levels of moral reasoning. According to Gilligan (1977, 1982), males and females develop morally along two different tracks closely related to socialization. For example, males are socialized to be more aggressive and assertive than females, resulting in a moral development that emphasizes the conflicts between individuals and the need for laws to resolve those conflicts, or what Gilligan refers to as the "morality of justice." On the other hand, females are socialized to be nurturant and understanding of the needs of others. This difference in socialization for females creates what Gilligan refers to as the "morality of care." Gilligan is careful to point out that neither the male morality of justice nor the female morality of care is superior to the other.

By interviewing 29 pregnant women about their current decision to have the child, Gilligan concluded that there are three levels of moral judgment: self-interest, self-sacrifice, and nonviolence. The first state, self-interest, is characterized by putting one's interest above other considerations. For example, the reasoning to have the child would be based on the probable interference the child would have in the woman's life. The woman might decide on an abortion if she thought the child would interfere with her future plans. The second stage, or self-sacrifice, is characterized by the woman's willingness to sacrifice her own interest in favor of the interest of others. In the third stage, women have moved beyond self-sacrifice to the belief that no one should be hurt. For example, a woman may elect to have an abortion if she thinks she would be having the child for the wrong reason.

As yet, researchers have failed to find consistent gender differences in the development of the levels of moral reasoning (Thomas, 1986). Although some differences may exist, researchers to date generally have concluded that in moral development males and females develop along similar tracks. Both males and females tend to use the morality of justice and the morality of care fairly equally rather than one being more the domain of males or females respectively (Walker, DeVries, & Trevethan, 1987). In reasoning about real-life moral situations, males and females respond compassionately and responsibly in similar ways (Smetana, Killen, & Turiel, 1991).

Psychosocial Perspective

The **psychosocial perspective,** largely associated with Erik Erikson (1963, 1968, 1982), takes the position that human development occurs within a social context. While Erikson's psychosocial perspective reflects the psychodynamic school of thought of which Freud is the originator, there are significant differences from Freud that appear consistent with a systems approach. One major difference is the focus on social rather than sexual forces. Erikson's theory goes beyond a one-sided focus on child egocentrism and views the child as an active creator of his/her environment rather than a passive recipient. This theory is broad enough to encompass the life cycle rather than focus only on the childhood and adolescent stages.

Psychosocial theory is based on the interaction of the individual with society. It has eight distinct stages and is based on a number of interlocking principles (Newman & Newman, 1991). The first principle is that stages of development refer to distinct periods in one's life cycle which represent a unique structure. Each stage is different, while it may be based on or directly follow from a previous stage.

Second is the concept of psychosocial crises, or demands of the environment to which the individual must adjust. These developmental crises are normal and generally anticipated by each member of a society. The assumption is that a child should master a crisis or conflict in sequence as it occurs. If mastery does not occur, the child is nevertheless swept along to the next crisis somewhat unprepared. For example, the first psychosocial stage, labeled "trust versus mistrust," represents about the first year of life. This first year requires that parents provide a consistent environment for the developing child.

During the second through the third years, the crisis to be mastered is "autonomy versus shame and doubt." The child must learn to express independent behavior, sometimes exerted through the terrible two's in terms of resistance and noncompliant behavior. Failure to achieve independence leads to the child's questioning his/her abilities. The third stage is referred to as "initiative versus guilt." A child who failed to acquire independent behavior might have problems in this stage in developing initiative to project him/herself socially. In the fourth stage, "Industry versus inferiority," the child must learn to achieve academically and relate socially to friends. Feelings of inferiority may result if the child fails at these endeavors. A child who has resolved these crises in a positive way probably will enter adolescence with a good chance of gaining self-identity without too much upheaval. The adolescent is prone to try various roles attempting to find a good fit for him/herself in establishing individual identity.

The remaining three stages are adult stages that are considered equally important to a person's sense of well-being and satisfaction. The sixth stage, "intimacy versus isolation," is the period in which the young adult selects a mate, establishes a career, and forms ties with the larger society. The middle adulthood years (ages 40–65) are characterized as a "generativity versus stagnation" crisis. A person must become productive in career choice, raising a family, community associations, and appreciation for one's culture. Failure to do so leads to stagnation and poorly prepares one to meet the last crisis, "ego integrity versus despair." The older person reviews his/her productivity and accomplishments and either feels relatively satisfied with the efforts or is disappointed by many unfulfilled and unrealized goals.

Life-Span Development

Life-span development refers to the systematic changes that occur in a person's life from birth to death. This developmental process is more than a single path leading to gradual deterioration, decline, and death. Rather, life-span developmentalists view development as a complex sequence in solving both growth and deterioration over one's lifetime (Kagan, 1986).

Life-span development involves a number of assumptions about how changes are understood during the course of a person's life that are consistent with a systems perspective (Baltes, Reece, & Lipsett, 1980). First, life-span development is a lifelong process. No longer is development thought of as ending or of being relatively unimportant after adolescence. Adult development is now considered extremely important for the total picture of the developing individual.

Second, life-span development is viewed in a historical context. An individual cannot be separated from his/her historical context. Each person has a history, which may share common experiences with others, such as wars and social and political changes, but this history also can be personal and specific. A child growing up in the United States today, though he/she has similar values and expectations as children in past periods, would have little in common with a child of the Depression years.

Third, life-span development allows for various directions in development. In contrast to viewing development as one locked-in sequence through which each person must travel, life-span developmentalists recognize that individuals are confronted with vastly different experiences and have significantly different resources and abilities to adapt. Because of the different developmental tracks, adults may have variant yet valid responses to the same stimuli (Baltes, Reece, & Lipsett, 1980).

In sum, although the theories of individual development presented here are not exhaustive, nor are they developed in great detail, they do share certain characteristics of human development that are consistent with a systems perspective. For example, the social dimensions of development and the individual's influence on development are represented in all of these theories. A critique of these theories and suggested ways that they could be incorporated into a systems paradigm of development will be presented later in the chapter.

Development Within the Family

The aforementioned models of individual development do not occur in isolation. The individual is embedded in a larger network including extended family, friendships, work, school, culture, and history. This larger context means that development must be viewed as circular or interactional rather than linear or unidirectional. Understanding a person's behavior in terms of both individual and family development allows the interdependence of the individual and his/her context to become more understandable (Becvar & Becvar, 1988).

Contextual Approach

A family process model of development is consistent with what the literature refers to as the **contextual approach** (Bronfenbrenner, 1979; Charlesworth, 1976; Lewin, 1954). This approach views development as bidirectional; that is, the individual develops within a context comprised of social groups which he/she participates in. This multidimensionality of development maintains that individuals act on their context while the context acts on them. Although both the individual and the environment are structurally unique, each is changing and affecting the other.

A contextual approach uses the concept of ecology as a central focus. For example, the child's behavior is not viewed as simply being shaped by the parents, but a consideration also is made for how the child's behavior influences the parent's behavior. The purpose of the child's behavior within a context must be understood. In addition, the parent/child relationship is influenced by the parent's spousal relation-

■ *To understand a member of the family, the researcher must analyze the interaction among various generations.*

ship as well as by extrafamilial relationships. The view that children can determine their own development has been examined in a number of studies (Bell & Harper, 1977). In this dynamic interindividual context, both "cause" and are "caused" by each other.

A number of studies support the belief that children are equally responsible for how they are treated by adults (Bell & Chapman, 1986). One study focusing on the behavior of aggressive children concluded that, during a play session, mothers of aggressive boys tend to relate in a negative and coercive way with their own sons, but in a calm and positive way with normal boys (Anderson, Lytton, & Romney, 1986).

This research suggests that these children shared responsibility with their mothers for the behavior they received.

Contextual development views developmental changes as a lifelong process (Hetherington & Baltes, 1988). While stages occur and cause individuals to change, no one stage takes primacy over another. Rather, development is viewed primarily as a gain/loss occurrence influenced by the interlocking of three factors. First, changes tend to be age-appropriate, or they occur at or near the same chronological age. Second, non-normative events, such as accidents, illnesses, family dissolution, or emotional problems are unprogrammed but increase the probability for a number of negative events, such as change in family socioeconomic status, residence, or job. Third, an individual exists within a changing historical context (Hetherington & Baltes, 1988).

The **historical context** is a powerful determinant of development (Parke, 1988). For example, raising a family with four children may be much different in the 1990s than during the Depression. Other situations actually may affect interdependency of the child and his/her environment. Certain situations have been known to affect family stability, such as taking care of a sick or disabled child (Tew, Lawrence, Payne, & Rawnsley, 1977).

Viewing the individual as embedded in a dynamic **social ecosystem** suggests a number of interesting considerations for parent/child relations. First, childhood experiences, while influential, cannot be viewed as the major prologue to adult life (Hetherington & Baltes, 1988). Second, the social ecosystem approach implies that intervention in the parent/child relationship should include both the individual and the environment. Based on the view that an active organism selects and evokes responses from his/her environment, intervention strategies should include shaping of the environment and other persons. In order to change oneself to fit different contexts, the individual must learn self-discipline and self-regulating behavior.

The Family Life Cycle: Normative Changes in the Family

The view that **normative,** or expected **changes** in the family cycle, such as the birth of a child or the first child leaving home, are seen as transitions has been advanced by a number of researchers (Carter & McGoldrick, 1980; Duvall, 1977) and family therapists (Haley, 1973). According to this view, the family proceeds through different stages similar to the individual's and each stage represents different developmental tasks that must be accomplished (see Table 2.1). The family moves through these stages sequentially much as the individual does in Erickson's individual development.

A number of researchers (Becvar & Becvar, 1988; Whiteside, 1982) have criticized this model of the family life cycle. Many families fail to fit neatly in the family life cycle because of divorce, single parenting, and more recently, voluntary childlessness. Whereas in the past these family forms were considered anomalies or deviant forms, today they are accepted as variant family forms in a more pluralistic society. This plurality of family forms raises an interesting question regarding the "normal" family and the viability of the family life-cycle concept.

Table 2.1 ■ The Revised Normal Family Life Cycle

Stage 1: *The Beginning Family.* Two persons come together for the purpose of forming an intimate relationship. This stage might include variant forms, such as cohabitators and gay and lesbian couples.

Stage 2: *Childbearing Families.* When the first child is born, the married couple moves to stage 2. For almost a fourth of all families, however, the childbearing stage is the first stage in the family life cycle because of the high rate of births to unwed mothers.

Stage 3: *Families with Preschool Children.* For married couples with young children, this stage is 3, but for never-married single-parent families, it is stage 2. For divorced and remarried families, this stage could represent stage 1 dynamics in that the family lacks cohesion and bonding and is without a biological child.

Stage 4: *Families with School-Age Children.* For traditional two-parent biological parents this stage represents the elementary school years. For single-parent families, it may represent stage 3; for remarried families, it could represent any of the stages depending on how long the family has been in existence.

Stage 5: *Families with Adolescents.* This stage begins when the first child reaches puberty. Again, the contemporary family with a teenager may be in any of the family life stages depending on remarriage, cohabitation, single-parent status, and never-married status.

Stage 6: *Launching.* This stage traditionally begins when adolescent children leave home. As noted earlier, however, depending on the variant family form, the family may be experiencing any stage.

Stage 7: *The Middle Years.* This stage has been referred to as the "empty nest syndrome" because children have left home. With increasing childless marriages and the remarriage of those with no children who are beyond the childbearing years, this stage could be viewed as any.

Stage 8: *Aging Families.* Again, depending on the circumstances, this family type could be considered in any stage.

The Revised Family Life Cycle: Non-normative Changes

The changing family form is noted through a number of specific facts. First, the divorce rate has increased and currently implies that almost 50% of married couples will divorce (Glick, 1984). Some differences are found for different groups, however, with the baby boomers being more divorce-prone (Norton & Moorman, 1987). Second, there are more single-parent families, partly because of the increased divorce rate and partly because of the births to unmarried women (Glick, 1984). Third, more women not only are now in the labor force but also consider their work as careers in much the same way as men traditionally have done. Fourth, over the past several decades a dramatic increase has occurred in the number of remarriages or reconstituted families (Santrock, Warshak, Lindbergh, & Meadows, 1982). The high remarriage rate suggests that marriage and family life are valued in American society, though it might take a variant form. These demographic changes in the American family suggest that the family life cycle should reflect a more pluralistic family than is usually presented.

As mentioned earlier, **non-normative changes** can interfere with the developmental progress in children. Researchers conclude that children are affected by divorce (Hetherington, Cox, & Cox, 1976, 1985; Wallerstein, 1987; Wallerstein & Kelly, 1974; Weiss, 1975). Children who have been triangulated into their parents' marital problems stand the greatest risk for experiencing the negative effects of divorce (Wallerstein, 1987). Young children typically respond by thinking the divorce was their fault. School-age children respond by experiencing depression or sadness and increasing acting-out behavior at home and school. Adolescents, because of greater cognitive understanding and social contacts outside the home, tend to make the best adjustment to divorce (Wallerstein & Kelly, 1976). Follow-up on past studies, however, indicates that the effects of divorce continue into adulthood and that the parents' divorce was the single most influential happening in their childhood memory (Wallerstein, 1987).

Many studies discuss changes in the parent/child relationship as a result of divorce (Wallerstein, 1987). Generally, the child loses contact and a feeling of closeness with the noncustodial parent, though loss of closeness may also happen with the custodial parent because of the change in family roles and a new social life for the custodial parent. Loss of job may affect the self-esteem and self-concept of a parent and, consequently, the way the parent interacts with the child.

The **single-parent family** results from divorce, pregnancy out of wedlock, or the death of a spouse. While some researchers have labeled the single parent a misnomer (Ahrons, 1983), citing that two parents do exist, these families appear to operate as one-parent families. Furstenberg (1980) found that 29% of single mothers remain in the family of origin, 24% move out to get married shortly after becoming pregnant, 15% move into their own apartment, and 11% return to the family of origin after marriage or divorce. Income is lower for the single mother than it is for single working women or married couples. Many single mothers must return to the family of origin or receive help from family and friends. Another source of support for the single mother is the paternal grandparents (Bolton, MacEachron, Laner, & Gai, 1987).

While the grandparents can provide support for the single parent, clinical literature demonstrates that dependency on the grandparents can undermine the authority of the single parent (Minuchin, 1974). The temptation would be for the grandparents to assume the parenting responsibility for the parent. Old grievances may arise and unresolved issues emerge that pit the single parent and the grandparents against each other in the battle over control. The child may respond by developing discipline problems or playing the parent against the grandparents.

The literature also suggests that a child in a single-parent home may take over the role of the departed or absent parent. This role-taking may be actual such as in the case of a teenager working after school to help support the family, or it may be psychological in providing emotional support for the parent. This child is robbed of being a

■ *Grandparents have a significant role in connecting the child with the total social context.*

child by taking on adult responsibilities too soon. Adulthood for such a person may be a series of unfinished growing-up experiences.

Divorced persons tend to remarry in high numbers (Glick, 1984). In addition, most single persons including single parents eventually marry (O'Flaherty & Eells, 1988). This definite preference for marrying/remarrying in American society suggests that most divorced and single parents are actively engaged in courtship. In fact, about 50% of divorced persons remarry by the third year after divorce.

Dating again is an initial shock for some divorced persons, but marriage occurs quicker than in first marriages (O'Flaherty & Eells, 1988). Less formality and the presence of children affect both the dating situation and the choice of a mate. Some women include their children on dates and use feedback from children in the process of selecting a mate (Roberts & Price, 1987).

Divorced persons who marry with children have been referred to in the literature as creating **blended,** reconstituted, or stepfamilies (Roberts & Price, 1989). Step-families may merge together neatly like the TV program *The Brady Bunch,* but that tends to be the exception rather than the rule. The rule tends to involve lack of cohesion, boundary problems, unclear roles, and problems with discipline. Adjustments tend to be enhanced when stepparents develop friendships first and slowly move into the parental role (Walker & Messinger, 1979). Children experience divided loyalties, sibling rivalry, and greater distance from both their custodial and noncustodial parents. Children also may find their birth-order role has changed. For example, a 10-year-old girl who was the older of two children in her family may find after a parent's remarriage that she is the middle child with older stepsiblings.

Developmentally, the family must establish a togetherness while allowing input and contact with a number of former members and new, previously unrelated members. Balancing the interplay among these various persons can be difficult and problematic for many couples. Clear boundaries that permit participation by a former husband, for example, but deny him interference in his ex-wife's remarried structure, would be seen as ideal (Whiteside, 1982).

The concept of family tasks defined as stage-specific problems and challenges seems to be particularly helpful in integrating a systems view and a developmental view of changes throughout the life course. These stages appear not only to be hierarchical, but also to increase in complexity as the family moves through time. These points will be elaborated on later in the chapter.

Internal Working Model

A family perspective of development also is concerned with the concept of the **internal working model,** or the child's or adult's inner representations of experience that can be used for initiating new social interactions (Kreppner, 1989). A child forms an internal repertoire of experiences that ensures some measure of consistency over time in relationship building. For example, the child's bonding with parents may form an internal working model of attachment that would affect his/her ability to form attachment outside the family. The internal working model includes both cognitive and affective dimensions, and it can change in reference to new experiences. Because it can change with new experiences, the internal working model is viewed as a disposition toward certain behaviors rather than a causal explanation for behavior. For example, children may be predisposed to forming attachment in certain ways, but not predetermined to do so.

Nonshared Environments

The concept of **nonshared environments** developed through research in the field of genetics, specifically with identical twins (Kreppner, 1989). Generally, the research on nonshared environments emphasized differences in siblings. The family environment appears to be different for each child. For example, the family environment would be different for a first child compared with a second child. Changes during the life cycle, such as divorce, may also affect children differently.

The extent of the nonshared environment in the family is such that two siblings from the same family can be considered as different as two unrelated children from the general population (Plomin, 1989). Although identical twins are more similar than other siblings, they are not exactly the same in all ways. The differences that do exist in identical twins are due to context.

In sum, the family is an important dimension for understanding development. Both the structure and the functional level of the family affect the development of individuals over the life cycle. A more thorough integration of these concepts will be discussed in terms of a systems perspective of parenting later in the chapter.

■ The Extrafamilial Context

The **extrafamilial context** refers to all influences on behavior that occur from sources outside the family, such as culture and race. Regarding the individual as having simultaneous membership in a variety of contexts is referred to as an **ecosystemic view** (Falicov, 1988). This view is based on the belief that individual and family development represents adaptations to ecological situations, or the notion of **ecological fit.** Family development is enhanced when the "fit" occurs, and family members may experience psychological stress when fit does not occur.

Models for an ecosystemic view of human development have emerged (Bronfenbrenner, 1979). In Brofenbrenner's model there are four levels of individual, family, and cultured interaction. The *microsystem,* intricate relationships within the family, is the level usually involved in family therapy. The second level, or *mesosystem,* involves the interrelations among such contexts as the extended family, school, peer group, and workplace. Institutions of society are referred to as the *ecosystem.* Finally, the prototype of the culture that sets the patterns for the interactions which occur in the three other levels is called the *macrosystem.* The interaction of these four levels determines a particular behavior in an individual. The family organizational structure and developmental patterns are viewed as adaptations that fit the other three levels (Falicov, 1988).

Family Structure and Organization and Culture

Family structure and organization differ according to culture. One main aspect of culture affecting the structure and organization of the family is social class, or socioeconomic status (SES), the position of the family or the individual in society according to such measures as educational level, occupational status, and income. Researchers have found that SES is related to different types of parenting behaviors (Maccoby, 1980). Higher-status parents talk more, use more complex language, and show more affection to their children. Lower-SES parents, on the other hand, are more restrictive in parenting style, and stress obedience and authority. Recently, a researcher concluded that lower-SES parents experience more stress in their lives, resulting in a diminished capacity to parent in a warm and supportive manner (McLoyd, 1990).

In the middle-class American society, especially among whites, the family is organized around the marital couple, referred to as the dominant dyad. The marital dyad has the position of most power in the family. Although both spouses may not be equal in all respects, their combined efforts make this dyad the driving force in the family. Although the marital dyad generally does not include the extended family, there have been situations in which the marital dyad is strengthened by involvement with the extended family. For example, in general among lower-SES parents, inclusion of the extended family is more accepted (Falicov, 1988). The inclusion may take the form of providing parenting or making decisions.

Culture and the Family Life Cycle

The family life cycle has been viewed as reflecting a cultural bias. The transitional crises related to the age of children are embedded in a cultural framework that dictates how those changes will be understood. While the life cycle is linked to certain biological events, such as marrying, having offspring, launching offspring, and retiring, the timing of the stages varies according to the cultural differences. In addition to the timing, how the rituals are performed may indicate a cultural bias. People mainly observe these rites and rituals in annual celebrations, such as holidays and anniversaries, and in rites of passage, such as weddings, graduations, and puberty rites (Falicov, 1988).

Cultural variations occur at various points in the family life cycle. One phase in the cycle that has received much attention is the leaving-home stage (Bowen, 1978; Haley, 1973). The generally accepted view is that differentiating from the family of origin is extremely difficult and is related to the development of schizophrenia or other debilitating mental and emotional problems. The belief that the schizophrenic behavior stabilizes the family so that the family does not have to deal with the threat of dissolution can be challenged by the observation that among some ethnic groups or working-class families, in which children typically leave home at later ages, there is no threat of family dissolution. Furthermore, some researchers have argued that in traditional families differentiation may occur later through marriage rather than through leaving home and establishing independence (Falicov, 1988).

Culture and Differences

Some researchers have found evidence that moral reasoning and maturity are related to cultural factors. For example, people who have graduated from college attain a higher level of moral reasoning than persons who graduated only from high school (Boldizar, Wilson, & Deemer, 1989). Other researchers have found that one can enhance moral development by interacting with others (Schlaefli, Rest, & Thoma, 1985) and by being in leadership roles (Tietjen & Walker, 1985).

Researchers have found that the family environment has some effect on the development of perception in children. For example, children raised by dominating parents who expected them to comply with rigid rules tend to be more distracted by irrelevant information in perceiving than children reared by less restrictive and less authoritarian parents (Witkin, Goodenough, & Oltman, 1979).

Cross-Cultural Studies

Research in cross-cultural studies provides a broader perspective for child development than is possible from a single culture (Rogoff & Morelli, 1989). These studies tend to focus on nonindustrial and non-Western cultures. An important advantage of cross-cultural studies is that one is able to stand back and view one's own culture dispassionately. Too often studies are biased because the researcher is also a subject within the same culture.

Western studies in child development have focused on the mother/child relationship, especially attachment, and stages of development. Cross-cultural studies generally have supported the stages of development expressed by Piaget and others (Rogoff & Morelli, 1989). Cross-cultural studies have found that children usually proceed through the same general stages, but at different rates. Of Piaget's stages, formal operations has received less support as being a universal stage. Piaget (1972), on the basis of evidence that the formal operations stage may not be universal, revised his theory to suggest that formal operations may represent individual competence (Rogoff & Morelli, 1989).

Perhaps the greatest contribution of cross-cultural studies is the link between culture and human behavior. One's behavior cannot be separated from the culture in which it exists. Studies have found that although some individuals in experimental settings may appear to be limited in cognitive skills, they are actually very skilled within their own daily activities (Rogoff & Morelli, 1989). This finding has led to the assumption that researchers should study the natural contexts in which individuals practice skills and behaviors.

Schooling.   Researchers have suggested that "schooling" or formal instruction may significantly contribute to differences in development. They believe that, as a variable in development, schooling is related to the development of such cognitive skills as logical reasoning and perception. In Western cultures, where schooling has greater influence, the more advanced cognitive and perceptual development may not reflect that Western children have real abilities which differ greatly from the abilities of children in other cultures where the cognitive and perceptual development is not as advanced. In real-life situations, children in non-Western cultures may perform just as competently as those in Western cultures. In contrast to everyday situations where the goal of the behavior guides the activity, in a school setting children have practice in carrying out a goal of completing an assignment by the teacher (Rogoff & Morelli, 1989).

Practice may also account for the physical differences that researchers note in cross-cultural studies. For example, African children develop sitting and walking skills earlier than Western children, who develop crawling and climbing stairs earlier (Rogoff & Morelli, 1989). African and American children are exposed to differences in contexts that tend to account for the difference. African children do not have stairs to climb and their parents encourage walking but not crawling skills, whereas American parents encourage their children to crawl and to learn to climb stairs.

Culture and Development

A cultural perspective of development is based on the notion that all members of a particular culture share the determinants of individual development. According to this perspective, biological or psychological factors are not adequate explanations for individual development. Rather, the individual is a product of his/her culture and, as such, is shaped by the culture. While some universal factors are evident, the steps in the developmental process clearly appear different for various cultures (Benedict, 1950).

According to Benedict (1950), some cultures tend to have age-appropriate expectations based on the acquisition of certain skills. These skills tend to be initiated in public ceremonies at the appropriate age. In contrast, cultures that do not have age-appropriate expectations also do not distinguish between the competencies of children and adults. The transition from childhood to adulthood occurs slowly and continuously.

Since the translation of his work into English, the Soviet Vygotsky (1978) has been influential in helping others understand the relationship of culture to development. His view of development emphasizes the interdependence of development and the social context. According to Vygotsky, much cognitive ability is the ability to use modern inventions. Children within a culture are skilled in using certain societal inventions. School, for example, is an invention in society when certain types of activity are practiced. When compared with children in other societies, children who have practiced certain skills appear more cognitively developed. Children learn in a society where more experienced adults model behavior. In this sense, "Culture and cognition create each other" (Cole, 1981).

For Vygotsky, development as represented by learning new skills occurred in a social context. A recent researcher found support for Vygotsky's theory. Freund (1990), working with 3- to 5-year-old children in an experimental setting of arranging furniture in a dollhouse, found that children were more competent in arranging the furniture when they had worked with their mother than when they had worked alone. Other researchers have found that children working with other children are better problem solvers than children working alone (Gauvain & Rogoff, 1989).

Vygotsky (1978) viewed language as an important factor in cognitive development and skills. A culture's language may partly determine the structure of cognitive ability and thinking. Combined with language is the importance of social interaction. As the child develops, the social interaction with the parent that determines the cognitive growth of the child may represent different outcomes in different cultures.

Vygotsky's view of language deviated from that of Piaget. Although both Piaget and Vygotsky believed that thinking preceded language, Vygotsky believed that thought and language merge and that nonsocial speech or private speech, called egocentric by Piaget, represents the transition from prelinguistic to spoken reasoning. Egocentric speech, according to Piaget, means little in terms of development. The child becomes progressively more social in speech as a consequence of being able to take on the role of others.

According to Vygotsky, nonsocial speech allows the child to better organize time and space. In contrast to Piaget, Vygotsky believed that nonsocial speech does not change to social speech as a dimension of development. Rather, it continues as a type of internal dialogue to organize and structure daily activity throughout one's life. Researchers have found that children consistently improve their performance as their nonsocial talk increases (Behrend, Rosengren, & Perlmutter, 1989). In addition, bright children tend to engage in more nonsocial talk than average children.

A Dialectical Approach to Development

A theoretical approach in the contextual perspective is **dialectical theory** (Riegel, 1976, 1979). The term **dialectical** refers to a dialogue or an experience where contradictory elements merge. The application of dialectical models to human behavior has a rich tradition in philosophy (Hegel, 1929) and in psychology in the development of gestalt therapy (Perls, 1969). The basic tenet of the dialectical model is the change that occurs when one statement or position (thesis) is challenged by its polar opposite (antithesis), forming a synthesis or resolution. The individual's state at any one time presupposes a contradictory state. The dialectical process is constantly in flux, and periods of equilibrium, or stages, are not evident.

Through the interplay of four distinct but interlocking dimensions—the inner/biological, the individual/psychological, the outer/physical, and the social/cultural—individual development takes place. The person cannot be separated from his/her environment and is in constant change. Developmental change results from conflict or tension between individuals and these four dimensions of development. This developmental process resembles a dialogue or conversation between the person and the environment where adjustments are made. This process is not predetermined, and the end result is not self-evident. Because the social and historical processes differ for individuals, maturation varies greatly.

Riegel's dialectical theory is both similar to and different from that of Piaget. For Piaget, development proceeds through stages that represent a period of equilibrium, or calm, which lasts for a period of time. During transitions between these stages, children are faced with contradictions between their understanding of the world and reality. Faced with conflict and disequilibrium, the child must devise new coping strategies. The child then moves to a new stage where a new equilibrium occurs. Riegel agrees that conflict and disequilibrium lead to a resolution and a brief period of stability, but he believes that equilibrium is short-lived. Universal stages with extended periods of equilibrium do not exist for Riegel. Rather, new discrepancies arise as soon as the conflicts are resolved. In the constant motion of the dialectic, one thing is met with its opposite to form a synthesis, which is encountered by its opposite, ad infinitum.

Critiquing the Theories of Development

Generally, the theories of development just discussed share concepts consistent with systems theory. The dialectical process involved in these theories fits with a systems perspective of change. For example, in these individual theories, the dynamic continuum between opposite points in Erickson's theory is similar in process to the theories of Piaget and Riegel. Erickson's dialectical process is not open-ended, however, and suggests that change is measured by the accomplishment of specific tasks. Kohlberg also implies that moral development must unfold toward a certain end point. Although dialectical in nature, the teleological view—that development appears to move toward an end point—implied in these theories would not be fully consistent with the systems notion that development may occur in different directions. Some modifications or alterations of the theories to make them more "systemic" are needed.

Contextualism, discussed in the section on family development, posits family relationships as extremely important for development. Serious students of development would not debate this point. What is open for debate, however, is more precisely how the family contributes to development. How does one explain, for example, the brilliant creative child who grew up to be world renowned in literature despite the fact that her parents were illiterate? To posit that the family, or the culture for that matter, is the cause of specific development in the child is a linear view of development and inconsistent with a systems paradigm. Although Vygotsky's claim that culture creates broad pathways for development that children by necessity incorporate, his ideas do not explain well the variety of development within a culture. His ideas appear to be dialectical in nature because change is understood as an ongoing, discontinuous process.

The question of dialectics requires further exploration. Although generally dialectical in nature, Piaget's theory has been criticized because it does not point to a true dialectical process (Lawler, 1975). Some researchers have argued that from Piaget's perspective cognitive development ends with the mastery of formal logical categories when there is no contradiction. From Riegel's point of view, it could be argued that the dialectical process which breaks down with the acquiring of formal logic is a rather static view of intelligence. Piaget's dialectical process tends to culminate in formal logic rather than lead to further development.

Other criticisms of Piaget's dialectical process have been made. Sameroff (1975) contends that Piaget's contradictions are between the cognitive structures and the input into these structures. He believes that Piaget's model is based on a coordination of structures at a lower level which leads to a new structure or level of development. For example, "The coordination of sucking, looking, and listening schemas produces the permanent object, or at a later stage the coordination of height and width concepts would produce conservation of mass" (p. 75). Furthermore, Piaget's basic dialectic appears to be between the individual and the environment, according to Sameroff, whereas Riegel's dialectical process is within the individual. Two contradictory cognitive inputs cause the individual to create a meaning system that can help him/her better understand the world.

Riegel's position is that change, rather than successive periods of equilibrium, is constant. This constant process defines and describes all life events, which are constantly in flux. When change occurs, the change involves both appearance and the structure of reality (Meacham, 1975).

Although Riegel's dialectical theory appears promising and consistent with a systems paradigm, some points in his theory should be expanded. Constant change certainly appears more appropriate for describing human interaction and behavior than is constant homeostasis. The uncertainty in Riegel's position, however, is that some processes do appear relatively stable over time. Personality appears to change little and, in fact, can be predicted in adulthood from the earliest emotional responses in the infant. Mental illness, especially schizophrenia, seems to continue regardless of the setting or circumstance.

In addition, Riegel does not specify the interactional dimension of the family in his four dimensions. No doubt, family interaction would be considered an aspect of the social/cultural dimension. From a systems perspective the intimate interactions within the family would call attention to the importance of these interactions for their role in the formation and maintenance of both functional and dysfunctional behavior. A fifth dimension could be added to Riegel's four dimensions labeled "family interactional system."

■ A Systems/Dialectical Theory of Development

The most consistent idea in the preceding discussion of the various theories of development is the notion of dialectics. The integration of systems theory and dialectical theory offers a unique way to view development.

Dialectics

A **systems/dialectical theory** views the basic dialectic as the tension arising between the desire to maintain a steady state and the desire to change, or homeostasis versus morphogenesis. These two opposite forces could form the basic background for all human behavior. This creative tension is present when the child learns to take the first step or when the elderly person learns to take the first step after suffering a broken hip.

This dynamic tension, or dialectic, though constantly occurring, is influenced by the power of each opposing position. While Riegel tends to suggest that the dialectic is an equal struggle by two opposing points, it is more likely that one point outweighs the other. The desire to change and the desire not to change differ in their power depending on the current event so that the resolution may be closer to the thesis than to the antithesis. For example, in a family where the wife wants to work outside the home and the husband is opposed, the resolution may be toward the husband's point of view because he has more power in the relationship. Resolutions therefore may appear almost indistinguishable from one of the opposing positions in the dialectic.

In applying these ideas to families, one could conclude that when families persist in a problem which appears unchanged, the appearance might be deceiving. Rather than acting out simply the rules of homeostasis, where irrational behavior is viewed as maintaining the family, many resolutions may have occurred but were little different from previous ones. It is not uncommon for families to say they have attempted many solutions, but nothing changed. The logical conclusion is that the resolutions tended to be toward the homeostasis end of the dialectic.

The process of development from this point of view modifies both Piaget's equilibrium view and Riegel's dialectical approach. It contends that equilibrium represents short periods similar to those suggested by Riegel, but perfect equilibrium is never reached. The polar forces of homeostasis and morphogenesis control the dialectical process. Some resolutions approximate previous ones on this continuum, producing little or no observable change, whereas other resolutions represent larger changes. Piaget referred to those resolutions producing little change as stages.

Development occurs within a context of the four dimensions discussed by Riegel and the familial dimension that this author suggested to add. When the child is met with experiences that are not understandable in one of the aforementioned dimensions, he/she attempts to resolve the conflict. Much experience, however, is not understood by the child, and the dialectical process of forming resolutions is in constant flux. Some resolutions tend to be very similar because better explanations cannot be found and because of the tendency to develop repeatable patterns. In this way, a "stage" appears to be protracted and the child appears to be in equilibrium. A new or novel resolution, one representing the morphogenetic end of the continuum, appears when the child makes a dynamic shift in understanding. New and novel resolutions do not appear as often because of the tendency to form repeatable patterns and rules, but when they do appear, dynamic shifts may result.

Moral Development and a Systems/Dialectical Model

In general, one can draw similar conclusions for conceptualizing moral development from a systems/dialectical model. This approach supports the belief that moral judgments are not permanent traits through the life cycle, but rather change in reference to the individual within a dynamic ecosystem (Meacham, 1975). A systems/dialectical perspective of moral development considers the interdependence of the individual's evaluation of the behavior, the contribution that other people or things outside the individual make to his/her moral judgment, and the larger cultural context. Behaviors are viewed as neither good nor bad but rather from a broad perspective depending on the context in which they appear.

Components of a Systems/Dialectical Model

While the preceding discussion should not be taken as a "new" theory, it is meant to integrate Riegel's dialectical theory in a systems framework. In integrating these concepts, one can make the following points for this model. First, development must be based on the context in which the individual develops—an idea that is expressed in the literature as "holism" (Reece & Overton, 1970). The researcher must investigate and acknowledge the contribution of parts within the context of the whole. The various dimensions of development must be viewed as contributing equally to the individual's development. In open systems, in which information passes back and forth between subsystems, the "whole" is constantly changing from the child to the dyad, to the family, to the culture and back to the child (Litowitz, 1983).

The context is not static or mere background, but dynamic. Development must be viewed as the interface of hierarchical coherent levels, linked by a feedback system with no level as the reference point. These hierarchical levels involved in human development include the inner/biological, the individual/psychological, the familial, the outer/physical, and the social/cultural (see Figure 2.1). No level of organization takes precedence over the other. The interaction among the levels comprises the process of human development. The organization of the levels at any one time in an individual's life is referred to as development.

This model posits that the argument about the interaction of the environment and nature is a moot one. Neither can take precedence over the other. Rather, the inner/biological interacts with the individual/psychological, the familial, the outer/physical, and the social/cultural to form a structure in which all levels contribute. The structure is such that both biological and contextual levels reciprocally influence each other. The interaction of the different levels, or systems, of the ecosystem attempts to maintain a balance among them that promotes "the survival both of the systems and the ecosystem" (Maddock, 1989). Balance in an ecosystem is the process of changing the relations among systems and ecosytems while maintaining the interdependence among them and "the integrity of the ecosystem in which they are a part."

Second, a systems perspective of development anticipates a **structural/functional perspective.** Structures develop through the individual's interaction with the environment and other people. Functions are patterns of behavior that occur consistently across the life cycle. Structures and their functions appear to mutually affect each other. The resolution of a conflict in the dialectical process represents both a structural and a functional change in the individual.

Structure applies to both biological and psychological patterns. Biological structures in an organism refer to cells, organs, and systems, and psychological structures refer to mental processes such as cognitive, moral, or emotional states. For example, Kohlberg's stages of moral development are a psychological structure.

When structures perform a certain purpose, they can be called functional. These functions can be either biological or psychological. For example, the structure labeled the eye may serve the function of seeing, or the structure of formal operations may serve the function of thinking in a logical pattern. The interaction of structure and function is related to changes throughout the life cycle.

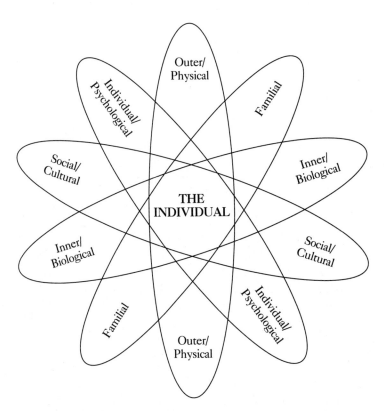

Figure 2.1 ■ **A Systems/Dialectical Model for Understanding Individual Behavior.**

Third, this model posits that the dialectical process, a change in structure rather than behavior, cannot be understood as resulting either from individual causes or from the context. Development can be viewed neither as directed by an end state, as would be the case with Piaget, nor as a consequence of external events, such as reinforcement or rewards, as might be true in a mechanistic model. Rather, development must be understood as a dynamic interaction of the individual and the context in which both are altered. Future development may be based on the past but is not dependent on it. New directions in development may occur at any period in the life cycle.

The dynamic interaction between the individual and the environment means that changes are likely to occur in the pathway that development follows (Sigman, 1982), sometimes referred to as relative plasticity. Over the life course, there is no single developmental pathway that all persons are expected to take. The pathway that does occur for an individual is the result of the interaction among the biological, psychological, and contextual dimensions of the person's life. Non-normative changes in the life cycle, discussed earlier in the chapter, affect the developmental pathway trajectory. For example, divorce and remarriage of parents could improve or lower the developmental trajectory.

Fourth, a systems/dialectical approach views change as both continuous, gradual or nonstage-like change, and discontinuous, stage-like or irreducible to previous elements. Some change appears to be continuous in that change can be predicted from earlier states. Other change in the system represents a change in the organization of the parts so that the new system has new, or "emergent," elements. In this regard both sameness and novelty can occur, and the reduction to antecedent events of a particular consequence is irrelevant.

A systems/dialectical approach to development suggests that most changes appear to be discontinuous rather than continuous. Because changes can occur at any time during the life cycle, predicting the specific pathway for change is very difficult. Changes occur over time as a consequence of the dynamic interaction of the individual and the environment. The best prediction for future change seems to be in terms of probable changes, referred to as probabilistic. Abilities that may be of little value at one period in a person's life may be of significant value at a later time.

Fifth, causality must be considered circular rather than linear. In mechanistic models, such as behaviorism, there is a unidirectionality of cause and effect, or one-way causality; that is, the effect depends precisely on the cause. Because of this unidirectionality of cause and effect, the S-R (stimulus-response) relationship can be identified for every behavioral change. The stimulus does not change and, in effect, stands outside the change process. Only the effect or response changes in the unidirectional model.

In contrast, a circular model is represented by reciprocal interaction in which each member affects and is affected by the other. This model, referred to as **bidirectional,** holds that an attempt to define one part of the change equation as cause and the other part as effect fails to explain the complexity of change. Because the structure has also changed, there is discontinuity and the equation cannot be reduced to an original S-R relationship.

In summary, from a systems/dialectical perspective, development is viewed as involving bidirectionality; that is, through circular feedback a child is influenced by and influences others. For example, children who have difficult temperaments, have sleeping problems, are irritable, and exhibit disruptive behavior tend to receive different behaviors from parents and teachers than children who have easy dispositions (Thomas & Chess, 1977). In this sense, children create their own development.

Feedback loops connect the individual with others and the environment, allowing the individual to be a self-regulating system. Flexibility helps the individual to cope with different situations. The change associated with flexibility could be seen as a kind of dialectic in which the new skill is needed or a different way of conceptualizing something is demanded. The dynamic tension between homeostasis and morphogenesis illustrates the constant demands to alter either oneself or one's context.

An implication of the frequent change in oneself and one's context is that a person is not the same over the life course. An adolescent is not the same as he/she was at 5 years old. The same behavior in a child may mean different things at different ages.

Because a person at any one time is so intertwined with the biological, psychological, familial, physical, and social dimensions of her world, her behavior may be expected to vary as these dimensions change. To say that a person "fits her context" is dynamic in that the person and the context must be thought of at a particular time.

■ Defining Conduct Disorders

To this point, the discussion has centered on human-development issues and these issues have been discussed within a systems perspective. The purpose of this section is to apply these developmental issues to parenting. For example, what is involved when children develop behavior that is noncompliant, destructive, and in opposition to parents and others around them? How different are these noncompliant children from children who relate well to parents, peers, and teachers?

Arrested Socialization

These questions can be answered in a number of ways. In general, age-appropriate behavior is a major consideration in determining misbehavior. For example, a 10-year-old having a temper tantrum in a store because the parents refused to buy him a toy would not demonstrate age-appropriate behavior. On the other hand, a 3-year-old having a temper tantrum in this same situation would be considered behaving in an age-appropriate way. If a behavior persists into another stage of development, most likely the child has formed a pattern in resolving conflict issues toward the homeostatic end of the continuum. Although the dialectical process is occurring, the resolutions are more similar than different.

Patterson (1982) refers to this tendency of behaviors to persist into a later stage of development as **arrested socialization.** The rate of severe conduct disorder has been identified by the President's Commission on Mental Health (1978) as between 5% and 15% of all children. A number of factors including age, sex, ethnic background, and type of disorder contribute to the rates of disorders (Kazdin, 1989). For example, boys (Graham, 1977), blacks and Hispanics (Langner, Gersten, & Eisenberg, 1974), and children from single-parent families (Gould, Wunsch-Hitzig, & Dohrenwend, 1980) tend to have high rates of conduct disorder.

The literature indicates that disorders such as temper tantrums, excessive fears, and the like are common in early childhood but tend to decrease through the process of development (Kazdin, 1989). There seems to be a consistent pattern among most children whose behavior exhibits conduct disorders. In addition, some problems disappear through the process of development but are replaced by other problems (Levitt, 1971). Although this phenomenon has not been well studied (Kazdin, 1989), it is clear that developmental determinants plot expected behavior along a certain continuum.

■ *Conduct disorder in children may reflect problems in the marital relationship.*

　　When children are referred to mental-health agencies for behavior problems, there is evidence that much more is occurring than a child's behavioral problem. For example, marital discord, a parent's severe depression, or other familial stressors may play a role. Many problems directly affecting children, such as child abuse, harsh punishment, or neglect, are either denied by parents or purposefully hidden by parents (Kazdin, 1989).

Factors Influencing Perception of Child Problems

A number of factors influence the perception of child problems. For example, research evidence suggests that parents are affected more by overt or acting-out behavior than by covert behavior such as truancy or lying (Loeber & Schmaling, 1985). Parents' lack of attention to covert behavior in children is reflected in researchers' lack of attention to this behavior. Most research instruments or checklists of misbehavior focus on overt behavior and do not measure covert behavior (Stouthamer-Loeber & Loeber, 1988).

　　Second, children do not present themselves to mental-health agencies with problems. Rather, children view the attention on them and their problems as externally motivated. Since children do not present themselves with problems, the focus on both the problem and the treatment has been on the parents (Kazdin, 1989). For example, strategies to help parents improve their skill in parenting focus on teaching parents how to change unwanted child behaviors. The literature on parenting over-emphasizes the parent's role in correcting the child's behavior.

Third, child problems cannot be separated from the context in which they appear. Typically, the child has been focused on for assessment and treatment. This focus is unidirectional and inadequate. In reviewing research in the parent/child interaction, Lewis and Lee-Painter (1974) conclude that parent and infant differ little in their ability to affect each other's behavior. They suggest that the infant shapes the parental behavior toward the infant. A bidirectional focus should equally scrutinize both the child's and the parent's behavior. Failure to identify and understand the parents' role in their child's misbehavior is correlated with poor outcomes in research (Griest & Wells, 1983).

A Systems/Dialectical Perspective of Conduct Disorder

What is needed is a focus on the total context of the child's misbehavior. There is some recent empirical emphasis in this direction, but it is only now beginning (Garmezy & Rutter, 1988). (See Table 2.2.) This total context includes the inner/biological, the individual/psychological, the familial, the outer/physical, and the social/cultural dimensions of development. Interaction of the individual in any of these dimensions is reflected by feedback loops. These feedback loops are self-regulating and operate in the manner of a dialectic where a resolution of opposing points occurs. This process is continual and may represent both incremental and dramatic changes. Although a child may appear to go through periods in which change is not recognized, small changes may be occurring.

In the case of chronic misbehavior, the self-regulating dialectic operates toward the homeostatic end of the continuum because this resolution is more operational than its competitor. The specific misbehavior may be maintained by familial relationships that prevent new or novel resolutions. In attempting to control unwanted behavior, the parent may inadvertently support the continuation of the misbehavior by persisting in the same kind of parental behaviors. When a misbehavior maintained within the family is changed, it can be expected that the family context has allowed a novel resolution to occur.

To change unwanted behaviors, parents may have to engage in **second-order parenting,** or behaviors that change the child, the parents, and the context simultaneously. Second-order parenting changes both the structure and the function of the parent/child relationship. For example, when parents are confronted with a 16-year-old boy who comes home late consistently after curfew, talks back to his parents, and openly smokes cigarettes and drinks alcohol in their presence, they are prone to handle it through increasing punitive behavior. Although punitive measures may be effective in the short-term, over the long-term they fail to be effective.

Table 2.2 ■ **Defining Conduct Disorder from a Systems/Dialectical Perspective**

- Conduct disorder is viewed as age-inappropriate behavior.
- Common disorders, such as temper tantrums and stealing, are more likely to occur at specific periods in development
- Marital and family problems may accompany the development of a child problem.
- Parents tend to ignore covert child behaviors but focus instead on overt behaviors.
- Treatment of child problems should focus on the total ecosystem rather than merely correct the child's behavior.
- Second-order parenting may be necessary to change chronic misbehavior.

In sum, many conduct disorders may represent deviations in normal developmental maturity. These so-called misbehaviors generally will disappear even if the parent does nothing to stop them. Parental overcontrol of these misbehaviors may be related to the development of behavior problems in children. When parents increase punitive control to curtail unwanted child behavior, the focus on the misbehavior may help create an ongoing or recurring pattern. The conduct disorder would be viewed as developing within a child and maintained through the social, psychological, physical, and familial subsystems in which the child lives. A dialectical process that changes in the context in which the child's misconduct occurs may be necessary to alter the behavior.

Parenting Proposition

Development is defined as change ocurring through a dialectical process that involves one or more of the following dimensions: the inner/biological, the outer/physical, the individual/psychological, the social/cultural, and the familial. These changes are related to both structural and functional aspects in the individual.

Answers to "Test Your Knowledge"

1.	F	4.	F
2.	T	5.	F
3.	F	6.	F

Key Concepts

child development

maturation

learning

process model of parenting

unidirectional model of parenting

cognitive development

equilibrium

schemata

adaptation

assimilation

accommodation

moral development

gender differences in moral development

stages of psychosocial development

life-span development

contextual approach

historical context

social ecosystem

normative changes

non-normative changes

single-parent families

blended families

internal working model

nonshared environment

extrafamilial context

ecosystemic view

ecological fit

dialectical theory

systems/dialectical theory

structural/functional perspective

bidirectional model of development

arrested socialization

second-order parenting

Study Questions

1 Compare and contrast current theories of child development with a systems/dialectical model of development

2 What is a unidirectional model of development? Give an example and cite research to back up your answer.

3 Briefly discuss Jean Piaget's theory of child development.

4 Briefly discuss Kohlberg's theory of moral development.

5 Briefly discuss life-span development. Give examples of life-span development.

6. Discuss the main tenets of the contextual approach of child development.

7 Describe the concept of arrested development. Give two examples.

8 Define *ecological fit*. Give several examples.

9 Define *life-cycle development*. What does *transitional crisis* refer to?

10 How valid is the belief that males and females differ according to the development of moral beliefs?

References

Ahrons, C. (1983). Divorce: Before, during, and after. In H. I. McCubbin & C. R. Figley (Eds.), *Stress and the family: Vol. 1. Coping with normative transactions* (pp. 102–115). New York: Brunner/Mazel.

Anderson, K. E., Lytton, H., & Romney, D. M. (1986). Mothers' interactions with normal conduct-disordered boys: Who effects whom? *Developmental Psychology, 22,* 604–609.

Baer, D. M. (1970). An age-irrelevant concept of development. *Merrill-Palmer Quarterly, 16,* 238–245.

Baltes, P. B., Reece, H. W., & Lipsett, L. P. (1980). Life-span developmental psychology. *Annual Review of Psychology, 31,* 65–110.

Becvar, D. S., & Becvar, R. J. (1988). *Family therapy: A systematic integration.* Boston: Allyn & Bacon.

Behrend, D. A., Rosengren, K., & Perlmutter, M. (1989). A new look at children's private speech: The effects of age, task difficulty, and parent presence. *International Journal of Behavioral Development, 12,* 305–320.

Bell, R. Q., & Chapman, M. (1986). Child effects in studies using experimental or brief longitudinal approaches to socialization. *Developmental Psychology, 22,* 595–603.

Bell, R. Q., & Harper, L. V. (1977). *Child effects on adults.* Hillsdale, NJ: Erlbaum.

Benedict, R. (1950). *Patterns of culture.* New York: New American Library.

Boldizar, J. P., Wilson, K. L., & Deemer, D. K. (1989). Gender, life experience, and moral judgement development: A process-oriented approach. *Journal of Personality and Social Psychology, 57,* 229–238.

Bolton, F. G., MacEachron, A., Laner, R. H., & Gai, D. S. (1987). *The adolescent family and child maltreatment: Perspectives on father, mother, and child.* Unpublished manuscript, Arizona Department of Economic Security.

Bowen, M. (1978). *Family therapy in clinical practice.* New York: Aronson.

Bronfenbrenner, U. (1979). *The ecology of human development.* Cambridge, MA: Harvard University Press.

Carter, E. A., & McGoldrick, M. (Eds.). (1980). *The family life cycle: A framework for family therapy.* New York: Gardner Press.

Charlesworth, W. (1976). Human intelligence as adaptation: An ethological approach. In L. B. Resnick (Ed.), *The nature of intelligence* (pp. 147–168). Hillsdale, NJ: Erlbaum.

Cole, M. (1981, September). *The zone of proximal development: Where culture and cognition create each other* (Report No. 106). San Diego, CA: University of California, Center for Human Information Processing.

Duvall, E. (1977). *Marriage and family development* (5th ed.). Philadelphia: Lippincott.

Elder, G. H., Jr., Liker, J. K., & Cross, C. E. (1984). Parent-child behavior in the Great Depression: Life course and intergenerational influences. In P. B. Baltes & O. G. Brim, Jr. (Eds.), *Life-span development and behavior* (Vol. 6). Orlando, FL: Academic Press.

Elkind, D. (1981). *The hurried child: Growing up too fast and too soon.* Reading, MA: Addison-Wesley.

Erikson, E. H. (1963). *Childhood and society.* New York: Norton.

Erikson, E. H. (1968). *Identity: Youth and crisis.* New York: Norton.

Erikson, E. H. (1982). *The life cycle completed: A review.* New York: Norton.

Falicov, C. J. (1988). Learning to think culturally. In H. A. Liddle, D. C. Brerentin, & R. C. Schwartz (Eds.), *Handbook of family training and supervision* (pp. 335–355). New York: Guilford Press.

Flavell, J. H. (1982). Structure, stages, and sequences in cognitive development. In W. A. Collins (Ed.), *The concept of development.* Minnesota symposium on child psychology (Vol. 15, pp. 1–28). Hillsdale, NJ: Erlbaum.

Freund, L. S. (1990). Maternal regulation of children's problem-solving behavior and its impact on children's performance. *Child Development, 61,* 113–127.

Furstenberg, F. F. (1980). Burdens and benefits. The impact of early child bearing on the family. *Journal of Social Issues, 36,* 64–87.

Garmezy, N., & Rutter, M. (Eds.). (1988). *Stress, coping, and development in children.* Baltimore, MD: Johns Hopkins University Press.

Gauvain, M., & Rogoff, B. (1989). Collaborative problem solving and children's planning skills. *Developmental Psychology, 25,* 139–151.

Gilligan, C. (1977). In a different voice: Women's conceptions of self and morality. *Harvard Educational Review, 47,* 481–517.

Gilligan, C. (1982). *In a different voice: Psychological theory and women's development.* Cambridge, MA: Harvard University Press.

Glick, P. C. (1984). Marriage, divorce, and living arrangements: Prospective changes. *Journal of Family Issues, 5,* 7–26.

Gould, M. S., Wunsch-Hitzig, R., & Dohrenwend, B. P. (1980). Formation of hypotheses about the prevalence, treatment, and prognostic significance of psychiatric disorders in children in the United States. In B. P. Dohrenwend et al. (Eds.), Mental illness in the United States: Epidemiological estimates (pp. 9–44). New York: Praeger.

Graham, P. J. (Ed.). (1977). *Epistemological approaches in child psychiatry.* New York: Academic Press.

Griest, D. L., & Wells, K. C. (1983). Behavioral family therapy with conduct disorders in children. *Behavior Therapy, 14,* 37–53.

Haley, J. (1973). *Uncommon therapy.* New York: Norton.

Hegel, G. W. F. (1929). *Science of logic.* New York: Macmillan.

Hetherington, E. M., & Baltes, P. B. (1988). Child psychology and life-span development. In E. M. Hetherington, R. M. Lerner, & M. Perlmutter (Eds.), *Child development in life-span perspective* (pp. 1–20). Hillsdale, NJ: Erlbaum.

Hetherington, E. M., Cox, M., & Cox, R. (1976). Divorced fathers. *The Family Coordinator, 25,* 417–428.

Hetherington, E. M., Cox, M., & Cox, R. (1985). Long-term effects of divorce and remarriage on the adjustment of children. *Journal of the American Academy of Child Psychiatry, 24*(5), 518–530.

Kagan, J. (1986). Presuppositions in developmental inquiry. In L. Cirillo & S. Wapner (Eds.), *Value presuppositions in theories of human development.* Hillsdale, NJ: Erlbaum.

Kazdin, A. E. (1989). Developmental psychopathology: Current research, issues, and directions. *American Psychologist, 44,* 180–187.

Kohlberg, L. (1969). Stage and sequence: The cognitive-development approach to socialization. In D. A. Goslin (Ed.), *Handbook of socialization theory and research.* Skokie, IL: Rand McNally.

Kreppner, K. (1989). Linking infant development-in-context research to the investigation of life-span family development. In K. Kreppner & R. M. Lerner (Eds.), *Family systems and life-span development* (pp. 33–64). Hillsdale, NJ: Erlbaum.

Langner, T. S., Gersten, J. C., & Eisenberg, J. G. (1974). Approaches to measurement and definition in the epidemiology of behavior disorders: Ethnic background and child behavior. *International Journal of Health Services, 4,* 483–501.

Lawler, J. (1975). Dialectical philosophy and developmental psychology: Hegel and Piaget on contradiction. *Human Development, 18,* 1–17.

Lerner, R. M. (1989). Developmental contextualism and the life-span view of person-context interaction. In M. Bernstein & J. S. Bruner (Eds.), *Interaction in human development* (pp. 217–239). Hillsdale, NJ: Erlbaum.

Levitt, E. E. (1971). Research on psychotherapy with children. In S. L. Garfield and A. E. Bergin (Eds.), *Handbook of psychotherapy and behavior change: An empirical analysis* (pp. 474–494). New York: Wiley.

Lewin, K. (1954). Behavior and development as a function of the total situation. In L. Carmichael (Ed.), *Manual of child psychology* (2nd ed.) (pp. 918–983). New York: Wiley.

Lewis, M., & Lee-Painter, S. (1974). An interactional approach to the mother-infant dyad. In M. Lewis and L. A. Rosenbaum (Eds.), *The origins of behavior: The effect of the impact on its caregiver* (pp. 21–48). New York: Wiley.

Litowitz, B. E. (1983). Context and continuity. Speeches from the Conference of the Erikson Institute, Chicago, April 29–30, 1983. ED 265 952 PS 015 613.

Loeber, R., & Schmaling, K. B. (1985). The utility of differentiating between mixed and pure forms of anti-social child behavior. *Journal of Abnormal Child Behavior, 13,* 315–336.

Maccoby, E. E. (1980). *Social development: Psychological growth and the parent-child relationship.* San Diego: Harcourt Brace Jovanovich.

McLoyd, V. C. (1990). The impact of economic hardship on black families and children: Psychological distress, parenting, and socioemotional development. *Child Development, 61,* 311–346.

Maddock, J. W. (1989). Healthy family sexuality: Positive principles for educators and clinicians. *Family Relations, 38,* 103–136.

Meacham, J. A. (1975). A dialectical approach to moral judgement and self-esteem. *Human Development, 18,* 159–170.

Minuchin, S. (1974). Families and family therapy. Cambridge, MA: Harvard University Press.

Newman, B. M., & Newman, P. R. (1991). *Development through life: A psychosocial approach* (5th ed.). New York: Brooks/Cole.

Norton, A. J., & Moorman, J. E. (1987). Current trends in marriage and divorce among American women. *Journal of Marriage and the Family, 49,* 3–14.

O'Flaherty, K. M., & Eells, L. W. (1988). Courtship behavior of the remarried. *Journal of Marriage and the Family, 50,* 499–506.

Parke, R. D. (1988). Families in life-span perspective: A multilevel developmental approach. In E. M. Hetherington, R. M. Lerner, & M. Perlmutter (Eds.), *Child development in life-span perspective* (pp. 159–190). Hillsdale, NJ: Erlbaum.

Patterson, G. R. (1982). *Coercive family process.* Eugene, OR: Castalia Press.

Perlmutter, M. (1988). Cognitive development in life-span perspective: From description of differences to explanation of changes. In E. M. Hetherington, R. M. Lerner, & M. Perlmutter (Eds.), *Child development in life-span perspective* (pp. 191–218). Hillsdale, NJ: Erlbaum.

Perls, F. S. (1969). *Ego, hunger, and aggression.* New York: Random House.

Piaget, J. (1950). *The psychology of intelligence.* New York: Harcourt Brace.

Piaget, J. (1952). *Judgement and reasoning in the child.* New York: Humanities Press.

Piaget, J. (1954). *The construction of reality in the child.* New York: Basic Books.

Piaget, J. (1972). Intellectual evolution from adolescence to adulthood. *Human Development, 15,* 1–12.

Plomin, R. (1989). Nature and nurture in the family. In K. Kreppner & R. M. Lerner (Eds.), *Family systems and life-span development* (pp. 129–148). Hillsdale, NJ: Erlbaum.

President's Commission on Mental Health Task Panel Reports (Vols. 1 & 2). (1978). Washington, DC: U.S. Government Printing Office.

Reece, H. W., & Overton, W. F. (1970). Models of development and theories of development. In L. R. Goulet & P. B. Baltes (Eds.), *Life-span developmental psychology* (pp. 111–145). New York: Academic Press.

Riegel, K. F. (1976). The dialectics of human development. *American Psychologist, 31,* 689–700.

Riegel, K. F. (1979). *Foundations of dialectical psychology.* New York: Academic Press.

Roberts, T. W., & Price, S. J. (1987). Instant families: Divorced mothers marry never-married men. *Journal of Divorce, 11,* 71–92.

Roberts, T. W., & Price, S. J. (1989). Adjustment in remarriage: Communication, cohesion, marital and parental roles. *Journal of Divorce, 13,* 17–43.

Rogoff, B., & Morelli, G. (1989). Perspectives on children's development from cultural psychology. *American Psychologist, 44,* 343–348.

Sameroff, A. J. (1975). Transactional models in early social relations. *Human Development, 18,* 65–79.

Santrock, J. W., Warshak, R., Lindbergh, C., & Meadows, L. (1982). Children's and parents' social behavior in stepfather families. *Child Development, 53,* 472–480.

Schlaefli, A., Rest, J. R., & Thomas, S. J. (1985). Does moral education improve moral judgement? A meta-analysis of intervention studies using the Defining Issues Test. *Review of Educational Research, 55,* 319–352.

Shaffer, D. R. (1989). *Developmental psychology: Childhood and adolescence* (2nd ed.). Pacific Grove, CA: Brooks/Cole.

Sigman, M. (1982). Plasticity in development: Implications for interventions. In L. A. Bond & J. M. Joffe (Eds.), *Facilitating infant and early childhood development* (pp. 98–116). Hanover, NH: University Press of New England.

Smetana, J. G., Killen, M., & Turiel, E. (1991). Children's reasoning about interpersonal and moral conflict. *Child Development, 62,* 629–644.

Stouthamer-Loeber, M., & Loeber, R. (1988). Parents as intervention agents for children with conduct problems and juvenile offenders. In D. H. Olson (Ed.), *Family perspectives in child and youth services* (pp. 127–148). Binghamton, NY: Haworth.

Tew, B. J., Lawrence, K. M., Payne, H., & Rawnsley, K. (1977). Marital stability following the birth of a child with spina bifida. *British Journal of Psychiatry, 131,* 79–82.

Thomas, S. J. (1986). Estimating gender differences in the comprehension and preference of moral issues. *Developmental Review, 6,* 165–180.

Thomas, A., & Chess, S. (1977). *Temperament and development.* New York: Brunner/Mazel.

Tietjen, A. M., & Walker, L. J. (1985). Moral reasoning and leadership among men in Papua New Guinea society. *Developmental Psychology, 21,* 982–992.

Vygotsky, L. S. (1978). *Mind in society.* Cambridge, MA: Harvard University Press.

Walker, K. N., & Messinger, L. (1979). Remarriage after divorce: Dissolution and the reconstitution of family boundaries. *Family Process, 18,* 185–192.

Walker, L. J., DeVries, B., & Trevethan, S. D. (1987). Moral stages and moral orientations in real-life and hypothetical dilemmas. Child Development, *58,* 842–858.

Wallerstein, J. S. (1987). Children of divorce: Report of a tenyear follow-up of early latency-age children. *American Journal of Orthopsychiatry, 57,* 199–211.

Wallerstein, J. S., & Kelly, J. B. (1974). The effects of parental divorce: Experiences of the preschool child. *Journal of American Academy of Child Psychiatry, 14,* 606–616.

Wallerstein, J. S., & Kelly, J. B. (1976). The effects of parental divorce: Experiences of the preschool child in later latency. *American Journal of Orthopsychiatry, 46,* 256–269.

Weiss, R. S. (1975). *Marital separation.* New York: Basic Books.

Whiteside, M. F. (1982). Remarriage: A family development process. *Journal of Marital and Family Therapy, 8,* 59–68.

Witkin, H. A., Goodenough, D. R., & Oltman, P. K. (1979). Psychological differentiation: Current status. *Journal of Personality and Social Psychology, 37,* 1127–1145.

Chapter 3

Parent Education from a Systems Perspective

Parenting Myth ■ The purpose of parent education is to teach parents skills in using strategies to change misbehavior in children.

Test Your Knowledge ■ The following questions were designed to test your knowledge prior to reading the material in this chapter. Answers appear at the end of the chapter.

1 Parent education is considered necessary for most parents in today's society. True or false?

2 The inconsistency principle in Parent Effectiveness Training (PET) suggests that being inconsistent in applying parenting strategies leads to poor outcomes in parent/child relationships. True or false?

3 Researchers have not verified the effectiveness of PET. True or false?

4 Physical punishment is usually regarded as a good means of gaining compliance from children. True or false?

5 From an Adlerian perspective, a cause of misbehavior in children is mistaken goals. True or false?

6 A systems perspective is different from other models of parenting because it posits reciprocal causality. True or false?

Assuming that parenting is a natural human behavior engaged in for millions of years, why do parents need to be trained to do something that comes naturally? The answer to this question is as complex as the question is and, perhaps, as unreassuring. While it is true that parents have been busy at parenting for quite some time, it is evident that parenting behaviors change according to societal situations. For example, one hundred years ago children were needed to help parents produce home-based artifacts and farm products. Working alongside their parents on a daily basis, children were socialized into expected child and adult roles. Child-care practices were handed down from one generation to the next with little alteration or concern about parenting per se. Parenting was "natural" in that generation after generation used similar methods. To suggest that parents needed to be educated to handle parent/child problems would have seemed laughable in those days.

In American society today, a number of factors unique to contemporary society influence parenting. Such factors as increased female participation in the work force, the increase in the number of single-parent families, gender differences in parenting, and remarried families combine to make the present period of parent/child relations quite different from the past.

■ Combining Employment and Parenting

Parenting in the 1980s and 1990s has little in common with parenting only a few generations ago. Today, more women with children 6 years of age and younger are in the labor force than stay home with the children (U.S. Bureau of the Census, 1989). The increase in mothers reentering the work force shortly after giving birth has quadrupled since 1950 (Hayghe, 1986). While women with young children have drastically increased their participation in the labor force, researchers have found that they still provide greater responsibility for child care than men do (Berardo, Shehan, & Leslie, 1987). Fathers provide only a small amount of time and activity with their children in comparison with mothers (Lamb, 1980). This lack of time and energy directed toward children by both parents affects the socialization process of children and parenting in particular.

Women return to work shortly after the birth of an infant for different reasons. Career-oriented women most often say that personal satisfaction and career development are the reasons for returning to work. Women with lower-status jobs return to work because of economic pressures (Volling & Belsky, 1993).

Researchers have found contradictory evidence about the mother's personal qualities related to the decision to return to work. Although some researchers have found that employed mothers with young children are more career oriented, less nurturant, and more organized in handling stress (Hock, Morgan, & Hock, 1985, cited in Volling & Belsky, 1993), other researchers have found that these characteristics are not significant in the mother's decision to return to work (Volling & Belsky, 1993).

While personal qualities of the mother may not be related to employment of mothers with young children, the mother's commitment to work prior to pregnancy appears to be a strong predictor of her returning to work within the first year. Career-oriented women have greater commitment to work than noncareer-oriented women. The father's prenatal participation in the family's division of labor and the amount of stress of the mother's job are important contextual factors related to the decision to return to work. Mothers are more likely to return to work shortly after the birth of a child if the father regularly participated in the household division of labor prenatally and if her job stress is low. It appears that women who do not return to work have less support from their husbands and are less satisfied in their work.

A number of researchers have found that the role of fatherhood among career-oriented men is stressful (Baruch & Barnett, 1986). For example, when fathers are active in child care they tend to feel more competent in their role as parent but feel more stress about their careers because the increase in child-care responsibilities decreases their time and energy for their careers. It appears to be very difficult for men to attain a satisfactory level at both high-quality parenting and high-quality career without feeling significant stress. Barnett, Marshall, and Pleck (1992) have found among white career-oriented men that both the quality of work and the quality of their parental roles are equally important for their psychological level of distress. Contrary to popular belief, the fathers in this study were quite concerned about their relationship with their children. The quality of the parent/child relationship rather than the circumstance of merely being a parent was the major predictor of the fathers' psychological level of distress.

This change in the way children are socialized affects parenting both in the amount of time that parents have available to take care of and interact with their children and in the quality of the parent/child relationship. Older children may form closer bonds with friends and peer group than with parents. When parents do have some time to spend with their children, they may find that they share little in common with their children except the same household.

Researchers have found some evidence that young children may be at high risk to form an insecure attachment with their mother if the mother works more than 20 hours a week and places them in a day-care center before the children reach 1 year of age (Belsky & Rovine, 1988). When linked with research concluding that older children in preschool and elementary school who have insecure attachments with their parents are more aggressive and noncompliant (Haskins, 1985), a concern about how parenting and work complement one another in families can be raised.

■ The Influence of Gender on Parenting

Concomitant with the issue of combining work and parenting, some researchers have found gender differences in parenting. For example, there is evidence that most couples believe that the wife is, or should be, more dominant in parenting. Husbands typically view their role as supportive to their wives, particularly to ensure the child's compliance (LaRossa, 1986). These roles, mothers involved more in nurturance and fathers involved more in control, evolved over time and are carried out without much conscious awareness. Socialization of boys and girls has much to do with these gender differences. For example, boys and girls are socialized toward different parenting roles. Girls are socialized toward child care and nurturance, whereas boys are socialized to be more assertive. Researchers have found that this gender difference is also evident in remarried families because stepfathers use more control than their wives (Santrock, Warshak, Lindbergh, & Meadows, 1982).

Single-parent mothers may have more difficulty with the control aspect of parenting than single-parent fathers. Some researchers have found that single-parent mothers do not use as much control as single-parent fathers (Santrock, Warshak, & Elliott, 1982). It appears that single-parent mothers may have more difficulty handling noncompliant behavior because of the female disposition and/or expectation to be more involved in nurturing than in controlling behavior. It would be expected that single-parent mothers use control proportionately to the amount of time they have been single parents. For example, single-parent mothers who have been single for ten years would tend to display more control than mothers who have been single for only a year.

■ The Effect of Family Structure on Parenting

The **nuclear family,** a family consisting of a father, a mother, and a child or children, accounts for only about one-fourth of today's families (White & Tsui, 1986). The American family can be characterized as **pluralistic,** or consisting of variant forms. A great increase in single-parent families has occurred since 1960, particularly among minorities. An estimated 86% of black children and 42% of white children experience a single parent in the course of growing up (Bumpass, 1984). Out-of-wedlock births to teenage mothers account for much of the increase of children reared in single-parent families. Among teenage mothers in 1984, 90% of black mothers and 48% of white mothers gave birth out of wedlock (National Center for Health Statistics, 1986).

The lack of resources and the concomitant effect on children's educational and occupational performance of single-parent families are well documented (Nock, 1988). Developmental delays and behavioral problems are more prominent in the preschool years in children raised in single-parent families than in children reared in two-parent families (Brooks-Gunn & Furstenberg, 1987). When children from single-parent families become adolescents, they have more problems in school and with drug use than children reared in two-parent families (Furstenberg, Brooks-Gunn, & Morgan, 1987).

The most common experience of out-of-wedlock births is poverty. Poverty, related to many ills in society including decreased effectiveness in parenting, has increased from 1970 to 1989 (U.S. House of Representatives, 1989). Compared to other children, children reared in poverty are at greater risk for developmental and behavioral problems (Fuchs & Reklis, 1992) and encounter more stress and negative life events (Hernandez, 1988). To counter the effects of poverty, various organizations and individuals have devised programs to improve the quality of the mother/child relationship by increasing knowledge of parenting and child development (Brooks-Gunn & Furstenberg, 1987).

The increase in remarried families means that a significant number of children are reared in homes with a stepparent. Generally, researchers have found that stepparents are not as bonded with stepchildren, provide less nurturance, and communicate less than biological parents (Astone & McLanahan, 1991). Thomson, McLanahan, and Curtin (1992) found that the amount and quality of the interaction of stepparents with stepchildren are significantly less than the amount of activities and quality of communication between biological parents and children. This research supports the contention that parenting by stepparents is qualitatively different from parenting by biological parents. The main reason for this difference is that stepparents are less likely to provide warmth and nurturance. Research with stepparents supports the contention that stepparenting can be more difficult than parenting one's biological children.

The Need for Parent Education in the 1990s

Instead of being natural, parenting has become a difficult role requiring that parents learn or be trained to parent effectively. But parents are not the only ones who benefit. Most clinicians and educators are aware of the benefits of parent education/training for the happiness and well-being of children. Some professionals have advocated compulsory parent education in both elementary and junior high school (Anastasiow, 1988). They believe that a proactive stance such as mandatory parent education would improve the chance of more normal developmental outcomes for children. Furthermore, the high number of children born to unwed mothers and the social problems experienced by those children might be lessened if parent education was mandatory. Parent education focusing on family involvement would be more desirable.

Some researchers have found evidence that a proactive stance can affect attitudes toward parenting. For example, Zoline and Jason (1985), using a group of high school seniors in a program providing behavioral skills training and child-development information, found that these students displayed significantly greater knowledge and positive expectations about parenting than did a control group that did not participate in the training.

The trend in developmental psychology over the past several decades toward a contextual, or interactional, perspective is based on the premise that development is plastic, or changeable. An impoverished beginning in life does not predispose the child toward lower developmental outcomes. Improved environmental contexts can change the developmental course at any stage of development or age (Vygotsky, 1978). The main emphasis in development is on the process of development, rather than final outcomes.

For the most part, researchers have supported the contention that parent-education programs improve the lives of children whose parent or parents participate. The best results of parent-education programs have come from middle-class subjects (Dumas & Wahler, 1983). Results indicate that the parent/child relationship is significantly improved through more open communication. Moreover, in recent years, parent-education efforts have been successful in the special-needs populations. For example, Pfander and Bradley-Johnson (1990) conducted a parent-education program for hospitalized infants in a neonatal intensive care unit. The purpose of the study was to determine if parent education was related to the quality of care for the infant and if mental development as measured by the Bayley Scales of Infant Development (BSID) was enhanced. Parents in the study displayed increased quality of care for the infant and the infants scored higher on the mental scale of the BSID, but the developmental assessment component of the scale did not enhance infant mental development.

Parent-education programs with children at high risk for abuse are popular in the literature. For example, videotape parent-education programs have increased in use because of both the application to large segments of the population and the low costs of conducting the programs. At the San Fernando Valley Child Guidance Clinic, a videotape parent-education program was used for abusive parents and parents at high risk for becoming abusive (Golub, Espinosa, Damon, & Card, 1987). Each week the videotape presentation showed a common problem of child rearing and a number of alternate parenting behaviors for the problem. After the videotape, parents met in groups and discussed the problem and its possible solutions. Parents who participated in the education program demonstrated increased knowledge of normal child development and alternatives to physical punishment, and they showed positive change in attitudes about children's misbehavior.

One group of researchers used a practical parenting approach with middle- and low-income families based on social-learning principles to increase parent skills in managing undesirable behavior (Thompson, Grow, Ruma, Daley, & Burke, 1993). Results indicated that these parents improved on seven of the eight indices used to test the effectiveness of the program. Furthermore, offering several locations and time periods for this program made it more accessible to low-income families. Make-up sessions were also available for parents who missed sessions. This research underscores the need for flexibility in providing parent education for low-income families.

In sum, the preceding discussion suggests that significant numbers of parents today have less time, energy, and other resources available to them, which makes it difficult for them to parent effectively. It also suggests that family structure is an important variable related to parenting. Single-parenting and stepparenting may offer unique challenges generally not present in two-parent families. Two-parent families, however, may have many parenting problems, not the least of which is related to increased female participation in the work force. To do a good job of parenting in the 1990s requires ongoing appraisal and development of parenting skills.

■ Parent-Education Models

Parent-education models have reflected three major theoretical positions. First, the humanistic model, characterized by showing understanding of the child's feelings, is best represented by the work of Haim Ginott (1969) and Thomas Gordon (1975). Parent Effectiveness Training (PET) (Gordon, 1975), one type of humanistic model, applies the work of Carl Rogers to parenting. Parents are taught in this model to respond to their child's feelings rather than use rewards, reinforcement, or consequences for behavior. Second, Adlerian theory has been applied to parenting (Dinkmeyer & McKay, 1976; Dreikurs & Soltz, 1964). This model is based on the principle that when children suffer the consequences of their misbehavior they learn to act responsibly. Third, the behavioral approach, emphasizing reinforcing desired behavior and punishing or extinguishing negative behavior, has been applied in a number of ways to parenting (Patterson, 1975, 1982; Smith & Smith, 1966).

Initially, these models were published in books or adapted to workshop format. More recently, the concepts in these models have been expanded and adapted for videocassettes. For example, Michael Popkin (1983) has developed a videotape package for parenting called "Active Parenting" based on the theoretical position of Alfred Adler (1927) and Rudolph Dreikurs (Dreikurs & Soltz, 1964). Using 40 vignettes, Popkin presents the concepts of active listening and effective communication skills. Another example is the work by Richard McDowell (1978), which uses a modified behavioral approach in presenting an abbreviated workshop of three primary meetings with one follow-up meeting to teach parents behavioral management techniques. Training materials include filmstrips, explaining the concepts of behavioral management, and a parent workbook that contains exercises, activities, and other material of help to parents.

For the most part, the behavioral approach discussed in this chapter will review the earlier work of Gerald Patterson (1975, 1982). Although Patterson (1986) presents a fuller account of family dynamics in later writings, his position is clearly a behavioral cause-and-effect paradigm. For example, his later writings suggest that deviant behavior in children reflects a breakdown in parental management skills, an increase in the child's negative behavior, and parental rejection of the child. (Patterson, Dishion, & Bank, 1984). These elements interact in a mutual cause-and-effect manner in that parent behaviors and child behaviors form a contingent reinforcement pattern where each depends on the other. Rather than being consistent with a systems paradigm, the real message in Patterson's later writings is the same as in the earlier writings: namely, behavior that is reinforced will continue. There is no more support for discussing novelty or unexplained behavior in the later writings than there was in the earlier writings.

While other models are available in the literature, only the humanistic, Adlerian, and behavioral models in parent education will be discussed in more detail in the next section of the chapter. These models will be critiqued using available research, and suggestions for a new model, incorporating a systems perspective, will be made. Then the advantages of a systems model for parenting over established models will be discussed. In addition, the few articles or book chapters referring to a systems perspective will be evaluated. The last section of the chapter will present a new and innovative model based on a systems/dialectical approach.

Parent Effectiveness Training (PET)

PET consists of a workshop format of eight weekly three-hour classes. It is based on a number of skills that are believed to be helpful in all human relationships. Thomas Gordon (1975) believes that healthy growth and development of children is closely related to the ability to communicate feelings. In this regard, Gordon's position is similar to that of other theorists such as Haim Ginott (1969). Although Gordon's position is based on Ginott's ideas of communication and feeling as the central parenting behaviors, Gordon expands the concepts and applicability of the theory.

Gordon's beliefs are also similar to those of Carl Rogers (1961), particularly in the need to create an accepting and respectful atmosphere. In fact, both Gordon and Rogers see parents somewhat as therapists for their children in both their accepting attitudes and their behaviors toward children. They believe that children are sufficiently competent to solve many of their own problems, but this competency requires that the parents create the proper atmosphere.

Gordon has applied Rogers's (1965) "client-centered theory" to parenting in the same way the therapist is instructed to reflect in a nonjudgmental way what the client is saying. The child's misbehavior signals that "dysfunctional communication" predominates between the child and the parent. Children naturally resist negative and coercive means of controlling their behavior. In fact, the child must try harder to defend the way he/she is against the onslaught of parental criticism (Gordon, 1975). In effect, the natural tendency to grow and develop is thwarted by such parental behavior.

The net result of negative parental behavior toward the child is a vicious cycle in which the misbehavior of the child is followed by punitive efforts to control him/her. The skills taught in PET are meant to enhance mutual satisfaction of parent and child and create a positive feedback cycle. For example, parents respond to the child by showing respect and empathy. In return, children are more likely to talk about problems and negotiate change. Children are expected to develop optimally from the consistent positive interactive cycle with the parents.

There are two basic principles of PET, the inconsistency principle and the problem ownership principle. Gordon (1975) believed that the tendency of parents to

■ *According to PET, parents must be good listeners to their children.*

emphasize consistency and form a united parental front may limit the parents' effectiveness. According to Gordon, it is far better for the parents to act naturally, recognizing that inconsistencies do occur and that parents often disagree about parenting. The **inconsistency principle** refers to parents attempting too hard to agree on matters in which agreement is difficult. The **problem ownership principle** refers to whether the behavior is acceptable to the parent, whether the behavior indicates the child's needs are being met, or whether the behavior is neither a parent nor a child problem. It is important to determine problem ownership because parental behavior should vary accordingly.

Active Listening.   By use of **active listening** a parent is able to show acceptance of the child, demonstrate a desire to hear the child's point of view, and perhaps most important, allow the child to emphsize his/her autonomy. Specifically, by using active listening, a parent allows the child to own his/her problem. And for the child, active listening provides the opportunity to explore his/her behavior in a caring and non-judgmental environment (Gordon, 1975).

The parent demonstrates active listening by reflecting, or feeding back, the feelings the child expresses. This is usually followed by greater exploration of the problem and more self-reflection on the part of the child. For example, if the child says, "I don't have any friends because nobody would play kick ball with me on the playground at school today," the parent would demonstrate active listening by responding, "You really felt left out playing today because no one wanted to play kick ball." This statement by the child followed by the parent's reflection can go on for some time, depending on the situation and the child's self-exploration (Gordon, 1975).

The use of active listening by a parent, however, is affected by the tendency to want to solve the problem for the child. In wanting to help their child, parents often move the exploration of feelings along too fast and prevent the child's self-exploration and taking responsibility for the problem. It takes practice to learn and implement active listening skills. Parents sometimes find this type of responding to their child's feelings to be unnatural and laborious (Gordon, 1975).

I-Messages.   Gordon (1975) recognized that active listening is not always enough to influence the child's behavior effectively. Taking more control of the situation is referred to as sending **I-messages.** When the parent is angry or irritated at the child, the parent may initiate the communication with the child by using an I-message, which consists of three specific parts: (1) a statement of how the parent feels, (2) a statement of what the feeling is based on, and (3) a statement of why the parent disapproves of the behavior. For example, a parent who is upset at the child's dawdling behavior in getting dressed to go with the parent to the store, may say, "I'm irritated that you didn't get dressed sooner because I will not have adequate time to shop."

The advantages of using I-messages are that they communicate the parent's need to the child and display empathy and caring. The honesty and straightforwardness of such an approach creates openness and honesty in return. Sometimes children will respond to I-messages by returning an I-message. The parent would then respond to the child's I-message through active listening (Gordon, 1975). For example, a parent might say to a child playing outside, "I want you to wear shoes when you are outside." The child might respond with "I don't like wearing shoes because my feet hurt." To this, the parent might say, "You prefer not wearing shoes when you are running because your feet hurt."

I-messages can also be used when there is no conflict between the parent and the child. For example, parents can use I-messages to express encouragement for the child's positive behavior. A parent might say, "I like it when you put away your dishes after dinner." A one-sided or too frequent use of I-messages by the parent could elicit a negative response from the child. A few appreciative I-messages can facilitate more effective communication. In addition, parents can use I-messages to prevent future misbehavior. For example, a parent may say to a child before going shopping, "I want you to stay near me in the store and I want you to walk and hold my hand in the parking lot" (Gordon, 1975).

No-Lose Solution.   Gordon (1975) believed that conflicts between parent and child should be resolved in a way that is not coercive to either through the practice of a **no-lose solution.** There are six steps in the no-lose solution: (1) defining the problem, (2) identifying alternate solutions, (3) evaluating alternate solutions, (4) deciding on a preferred solution, (5) carrying through on the decision, and (6) a follow-up evaluation.

The no-lose solution begins with the parent describing his/her feelings about the problem and asking the child to do the same. Considerable time and effort should go into defining the problem and selecting alternate solutions. Instead of force being used to arrive at a solution, necessary time is allowed for each person to feel comfortable with and agree on one solution.

When agreed-on solutions are broken by children, the parent may use an I-message to express irritation or anger. Using an I-message is preferred over the use of punishment. Parents who attempt to gain compliance to an agreed-on solution through punishment will find that they have undermined the relationship.

Evaluation of PET. A number of researchers have found positive outcomes in parenting effectiveness for parents who use PET. For example, Hills and Knowles (1987) found that parents who have been trained in PET provided more warmth and acceptance of their child when compared with a control group. In addition, research has indicated that parents in a PET workshop showed more liberal child-rearing attitudes than did control subjects or subjects who read the book but were not involved in the workshop (Mitchell & McManis, 1977).

On the other hand, some researchers have been critical of PET (Doherty & Ryder, 1980). One major criticism is directed at the underlying assumption that parents should be therapists for their children. In the parent/child dyad, the input of the parent is much greater than that of the child. The resulting model is unidirectional, suggesting that the flow of influence is from parent to child exclusively. There is little or no consideration for family dynamics. Not only is the behavior of other family members not given proper attention in the influence on the child's misbehavior, but no attention is given to siblings who aren't misbehaving. Nor is there discussion of the role of the marital dyad in misbehavior.

While the PET model ignores family dynamics, it also ignores landmarks in child-development research. For example, some researchers criticize PET for being simplistic in its lack of attention to age differences and cognitive development of children. There is no indication that personality theory is represented in this model.

In reviewing the research on the effectiveness of PET, Levant (1983) summarized 23 studies, many of which were unpublished dissertations. He found that most of the studies used pretest and posttest designs and only a few used longitudinal designs. The subjects generally were middle-class families with children who were disabled; families with emotionally disturbed and high-risk children; single parent families; and highly educated families.

Levant (1983) summarized the findings as follows:

> Overall, the results these 23 studies are not encouraging. Eleven studies compared PET to a nonattendant comparison or control group. . . . Out of a total of 100 comparisons, 53 (53%) showed no significant differences, 36 (36%) favored PET, and 11 (11%) favored the comparison group. Twelve studies compared PET to an alternative treatment. . . . Two of these studies were not included in this overall analysis. . . . In the remaining 10 studies, out of a total of 49 comparisons, 34 (69%) showed no significant differences, 12 (25%) favored PET, and 6 (3%) favored the alternate treatment.

However, this bleak picture is misleading because so many of the studies are rife with serious methodological problems. In fact, there are only three studies which met the following minimal criteria of methodological adequacy: use of a nonattendant control group, random assignment to condition, use of standard PET procedures, and appropriate use of inferential statistical tests. . . . These three studies compared PET to a control group, using a pre-post design and self-report measures. Out of 35 comparisons, 24 (69%) favored PET over the control group, 0 (0%) favored the control group, and 11 (31%) showed no significant differences. Another recent review of research of PET concludes that most studies have been methodologically weak. The failure to demonstrate appropriate research outcomes drastically weakens the application of PET as a parent-training model (p. 41).

One final criticism of PET is "that Gordon has confused, equated, and interchanged terms of authority, parental power, and excessive punishment" (Barr, 1987, p. 95). Barr views the PET warning against the use of parental power as exaggerated and criticizes Gordon for not distinguishing between parental power and parental abuse. According to Barr, a qualitative difference exists between parental abusive behavior and parental power. The former is correlated with certain negative behaviors in children such as stubbornness, poor impulse control, and aggressive behavior (Green, 1978, cited in Barr, 1987), whereas the latter is correlated with highly functional behavior in children. Based on these criticisms, Barr suggests that Gordon either conduct research to substantiate his claims or not make them.

Adlerian Parent Education

Alfred Adler (1927), a contemporary of Sigmund Freud, has been very influential in parent-education models. His basic assumptions lend themselves to the application of parenting techniques because they are based on how to behave responsibly within a social group. Specifically, he was concerned with development of personality through self-directed achievements. He also believed that humans are goal directed or future oriented. When these concepts are applied to parenting, it becomes clear that children are goal oriented in behavior and that even misbehavior must be understood in terms of its purpose. **Adlerian parent education** helps parents understand the goal of their child's misbehavior. Strategies focus on helping the child learn to act responsibly.

The Goal of Misbehaving.   A follower of Adler, Dreikurs developed the parenting model most associated with Adler (Dreikurs & Soltz, 1964). The misbehaviors of children are described as **goal directed** in that these misbehaviors represent attempts at belonging, misguided as they are. These **mistaken goals**—attention, power, revenge, or inadequacy—increase in severity in response to the child's feeling of belonging.

Dreikurs believed that children as well as adults have resources needed to meet any crisis and that parents should provide children with experiences that develop their resources and provide a challenge. For example, parents must encourage independent self-direction in their children, which, according to Dreikurs, will help build the child's competency and ability to live in a society that requires order and restraint. Showing the child respect from birth sends a message that he/she is a valued member of society (Dreikurs & Soltz, 1964).

According to the Adlerian model, families should adopt the principle of **democracy,** allowing all members to have equal rights to be respected and listened to. The welfare of the family is everyone's duty including children's. Working for the common good of all is an expected behavior to live successfully within a social order. In order to accomplish the common good, the family must be structurally organized and governed by a set of rules (Dreikurs & Soltz, 1964).

By encouraging appropriate behavior, parents allow their children to accept responsibility for their behavior. When children are prevented from making or fail to make a social contribution, they seek other, less desirable ways to accomplish a desirable end. For example, a child, naturally desiring attention, will talk or act aggressively in order to obtain a response from the parent. If the child is denied appropriate attention, particularly as it becomes a pattern in the parent/child relationship, the child will use other means to attain the goal (Dreikurs & Soltz, 1964).

This second round of misbehavior is referred to as a power struggle, which is a deliberate attempt of the child to win in a dispute with the parent. The dispute may be over mealtime, TV watching, snacking between meals, bedtime, or a host of other situations in which the child can attempt to assert dominance. Power struggles with a child are more difficult to resolve than the desire for attention (Dreikurs & Soltz, 1964).

Failing in the power struggle, the child may intensify the struggle with the parent and increase his/her resistive behavior. Having given up the hope of attaining desired goals through positive behavior, the child pits his/her will against the parents in deliberate acts of sabotage or noncompliance. To this child, getting even is more important than fitting in and belonging (Dreikurs & Soltz, 1964).

Children who have failed to attain their goals resort to demonstrating inadequacy, or giving up of any appropriate pursuit of positive behavior. Parents of such children, according to Dreikurs, are angry and locked in to certain behaviors that they believe will improve the situation. Over the long run these parents are punitive and not accepting of the child. Dreikurs believed that it is necessary for parents to be more accepting of the child when the child is misbehaving than at other times (Dreikurs & Soltz, 1964).

Natural and Logical Consequences. The parent can respond in a number of ways to the child's misbehavior. First, the parent can use **natural consequences,** or consequences the child brings on him/herself as a result of the misbehavior. For example, a child refusing to wear a coat to school on a very cold day may learn the hard way by being cold rather than the parent getting into a struggle for control by attempting to force the child to wear the coat. Dreikurs and Soltz (1964) view natural consequences, however, as limited in responding to many child misbehaviors, such as running into the street.

Parent involvement that provides more direct input to change the child's behavior is called **logical consequences.** Although logical consequences are placed on the child by the parent, they are not equated with punishment. A punishment is a penalty placed on the child as a result of the child's misbehavior, whereas a logical consequence is a circumstance that follows logically from the child's behavior. For example, a child's not coming to dinner on time could result in the food being put away and the child receiving no dinner. In such situations, the parent must be firm without engaging in a power struggle and must not respond verbally or nonverbally in a punitive manner. Dreikurs believed that the consequences of the misbehavior are enough for the child to learn appropriate behavior and that lecturing or criticizing the child are ineffective. Children who are responded to with logical consequences will learn self-control and to take responsibility for their own behavior (Dreikurs & Soltz, 1964).

Dreikurs encouraged the use of regular **family meetings** in which all family members participate equally to discuss and make decisions about particular family issues. Problems facing the family or particular members are discussed openly, and decisions are made by the family as a group. Resolving problems in this manner creates cooperation and group cohesiveness. If problems occur between meetings, no decision is to be made until it can be fully discussed at the next family meeting (Dreikurs & Soltz, 1964).

Systematic Training for Effective Parenting (STEP) is an Adlerian approach based on the work of Dreikurs (Dinkmeyer & McKay, 1976). This training model, lasting approximately two hours for nine sessions, is limited to 12 participants. Each session is concerned with a specific parenting technique. Although relationships among family members are considered important, the major thrust is toward the parent gaining skill in dealing with specific misbehavior.

Evaluation of Adlerian Parenting.   Considerable research has been conducted on the Adlerian approach. In a comparative study of PET with STEP and other Adlerian approaches, none was found more effective than the others (Hills & Knowles, 1987). In a review of 21 studies evaluating parent-education programs from an Adlerian perspective, Burnett (1988) concluded that generally there is support for the Adlerian position. Positive effects on children's behavior and self-concept and parental attitudes were found. For the most part these 21 studies were methodologically sound but could have been strengthened by using control groups and randomized sampling. Weaknesses included poor follow-up and evaluation of the long-term effects of participating in an Adlerian parent-education program. None of the studies used family variables, such as intact versus divorced, the level of conflict, or the degree of satisfaction with relationships, in determining the effect of change in family functioning. Extrafamilial variables, such as the social network including school, work, extended family, or society, were not considered. Although Adlerian approaches have some methodological problems, researchers conclude that they are more sound than studies of PET or behavioral theories (Krebs, 1986). These methodological problems and weaknesses, however, make it impossible to determine the long-range effects of Adlerian parent education on families.

Behavioral Model of Parenting

The **behavioral model of parent education** is based on the view that all behavior is learned through social interactions with significant others. Behavior is either **reinforced** by others or eliminated for lack of reinforcement. **Punishment** is viewed as a powerful means of control of behavior, but it must be used according to specific guidelines (Clark, 1985; Patterson, 1982). A child's misbehavior, simply put, is the degree to which the child's behavior has been reinforced or rewarded by the parent in the absence of appropriate punishment.

Parent-education models from the behavioral approach attempt to teach parents specific skills in parenting. The child's misbehavior is seen as resulting from deficits in social learning or socialization rather than as personality or emotional disorders. The parent, as the main agent of socialization for the children, must be alert to reeducating his/her child.

Techniques of Child Management.   The behavioral model trains parents in specific techniques of managing the child's behavior. Generally, these techniques focus on specific targeted behaviors of the child. Recognizing that children are not always able to act accordingly to rewards, parents are informed how to break down behaviors into smaller units to **shape** the child's behavior gradually over time. In addition to shaping behavior, parents themselves are models that children imitate.

In giving rewards to shape behavior, parents are advised to reward immediately after the child performs the desired behavior. **Rewards** are of three basic types: social, or smiles, hugs, praise, and attention; material rewards of gifts, special treats, and food; and privileges such as special purchases, surprises, and outings. Because children are different, some rewards may be more effective with one child than with other children. Behaviorists believe that social rewards are generally the most effective because of their cohesive function for family members. When families have a long history of poor parent/child relations, however, it might be more appropriate to use material rewards or privileges until the social relation has altered in a more positive direction (Patterson, 1982).

In order to firmly establish a behavior, the parent should reward it regularly at first until the desired behavior is established, then reward it not as often. Behaviorists teach parents specifically how to give rewards to their children. The following is a list of recommended steps presented by Jane Brooks (1987).

1. Make eye contact with your child. Direct eye contact makes the statement a more personal one.
2. Be physically close to your child. Praise given at close range has more impact.
3. Smile. Sometimes a smile alone is praise, but it should accompany the verbal message so that the child sees your pleasure on your facial expression.
4. Comment on positive behaviors. Send I-messages telling the child what you like about his/her behavior—"I like it when you help me carry in the groceries." Express appreciation when the child does you a favor—"Thank you for mailing my letter." Children blossom under this attention.
5. Focus on behavior, not on the child. Like every other strategy presented, behaviorists recommend comments on specific behaviors on the child's

■ *Time-out is a frequently used method of discipline by behaviorists.*

characteristic. "Doing dishes is a big help to me, Linda, and I appreciate it," not "What a good girl you are."

6. Show affection. How we handle our bodies—our gestures, moves, tone of voice—can increase the value of the praise and make the child feel very special. Again, tailor the affectionate demonstration to the child.

7. Immediately deliver reward. The faster the reward is given, the more effective it is. (pp. 76–77)

Behaviorists recognize that praise and reward may not be adequate to shape a child's behavior in the desired direction. Consequently, they have developed a number of techniques that could be used for eliminating undesirable behavior. One technique is for parents to state specific expectations of their children in specific behavioral terms so that the child has no misunderstanding. When the child deliberately behaves in undesired ways, the parent must observe both the child and his/her own behavior. This observation helps the parent determine a strategy to change the child's behavior and, perhaps, his/her own behavior. In setting up a plan of action, the parent might include rewards or punishments, perhaps even ignoring the child's misbehavior, depending on the situation (Clark, 1985).

Evaluation of Behavioral Theory.   A considerable amount of research has demonstrated the effectiveness of the behavioral model. In a review of the literature, Pinsker and Geoffray (1981) found that parents easily learn and implement the behavioral approach, requiring few professionals. In comparing behavioral approaches to other approaches, they found the behavioral model to be more effective in decreasing problem behavior. In addition, this same study revealed that there is a greater tendency for parents using a behavioral approach to exert more parental control than parents who are using the two other approaches.

Some researchers have severely criticized the behavioral approach. For example, Cagan (1980) pointed out the mechanistic underpinnings of this approach. The parent/child relationship is constructed so that the parent is the reinforcer of the child's behavior, whereas the child is not considered of equal importance in the parent/child dyad. The reciprocal role of the parent and child in interaction with each other is not considered. This one-sided emphasis on the dominance of the parent over the child ignores literature emphasizing the importance of reciprocity in the parent/child relationship.

Recent research has found that children may not persist in desired behaviors unless those behaviors are rewarded (Fabes, Fultz, Eisenberg, May-Phumlee, & Christopher, 1989). The more parents use rewards, apparently the more they are forced to use rewards. For example, when parents use a reward system to get children to do chores, they may discover that children are not doing their chores after rewards cease. As parents rely on rewards, the creativity in solving problems and other positive outcomes in parent/child relationships may be curtailed (Schwartz, 1986).

The use of rewards to motivate change in children appears to be a form of bribery, though not according to a strict definition. For example, when a parent rewards a child for going to bed early by reading two additional stories, the right result is obtained but for the wrong reason. A parent who uses this kind of reward would be expected to reward certain behaviors but fail to create self-motivation on the part of the child (Boggiano & Main, 1986). Most activities that a child repeats have some intrinsic value for the child in addition to the reward from the parent. For example, when a child plays a game very hard and is creative and innovative in doing so, the reward is the enjoyment derived from this activity. Behaviorists do not consider these internal sources of "reward" an important variable.

■ ## Parent-Education Models: A Critique

Weaknesses of Adlerian, Humanistic, and Behavioral Models

These three approaches to child rearing are dissimilar but share some of the same weaknesses. Although all models tend to be validated by some research findings, the following criticisms are based on the belief that outcomes have focused on limited variables, failing to consider the interdependence of the child's behavior and the behavior of other family members. For all three approaches, seven criticisms can be made. First, outcome studies tend to look at either the parent variable or the child variable, but not at the long-term effects of parent education on the family. In addition, the focus on specific child behaviors without regard to age or developmental appropriateness of the child has been criticized as a "cookbook" approach to eradicating the unwanted behavior of the child (Griffore, 1980).

Second, all three parenting approaches are based on a cause-and-effect, or linear, model of reality. In a **linear model**, A causes B where A precedes the response of B, referred to as the billiard ball approach to causality. These three approaches tend to make the parent's behavior the cause of the child's behavior. When the parent changes approaches to the child, the child changes behavior. For example, a parent may find that the child's temper tantrum is not a problem after he/she stops giving in when the child escalates the screaming.

Although recent attempts have been made to integrate systems theory and Adlerian theory into a compatible approach (Dinkmeyer & Dinkmeyer, 1991; Sherman & Dinkmeyer, 1987), researchers have not addressed basic differences in the two models regarding how they conceptualize causality and the nature of change. For example, Adlerian theory suggests that the child learns to act more responsibly because of suffering the natural or logical consequences of behavior. These consequences result from the child's own behavior or the parent devising consequences to fit the behavior. The change that takes place is in how the child views his/her own behavior. This view of change is not consistent with a systems perspective of bidirectional change; that is, both parent and child change.

Third, these models tend to err in that they suggest there are specific parental behaviors for specific child behaviors. When parent/child relations are viewed in this way, the behavior of both child and parent is lifted from the current context. For example, a temper tantrum is to be responded to in the same way in all circumstances, and a dawdling child must be responded to in a certain way. This gives the impression that a parent can simply look up a description of a misbehavior and apply certain techniques, which result in immediate change. While parents and professionals generally support this "cookbook" approach, this false sense of "correct" parental behavior is portrayed as the appropriate, or only, parental behavior. Parents may actually come out of these experiences disillusioned because they are unable to "perform" as the experts advise (Doherty & Ryder, 1980). Alternate parent-education programs are needed that are relevant to parents' specific concerns and backgrounds (Brems, Baldwin, & Baxter, 1993).

Fourth, evidence is beginning to emerge that parent education can negatively affect family stability (Getz & Gunn, 1988). This greater disruption of families who have been in a parent-education class results from only one parent, usually the mother, participating in the training (Levant & Doyle, 1981). Mothers who participate in parent-education classes may exhibit better parenting skills and have a better relationship with their child, but be less satisfied with their partner. Furthermore, Noller and Taylor (1980) have noted that the marital relationship suffers when only one spouse has received parent education. Obviously, any model of parent education should address the negative side-effects.

Fifth, these three models are reductionistic in that they fail to appreciate the complexity in the parent/child relationship, particularly relationships with other family members and extrafamilial relationships. The larger social network, the eco-system of the family including peers, work, and culture, is not even discussed as a possible molder of family interaction. Cross-cultural comparisons emphasize the need for grounding individual behaviors in a broader context than even the family.

Sixth, researchers generally have found that no approach is superior in effectiveness. While short-term gains have been demonstrated in outcomes in child behavior (Powell, 1986), little is known of the lasting effects of these changes. Seckinger and Day (1986) suggest that the failure to find a superior content may reflect the lack of attention in all programs to the disregard for the specific needs of different families represented in the parent-education programs.

Finally, models of parenting tend to focus on either the nurturing function or the control function of parenting but to ignore the interactive or ecological aspects of parenting. For example, Adlerians tend to focus on both nurturance and control by allowing natural consequences and by placing logical consequences on the child's misbehavior. The consequences act to reinforce certain appropriate goals in the child and to teach the child responsibility. The parent's attitude is both nurturing and controlling. It is **nurturing** in that the parent maintains a high level of respect for the child, a decreased level of authority, and demonstrates democratic practices. On the other hand, it is **controlling** because parents use their authority to set up consequences to influence behavior. The humanistic position tends to focus on nurturance rather than control. In fact, the parent tends to gain control through nurturant acts of showing understanding and empathy. Adherents to a systems approach focus primarily on the **interactive model** as being formative for both nurturance and control functions of parenting. For example, interaction within the family through play, storytelling, or family rituals provides a naturalistic structure for both building cohesion and influencing behavior.

The Need for a New Parent-Education Model

Based on the preceding weaknesses of current parent-education models, a new paradigm for training parents is needed. A number of researchers have pointed out the need for a paradigm shift that emphasizes the individual in context (Getz & Gunn, 1988; Osborne, 1989). While Osborne has written specifically about the need for a parent-education model from a systems perspective, to date not one model has emerged. Other researchers have suggested that traditional parent-education models be revised to include children and parents interacting together (Coleman & Ganong, 1987).

No doubt a systems perspective of parent education would be difficult to evaluate. Only a few instruments are currently available to determine outcome variables of family members and family functioning. In addition, parent education must shift in focus toward "family" education; that is, the context in training must include both parents and nonsymptomatic siblings. A circular view of seeing the child in context emphasizes the reciprocity between the child's behavior and the parent's behavior (Osborne, 1989). A **circular model** takes the position that children and parents are subjectively reactive. When the parent does something to the child, the effect on the child is determined by his/her subjective reactivity to the parent. This means that one person may respond to a situation or person differently than another may respond. Consequently, parent training must be tailored to meet the specific needs of family members (Getz & Gunn, 1988). It may be necessary to determine how individual behavior "fits" in the family ecosystem. This ecosystem may be the necessary point of emphasis. Change may, therefore, represent a complex pattern of relationships in the family ecosystem.

The goal of parent education from a systems perspective would be to develop functional families. The goal in behavioral, Adlerian, and humanistic approaches is to reduce a child's misbehavior and help the parent gain confidence in meeting the challenge of parenting. Gaining new skills in communicating, problem solving, and nurturing no doubt are helpful to parents. The concern, however, is that the underlying family ecosystem is not a focus of the behavioral, Adlerian, and humanistic models. Learning skills without applying them to a specific context appears to be an extremely simplistic maneuver.

Other forms of family interaction, such as play, storytelling, or family rituals, are not discussed in current nonsystems models of parent education. The application of play as a specific parenting behavior is underdeveloped in the literature with the exception of its use in counseling or therapeutic settings. Storytelling, offering a unique and creative way to communicate and influence the behaviors of both parent and child, has rarely been applied to parent education. The potential for using storytelling and play in influencing positive parent/child relations appears unlimited.

To date there is one published article on parent education from a systems perspective (Getz & Gunn, 1988). That article argues effectively that a systems perspective is needed for parent education. How a systems perspective is integrated in parent education, however, is not adequately developed. In fact, in suggesting that a particular parent/child problem first be analyzed in terms of family dynamics, followed by applying a specific Adlerian or PET technique, undermines a systems perspective. No doubt the lack of specificity in systems theory lends itself to borrowing techniques from other positions. My position, however, is that borrowing such techniques from other positions undermines the significant contribution of a systems approach. Mixing a circular paradigm and a linear paradigm only contributes to more confusion and adds little to understanding the total ecosystem.

Attempts to Apply Systems Theory to Parenting

Several publications have attempted to apply systems therapy to parenting issues. One such application was a chapter in a book on strategic therapy (Efron, Rowe, & Atkison, 1986). While the authors are to be commended for their efforts to apply

■ *In the early years, the parental role reflects teaching and guiding behaviors.*

strategic therapy to the parent/child relationship, they fail to address a number of problems. First, they make the same mistake as Getz and Gunn (1988) in integrating techniques developed in behavioral or Adlerian perspectives. A systems perspective offers a unique approach in that it does not focus on technique. This orientation of parents learning particular skills for the purpose of controlling or changing the child's behavior must not be incorporated into a systems perspective.

Second, the aforemented strategic application departs from a truly systemic or circular approach. It takes the position that the therapist is the knowledgeable person and should not share his/her views of family dynamics with the family. This lack of trust in how the family would use, or resist, such information necessitates a third party, namely the therapist, guiding or directing change from outside the family. The position taken in this book is that families must be empowered from within to direct, monitor, and change. Parent education must be conducted in such a way as to enhance family functioning through empowering families to be their own change agent.

A systems/dialectical perspective of parent education would focus on the functional aspects of the child's misbehavior for the family. This aspect of the family can be referred to as an ecological fit in that a child's misbehavior is viewed as "fitting" the context of the family in the sense that the misbehavior is the child's attempt to resolve a conflict in his/her ecosystem. In this sense the child's behavior is viewed as **context dependent.** In contrast to behaviorism, which tends to view humans in terms of simple and proximate situations, systems theory does not separate the individual from the environment and regards child learning and behavior as occurring in the naturalistic setting (Ballard, 1986; Bronfenbrenner, 1977).

Finally, from a systems perspective, each family would be viewed as unique, which would allow what is learned from a training session to be carried over to the real family situation. Research indicates that models utilizing a "personal-meaning approach"—that is, associating the technique with individual application—have resulted in more effective parental learning and use of the techniques than in traditional models (Hills & Knowles, 1987). Participants in a systems approach would be able to bring their own family experiences and dynamics into the learning process.

Table 3.1 compares systems/dialectical, Adlerian, behavioral, and humanistic (PET) models of parent education.

■ A Parent-Education Program from a Systems Perspective

In this model, the concept of circular causality is applied to parent education and parenting behavior is viewed as not essentially different from other parent/child interaction. Training sessions should include both parents in two-parent families, and in single-parent families, all persons involved in parenting should be included. In order to address specific family needs, parents should be assigned to one of three groups according to the age of the misbehaving child: parents with an infant or preschool child; parents with an elementary school child; and parents with an adolescent. Assigning families in this way facilitates sharing of information and helps build cohesiveness in the groups. Evaluation of the model may need further elaboration and development because existing measures are inadequate to evaluate it.

This model, consisting of sessions 2½ hours long over a 12-week period, would be limited to five families and all family members would be expected to participate. The goal would be to improve overall family functioning through better relationships.

Table 3.1 ■ Comparing Systems/Dialectical, Adlerian, Behavioral, and Humanistic (PET) Models of Parent Education

	S/D	Adlerian	Behavioral	PET
Considers developmental issues	yes	no	no	no
Considers age of child	yes	no	no	no
Prescribes specific techniques regardless of the current situation	no	yes	yes	yes
Requires participation of both parents in parent-education classes	yes	no	no	no
Considers other social and cultural factors related to the child's misbehavior	yes	somewhat	somewhat	no
Assumes that if parents change their behavior the child will change his/her behavior	no	yes	yes	yes
Advocates good communication skills between parent and child	yes	yes	yes	yes

Note: These issues are compared according to their occurrence in the different strategies used by parents.

The evaluation of parent-education models should consider the total ecological situation including the child, the family, and the culture (Weiss & Jacobs, 1984). Such frequently used instruments as the following should be used: Child Behavior Checklist (CBC) (Freeman, 1975), Parent Attitude Survey (PAS) (Hereford, 1963), Family Adaptability and Cohesion Scale (FACES-II) (Olson et al., 1982), Dyadic Adjustment Scale (DAS) (Spanier, 1976), and Parents' Ratings of Program Effectiveness (PREPE) (Noller & Taylor, 1989). The individual child measures, commonly used by researchers, are included mainly for comparison because other parent-education measures use only individual measures. The point of main interest is the use of family measures to determine the impact on the family. To date, parent education routinely uses individual measures exclusively. All subjects would be given the measures at pretest, posttest following the training, six months after training, and one year after training.

This model consists of three distinct stages. Stage one consists of an initial interview with each participating family. A facilitator collects demographic data on each family, and assesses family strengths and goals. The goals will help tailor the training toward particular needs. Stage two consists of 12 sessions each 2½ hours long. These sessions are described in more detail below. Stage three consists of follow-up evaluations at the last session, six months later, and one year after training.

Session 1: This 2½ hour opening session focuses on helping family members understand how behavior in the family is reciprocal. The concept of circular causality is presented in concrete terms and examples given. A videotape demonstration is presented followed by group discussion. In a group session, each family is asked to apply these concepts to their own situation, particularly to the identified misbehavior.

The purpose of this session is to introduce participants to the idea that the child's misbehavior occurs within a context of mutually interacting persons. Furthermore, it is meant to reframe the child's behavior problem in terms of misguided efforts by both the child and the parents to adjust or overcome the problem. The tendency to determine blame or fault in relationships is altered by the view of reciprocal causality.

This session also includes a discussion on cultural patterns and other influences on the family, including work, school, and community. The idea of how the family and individuals fit their total ecosystem is presented. Each family probes their own background to find links with the current situation.

Session 2: Because most parents lack understanding of developmental issues, this session focuses on increasing knowledge of developmental issues including physical and cognitive development through the life cycle. Specific developmental issues are highlighted according to the three problem groups mentioned earlier, and the concept of "transition" is emphasized. Developmental stages are discussed for infancy, toddlerhood, preschool age, school age, and adolescence. The discussion on infancy focuses on physical development of expected behaviors during the first year, including teething, crawling, walking, and sitting independently. For the toddlerhood stage, expected physical development, intellectual development, and social/emotional development are discussed and specific issues such as autonomy versus doubt, separation from parents, and toilet training are highlighted. Initiative versus guilt, sex role and identity, play, fears, and imaginary friends are emphasized in the preschool-age years, ages 3 to 6. Making friends, learning new skills, self-evaluation, team play, and Erikson's (1963) psychosocial crisis industry versus inferiority characterize the school-age years. Adolescent development focuses on physical changes at puberty, peer group relationships, sexual relationships, and identity versus alienation.

Session 3: This session continues the previous discussion by applying moral development theory to parenting (Gilligan, 1981; Kohlberg, 1981). Parents and children could be inspired to reason at higher levels of moral reasoning through exercises in moral dilemmas (Winsor & Lower, 1989). Although the application of the various levels of moral reasoning to specific child misbehavior has not been emphasized in the literature, it seems clear that parents must communicate moral reasons for behavior on a level that the child can easily comprehend. For example, a child reasoning on level one would have much difficulty understanding the concept of "turning the other cheek" when a child borrows his favorite toy and loses it. Communications problems between parents and child may reflect their different levels in moral reasoning; knowledge and understanding of the different levels could help resolve these problems.

Session 4: This session is the communication component, and it emphasizes problem-solving skills rather than merely reacting emotionally. Family members are helped to reduce negative communicating and learn ways of pooling resources to solve problems. All members in a family must be able to communicate clearly. Unfortunately, most methods of teaching communication skills are based on adult levels of cognitive reasoning. Younger children have greater difficulty communicating critical information that a listener needs in order to differentiate one piece of information from another (Kahan & Richards, 1986). As children age they anticipate better what listeners need and direct their statements accordingly. For example, 9- to 10-year-old children provide repeated information to fill in gaps for the listener more often than 6- to 7-year-old children (Sonnenschein, 1986). There is also evidence that younger children overlook problematic statements because they assume that the speaker has stated a clear message, whereas 8- to 10-year-old children ask more often for clarification. Young children can improve their communication skills by being helped to differentiate one piece of information from another. In addition, young children can be encouraged to listen more attentively to statements and ask for clarification. Reading and writing exercises can help school-age children improve their communication skills (Olson & Hildyard, 1983). At the end of this session, a videotape demonstration is presented followed by group discussion of applying these concepts to their own families.

Session 5: The purpose of this session is to improve the marital relationship and improve sibling relationships. Although marital and family therapists have known that child problems are related to conflictive marriages, no parent-education program addresses this important issue. Parents are in one group and children in a second group. The parent group is presented information about unhealthy marital relationships. Of particular interest is how spouses allow their conflicts to interfere with their parenting. The overinvolved/underinvolved spousal split in parenting, respectively, may represent an underlying marital problem instead of a child problem. This mishandling of the marital problem complicates and inhibits appropriate parenting strategies. This problem is particularly exacerbated when the spouses have divergent family backgrounds and maintain loyalty to those backgrounds in parenting. When one parent uses his/her power to undermine the other parent, the child probably will develop behavioral problems. Parents are encouraged to agree on their parenting approach or, at least, not to undermine the partner's authority with the child. Videotape examples show how a fused relationship by the spouses may be reflected in child problems. The children's group focuses on sibling relationships and the importance of understanding one's role as sibling.

Session 6: This session focuses on the development and maintenance of triangles in the family. The basic theory of a triangle—when dyadic relationships reach a certain level of tension, a third party is invited into the relationship—is discussed. A number of examples are used to show the classic formation of familial triangulation of the conflict between husband and wife being defused through the child. Videotape examples show how parents and children form triangles and their destructive uses. Families have an opportunity to discuss and apply these concepts in a group setting.

Session 7: This session focuses on family boundaries. Instructional material is presented on the concept of boundaries, emotional barriers that protect and identify the integrity of individual members, subsystems, and families. Clear boundaries, which are open and flexible, are correlated with healthy families. Spouses must form a boundary around their relationship while allowing for interaction with the children. When a parent becomes closer to a child than to the spouse, he/she has violated a spousal boundary. Videotape examples are shown, and families have the opportunity to discuss and apply these concepts to their own families.

Session 8: This session focuses on Bowen's (1978) concept of **differentiation,** the process by which a person controls his/her emotional reactions to family members. Developing autonomous individuals who are connected but also capable of thinking and acting autonomously are presented. When members of the family are emotionally reactive and become distanced through conflicts, they are characterized as being undifferentiated. Undifferentiated persons fail to separate thought from feeling and find their intellect overrun with emotions, preventing rational or objective thinking. In families characterized by lack of differentiation, members maintain the fusion through rigid boundaries or through inappropriate attempts at independence, such as emotional cutoffs (that is, creating physical distance in an attempt to differentiate). Parents are encouraged to make differentiation a goal of parenting. The time when children leave home is discussed in this session as a primary problem for undifferentiated families (Haley, 1963). Videotape examples and discussion of the issues and application to one's family will follow.

Session 9: This session focuses on unwritten family rules and on the development of family roles. The concept of rules is defined and discussed. A family, according to systems theory, is a rule-governed system. Behavior does not occur randomly; rather, behavior conforms to certain rules. Dysfunctional behavior reflects an inflexible set of rules, most of which are nonverbal and covert. Families are encouraged in this session to make their rules explicit and negotiable through family interaction. Helping members define and evaluate their current roles are also an emphasis of this session. The perpetual behavior imposed on a family member due to the complex interactional patterns within the family is referred to as a role. When a family is stuck with inflexible roles, symptomatology, such as misbehavior in a child, often develops. "The sick one" or "the bad child" are roles maintained by family interaction (Bell, 1975). Videotape examples are shown and discussed.

Session 10: This session again divides parents and children into two groups. Parents focus on the beneficial effects of play with children and the utilization of play in creating cooperative family relations. Play has been applied to therapy (Axline, 1947) and to learning (Bergen, 1988; Sponseller, 1974), but rarely has been applied to parenting strategies, including control of behavior. Parents are taught how to use play to gain cooperation and create patterns of mutual enjoyment and satisfaction. The children's group is a discussion of play followed by individual and group play activities.

Session 11: This session focuses on storytelling as an underdeveloped and underutilized parental behavior activity. Again parents and children are separated by group. Parents learn how to use storytelling to direct children's behavior and gain cooperation. The children's group discusses storytelling, and each child writes/tells a story about his/her family experiences.

Session 12: This is the concluding session in which families discuss and evaluate their family goals. They evaluate how this training has affected each member of the family. A posttest evaluation using the same instrument as the pretest is given. A follow-up at six months and one year will be done.

While the preceding proposed model is only one of many that could be devised for addressing parent education from a systems perspective, this model has a number of advantages over traditional ones discussed earlier. First, the family ecosystem maintains behavior and action within the bounds of its context. The family is viewed as an interactive system that is responsible for individual behavior. Correcting the individual necessitates participation of the entire family unit. The focus of training is the ecosystem itself and not individual behavior. This model is true to a systemic paradigm, which views behavior as reflecting circular rather than linear causality.

Second, the outcome of training should be improvement in the family system. The long-term effects will be evaluated rather than the short-term improvement in the child's behavior. Satisfaction in the marital relationships will be evaluated as part of the follow-up. This outcome will address a crucial factor in parent/child relations—that is, the marital dyad. Outcomes in parent education training in which the child's behavior is improved, but the marital or family situation is worse, would be considered failures.

Parenting Proposition

Parent education should consider the whole family and aim to improve the family's level of functioning. All members of the family should be present. The focus should be to help the family monitor itself and be able to both understand itself better and solve its own problems.

Answers to "Test Your Knowledge"

1. T   4. F
2. F   5. T
3. T   6. T

Key Concepts

nuclear family

pluralism

parent-education models

Parent Effectiveness Training (PET)

inconsistency principle

problem ownership principle

active listening

I-messages

no-lose solution

Adlerian parent education

goal-directed behavior

mistaken goals

democracy	shaping behavior
natural consequences	reward
logical consequences	linear model
family meeting	nurturing function of parenting
Systematic Training for Effective Parenting (STEP)	control function of parenting
	interactive model of parenting
behavioral model of parent education	circular model
reinforcement	context-dependent behavior
punishment	differentiation

Study Questions

1 Compare and contrast parenting today with parenting in earlier periods of American history.

2 Discuss the phrase "Parenting is not a natural behavior." Give a rationale for your answer.

3 PET is considered a humanistic approach to parenting. Explain why it would be considered humanistic.

4 Discuss the strengths and weaknesses of PET.

5 Discuss Adlerian parent-education principles. Define such concepts as mistaken goals, democracy, natural and logical consequences, and family meeting.

6 Discuss the basic principles of behavioral parent education.

7 Compare and contrast parenting from a systems perspective to PET, Adlerian, and behavioral perspectives.

8 Discuss the advantages of a systems perspective of parent education.

9 Discuss errors in applying a systems perspective to parenting.

10 Outline a 12-week training session for parenting from a systems perspective.

References

Adler, A. (1927). *The practice and theory of individual psychology.* Harcourt, Brace, & World.

Anastasiow, N. (1988). Should parenting education be mandatory? *Topics in Early Childhood Special Education, 8,* 60–72.

Astone, N. M., & McLanahan, S. S. (1991). Family structure, parental practices, and high school completion. *American Sociological Review, 56,* 309–320.

Axline, V. M. (1947). *Play therapy: The inner dynamics of childhood.* New York: Houghton Mifflin.

Ballard, K. (1986). Child learning and development in context: Strategies for analyzing behavior-environment interactions and a proposal for research into everyday experiences. *Educational Psychology, 6,* 123–137.

Barnett, R. C., Marshall, N. L., & Pleck, J. H. (1992). Men's multiple roles and psychological distress. *Journal of Marriage and the Family, 54,* 358–367.

Barr, R. T. (1987). Parent effectiveness training and parental authority: A critique. *Family Therapy, 14,* 91–96.

Baruch, G. K., & Barnett, R. C. (1986). Role quality, multiple role involvement, and psychological well-being in midlife women. *Journal of Personality and Social Psychology, 51,* 578–585.

Bell, J. E. (1975). *Family therapy.* New York: Jason Aronson.

Belsky, J., & Rovine, M. (1988). Nonmaternal care in the first year of life and security of infant-parent attachment. *Child Development, 59,* 157–167.

Berardo, D. H., Shehan, C. L., & Leslie, G. R. (1987). A residue of tradition: Jobs, careers, and spouses' time in housework. *Journal of Marriage and the Family, 49,* 381–390.

Bergen, D. (1988). *Play as a medium for learning and development: A handbook of therapy and practice.* Portsmouth, NH: Heinemann.

Boggiano, A. K., & Main, D. S. (1986). Enhancing children's interest in activities used as rewards: The bonus effect. *Journal of Personality and Social Psychology, 51,* 1116–1126.

Bowen, M. (1978). *Family therapy in clinical practice.* New York: Jason Aronson.

Brems, C., Baldwin, M., & Baxter, S. (1993). Empirical evaluation of a self psychologically oriented parent education program. *Family Relations, 42,* 26–30.

Bronfenbrenner, U. (1977). Toward an experimental ecology of human development. *American Psychologist, 32,* 513–531.

Brooks, J. (1987). *The process of parenting* (2nd ed.). Mountain View, CA: Mayfield.

Brooks-Gunn, J., & Furstenberg, F. F. (1987). Continuity and change in the context of poverty: Adolescent mothers and their children. In J. J. Gallagher & C. T. Ramey (Eds.), *The malleability of children* (pp. 171–188). Baltimore: Brookes.

Bumpass, L. L. (1984). Children and marital disruption: A replication and update. *Demography, 21,* 71–82.

Burnett, P. C. (1988). Evaluation of Adlerian parenting programs. *Individual Psychology, 44,* 63–76.

Cagan, E. (1980, January/February). The positive parent: Raising children the scientific way. *Social Policy,* 40–48.

Clark, L. (1985). *SOS! Help for parents: A practical guide for handling common everyday behavior problems.* Bowling Green, KY: Parents Press.

Coleman, M., & Ganong, L. (1987). An evaluation of the stepfamily self help literature for children and adolescents. *Family Relations, 36,* 61–65.

Dinkmeyer, D., Jr., & Dinkmeyer, D., Sr. (1991). Adlerian family therapy. In A. M. Horne & J. L. Passmore (Eds.), *Family counseling and therapy* (pp. 383–402). Itasca, IL: Peacock.

Dinkmeyer, D., Sr., & McKay, G. (1976). *Parent's handbook (A part of the complete STEP Program).* Circle Pines, MN: American Guidance Service.

Doherty, W. J., & Ryder, R. (1980). Parent effectiveness training (PET): Criticisms and caveats. *Journal of Marital and Family Therapy, 6,* 409–419.

Dreikurs, R., & Soltz, V. (1964). *Children: The challenge.* New York: Hawthorne.

Dumas, J. E., & Wahler, R. G. (1983). Predictors of treatment outcome in parent training: Mothers' insularity and socioeconomic disadvantage. *Behavioral Assessment, 5,* 301–313.

Efron, D. E., Rowe, B., & Atkison, B. (1986). Strategic parenting. In D. E. Efron (Ed.), *Journeys: Expansion of the strategic systemic therapies.* New York: Brunner/Mazel.

Erikson, E. H. (1963). *Childhood and society* (2nd ed.). New York: Norton.

Fabes, R. A., Fultz, J., Eisenberg, N., May-Phumlee, T., & Christopher, F. S. (1989). Effects of rewards on children's prosocial motivation: A socialization study. *Developmental Psychology, 25,* 509–515.

Freeman, C. W. (1975). Adlerian mother study group: Effects on attitudes and behavior. *Journal of Individual Psychology, 31,* 37–50.

Fuchs, V. R., & Reklis, D. M. (1992). America's children: Economic perspectives and policy options. *Science, 255,* 41–46.

Furstenberg, F. F., Brooks-Gunn, J., & Morgan, P. (1987). *Adolescent mothers in later life.* New York: Cambridge University Press.

Getz, H., & Gunn, W. B. (1988). Parent education from a family-systems perspective. *The School Counselor, 35,* 331–336.

Gilligan, C. (1982). *In a different voice: Psychological theory and women's development.* Cambridge, MA: Harvard University Press.

Ginott, H. (1969). *Between parent and child.* New York: Avon.

Golub, J. S., Espinosa, M., Damon, L., & Card, J. (1987). A videotape parent education program for abusive parents. *Child Abuse and Neglect, 11,* 255–265.

Gordon, T. (1975). *P.E.T.: Parent Effectiveness Training.* New York: New American Library.

Green, A. H. (1978). Child abuse. In B. B. Wolman (Ed.), *Handbook of treatment of mental disorders in childhood and adolescence.* Englewood Cliffs, NJ: Prentice-Hall.

Griffore, R. (1980). Toward the use of child development research in informed parenting. *Journal of Clinical Child Psychology, 9,* 48–57.

Haley, J. (1963). *Strategies of psychotherapy.* New York: Grune & Stratton.

Haskins, R. (1985). Public school aggression among children with varying day-care experience. *Child Development, 56,* 689–703.

Havemann, E., & Lehtinen, M. (1986). *Marriages and families: New problems, new opportunities* (2nd ed.). Englewood Cliffs, NJ: Prentice-Hall.

Hayghe, H. (1986). Rise in mothers' labor force activity includes those with infants. *Monthly Labor Review, 109,* 43–45.

Hereford, C. F. (1963). *Changing parental attitude through group discussion.* Austin: University of Texas Press.

Hernandez, D. J. (1988). Demographic trends and the living arrangements of children. In E. M. Hetherington & J. D. Arasteh (Eds.), *Impact of divorce, single-parenting and step-parenting on children* (pp. 3–22). Hillsdale, NJ: Erlbaum.

Hills, M., & Knowles, D. (1987). Providing for personal meaning in parental education programs. *Family Relations, 36,* 158–162.

Hock, E., Morgan, K., & Hock, M. (1985). Employment decisions made by mothers of infants. *Psychology of Women Quarterly, 9,* 383–402.

Kahan, L. D., & Richards, D. D. (1986). The effects of context on referential communication strategies. *Child Development, 57,* 1130–1141.

Kohlberg, L. (1981). *Essays on moral development* (Vol. 1). New York: Harper & Row.

Krebs, L. L. (1986). Current research on theoretically based parenting programs. *Individual Psychology: Journal of Adlerian Theory, Research, and Practice, 42,* 375–387.

Lamb, M. E. (1980). The development of parent-infant attachments in the first two years of life. In Federson (Ed.), *The father-infant relationship.* New York: Praeger.

LaRossa, R. (1986). *Becoming a parent,* Beverly Hills, CA: Sage.

Levant, R. F. (1983). Client-centered skills-training programs for the family: A review of the literature. *Counseling Psychologist, 11,* 29–63.

Levant, R. F., & Doyle, G. F. (1981). *Parent education for fathers: A personal developmental approach.* Unpublished manuscript, Boston University.

McDowell, R. (1978). *Managing behavior: A parent involvement program.* Torrance, CA: Winch and Associates.

Mitchell, J. & McManis, A. (1977). Parent effectiveness training: A review. *Psychological Reports, 41,* 215–218.

National Center for Health Statistics. (1986). Advance report of final natality statistics, 1984. *Monthly Vital Statistics Report, 35.* Hyattsville, MD: Public Health Service.

Nock, S. L. (1988). The family and hierarchy. *Journal of Marriage and the Family, 50,* 957–966.

Noller, P., & Taylor, R. (1989). Parent education and family relations. *Family Relations, 38,* 196–200.

Olson, D. H., McCubbin, H. I., Barnes, H., Larsen, A., Muxen, M., & Wilson, M. (1982). *Family inventories: Inventories used in a national survey of families across the family life cycle.*

Olson, D. R., & Hildyard, A. (1983). Writing and literal meaning. In M. Martlew (Ed.), *The psychology of written language: A developmental approach.* New York: Wiley.

Osborne, P. (1989). *Parenting for the 90s.* Intercourse, PA: Good Books.

Patterson, G. R. (1975). *Families: Applications of social learning to family life.* Champaign, IL: Research Press.

Patterson, G. R. (1982). *A social learning approach to family interventions: Vol. 3. Coercive family process.* Eugene, OR: Castalia.

Patterson, G. R. (1986). Maternal rejection: Determinant or product for deviant child behavior. In W. W. Hartup & Z. Rubin (Eds.), *Relationships and development* (pp. 73–94). Hillsdale, NJ: Erlbaum.

Patterson, G. R., Dishion, T. J., & Bank, L. (1984). Family interaction: A process model of deviancy training. *Aggressive Behavior, 10,* 253–267.

Pfander, S., & Bradley-Johnson, S. (1990). The effects of an intervention program and its components on NICU infants. *Children's Health Care, 19,* 140–146.

Pinsker, R., & Geoffray, K. (1981). A comparison of parent effectiveness training and behavioral modification parent training. *Family Relations, 30,* 61–68.

Popkin, M. (1983). *Active parenting*. Atlanta: Active Parenting.

Powell, D. (1986). Parent education and support programs. *Young Children, 41,* 47–53.

Rogers, C. (1961). *On becoming a person*. Boston: Houghton Mifflin.

Rogers, C. (1965). *Client-centered therapy: Its current practice, implications, and theory*. Boston: Houghton Mifflin.

Santrock, J. W., Warshak, R., & Elliott, G. L. (1982). Social development and parent-child interaction in father custody and stepmother families. In M. E. Lamb (Ed.), *Nontraditional families: Parenting and child development* (pp. 289–315). Hillsdale, NJ: Erlbaum.

Santrock, J. W., Warshak, R., Lindbergh, C., & Meadows, L. (1982). Children's and parent's observed social behavior in stepfather families. *Child Development, 53,* 474–480.

Schwartz, B. (1986). The battle for human nature: *Science, morality, and modern life*. New York: Norton.

Seckinger, D., & Day, M. (1986). Parenting education: The way we were. *Lifelong Learning, 10,* 8–10, 23.

Sherman, R., & Dinkmeyer, D. (1987). *Systems of family therapy: An Adlerian integration*. New York: Brunner/Mazel.

Smith, J. M., & Smith, D. E. (1966). *Child management: A program for parents*. Ann Arbor, MI: Ann Arbor Publishers.

Sonnenschein, S. (1986). Development of referential communication skills: How familiarity with a listener affects a speaker's production of redundant messages. *Developmental Psychology, 22,* 549–555.

Spanier, G. B. (1976). Measuring dyadic adjustment: New scales for assessing the quality of marriage and similar dyads. *Journal of Marriage and the Family, 38,* 15–28.

Sponseller, D. (Ed.). (1974). *Play as a medium of learning*. Washington, DC: National Association for the Education of Young Children.

Thompson, R. W., Grow, C. R., Ruma, P. R., Daley, D. L., & Burke, R. V. (1993). Evaluation of a practical parenting program with middle- and low-income teens. *Family Relations, 42,* 21–25.

Thomson, E., McLanahan, S. S., & Curtin, R. B. (1992). Family structure, gender, and parental socialization. *Journal of Marriage and the Family, 54,* 368–378.

U.S. Bureau of the Census (1989). Women in the American economy, by C.M. Taeuber & V. Valdisera. *Current Population Reports* (Ser. p. 23, No. 146). Washington, DC: U.S. Government Printing Office.

U.S. House of Representatives, Select Committee on Children, Youth and Families. (1989). *U.S. children and their families: Current conditions and recent trends, 1989*. Washington, DC: U.S. Government Printing Office.

Volling, B., & Belsky, J. (1993). Parent, infant, and contextual characteristics related to maternal employment decisions in the first year of infancy. *Family Relations, 42,* 4–12.

Vygotsky, L. S. (1978). *Mind in society: The development of higher psychological processes*. Cambridge, MA: Harvard University Press.

Weiss, H., & Jacobs, F. (1984). *The effectiveness and evaluation of family support and education programs*. A final report to the Charles Stewart Mott Foundation by the Harvard Family Research Project, Cambridge, MA.

White, M. J., & Tsui, A. O. (1986). A panel study of family-level structural change. *Journal of Marriage and the Family, 48,* 435–446.

Winsor, J. L., & Lower, F. (1989, March). *An application of Kohlberg's moral reasoning theory to understand problems of marital and family communications.* A presentation at the Fourth Annual Symposium on Building Family Strengths, Jonesboro, AR.

Zoline, S. S., & Jason, L. A. (1985). Preventive parent education for high school students. *Journal of Clinical Child Psychology, 14,* 119–123.

Chapter 4

Parenting the Infant

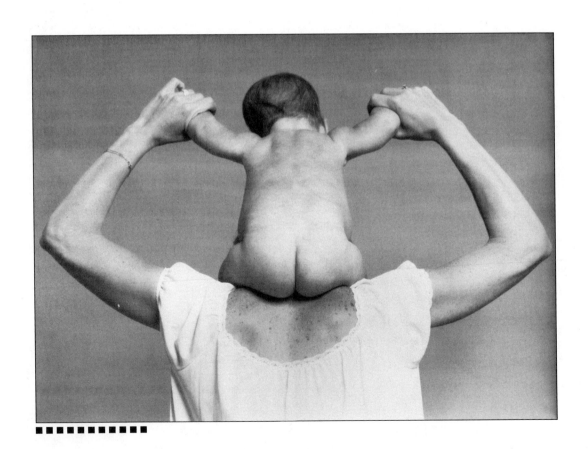

Parenting Myth ■ Attachment of the infant to the mother has more to do with the mother's behavior than with the infant's behavior.

Test Your Knowledge ■ The following questions were designed to test your knowledge prior to reading the material in this chapter. Answers appear at the end of the chapter.

1 Researchers have recently found that marital satisfaction for a father is enhanced when he is more involved in child care. True or false?

2 Researchers have found that women who have partners, regardless of marital status, have less stress related to the birth of a child. True or false?

3 The unique role of motherhood in child care may reflect more the intentional learning related to the close interaction between mother and child than it reflects any other factor. True or false?

4 Some researchers have found that fathers are affected more in their parenting roles by mothers than mothers are affected by fathers. True or false?

5 The concept of the emerging perspective on fathers has been challenged on the basis that fathers have not changed their behaviors about equal participation in child care and household responsibilities relative to their change in attitude toward such participation. True or false?

6 Temperamentally difficult children respond favorably when parents are patient. True or false?

T his chapter addresses the issues related to parenting the infant. The first section discusses biological and physical development. Later sections deal with issues involved in the decision to have children, the effects of children on the marriage, parent/child attachment, and child temperament. Although parenting begins long before the birth of the child, the delivery is the time often ascribed to the beginning of parenting. The process of parenting, involving many interrelated factors, is significant in the success or failure of the parenting experience. In this chapter, a systems perspective of parenting the infant attempts to show the interrelatedness of these factors.

■ Biological and Physical Development of the Infant

From birth to 2 years of age, phenomenal physical and mental growth takes place. Shortly after birth, infants must begin adapting to the outside world. They begin to establish routines around eating, sleeping, observing others, and crying. The infant, learning to adjust to these and other events, is completely dependent on parents for meeting physical and psychological needs.

Infants are similar in appearance at birth, being covered with a substance called vernix caseosa and having a large head, short neck, and protruding stomach. Shortly after birth, however, the differences in facial features and temperament, characteristic patterns of interaction with the environment, begin to emerge. The combination of genetic makeup and interaction with the environment begins to shape an infant and distinguish it from other infants (Plomin, 1989).

The early survival of the infant depends on adequate care by the parents. Aiding survival of the infant is inborn responses to the environment called reflexes, some of which may disappear after several months. These inborn reflexes, such as sucking, coughing, or crying, are not learned and help the infant adapt to life outside the womb. The rooting response, turning the head and initiating sucking at being touched on the corner of the mouth, more readily occurs when the infant is hungry (Prechtl, 1982).

Other reflexes include the Moro, or startle, response: the infant throws out its arms and clenches its fingers as if to catch itself when turned upside down. The Babinski response refers to the toes of the infant spreading out in response to the sole of the foot being rubbed. When placed in the upright position with feet on the floor, the infant will appear to take steps and it will make swimming motions when placed horizontally in a tub of water. The infant will grasp a finger placed in its palm.

Infants weigh on average 7½ pounds at birth and are about 20 inches long. Infancy is characterized by rapid growth, but all infants do not grow at the same rate (Lampl & Emde, 1983). The growth in infants represents both size and weight and proportions (Timiras, 1972). The most noticeable change is in the size of the head relative to the body and the length of the legs. For example, the head accounts for

Table 4.1 ■ Language Development in Infants

- At birth infants cry to communicate hunger, pain, and anger.

- At 3 weeks they also cry merely to make a noise.

- Infants begin to "coo," or repeat vowel sounds, in states of satisfaction.

- At 4–6 months, they begin to produce consonant sounds, referred to as babbling. These sounds combine vowels and consonants into sounds like "baba." Even deaf infants develop the same to this point.

- By 8 months the babbling begins to sound like the language patterns they have been exposed to.

- Shortly before age 1 year, infants appear to understand many words they hear.

- In their first year, infants seem to be learning the basic pragmatics of speaking. For example, they master conversational turn-taking by speaking and pausing for a response.

- First words, or holophrases, tend to represent an entire sentence in one word.

- Most first words are about familiar objects.

- Infants tend to learn words one at a time initially, but by 24 months they have an average vocabulary of 186 words.

- Two-word sentences usually begin between 19 and 24 months.

Source: Bates, O'Connell, and Shore, 1987; Oller and Eilers, 1988.

about one-fifth the length of the infant and only one-eighth the length of the adult. Legs in the adult are also proportionally longer than those in the infant.

The infant's brain, not fully developed at birth, has much plasticity, which means it is influenced by both growth-enhancing and growth-decreasing stimuli. The infant's brain grows because neurons are becoming interconnected and taking on specialized functions, such as in the development of language (see Table 4.1). Although neuron development continues throughout the infancy period, many of the neurons do not survive, mainly because of lack of use (Shepherd, 1988). There is evidence that an enriched environment influences neuron development in a positive way not only in infancy but throughout life as well (Greenough, 1986).

■

The Marital Relationship and the Transition to Parenthood

A systems perspective of parenting must begin with the couple's relationship. Upon marrying, a couple forms a unique dyadic system that requires cooperation and

■ *The marriage prior to children is a time of bonding and togetherness. Marital satisfaction is generally high in early marriage.*

problem-solving ability. The more the couple **bonds** together and creates a relationship boundary that separates it from others, the more functional the system is in meeting the needs of the spouses. The period of the family life cycle before children are born is considered the happiest period in the couple's marriage (Nock, 1979). When this prechild period is beset with problems, there is evidence that the marriage will have even more problems after a child is born.

Teenage marriages and marriages in which children are born in the first several years of marriage are viewed as occurring before the couple has formed a boundary around their relationship. This lack of a firm relationship boundary may directly relate to difficulty in accepting the parent role. How specific couples achieve marital adjustment or happiness in the first few years of marriage is open to debate. Likewise, delineating the various dimensions of marital adjustment is equally challenging (Neal, Groat, & Wicks, 1989).

Effect of the Child on the Marital Relationship

The quality of the marital relationship is extremely important in the early months and years. The effect of the child on the quality of the marital relationship and the effect of the marital relationship on the **transition to parenthood** has been given some attention in the literature. Generally, adjustment to the transition to parenthood tends to be better when there is a good marital relationship (Tietjen & Bradley, 1985). In fact, in families where marital strife is present, neither parent is viewed as effective in caring for their 5-month-old infant (Main & Weston, 1981).

A systems perspective of the transition to parenthood focuses on the formation and maintenance of the marital dyad. This dyadic relationship should be sufficiently strong to bind the couple together, yet flexible enough to permit a child's entrance into the family. The stronger the marital bond before marriage, the greater the likelihood the couple will experience satisfaction in the transition to parenthood period.

Even in marriages where the couple has formed an appropriate marital bond, researchers have viewed the addition of a child as disruptive to the communication patterns of the marital dyad. This disruption reduces intimacy and **marital satisfaction,** the degree of happiness or contentment in the way the couple communicates and interacts together (Belsky, Spanier, & Rovine, 1983). The reduction in marital satisfaction reported after the birth of a child is consistent with the majority of research addressing family life-cycle issues. Researchers of the family life cycle have generally found that marital satisfaction varies relative to a specific stage (Nock, 1979). The usual pattern is to find a decrease in marital satisfaction with the presence of children and a higher degree of marital satisfaction before children are born and after they leave home. Couples in **childless marriages** score higher on marital-satisfaction inventories than those who have children.

Different reasons have been given for the relationship between marital satisfaction and the presence of children. For example, some researchers have found that the presence of children reduces marital satisfaction because it reduces companionship (Miller, 1976). Spouses have less time for each other and suffer a loss of support. Other researchers have concluded that the sex of the child (Abbott & Brody, 1985) and the spousal loss of privacy (Hoffman & Manis, 1979) affect marital satisfaction. Spouses experience some distress when, for example, they want a girl but have a boy. In addition, having a child interferes with the amount of privacy in the couple's relationship. The couple's relationship with each other and the child introduces the problematic triangle in family relationships that will be discussed later. Still others have suggested that parental disagreement about child-rearing practices is highly correlated with marital dissatisfaction (Roberts, Block, & Block, 1984). The differences in parenting styles may create a unique set of variables regarding the marital relationship. Disagreeing about discipline may affect other areas of the relationship, particularly problem solving.

While most researchers adhere to the belief that the presence of children disrupts the marital relationship resulting in lower overall satisfaction, some have questioned this notion. Most research in the area of marital satisfaction and the presence of children has failed to have proper control by including a childless group (White & Booth, 1985). As a result, the conclusions of most researchers may represent only the normative or expected changes rather than reflect parental status (Belsky & Pensky, 1988).

■ *Marital discord reduces the parenting effectiveness of both parents.*

Research on Marital Satisfaction

The above suggests that research methodologies may have contributed to discrepancies in the findings that marital satisfaction varies over the life cycle. Not only have most of the studies failed to classify parental status, recent researchers have criticized past studies because they followed up only during the first postpartum year (Belsky & Rovine, 1990). Had researchers followed up at intervals, a different picture may have emerged.

In a study designed to correct the past inadequacy of research, Belsky and Rovine (1990) attempted to determine the differences among four distinct types of change in marital satisfaction: linear deterioration, or gradual deterioration of the relationship over time; accelerating deterioration, or deterioration due to a sudden change or crisis; no change; and modest positive increase. The researchers investigated the impact of demographic, personality, and marital information to determine if the four marital types changed significantly from the last trimester of pregnancy through the child's third birthday. Two additional factors also were considered important: stressful life events and changes in the family's income through the child's first three years.

The findings of this study concluded that marital satisfaction declines slightly during the first three years after the birth of a child. These changes occur systematically and can be predicted from the information collected prenatally. Thus, the change itself is predicated on factors indigenous to the marriage, not on the fact that the couple has a child. Adjustment to parenthood was described as a complex phenomenon, which some persons are well suited for and others are not (Belsky & Rovine, 1990). This research tends to be consistent with findings that satisfying marital relationships before the birth of a child have been found to be satisfying after the birth and that dissatisfying relationships before the birth of a child tend to be the same or worse after the birth (Lewis, 1987).

Recently, other researchers have focused on the concept of marital happiness or adjustment in the literature (Crohan & Veroff, 1989). Generally, the literature has not reflected a consensus of defining the concept of marital quality. Most instruments have been self-reports and/or have combined behaviors with cognitive and affective dimensions of the marriage. This mixing of behaviors with cognitions and affect confuses the attempt to determine antecedent and consequence factors in research.

Crohan and Verhoff (1989) attempted to determine the underlying structure of marital quality for the newlywed by focusing on the subjective affect of the relationship rather than the descriptions of behavior. Citing other recent researchers, Crohan and Verhoff attempted to obtain a global rather than a specific rating of quality. They evaluated four dimensions of quality: marital happiness, equity, competence, and control.

Findings indicated that the happiness factor included not only affective items in a factor analysis but also commitment to the relationship, an item not expected to be representative of the early marriage. The competence factor was related to negative items while the control factor was related to positive items. The researchers determined all four dimensions to be distinct. They determined the happiness factor, however, to be a more general factor that included aspects of the other three. Commitment is expected to emerge as a factor later in the marriage but not during the first year.

Becoming a Parent

The Decision to Have a Child.   A major consideration in parenting today is the decision to have a child. In the past decade, an increasing number of couples have decided to remain childless (U.S. Bureau of the Census, 1989). In 1971, 45% of married women in the United States expected to have two or more children. By the early 1980s almost 70% of U.S. women expected to have only two or fewer children (U.S. Bureau of the Census, 1973; 1983). This expectation together with the statistic that 13% of women 40–44 years of age in 1986 will not bear children (U.S. Bureau of the Census, 1987) suggests that the value placed on having children in U.S. society may have changed.

This change in the value of children may represent underlying beliefs about the symbolic meaning of children for society at large (Neal, Groat, & Wicks, 1989).

Whereas past generations developed institutions specifically to meet the needs of children, who formed a continuous link from one generation to another, children in today's society are met with ambivalence. One family researcher has concluded that children mean little to parents except in the way of providing them with psychological or emotional satisfaction (Ryder, 1979).

This negative view of children is demonstrated in numerous images of children in U.S. society. For example, the number of children living in poverty has increased dramatically in the past three decades. Furthermore, increased numbers are fatherless, suffer from poor prenatal and postnatal care, and have higher risks of infant mortality rates (Neal, Groat, & Wicks, 1989). And popular culture has exacerbated the negative image of children through exploitations such as movies, books, pornography, and violence toward children.

Some researchers have viewed the decision not to have children as based on hedonistic values and self-interest (Preston, 1984). A study examining the decision to have children indicates that ambivalence in the decision-making process is related to the perceived reward in having children. For example, having a neat house, hobbies, and alternatives for generating extra income were rated as highly as having a child. Furthermore, the lack of value placed on having children may be correlated with a decrease of integration and commitment to institutionalized behavior. Alienation from societal and family expectations is an important variable in the decision to remain childless (Neal, Groat, & Wicks, 1989).

An alternate view for understanding the decision to not have children, however, might represent a more positive or functional interpretation. For example, couples who decide not to have children may be less inclined to be influenced by others in contrast to the popular view that the couple is selfish and lacks nurturance. Persons who resist social pressure to have children are capable of making decisions independently and are autonomous as a couple. In systems terms, the childless marriage could be seen as a well-defined and supportive marital bond which, paradoxically, may function well as a parental unit at a later date.

The Change in Role from Nonparent to Parent.   The birth of the first child changes the marital relationship by conferring a new role on the couple. In addition to the role of spouse, the couple must now take on the role of parent. New and unfamiliar roles are correlated with an increase in family stress. Past researchers referred to this change as a "crisis" (Miller & Sollie, 1980). The greatest stress tends to come with an unplanned pregnancy (Hobbs & Wimbish, 1977). When the pregnancy is unplanned, the shock of parenting, in addition to perhaps not even wanting a child, can result in anxiety and depression. When both parents are prepared for the birth, they experience greater adjustment to their new role. This preparation seems especially true for men, who derive greater satisfaction from the parent role when they have read books or attended classes pertaining to the birthing process (Russell, 1983).

The transition to motherhood involves defining and redefining relationships with significant others. Problematic intimate relationships are correlated with a host of negative pregnancy outcomes (Liese, Snowden, & Ford, 1989). Psychological conflicts in interpersonal relationships have been determined to have detrimental consequences for the fetus (Lederman, Lederman, Work, & McCann, 1981). Adequate mothering, therefore, tends to be reflective of and influenced by the mother's relationships with significant others, such as her husband or partner.

Researchers have found that married mothers have significantly less stress than unmarried mothers, a circumstance that may be directly related to a more enhancing psychological attitude for the infant (Tilden, 1983). The degree of the stress reaction appears to be related to what kind of support the mother receives from her husband or partner. There are two types of support, instrumental and emotional. Instrumental support refers to help with housekeeping, meals, and other related activities, and emotional support refers to understanding, empathy, and acceptance. Researchers have found that women making the best adjustment to pregnancy have greater instrumental and emotional support (Mercer, Hackley, & Bostram, 1983).

Recently, researchers have concluded that such categories as married versus unmarried may have mislabeled a group of unmarried women who have adequate relationships (Liese, Snowden, & Ford, 1989). These researchers investigated women who were "partnered" versus women who were "not partnered"—that is, women in an intimate married or unmarried relationship versus those not in an intimate relationship. The findings indicate that the differences exist between partnered versus nonpartnered rather than between married versus unmarried.

The father's ability to cope with the stress associated with pregnancy and childbirth is related to a number of factors. For example, fathers who scored high on a flexibility measure have higher levels of marital satisfaction during the critical transition to parenthood (Lazarus & Folkman, 1984). In addition, the father's inability to cope with stress may be related to his perception of his parents' marital relationship. Although developmental issues have been mainly ignored by researchers, there is evidence that the happier a person perceives his/her parents' marital relationship to be, the higher the quality of the marital relationship is in the transition to parenthood (Belsky & Isabella, 1985).

■ Parent/Child Attachment

A major parenting task from a systems perspective is making room for the infant in the marital dyad. The first bonding in the family is between the spouses. As stated earlier, the quality of the marital relationship and the family depends on the strength of the marital bond. When a child is born to a couple who have not formed a satisfying marital bond, one or both spouses may form a closer bond with a third party than with each other (Bowen, 1988).

Attachment refers to the formation of bonds, or positive emotional intimacy with others. Parents who are positively bonded with each other also must bond with their child. Attachment between parent and child keeps the infant close to the caregiver and provides for the reciprocal response of nurturing or parenting the child (Bowlby, 1988). Infants display attachment to the caregiver by maintaining contact, showing distress when separated, and appearing at ease when the parent is present (Ainsworth, 1973).

Table 4.2 ■ The Emotional Life of the Infant

- Babies are believed to be born with a generalized excitement that becomes more specialized after birth into positive and negative aspects.
- The baby's smile indicates a communicative desire.
- There are three stages of smiling: endogenous, from internal states; exogenous, from external triggers; and selective social, or smiling at familiar persons at about 5–6 months.
- Infants also express fear during the first year of life: stranger fear, fear expressed when presented to an unfamiliar person; and separation anxiety, when separated from mother.

Source: Jones and Raag, 1989; Tronick, 1989.

Formation of Attachment

Attachment of the infant to the parent follows a series of stages from birth to 1 year and beyond (see Table 4.2). Initially, such infant behaviors as rooting, sucking, grasping, gazing into the eyes, and visual tracking tend to keep the parent caregiver close to and responding reciprocally to the infant. These infant attachment behaviors last until about 3 months of age and generally are not directed toward specific persons. In the second stage, from 3 months to 6 months of age, infants target specific familiar persons with such behavior as smiling and showing interest at the arrival and distress at the departure of familiar persons (Ainsworth, 1985).

During the third stage, from 6 to 9 months, the infant is able to use its own mobility to maintain closeness with the attachment object. In the fourth stage, from 9 months to 1 year of age, the infant not only uses its mobility to enhance attachment but also begins to internalize the objects of attachment (Ainsworth, 1985). By internalizing the objects of attachment the infant gains control over the anxiety experienced when the object fails to perform adequately in meeting certain ego needs (Fairbairn, 1954).

Two terms related to the formation of attachment are "stranger anxiety" and "separation anxiety." **Stranger anxiety** refers to the amount of distress an infant may feel in the presence of unfamiliar adults and appears rather suddenly about the seventh month. **Separation anxiety** appears later than stranger anxiety, usually between 12 and 18 months. Cross-cultural studies indicate that differences in both stranger anxiety and separation anxiety exist for different cultural groups (Ainsworth, 1973).

There is evidence that cognitive development plays a role in both stranger anxiety and separation anxiety. For example, before the infant can feel anxious about a stranger, it must be able to recognize familiar objects and differentiate them from unfamiliar ones. Perhaps more important, however, is that the infant must grasp the concept of object permanence, or the knowledge that the attachment object continues when removed from sight. One can assume that after developing object performance infants would protest less when the attachment object disappeared. Researchers have found that infants react less to being left at home than being taken out

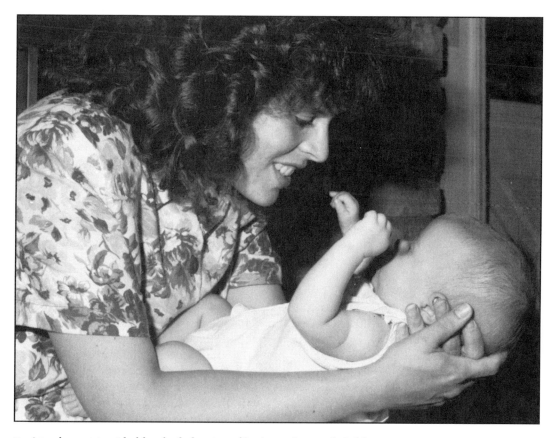

■ *Attachment is aided by the behavior of both mother and child.*

of the home if the mother leaves through a frequently used door (Littenberg, Tulkin, & Kagan, 1971).

The specific way the infant expresses attachment may represent cognitive developmental changes in him/her. The physical departure of a parent may not be as upsetting as the child reduces the need for physical closeness to the parent. For example, researchers have concluded that children who have been informed that the mother was leaving played better in her absence than did children who were not informed about her leaving (Weinraub, 1977).

Quality of Attachment

The quality of the infant's attachment to the caregiver may vary according to a number of factors. First, it depends on the quality of the responses from the caregiver. For example, to become **securely attached** to the caregiver an infant must receive a consistent and warm response from him/her as it passes through the stages of attachment. Infants classified as **anxious/resistant** tend to have caregivers who, despite efforts to be securely attached to the infant, frequently misinterpret the infant's messages. This breakdown in the communication between caregiver and infant is related an increase in frustration and **insecure attachment.** The infant might experience this inconsistency not only as confusing but also as proof that the caregiver was inadequate (Belsky, Rovine, & Taylor, 1984). **Anxious/avoidant** infants tend to have caregivers who are unresponsive to their needs and display overt anger and hostility to them. These mothers tend to reject their infants and be selfish and self-centered individuals (Ainsworth, 1979).

Research on the quality of attachment between the mother and her infant is based on the "stranger situation test," in which a mother and her infant are introduced to an experimental room by an observer who subsequently leaves. Mother and infant are then observed for three minutes while the baby explores. A stranger enters the room and remains silent for the first minute, converses with mother for a minute, and the third minute approaches the infant while mother leaves the room. For the next two to three minutes, the stranger focuses his/her attention on the infant. The mother enters the room and is reunited with the infant and attempts to soothe and play with it. Mother again leaves, but this time saying "bye-bye." The infant is alone about three minutes when the stranger enters again and plays with the infant. Mother enters, picking the infant up, while the stranger leaves. The infant's reactions to the stranger compared with the relation to the mother can be observed and analyzed.

Recently, the debate over secure attachment has centered on the nature of the stranger test. Kagan (1984) has concluded that the stranger test is a better indicator of internal attributes of the infant—that is, temperament—than the quality of the mother/infant attachment. For example, a temperamentally difficult child may respond in a less consoling way to the mother in the stranger test because of negative reaction to the stranger and the constraints of the test situation. From Kagan's point of view, on the basis of the stranger test, a temperamentally difficult child may be labeled anxious/avoidant. Kagan concludes that the child's temperament is more important in determining the attachment relation than the type of caregiving by the mother. Other researchers, however, tend to support the assertion that the type of caregiving received by the infant was the most significant factor in attachment (Belsky, Rovine, & Taylor, 1984). Even temperamentally difficult infants establish secure attachments when their mothers have adequately responded to their needs (Goldberg, Perrotta, Minde, & Corter, 1986).

Other assessments of the stranger test have been performed in the context of multiple association with adults, such as children in day-care centers, who have less contact with the primary attachment object (usually the mother) while having increased contact with secondary caregivers. The increased contact with "strangers" on a regular basis may compromise the effectiveness of the stranger test. There is also the question of whether such contact with secondary persons has a detrimental effect on the primary attachment relationship. In general, researchers have found that children prefer their mother over day-care workers when given a choice (Clarke-Stewart & Fein, 1983).

In recent research, the stranger test has been revised to focus exclusively on the mother/child relationship rather than the mother/child/stranger relationship. This revision was made in part because of the preceding questions regarding the validity of

Box 4.1	■■■■■■■■■■
	Infants at Social Risk

In recent studies, low socioeconomic status (SES) is used to identify infants who are at risk for having developmental, language, school, and emotional problems. Other factors associated with low SES include teenage parenthood, premature birth, and parental emotional problems. With successive additional risks, these risk factors are correlated multiplicatively rather than additively making the most impaired group the children in multirisk families. Researchers have found that classroom-based preschool programs have been effective in improving children's language and cognitive skills. Long-term follow-up studies have suggested that social and motivation effects of early intervention may be a more important factor in helping disadvantaged children develop these competencies than are the structured learning exercises.

Recently, investigators have attempted to determine if home-based intervention services could assist infant development in the most highly stressed families. Subjects who met the criteria of most distressed were referred to the study from various community agencies. A control group of an equal number of families (35 families) was selected from the same neighborhood. These families, labeled the community group, had never sought or received social services from the community. Subjects were asked to complete demographic data regarding race, education, per-person weekly income, mother's age at child's birth, social-service support, and number of siblings under age 6. Maternal depression was determined by the Center for Epidemiological Studies Depression Scale (CES-D), administered verbally. Maternal IQ was determined by the Similarities Subscale of the Wechsler Adult Intelligence Scale. Maternal behavior at home was determined by analyzing 40 minutes of mother/infant behavior in a natural setting. Other measures included a sensitivity scale, infant development scale, and infant attachment security scale.

The findings of this study suggest that home-visiting services for developmentally at-risk families have a significant impact on infant development. Infants of depressed mothers who participated in home-visiting services outperformed infants of nonparticipating mothers by 10 points. In addition, infants whose mothers participated were twice as likely to be classified as securely attached.

Source: Lyons-Ruth, Connell, Grunebaum, and Botein, 1990.

the stranger test when strangers are constantly coming in contact with children in day-care centers. Research focusing on the reunion of the mother/child dyad after a separation has revealed that many infants less than 1 year of age appear anxious for some time after their mother returns. In fact, many infants appear upset by their mother's presence and do not calm down for quite some time after her arrival (Belsky

■ *There is a continuing debate about the attachment of infants to their mothers when infants are cared for in day-care centers.*

& Rovine, 1988). If the mother worked fewer than 20 hours a week during the first year of life and the child was in a day-care center no more than 20 hours a week, the attachment bond was not affected.

In general, researchers have also found evidence that a child's experience in a good day-care center can be an advantage over being at home with the mother. This advantage is expressed through better social skills, particularly when the child is from a poor home environment (Clarke-Stewart & Fein, 1983). In addition, the intellectual climate in the day-care setting may be of greater stimulation for children from disadvantaged backgrounds (Ramey, Bryant, & Suarez, 1985). In contrast to Belsky and Rovine's findings, some researchers have found that high-quality day-care centers are no threat to the attachment to the mother. Infants younger than 5 months of age who were cared for in a day-care center were found to be no different from infants whose mothers cared for them (Kagan, Kearsley, & Zelazo, 1977). Other researchers have found that infants cared for in a day-care setting from birth may be more aggressive and less cooperative with adults compared with children who entered day care as toddlers (Haskins, 1985). Generally, it seems that children tend to fare well in day care when they are older than 1 year and attend a high-quality center, or if they are younger than 1 year of age and attend the center no more than 20 hours a week.

A Systems Perspective of Attachment

From a systems perspective, the attachment of parent and child is not unlike other relationships that develop throughout one's lifetime. In contrast with Freudian theory that emphasized the early years as far more important than other periods of development, a systems perspective regards the early developmental period as one among others. Not only is the parent/child relationship similar in process to the formation of other relationships, the interdependence of the relationship of parents and child means that to study the mother/child relationship exclusively while ignoring the father's role or contribution is fragmenting and compartmentalizing the process of attachment.

The Bidirectional Nature of Attachment.   The interaction between parent and child progresses bidirectionally where both persons initiate and respond interdependently. For the infant, the primary caregiving parent is the context in which his/her world unfolds. The infant coos or babbles in a particular sequence to certain responses from the caregiver. Likewise, the caregiver talks softly to and smiles at the infant, or engages in particular interactions to which the infant responds. This process is continuous and initiated by either caregiver or infant. Because the caregiver is the most salient figure in the infant's life, the infant must develop a relationship that meets physical, emotional, and personal needs.

Attachment cannot be understood apart from the development of the context of interaction, which has a number of properties. First, interacting persons must have enough in common to warrant their reciprocal actions toward each other. Over time a dyad may exhibit an intense closeness and distinct pattern of interaction. For example, the mother/child dyad develops through an intense emotional exchange over an extended period of time and becomes a solid pattern that represents a basic interactional structure (Cairns, 1977). This interactive process is dialectical in nature with each new parent/child interaction providing a new possibility.

The attachment security that the infant attempts to establish, as discussed by Ainsworth (1979) and others, results from the relative importance that the infant and the caregiver form for each other as the major interactive context. Although security feels more comfortable for both caregiver and infant, it is one of a number of possible outcomes. As the interaction continues between caregiver and infant, the relationship forms boundaries that separate it from other relationships and define its structure. Both caregiver and infant begin to form a concept of the relationship and of themselves as a result of the ongoing relationship. Certain behaviors are expected to occur on the basis of past behaviors. Both caregiver and infant feel both acceptance and rejection, security and insecurity, comfort and discomfort, and a myriad of other feelings and their opposites.

Feedback loops maintain these relationship boundaries and determine the amount of new information allowed into the system. The shared image of the relationship through communication feedback loops both directs and is directed by the same process. For example, when the caregiver and the infant communicate in expected ways, both feel secure and comfortable. When the feedback loop changes, they may feel insecure or uncomfortable because the shared concept of the relationship may shift.

The relationship between mother and child is viewed as equal, although the mother is superior in social, cognitive, and emotional expression. The process of influencing one another, however, is equally shared by both mother and child. This interaction is expected to exhibit unique characteristics as a function of the particular feedback loops of the mother and the infant. The same mother may form unique relationships with different children because of the feedback structure for each relationship. This process is viewed as a unique structure that continues to develop and regulate itself over time.

The relationship between mother and child, while important in influencing the formation and style of other relationships, is not considered to be the prototype for other relationships. In fact, the correlation between the mother/child connection and other relationships is parallel rather than cumulative. While forming a relationship with the mother, the infant is forming an attachment with other persons, including father, siblings, grandparents, baby sitters, and any other person who interacts with him/her. Researchers have found that infants use the same process to form relationships with peers that they used to form the relationship with their mother (Hay, 1985).

The uniqueness of the mother/child relationship in the literature may be better explained as **intentional learning,** which is the development of attachment, in contrast to Ainsworth's belief, through a deliberate act of the parent. This deliberate attempt to teach the child to relate intimately may be the basis for the uniqueness given to the mother/child relationship. This conclusion suggests that the focus on the mother/child relationship has resulted from the mother's interest and deliberateness in forming it.

The stranger test can be criticized from the point of view that separation from and reunion with the mother is an ongoing process requiring continual adaptation of both mother and child. The stranger test views the child as inflexible and somewhat changeless. In contrast to this point of view, the infant and/or mother adjust to the change brought about by the life circumstance over a period of time. According to a systems perspective, both the infant and the mother are open, changing organisms that adapt to changing life circumstances through a dialectical process. Infants are not viewed as reflecting a fixation process in which the early period of development is more important than later periods (Cairns, 1977).

The stranger test is presented in a certain sequence where the infant is not allowed to adapt before moving to another step. The test, therefore, is useless for determining normative changes in the infant in relation to either mother or stranger. From this perspective, the stranger test can best be viewed as a stress test for infants but not an accurate experiment for understanding the mother/child relationship (Hay & Vespo, 1988).

The stranger test seems to describe the mother/child relationship from the standpoint of the child rather than from the relationship between mother and child. The test asserts that a relationship is measured rather than the internal characteristics of the child, the mother, or the father. As such, it could be expected that the relationship with the mother might be secure whereas the relationship with the father might be insecure. It is the child's perspective of feeling or acting insecure that is emphasized, not the "relationship" with the mother or the father. The attempt to understand the infant's insecurity from the stranger test appears very similar to other theories that are unidirectional. The mother's effect on the child, which tends to be the predominate paradigm in parent/child behavior, is the underlying focus of concern for the stranger test. It is a small step from the stranger test to blaming the mother for the infant's insecurity (Hay & Vespo, 1988).

A systems or bidirectional approach to the mother/child relationship concludes that both mothers and infants are active organisms and participate equally in the development of attachment. Infants affect mothers and are affected by mothers in an ongoing and recursive manner. As an active participant in the mother/child relationship, the infant selects certain input from the mother to respond to. Rather than merely responding to the stimulus, infants partly create the outcome by selecting which stimulus to respond to. Likewise, mothers, as active organisms, can also influence the outcome by focusing on certain actions by the infant while ignoring other actions (Hay & Vespo, 1988).

The Social Nature of Attachment.   Another aspect of the bidirectional approach is the social nature in which the mother/child relationship develops. The mother/child relationship conforms to the structure that underlies the give and take of all social relationships in that it is a mutual, reciprocal, and interdependent endeavor that evolves over time and events. This approach suggests that the mother/child relationship is not limited to the first two or three years of life but rather is a lifelong process in which each changes and the concept of the relationship changes (Hay & Vespo, 1988).

Social Class and Attachment.   A major influence on the family in American society is social class, the status of the family as a consequence of a number of factors including education, income, and occupation. Social class, especially that of the mother, may also influence child development. Poor nutrition, inadequate stimulation, isolation, poor health, and other numerous hardships are highly related to social class. Some researchers suggest that poor mothers do as well as middle-class mothers with children before age 2, but thereafter they do not provide the resources children need (Birns & Golden, 1972). This finding indicates that the effects of poverty may be cumulative and interact with a number of other factors.

■
The Mother's Experience of Parenthood

Researchers have found that mothers experience parenthood more intensely than fathers do (Wilkie & Ames, 1986). Pregnant women tend to behave in more traditional roles than women who are not pregnant. For example, researchers have

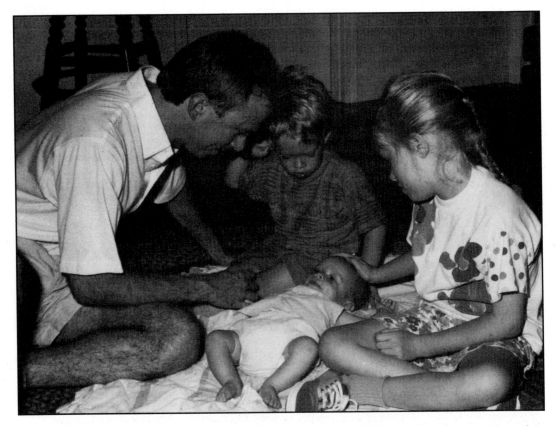

■ *The attachment of the infant to the father and siblings has been neglected in literature.*

found that pregnant women feel more "feminine" than nonpregnant women and are more likely to participate in traditionally feminine activities. This behavior continues throughout the pregnancy and delivery periods, resulting in a more secure attachment between mother and infant (Ainsworth, 1979).

Research in the past tended to place mothers in the limelight in the parenting role. As recently as the late 1970s, some child-development experts believed that the mother has the central role in parenting. Fraiberg (1977), for example, claimed that the mother's role constitutes a birthright for every child and lobbied for social programs that would allow mothers receiving welfare to stay home with their children. The love expressed by the infant for its mother was assumed to be so important that the child could be permanently damaged psychologically and emotionally by the lack of close contact with her.

Recently, researchers have addressed the relationship between the child's attachment to the mother and antisocial behavior in the child. In the stranger test, the type of insecurity most associated with future behavior problems is the avoidant type. The avoiding child may be angry and using the avoidance as a type of defense against the

---

Box 4.2	■ ■ ■ ■ ■ ■ ■ ■ ■ ■

Can Psychotherapy Improve Mother/Infant Attachment?

S tudies have demonstrated that anxious attachments in infancy are associated with decreased emotional and social functioning of toddlers. A recent study investigated the relation between mother–infant psychotherapy and improved emotional and social adjustment in the infant and the quality of attachment between the mother and the infant. Subjects included 100 low SES, Spanish-speaking mothers from Mexico or Central America and their 1- to 2-year-old infants. The researchers classified mother/infant relationships by the Stranger Situation and assigned anxiously attached infants to either the intervention or the control groups. The intervention group received weekly 1½ hour sessions with a therapist in the home. The therapist's main task was to focus on the affective experiences of the mother and the infant. The therapist also provided individualized developmental information.

Infants in the intervention group were significantly lower in avoidance, resistance, and anger than the nonintervention group and higher in partnership and cooperation with their mothers. No differences were found in maternal child-rearing attitudes.

Although this study finds evidence to support improvement in the infant, the long-term effects are not known. Furthermore, the mother/child dyads were not categorized according to the presence or absence of the father or other supportive family members. The findings in this study should be viewed as tentative without more analysis of the family variables, particularly the presence and relationship of the father.

Source: Lieberman, Weston, and Pawl, 1991.

---

anger, resulting in the child's greater risk for noncompliant or aggressive behavior (Belsky & Rovine, 1988). One study tested the hypothesis that avoidant insecure infants have greater social and behavior problems (Fagot & Kavanagh, 1990). The researchers obtained the stranger situation test on all subjects at 18 months and included in the study 81 infants who fit the criterion of avoidant. They observed the children in their homes with their families and in playgroups at 18 and at 30 months. The only significant finding was that avoidant-classified girls were rated as more difficult and having more social problems than girls who were classified as secure.

This view of the central importance of the mother's role has led to a tendency to blame mothers for poor outcomes in parent/child relationships (Chess, 1982). The clinical literature, particularly the psychoanalytic, has viewed the mother as causing the maladjustments in their children. The appeal of systems theory in the 1950s and 1960s, no doubt, was a reaction to the attempt to find "causes" of mental illness and a change to conceptualizing mental illness as the product of a social system.

Although the mother's role is of great importance in the child's development, some researchers have regarded the mother's role as less pivotal in the child's life than previously. For example, in studying nurseries staffed by rotating nursing students where children were placed after being removed from their homes, Tizard (1977) determined that the children were within normal limits on certain measures, such as IQ or behavior checklists. In fact, it was difficult to predict children functioning at age 8 after being adopted or returned to their mother on the basis of the earlier tests. Adopted children were functioning better at age 8 than children who had been returned to their mothers. This research indicates that while the mother's role is extremely important, other factors also influence the child's adjustment.

Marked differences exist between mothers in their twenties and thirties and adolescent mothers. Adolescent mothers display much less maternal behavior than do older mothers and seem to have fewer resources to depend on. Furthermore, the home environment of adolescent mothers is less intellectually stimulating than that of older mothers (Ragozin, Basham, Cronic, Greenberg, & Robinson, 1982).

There is evidence that even in egalitarian couples mothers are far more involved in child care than fathers are (Parke & Tinsley, 1984). Even working mothers with very young children do the majority of child care along with other duties in the home (Coverman & Sheley, 1986). Mothers typically hold, talk to, soothe, and generally care for infants more than fathers do.

■ The Father's Experience of Parenthood

Although mothers are more involved with infants initially, fathers are involved especially during the first few months after birth (Easterbrooks & Goldberg, 1984). Early research into the father role demonstrated that fathers were competent in holding, soothing, and responding to the infant's needs (Parke & O'Leary, 1976; Parke & Sawin, 1976). Although mothers were found to be more involved in feeding infants, they were not viewed as more responsive to the infant coughing or choking. While fathers have been viewed as potentially competent as mothers, both the amount and quality of involvement is sharply different from that of mothers. Observing mothers and fathers in naturalistic settings, researchers have concluded that mothers exceed fathers in all but one observed category of involvement with the child (Belsky, Gilstrap, & Rovine, 1984). Other researchers have suggested that fathers engage more in play activities as a percent of the total time with the child and less in caregiving activities (Kotelchuck, 1976), although the total amount of play time is greater for mothers than for fathers.

Fathers not only have spent less time in rearing children but also spend less time as children get older (Pleck, 1983). Fathers, like mothers, are much more involved in child responsibilities when children are younger and less as children age. This decreased contact with teenagers may reflect as much the teenagers' desire to be autonomous as it reflects any specific parental reason. In addition, fathers tend to spend more time with their sons at any age compared with the amount of time they spend with their daughters.

In play activities, fathers generally take the role of special playmate and hence are in a unique position of influencing the types of play activities the child engages in (Barnett & Baruch, 1987). For example, very early in development fathers tend to encourage boys and girls to play with different toys (Snow, Jacklin, & Maccoby, 1983). Boys are encouraged to play with cars, trucks, and balls, whereas girls are encouraged to play with dolls and dishes. Although fathers may be more sex stereotyped than mothers, past researchers have concluded that fathers have affected sex-role development in their sons through a warm and supportive relationship rather than through their "masculine" traits (Mussen & Rutherford, 1963). The impact of the past studies on the present suggests that present-day warm and supportive fathers would influence their sons' sex role in more androgynous than masculine ways (Lamb, 1987). It is worth noting, however, that the father's warmth, not his masculine traits, is the important factor in the son's appropriate sex-role development.

The "father absent" literature tends to support the important role fathers play in the sex-role development of the son (Lamb, 1987). Attempts have been made to interpret the findings of researchers of absent fathers in terms of why some boys appear unaffected while others suffer severe problems. Generally, the reduction in co-parental support may overtax the single parent's resources and ability to cope with problems. This lack of emotional support may also be associated with a reduction of income and greater economic disadvantage. Overall, the amount of time children spend with parents is much less today compared with earlier times because both parents are much busier dealing with nonfamily matters than in the past. Consequently, the child may be more affected by the social and economic impact of the father's absence than by the impact on learning sex roles.

Although the father role has been given more attention in recent years, research has not always focused on the father in the broader context of interaction, including relationship with wife, work, and extrafamilial interactions. It is necessary to adopt a systems approach in viewing any part of the family interaction, such as the father/child interaction, or run the risk of making misleading interpretations. For example, when discussing the amount of time the father spends with the child, it would be pertinent also to know how much time the mother was spending with the child. Work commitments may also enhance or curtail both the amount of time and the type of activity. Social and cultural considerations may also influence a father's time spent with and caring for his child (Lamb, 1987).

A systems perspective of parenting views the father emerging within a context of interdependent relationships. The transition to parenthood generally portrays the role of fatherhood emerging in a vacuum rather than as part of an interlocking system. It appears more accurate to view the family as involved in an intricate balancing act where roles are interrelated and developed through the process of interaction. The fatherhood role can be seen as neither static nor self-contained but as emerging through the **dialectical process** of family interaction, which refers to the nature of change as being influenced through the synthesis of opposing positions.

A general focus has been on the changing role of the father in reference to the dramatic changes in the role of women. One way fathers have changed is by participating in domestic activities (Daniels & Weingarten, 1982). Furthermore, fathers are more motivated than in the past to be actively involved in parenting (Quinn & Starnes, 1979). This greater desire, however, correlates to greater need when the mother is employed outside the home. The changing image of masculinity—that is, men can be warm and supportive—creates a greater sense of confidence that men can build on while fulfilling their parenting responsibilities.

This perceived change in the father's role has been referred to as the **androgynous father** (Rotunda, 1985) and the **emerging perspective on fathering** (Fein, 1978). According to this view, this new role for fathers creates positive outcomes for all family members. Fathers benefit because of the stronger bond with their children, mothers have more time and energy to pursue individual interests, and children have two involved parents.

Arguments have been made against this assumption by LaRossa (1988), who claims that while values have changed about men's parenting, little or nothing has changed in significant behaviors of men. LaRossa believes that fathers are caught in a kind of double bind in that they want to perform in the manner that society expects but are not able to behave as such. Studies have been somewhat supportive of LaRossa's views. For example, family satisfaction does not seem to be correlated with greater father involvement (Russell & Radin, 1983). Research on dual career families has shown that there is reduced marital satisfaction and greater conflict when the father is actively involved in child care (Crouter, Perry-Jenkins, Huston, & McHale, 1987). In addition, researchers have found a decrease in the father's self-esteem as a result of greater involvement in child care (Hawkins & Belsky, 1989). One can conclude that when the father is more involved in child care, there are some negative consequences for the family, such as the father making sacrifices in his career and being dissatisfied in the marriage.

Some researchers have concluded that not all mothers have accepted the increase in the father's participation in parenting (Quinn & Starnes, 1979). This indicates that forces within the family may influence the employment roles more than any other factor. One longitudinal study suggests that divorce occurs more frequently when the father is highly involved in child care. This finding should not be dismissed lightly and should generate other research to attempt to discover the parameters associated with the success or failure of families with highly involved fathers.

Recently, researchers have attempted to determine the correlates that define father involvement in parenting. Some researchers have found that the amount of time the father gives to parenting correlates with his employment responsibilities and those of his spouse (Barnett & Baruch, 1987). Lamb (1986) distinguished three types of father involvement. The first type, "interactive," refers to the amount of time the father spends in face-to-face interaction with his child. The second, "accessibility," includes activities related to the child other than direct contact, such as washing the child's dirty clothes or fixing a broken toy. The third type, "parental responsibility," refers to the amount of time the father takes responsibility for child-care activities, such as baby sitting or arranging for/transporting to doctor's appointments. These paternal behaviors differ in reference to various circumstances.

A study by Volling and Belsky (1991) attempted to answer some of these concerns, specifically, to determine the multiple correlates of the father's involvement in parenting in both single-earner and dual-earner families. They found that positive marital relations were associated with increased participation by fathers in both single-earner and dual-earner families. The father's high self-esteem, his perception of the infant as less difficult, and his sensitivity to others were related to higher levels of responsiveness and affection expressed to the infant. The division of labor in the family worked out before the infant's birth was found to be the most significant factor related to the father's involvement in child care after birth. The more involved fathers in **dual-earner families,** however, experienced more problems in managing their work and family roles, resulting in greater dissatisfaction and marital conflict.

In another study attempting to determine the relation between the father's involvement in child care and the marital relationship, researchers concluded that positive marital change is associated with positive child behavior and negative marital change is associated with negative child behavior (Belsky, Youngblade, Rovine, & Volling, 1991). Furthermore, these researchers found that fathers who decreased their love feelings for their spouse related in more negative and intrusive ways with their children. Mothers, on the other hand, related more positively to their children as a result of a decline in satisfaction in the marital relationship. This increase in positive behavior by the mother toward the child was an attempt to compensate for the father's insensitivity.

Fathers, viewed from a systems perspective, would provide more of a context than simply an effect on the mother/child interaction. As indicated earlier, the mother/father relationship, the mother/child relationship, and the father/child relationship are all interdependent. For example, in their longitudinal study of the mother/father/infant triad, Belsky, Gilstrap, and Rovine (1984) found that fathers were involved more with the infant as a function of their marital involvement than mothers were. Positive and healthy marital communication contributes to greater father involvement in parenting.

In a later study to further explore the mother/father/child triad, Belsky and Volling (1987) concluded that maternal behavior tends to influence paternal behavior, but not vice versa. Likewise, in addressing the influence of marriage and parenting, these researchers found that mothers influence fathers, but not vice versa. Why fathers tend to be more influenced by their wives was not determined in this study. These researchers speculated that future studies might address this pliability of fathers in more detail. One obvious assumption is that because fathers are less socialized into the parenthood role and because the fatherhood role is less defined, fathers are more easily influenced by their wives.

As previously stated, although researchers have consistently found that fathers are neither as involved nor provide the same quality of parenting as mothers, the most common assumptions that fathers are lacking in skills, more interested in their jobs than in parenting, or uninterested in parenting are viewed as an inadequate interpretation of the findings. In fact, most researchers have concluded that fathers appear highly motivated for the actual involvement they do have with parenting. A more plausible explanation for why they are not as active is that barriers within the family system prevent fathers from assuming a more active role (Cowan & Cowan, 1987).

One factor that influences the amount of time fathers spend with their children is the role model their own father provided. Generally, fathers have not had an involved role model to emulate, so they have had to learn how to parent on their own. Although some fathers make efforts not to repeat patterns established in their family of origin, this attempt to overcome past influences may or may not be successful because fathers know only what they do not want to repeat (Cowan & Cowan, 1987).

Families are also influenced by **transgenerational patterns**—those that continue from previous generations. Traditional roles established in the family of origin influence new mothers and fathers both through their experiences of family life and through contact with parents. It is evident that parents continue to influence their children through certain expectations. For example, parents may believe in the more traditional roles of "breadwinner" and "homemaker" and exert certain subtle but pervasive influence so that their children will continue these roles in their own marriages. When not met, these expectations may result in conflict between and within the generations (Cowan & Cowan, 1987).

Researchers have found that the father's sense of self-esteem in parenting is related to his feeling of competence and cannot be separated from the parent/child relationship or the couple's relationship. Certain natural barriers are related to the father's feelings of competence, such as the inability to breast-feed the infant. Another barrier is that infants respond more readily to the female voice, which may provide a subtle reminder that the father is not as competent as the mother.

The father's work may also distance the father from the infant. Work roles in American society still favor male career development. Many jobs, requiring overnight travel, have been exclusively male despite the growing equality of females in traditional male careers. Employers do not recognize paternity leave as equal to maternity leave, thus limiting the father's involvement through the sanctioning of the work force. If fathers were allowed more time away from work for birth and other child-care activities, increasing numbers of fathers probably would take advantage of it (Cowan & Cowan, 1987).

The marital relationship itself may limit the father's involvement in child care. A casual observation of the marital relationship is enough to warrant the conclusion that many mothers not only assume the major role of caregiver but are uneasy and uncomfortable when the father assumes the major role. Most women want their husbands to "help" in child care at their direction. Many mothers who are prevented from taking the major role in child care feel a sense of guilt and irresponsibility.

From a systems perspective, mothers and fathers must work out their parenting roles in a manner that pleases both. There is no right or wrong way to determine what the couple should decide, and the process of working out the arrangement is as important as the outcome. How couples communicate, support each other, and offer assistance is more important than attempts to force a particular outcome because it is viewed as more functional. What is functional in one family could be dysfunctional in another.

Nugent (1991) has attempted to focus on the father within a larger context than the traditional father/child relationship. In reviewing the literature, he noted that recent cross-cultural studies of Chinese, Mexican, and British fathers depict the father in less traditional roles and more involved in child rearing. Although a number of factors may be involved in increasing the father's role in child rearing, changing economic and social conditions may account for much of the increase.

Nugent (1991) studied the nature of the Irish father's involvement in the socialization of children and the relationship between paternal involvement in caregiving and infant development. The findings contrast sharply with previous research which found that Irish fathers are emotionally uninvolved and provide little assistance to their wives in child care. Irish fathers of urban working-class status were found to be actively involved in child care throughout the first year. A concern about Nugent's study was the small sample size and the self-report instrument.

In sum, researchers have found that the type of relationship an infant has with the mother has little or no effect on the relationship with the father (Main & Weston, 1981). In fact, the relationship with the father has been seen as reducing the negative effects of an insecure attachment. This finding may mean that the attachment to each parent is unique and that the attachment to one parent may be good and it may be bad to the other. Infants who appear to be the most socially competent, however, seem to be securely attached to both parents. In addition, the concept of attachment must be expanded to include attachment to grandparents, siblings, baby sitters, and day-care workers. The interdependence of all these relationships must form the basis for future research on attachment.

■ ## Child Temperament and Marital Satisfaction

Child temperament has been described as easy, difficult, or slow-to-warm-up (Chess & Thomas, 1987). A child who sleeps, appears responsive, and cries little is **temperamentally easy,** whereas a child who cries, sleeps little, and demands frequent parental attention is **temperamentally difficult.** Slow-to-warm-up children are active and moody, sharing these and other characteristics of difficult children. Some researchers have concluded that adjustment to the transition to parenthood depends on the temperament of the child primarily because of the amount of time required in taking care of the child and responding to his/her needs (Thomas, Chess, & Birch, 1970).

In a longitudinal study, Chess and Thomas (1984) found that about 40% of a sample of infants were easy, 10% difficult, and 15% slow-to-warm-up. They could not clearly characterize the remaining infants, who shared characteristics of more than one group. In addition, the researchers found that these early patterns of temperament continued throughout childhood, adolescence, and early adulthood. Being difficult or easy in infancy predicted being easy or difficult in temperament as an adult. Of special importance was the way parents responded to the difficult child.

Responding in impatient, inconsistent, and demanding ways was correlated with difficult temperaments as adults regardless of the childhood temperament. The same
seemed to be true for slow-to-warm-up children—the more patient and reassuring
the parents, the more readily the child develops along an easy path.

Sirignano and Lachman (1985) have concluded that a child's temperament
affects the perception that parents have of themselves. For example, parents of a child
labeled as having an easy temperament view themselves more positively than do parents of a child whose temperament is labeled difficult. This easy temperament of the
child leads to a feeling of competency in that parents are able to obtain compliance.
When positive feedback occurs, both parent and child can change accordingly.

Researchers view temperamentally difficult children as creating a risk for the
normal family that is greater than expected. It is this increase in marital and family
stress that is related to parental and marital dissatisfaction. The outcome is decreased
spousal support coupled with an increase in conflict. Likewise, the parents' sense of
competency in the parenting role suffers, resulting in ineffectiveness in parenting
strategies. A vicious cycle develops in that the parenting ineffectiveness leads to further perceptions that the child is difficult (Stoneman, Brody, & Burke, 1989).

In a study attempting to determine the risk to marital satisfaction and family
functioning that the temperament of a child poses for the family, Stoneman, Brody,
and Burke (1989) hypothesized that children defined as temperamentally difficult
would reside in families where marital satisfaction was low and marital conflict was
high, the family environment was considered unhealthy, and parents generally appeared depressed. The study also addressed an issue usually neglected by researchers, that is, how does the presence of multiple children, one or more of whom
may be diagnosed as difficult, affect family relations? The crucial issue for parents is
how to simultaneously parent normal children and those who are temperamentally
difficult. It seems logical to assume that parenting a temperamentally difficult child
would lead to problems with parenting other, temperamentally easy children and,
furthermore, that parenting more than one temperamentally difficult child would be
especially stressful.

The strongest finding in this study was the relationship between the oldest daughter, described as temperamentally difficult, and marital dissatisfaction in a
compromised family environment. Parental depression was reported for families in
which the oldest daughter was considered temperamentally difficult, and marital conflict was highest when two daughters were considered to be temperamentally difficult.
Mothers of girls were found to have high marital satisfaction when both daughters
were described as temperamentally easy. Fathers of boys had the least marital satisfaction when both boys were temperamentally difficult and the least marital conflict
when both boys were temperamentally easy (Stoneman, Brody, & Burke, 1989). Generally, when the father viewed the oldest child as temperamentally difficult, there was
greater marital and family distress than when the mother viewed the oldest child as
difficult.

Some researchers have posited a biological basis for the temperaments of children. Kagan (1984) concluded that fearfulness in 21-month-old infants predicts
fearfulness at 4 years of age. The problem with viewing development as biologically

linked is that there is a tendency to ascribe fixed changes and causes for behavior. A systems view of development sees biology as one of the factors affecting development, more from the chain of events that are set in motion than a causal link.

The view taken in this chapter is that a cluster of determinants are related to both positive and negative outcomes in child development. Positive outcomes are more often correlated with highly responsive caregiving, satisfaction in the marital relationship, a warm and supportive father, a supportive social structure, and comfortable economic status. On the other hand, negative outcomes are related to poor attachment, poor marital relationship, a distant and uninvolved father, poor economic status, lack of social support, among other factors.

While these general conclusions can be made, one must also keep in mind that child development is not an assembly line where mothers and fathers are producing products. When studying the development of a particular child, the researcher must consider the father, the marriage, siblings, the extended family, friends, and the social milieu. Children must be viewed not only as responding to the control and regulation of others but also as regulating their own world. This regulatory factor is both between the parent and child and within the child. The feedback loops of communication between the child and parents regulate continuing interaction and behavioral outcomes (Tronick, 1989).

Family Portrait ■■■■■■■■■■

W ade and Donna have been married for six years and have a 14-month-old son. Both parents are employed. Donna has worked for the past two years as a regional manager for a large drug company. Her job takes her out of town overnight on average three nights a week. Before their son, Corky, was born there was little problem associated with her job. In fact, Wade enjoyed his nights alone and usually spent them on hobbies, such as writing or painting. Occasionally he went out with male friends for a few drinks.

Since the birth of Corky, Wade has been home every evening with him while Donna has continued her employment and frequent overnight business trips. Although Wade is extremely attached to Corky and describes himself as the "house-husband," he has some problems accepting Donna's decision to continue her present employment. Donna feels guilty about her lack of presence at home and even worries that Corky will be affected by it. To make matters worse, Donna is usually extremely tired when she returns from a trip and needs the time at home to recuperate before taking another trip.

Corky seems unaffected in the sense that he prefers Wade to Donna in such parental activities as feeding, rocking to sleep, soothing when sick, and playing with favorite toys. When awakened in the middle of the night, Corky insists that Wade get up and see about him. Donna's feelings of inadequacy in taking care of Corky are accentuated when family and friends comment about Corky's lack of attachment to her. She feels most bothered by it when she picks him up from day care and he appears uninterested in going to her. Because of the guilt feeling, Donna has indulged Corky more than Wade has and she has allowed him excessive freedom in playing with toys, even though he may bang them or damage furniture. When she does attempt to stop him and he protests, she is prone to allow him to continue.

Like many first-time parents, both Wade and Donna are very concerned by every detail of parenting and do not want to make any mistakes. They have attempted to do many things as a family when Donna is in town. Recently, Donna has begun looking for other employment that would not require travel.

Compare and Contrast

This case has some most interesting facts. For one thing Corky is more attached to his father than to his mother. Although there is no implied problem with this circumstance, the expectation is that Donna would be more attached to Corky than Wade would be. Both Wade and Donna expect that she would be at least as involved as Wade regardless of her business travel.

Comparing this case from systems, Adlerian, behavioral, and humanistic perspectives gives interesting conclusions. A systems perspective analyzes that interaction from the standpoint of the father and son while the mother is out of town. The son has formed a close attachment with the father because the majority of the contact is with the father. From this perspective, there is no expectation that the attachment with the mother should be greater than with the father. Rather, the more involved parent is expected to have the greater attachment. Donna and Wade should be helped to understand that neither makes a better parent nor will damage occur as a result of Corky's greater attachment with the father.

Donna's guilt about not being as attached as she expects does prevent her from setting appropriate limits with Corky. Instead of forcing a relationship with Corky, Donna should relax and allow a natural relationship to occur over time, with Corky setting the parameters of the relationship. She should be warm and allowing, but also set limits when Corky is playing inappropriately with his toys. Wade and Donna might view the closeness between Wade and Corky as normal and healthy and part of a necessary stage in Corky's development.

Adlerians (Dreikurs & Soltz, 1964) would view the problem differently. They would be concerned that Corky is being held too much or relies too much on Wade, who obviously organizes his time around Corky. Corky must learn to do things on his own and not rely so much on his father. Corky should be given toys and then left alone to play by himself for extended periods of time. When Corky is crying for an object that Donna has taken away, she should allow him to cry for it if redirection does not change the crying. She might allow him to cry and ignore him for short periods of time. Addressing Corky's crying in this manner would emphasize to Corky that it would be better to cooperate than to continue his behavior.

Behaviorists (Patterson, 1976) would view Corky's attachment to his father as functional in the sense that this relationship is more satisfying and rewarding than the relationship with his mother. Because the father has fed Corky from a very early age and interacted in large blocks of time, attachment with the father would be considered the norm. From a behavioral perspective, Donna should not view this lack of attachment to her in a negative way.

Behaviorists (Patterson, 1976) would be concerned that Donna inadvertently rewards bad behavior, as, for example, when she gives in to Corky. She could either punish Corky by putting him in time-out or ignore his crying spells. Behaviorists would not be concerned about Donna's guilt related to her work schedule.

The humanistic approach of Gordon (1975) attempts to determine who owns the problem. In this case, the problem would be Donna's. Her guilt about the overnight travel and her resulting ineffectiveness in structuring Corky in activities must be addressed as the central issue. She cannot expect Corky to behave better until she is able to structure him without feeling guilty.

Although there are similarities in how these approaches would view Donna and Wade's parenting of Corky, only a systems approach is concerned with the context in which these "misbehaviors" are occurring. Certainly, Wade and Donna should discuss their situation openly and nondefensibly. In viewing their situation as normal, but having reversed roles, Donna and Wade could relax and enjoy their unique relationship with Corky.

■■■■■■■■■■■

Parenting Proposition

Attachment of the child to parents is a reciprocal process and bidirectional in nature.

Answers to "Test Your Knowledge"

1. F	4. T
2. T	5. T
3. T	6. T

Key Concepts

the marital bond	insecure attachment
transition to parenthood	intentional learning
marital satisfaction	dialectical process
childless marriages	androgynous father
attachment	emerging perspective on fathering
stranger anxiety	dual-earner families
separation anxiety	transgenerational patterns
secure attachment	child temperament
anxious/resistant infant	easy temperament
anxious/avoidant infants	difficult temperament

Study Questions

1 From a systems perspective, how is the marital relationship related to effective parenting?

2 Why is the transition to parenthood so important from a systems perspective? Compare and contrast couples who decide to have children and those who choose to remain childless. How is the decision to have a child different for a woman who is not married?

3 Discuss the concept of attachment between child and mother. How does a systems perspective challenge commonly held beliefs about attachment?

4 Discuss recent findings in the fatherhood literature. How accepted is the belief among researchers that fathers have changed their behaviors with reference to child care?

5 How can the concept of attachment be applied to the father/child relationship?

6 Discuss the concept of motherhood. How does a systems perspective challenge commonly held beliefs?

7 Discuss the concept of transgenerational patterns.

8 Define the concept of child temperament. How is child temperament related to effectiveness in parenting?

9 In what ways may children change temperament in reference to parenting behaviors?

10 Critique the stranger test from a systems perspective.

References

Abbott, D. A., & Brody, G. H. (1985). The relation of child age, gender, and number of children to the marital adjustment of wives. *Journal of Marriage and the Family, 47,* 77–84.

Ainsworth, M. D. (1973). The development of infant-mother attachment. In B. M. Caldwell & H. N. Ricciuti (Eds.), *Review of child development research* (Vol. 3). Chicago: University of Chicago Press.

Ainsworth, M. D. (1979). Infant-mother attachment. *American Psychologist, 34,* 932–937.

Ainsworth, M. D. (1985). Patterns of infant-mother attachments: Antecedents and effects on development. *Bulletin of the New York Academy of Medicine, 61,* 771–791.

Barnett, R. C., & Baruch, G. K. (1987). Determinants of father's participation in family work. *Journal of Marriage and the Family, 49,* 29–40.

Bates, E., O'Connell, B., & Shore, B. (1987). Communication in infancy. In J. O. Osofsky (Ed.), *Handbook of infant development* (2nd ed.). New York: Wiley.

Belsky, J., Gilstrap, B., & Rovine, M. (1984). The Pennsylvania Infant and Family Development Project, Vol. 1: Stability and change in mother-infant and father-infant interaction in a family setting at one, three, and nine months. *Child Development, 55,* 692–705.

Belsky, J., & Isabella, R. A. (1985). Marital and parent-child relationships in family of origin and marital change following the birth of a baby: A retrospective analysis. *Child Development, 56,* 342–349.

Belsky, J., & Pensky, E. (1988). Marital change across the transition to parenthood. *Marriage and Family Review, 12,* 133–156.

Belsky, J., & Rovine, M. (1988). Nonmaternal care in the first year of life and the security of infant-parent attachment. *Child Development, 59,* 157–167.

Belsky, J., & Rovine, M. (1990). Patterns of marital change across the transition to parenthood: Pregnancy to three years post-partum. *Journal of Marriage and the Family, 52,* 5–19.

Belsky, J., Rovine, M., & Taylor, D. G. (1984). The Pennsylvania Infant and Family Development Project, Vol. III: The origins of individual differences in infant-mother attachment—maternal and infant contributions. *Child Development, 55,* 718–728.

Belsky, J., Spanier, G. B., & Rovine, M. (1983). Stability and change in marriage across the transition to parenthood. *Journal of Marriage and the Family, 45,* 553–556.

Belsky, J., & Volling, B. (1987). Mothering and fathering and marital interaction in the family triad during early infancy: Exploring family systems processes. In P. Berman & F. A. Pedersen (Eds.), *Men's transition to parenthood: Longitudinal studies of early family experiences.* Hillsdale, NJ: Erlbaum.

Belsky, J., Youngblade, L., Rovine, M., & Volling, B. (1991). Patterns of marital change and parent-child interaction. *Journal of Marriage and the Family, 53,* 487–498.

Birns, B., & Golden, M. (1972). Prediction of intellectual performance at 3 years on the basis of infant tests and personality measures. *Merrill-Palmer Quarterly, 18,* 53–58.

Bowen, M. (1978). *Family therapy in clinical practice.* New York: Janson Aronson.

Bowlby, J. (1988). *A secure base: Parent-child attachment and healthy human development.* New York: Basic Books.

Cairns, R. B. (1977). Beyond social attachment: The dynamics of interactional development. In T. Alloway, P. Pliner, & L. Kramer (Eds.), *Attachment behavior.* New York: Plenum.

Chess, S. (1982). "Blame the mother" ideology. *International Journal of Mental Health, 11,* 95–107.

Chess, S., & Thomas, A. (1984). *Origins and evaluation of behavior disorders: From infancy to early adult life.* New York: Brunner/Mazel.

Chess, S., & Thomas, A. (1987). *Know your child.* New York: Basic Books.

Clarke-Stewart, K. A., & Fein, G. G. (1983). Early childhood programs. In P. H. Mussen (Ed.), *Handbook of child psychology: Vol. 2. Infancy and developmental psychology* (pp. 917–1000). New York: Wiley.

Coverman, S., & Sheley, J. F. (1986). Change in men's housework and child-care time, 1965–1975. *Journal of Marriage and the Family, 48,* 413–422.

Cowan, C. P., & Cowan, P. A. (1987). Men's involvement in parenthood: Identifying the antecedents and understanding the barriers. In P. W. Berman & F. A. Pedersen (Eds.), *Men's transitions to parenthood: Longitudinal studies of early family experience.* Hillsdale, NJ: Erlbaum.

Crohan, S. E., & Veroff, J. (1989). Marital well-being among white and black newlyweds. *Journal of Marriage and the Family, 51,* 373–384.

Crouter, A. C., Perry-Jenkins, M., Huston, T., & McHale, S. M. (1987). Processes underlying father involvement in dual-career and single-career families. *Developmental Psychology, 23,* 431–440.

Daniels, P., & Weingarten, K. (1982). *Sooner or later: The timing of parenthood in adult times.* New York: Norton.

Dreikurs, R., & Soltz, V. (1964). *Children: The challenge.* New York: Hawthorn.

Easterbrooks, M. A., & Goldberg, W. A. (1984). Toddler development in the family: Impact of father involvement and parenting characteristics. *Child Development, 55,* 740–752.

Fagot, B. I., & Kavanagh, K. (1990). The prediction of antisocial classifications. *Child Development, 61,* 864–873.

Fairbairn, W. R. (1954). *An object-relations theory of personality.* New York: Basic Books.

Fein, R. (1978). Research in fathering: Social policy and an emergent perspective. *Journal of Social Issues, 34,* 122–126.

Fraiberg, S. (1977). *Every child's birthright: In defense of mothering.* New York: Basic Books.

Goldberg, S., Perrotta, M., Minde, K., & Corter, C. (1986). Maternal behavior and attachment in low-weight twins and singletons. *Child Development, 57,* 34–46.

Gordon, T. (1975). *P.E.T.: Parent Effectiveness Training.* New York: New American Library.

Greenough, W. T. (1986). What's special about development? Thoughts on the bases of experience-sensitive synaptic plasticity. In W. T. Greenough & J. M. Juraska (Eds.), *Developmental neuropsychology.* Orlando, FL: Academic Press.

Haskins, R. (1985). Public school aggression among children with varying day-care experience. *Child Development, 56,* 689–703.

Hawkins, A. J., & Belsky, J. (1989). The role of father involvement in personality change in men across the transition to parenthood. *Family Relations, 38,* 378–384.

Hay, D. F. (1985). Learning to form relationships in infancy: Parallel attainments with parents and peers. *Developmental Review, 5,* 122–161.

Hay, D. F., & Vespo, J. E. (1988). Social learning perspectives on the development of the mother-child relationship. In B. Birns & D. F. Hay (Eds.), *The different faces of motherhood* (pp. 73–100). New York: Plenum Press.

Hobbs, D. F., & Wimbish, J. M. (1977). Transition to parenthood by black couples. *Journal of Marriage and the Family, 39,* 677–689.

Hoffman, L. W., & Maris, J. D. (1979). The value of children in the United States: A new approach to the study of fertility. *Journal of Marriage and the Family, 41,* 583–596.

Jones, S. S., & Raag, T. (1989). Smile production in infants: The importance of social recipient for the facial signal. *Child Development, 60,* 811–818.

Kagan, J., Kearsley, R. B., & Zelazo, P. R. (1977). The effects of infant day care on psychological development. *Educational Quarterly, 1,* 109–142.

Kagan J. (1984). The idea of emotion in human development. In C. E. Izard, J. Kagan, & R. B. Zajonc (Eds.), *Emotions, Cognition, and Behavior* (pp. 38–72). Cambridge University Press.

Kotelchuck, M. (1976). The infant's relationship to the father: Experimental evidence. In M. Lamb (Ed.), *The role of the father in child development* (pp. 123–157). New York: Wiley.

Lamb, M. E. (1986). The changing roles of fathers. In M. E. Lamb (Ed.), *The role of the father in child development* (2nd ed.). New York: Wiley.

Lamb, M. E. (1987). *The father's role: Cross-cultural perspective.* Hillsdale, NJ: Erlbaum.

Lampl, M., & Emde, R. (1983). Episodic growth spurts in infancy: A preliminary report on length, head circumference and behavior. In K. Fischer (Ed.), *Levels and transitions in children's development.* San Francisco: Jossey-Bass.

LaRossa, R. (1988). Fatherhood and social change. *Family Relations, 37,* 451–457.

Lazarus, R. S., & Folkman, S. (1984). *Stress, appraisal, and coping.* New York: Springer.

Lederman, E., Lederman, R. P., Work, B. A., & McCann, D. S. (1981). Maternal psychological and physiological correlates of fetal-newborn health status. *American Journal of Obstetrics and Gynecology, 139,* 956–958.

Lewis, M. (1987). Social development in infancy and early childhood. In J. D. Osofsky (Ed.), *Handbook of infant development* (2nd ed.) (pp. 419–555). New York: Wiley.

Lieberman, A. F., Weston, D. R., & Pawl, J. H. (1991). Preventive intervention and outcome with anxiously attached dyads. *Child Development, 62,* 199–209.

Liese, L. H., Snowden, L. R., & Ford, L. K. (1989). Partner status, social support, and psychological adjustment during pregnancy. *Family Relations, 38,* 311–316.

Littenberg, R., Tulkin, S., & Kagan, J. (1971). Cognitive components of separation anxiety. *Developmental Psychology, 4,* 387–388.

Lyons-Ruth, K., Connell, D. B., Grunebaum, H. U., & Botein, S. (1990). *Child Development, 61,* 85–98.

Main, M., & Weston, D. R. (1981). The quality of the toddler's relationship with mother and with father: Related to conflict and the readiness to establish new relationships. *Child Development, 52,* 932–940.

Mercer, R. T., Hackley, K. C., & Bostram, A. G. (1983). Relationship of psychosocial and perinatal variables to perception of childbirth. *Nursing Research, 32,* 202–207.

Miller, B. C. (1976). A multivariate developmental model of marital satisfaction. *Journal of Marriage and the Family, 35,* 643–658.

Miller, B. C., & Sollie, D. L. (1980). Normal stresses during the transition to parenthood. *Family Relations, 29,* 459–465.

Mussen, P. H., & Rutherford, E. (1963). Parent-child relations and parental personality in relation to young children's sex role preferences. *Child Development, 34,* 589–607.

Neal, A. G., Groat, T., & Wicks, J. W. (1989). Attitudes about having children: A study of 600 couples in the early years of marriage. *Journal of Marriage and the Family, 51,* 313–328.

Nock, S. L. (1979). The family life cycle: Empirical or conceptual tool? *Journal of Marriage and the Family, 41,* 15–26.

Nugent, J. K. (1991). Influences on the father's role in infant development. *Journal of Marriage and the Family, 53,* 475–486.

Oller, D. K., & Eilers, R. E. (1988). The role of audition in infant babbling. *Child Development, 59,* 441–449.

Parke, M., & Sawin, D. (1976). The father's role in infancy: A reevaluation. *The Family Coordinator, 25,* 365–371.

Parke, R. D., & O'Leary, S. (1976). Family interaction in the newborn period: Some findings, some observations, and some unresolved issues. In K. Riegel & J. Meacham (Eds.), *The developing individual in a changing world: Vol. 2. Social and environmental issues* (pp. 49–62). The Hague: Mouton.

Parke, R. D., & Tinsley, B. R. (1984). The early environment of the at-risk infant. Expanding the social context. In D. Bricker (Ed.), *Intervention with at-risk and handicapped infants: From research to application* (pp. 153–177). Baltimore: University Park.

Patterson, G. R. (1976). *Living with children* (Rev. ed.). Champaign, IL: Research Press.

Pleck, J. H. (1983). Husband's paid work and family roles: Current research issues. In H. Lopata & J. H. Pleck (Eds.), *Research in the interweave of social roles: (Vol. 3). Families and jobs.* Greenwich, CT: JAI Press.

Plomin, R. (1989). Environment and genes: Determinants of behavior. *American Psychologist, 44,* 105–111.

Polkowitz, R. (1984). Parental attitudes and father's interaction with 5-month-old infants. *Developmental Psychology, 20,* 1054–1060.

Prechtl, H. F. R. (1982). Assessment methods for the newborn infant: A critical evaluation. In P. Stratton (Ed.), *Psychobiology of the human newborn.* New York: Wiley.

Preston, S. H. (1984). Children and the elderly: Divergent paths for America's dependents. *Demography, 21,* 435–457.

Quinn, R. P., & Starnes, G. L. (1979). *The 1977 Quality of Employment Survey.* Ann Arbor, MI: Survey Research Center.

Ragozin, A. S., Basham, R. B., Cronic, K. A., Greenberg, M. T., & Robinson, N. M. (1982). Effects on maternal parenting role. *Developmental Psychology, 18,* 627–634.

Ramey, C. T., Bryant, D. M., & Suarez, T. M. (1985). Preschool compensatory education and the modifiability of intelligence: A critical review. In D. K. Detterman (Ed.), *Current topics in human intelligence: Vol. 1. Research Methodology.* Norwood, NJ: Ablex.

Roberts, G. C., Block, J. H., & Block, J. (1984). Continuity and change in parents' child rearing practice. *Child Development, 55,* 586–597.

Rotunda, E. A. (1985). American fatherhood: A historical perspective. *American Behavioral Scientist, 29,* 7–25.

Russell, G. (1983). *The changing role of fathers?* St. Lucian, Queensland: University of Queensland Press.

Russell, G., & Radin, N. (1983). Increased paternal participation: The father's perspective. In M. E. Lamb & A. Sagi (Eds.), *Fatherhood and Social Policy* (pp. 139–165). Hillsdale, NJ: Erlbaum.

Ryder, N. B. (1979). The future of American fertility. *Social Problems, 26,* 359–370.

Shepherd, G. B. (1988). *Neurobiology.* New York: Oxford University Press.

Sirignano, S. W., & Lachman, M. E. (1985). Personality change during the transition to parenthood: The role of perceived infant temperament. *Developmental Psychology, 21,* 558–567.

Snow, M. E., Jacklin, C. N., & Maccoby, E. E. (1983). Sex of child differences in father-child interaction at one year of age. *Child Development, 54,* 227–232.

Stoneman, Z., Brody, G. H., & Burke, M. (1989). Sibling temperaments and marital and family functioning. *Journal of Marriage and the Family, 51,* 99–114.

Thomas, A., Chess, S., & Birch, H. (1970, August). The origin of personality. *Scientific American, 223,* 102–109.

Tietjen, A. M., & Bradley, C. F. (1985). Social support and material psychosocial adjustment during the transition to parenthood. *Canadian Journal of Behavioral Science, 17,* 109–121.

Tilden, V. (1983). The relation of life stress and social support to emotional disequilibrium during pregnancy. *Research in Nursing and Health, 6,* 167–174.

Timiras, P. S. (1972). *Developmental physiology and aging.* New York: Macmillan.

Tizard, B. (1977). *Adoption: A second chance.* London: Open Books.

Tronick, E. Z. (1989). Emotions and emotional communication in infants. *American Psychologist, 44,* 112–119.

U.S. Bureau of the Census (1973). Birth expectations and fertility: June 1972. *Current Population Reports* (Series P-20, No. 248). Washington, DC: U.S. Government Printing Office.

U.S. Bureau of the Census (1983). Fertility of American women: June 1983. *Current Population Reports* (Series P-20, No. 395). Washington, DC: U.S. Government Printing Office.

U.S. Bureau of the Census (1987). Population profile of the United States: 1984–85. *Current Population Reports* (Series P-23, No. 150). Washington, DC: U.S. Government Printing Office.

U.S. Bureau of the Census (1989). *Statistical abstract of the United States: 1989* (109th ed.). Washington, DC: U.S. Government Printing Office.

Volling, B. L., & Belsky, J. (1991). Fathers' involvement with infants in single- and dual-career families. *Journal of Marriage and the Family, 53,* 461–474.

Weinraub, M. (1977, March). *Children's responses to maternal absences: An experimental study.* Paper presented at biennial meeting of the Society for Research in Child Development, New Orleans.

White, L. K., & Booth, A. (1985). The quality and stability of remarriages: The role of stepchildren. *American Sociological Review, 50,* 689–698.

Wilkie G., & Ames, E. (1986). The relationship of infant crying to parental stress in the transition to parenthood. *Journal of Marriage and the Family, 48,* 545–550.

Chapter 5

Parenting the Toddler and Preschool Child from 2 to 4 Years Old

Parenting Myth ■ Parents must control the child's behavior by being willing to engage in certain behaviors, such as "breaking the will" of the resistive child who deliberately misbehaves.

Test Your Knowledge ■ The following questions are designed to test your knowledge before reading the material in this chapter. Answers appear at the end of the chapter.

1 Play is generally viewed as a pleasurable activity for children, but it has no other useful purpose. True or false?

2 Researchers have found that a permissive parenting style is correlated with problems that are similar to those of authoritarian parenting. True or false?

3 Toilet training represents a developmental milestone rather than a self-help skill. True or false?

4 Toddlers who are more intelligent and socially developed differ little from other toddlers. True or false?

5 The induction type of parental behavior toward children has no advantages over other methods. True or false?

6 Toddlers are not capable of fantasy play. True or false?

In the infant stage, parents are concerned with making a place for the infant in the family through attachment. Little or no discipline is required in this stage. Parents spend the majority of their time with the infant in behaviors that result in the infant learning to feel loved and accepted. There is nothing comparable in parenting to the pleasure the parent receives in this period. Even parents who have difficulty with the amount of caregiving and attention needed by the infant may express a degree of disappointment in moving on to the next phase of parenting.

During the second year of life, called **toddlerhood,** parenting takes on a new focus. Parents spend less time caring for the infant and more time controlling and restricting his/her behavior. Whereas the infant was somewhat immobile, the toddler is highly mobile and engaged in nonstop activity. The toddler is constantly learning new behavior and increasing cognitive abilities. Phenomenal growth in both physical and mental abilities is taking place (see Table 5.1). While the toddler is learning and initiating new behaviors, he/she, unfortunately, does not come equipped with a set of instructions for self-regulation. As a result, the early years can be a period of dissatisfaction for both parents and children.

This process whereby parents are directly involved in teaching children how to behave within the guidelines of a particular society is called **socialization.** While parents have logical and well thought out reasons for doing the things they do, the toddler does not necessarily see their behavior that way and may, in fact, insist that parents change the way they deal with him/her. Further, parents who have low self-concepts are especially vulnerable to the stress produced by the toddler's attempts to master and control his/her environment.

Although the family is the focal point in the socialization of the child, the society's influence cannot be minimized. A later chapter will discuss in detail the contributions of the larger social network. A family, situated within a particular social and cultural network, sets the pattern of behavior and the expected values and attitudes of the particular family members. Standards of behavior differ according to certain demographic variables, such as attitudes, socioeconomic class, religion, education, and the gender of the parent.

Viewing the family as an interactional system means that children affect the socialization process while they are being molded by it. A systems perspective assumes that parents also change in this process of socialization (Bell, 1968). For example, a parent who begins by scolding a child may turn to taking away privileges or spanking, but may find none of these effective punishments. The parent's ineffectiveness in controlling an active child can escalate into a series of behaviors in the child that affect the parent's self-perception and sense of self-worth.

Socialization of the child involves a number of dimensions. The use of language to communicate and express oneself cognitively and affectively is of primary significance to parenting. The toddler's play activity is considered extremely important for the cognitive and social development of the child. In addition, a neglected aspect of play is guidance and redirection of unwanted behavior. Parents also socialize children through teaching self-help skills, such as dressing, eating, and toilet training. Finally, parents socialize children through specific strategies meant to control and redirect unwanted behavior.

■ *The mobility of toddlers and their interest in exploring make it difficult for parents to keep up with them.*

This chapter summarizes the biological and physical development of the toddler and discusses the role and function of play and social development. Although an in-depth discussion of these issues is impractical, I cite the most relevant research.

■
Biological and Physical Development

During toddlerhood, the child rapidly gains weight and increases in height (Eichorn, 1979). On average, the changes in weight and height from age 2 to 6, however, are not as dramatic as the changes during infancy. During this time, the toddler's

Table 5.1 ■ **Developmental Milestones**

Age	Milestone
1½ to 2 years	Language development—puts several words together Motor skills—builds tower of five to six blocks
2 years	Dressing—puts on socks, shoes, and pants Motor skills—builds tower of up to seven blocks Toilet training—dry during day
3 years	Motor skills—builds tower of nine blocks; jumps with two feet; rides tricycle; stands on one leg Speaks in short sentences Knows own gender Toilet trained

facial and skeletal features begin to resemble how they will appear in adulthood. The change in skeletal maturity that continues into adolescence is referred to as **ossification,** the replacing of cartilage by bone. Without this process, children would not be able to engage in physically strenuous activity.

In addition to skeletal growth during toddlerhood, the brain continues to grow in size and functions. This growth in functions is generally referred to as **lateralization,** or the specialization of certain functions in different hemispheres in the brain (Kolb & Wishaw, 1985). Generally, the right hemisphere is the center for visual, tactile, and spatial information whereas the left hemisphere is the center for processing language and linguistic information and analyzing situations. Although these functions are specialized in different hemispheres of the brain, there is some evidence that one hemisphere may fill in for the other in certain instances, such as after an injury to one hemisphere (Springer, 1989). Researchers generally conclude that some lateralization is present at birth because when lying on their back infants prefer to turn over on their right rather than their left (Kinsborne & Hiscock, 1983), and almost all show a preference for using their right hand (Ramsay, 1984).

During this period, the toddler begins to develop both gross motor skills—the use of the large muscle group—and fine motor skills—the use of the small muscles in the hands and the feet. Fine motor skills are related to brain maturation and occur after gross motor skills develop. The use of fine motor skills is illustrated in the development of drawing and through practice in different types of play (Hughes, 1991). Practice of a motor skill tends to help in both the mastery of it and in learning new skills.

Although males and females develop similarly during toddlerhood, there are some differences. For example, girls maintain more body fat from infancy through the toddler stage than do boys, while boys develop greater height and strength. There is some evidence that parental focus on sex differences may encourage boys and girls to engage in different types of activities related to physical differences (Jacklin, 1989). For example, boys are encouraged to run and use more gross body muscles than girls are.

■ *Toddlers should be allowed to eat the foods they like and at their own pace.*

■ Self-Help Skills

Learning **self-help skills** can be a time of extreme satisfaction and accomplishment for the toddler. Of course, eating is one of the first things that parents begin helping the child master. The infant typically begins eating by using fingers and later a spoon. Although some children learn to feed themselves easily, others have difficulty learning this skill. The latter case can cause problems in the family.

The problem for the toddler in eating is a skill deficit. Too many parents view messy eating as willful disobedience. When toddlers are allowed to eat the food they prefer and to eat at their own rate, they tend to learn faster. Forcing toddlers to eat certain foods or to eat in certain quantities may have the opposite effect. Parents should not create a control issue or power struggle in getting their children to eat.

Dressing is another skill that toddlers must begin to master. Dressing problems in the toddler period may be more related to the lack of skill than to any other problem. And when they experience difficulty in dressing, or any other activity, they may refuse to participate. Typically, when the parent is in a hurry to go someplace, the toddler will refuse to cooperate in dressing. Consequently, the parent forces the toddler to comply, resulting in anger and resentment by both parent and child. The best parenting strategy for dealing with dressing problems is to be patient and to allow the child autonomy. Parents should see themselves as teachers in the process of skill development rather than enforcers of particular behaviors.

In the past, child-development experts considered **toilet training** an extremely important aspect of parenting the toddler, but the focus on the development of this skill has declined in recent years. The reason career-oriented parents do not focus as much on toilet training probably stems from less focus by pediatricians and child-development specialists. Child psychologists view toilet training as a skill the child develops according to his/her internal timetable (Brazelton, 1974). When the toddler demonstrates a regularity of bowel movement and can connect the wetness in his/her diapers with bodily functions, it is usually time to begin encouraging the toddler to work jointly to master this skill. On the other hand, when children appear resistive and continue to soil their pants, it may signal that the parent is attempting to force the toddler. Such parental pressure may result in greater frustration for both toddler and parent.

Self-Control

The toddler's control over impulsive behavior is usually an area of concern for most parents. As the toddler develops a sense of continuity of events and better time perspective, he/she is more patient and can delay gratification (Vaughn, Kopp, & Krakow, 1984). More intelligent and more socially developed toddlers tend to be among those who are able to delay gratification (Mischel, Shoba, & Rodriguez, 1989). In addition, these differences have been noted at later ages, suggesting that the differences may represent unique personality and interactional structures. The frequency of aggressive acts tends to decline as the toddler learns to control his/her impulses (Cummings, Iannotti, & Zahn-Waxler, 1989).

Certain types of toddler behaviors, such as refusal to cooperate, tend to cause different parental responses. For example, a child who frequently refuses to do what the parent wants may be extremely upsetting to the parent. On the other hand, many normal behaviors may not be recognized as such by parents. This overall lack of knowing what is normal behavior and what is abnormal behavior may be related to reduced competencies in parenting.

Language Development

Vocalizations begin to appear very early. By 6 months, infants are mixing cooing and babbling noises. Babbling, or one-syllable words, over time tends to represent specific sounds the infant hears frequently (Lenneberg, 1967). By 1 year of age, the infant is babbling sounds in its own language versus a generic language. Evidence suggests that language and thought may develop along similar but parallel tracks. Many behaviors, such as grasping and reaching, signify thought processes without accompanying language (Best, McRoberts, & Sithole, 1988).

Infants tend to use sounds in ritualized fashion to obtain specific outcomes. For example, they may express emotions through certain repetitions of sounds. Likewise, in order to get the mother's attention, infants may develop repeatable sounds that tend to produce targeted behavior in the mother (Bates, O'Connell, & Shore, 1987). Researchers have found that infants appear to understand language before they are able to vocalize specific words or related sounds.

During toddlerhood there is an explosion in the development of using words to convey meanings (Rice, 1989). **Language development** in toddlers consists of four dimensions: **phonology,** or the sound system; **semantics,** or the meaning system; **morphology,** rules of word formation; and **syntax,** the rules of sentence formation. One syllable can convey an entire sentence of meaning for the toddler. For example, "Ba" may mean "Get me the bottle." This acquiring of a vocabulary of functional words in such a short time frame represents the toddler's ability to understand new words through their connections with familiar words in repetitive sentences (Rice & Woodsmall, 1988). The toddler forms a type of "gestalt" for understanding meanings in the context in which they are used. The combining of two words to make a sentence begins soon after single-word thoughts. Researchers have found that toddlers vary in the degree to which they gain mastery of language and in their patterns of combining words (Ferguson, 1989).

Researchers have concluded that the toddler's interaction with the mother or other caregiver is the single most influential factor affecting his/her acquisition of language (Snow, 1984). Adults tend to alter their speech patterns to fit the level of the toddler after he/she begins to talk (Rice, 1989). The interaction of the mother with the child has been referred to in the literature as **motherese,** which is characterized by frequent repetitions, short sentences, a slow rate of speech, and frequent pauses between utterances. This style of interaction tends to characterize the conversation of white, middle-class mothers. Motherese does not seem to characterize rural Southern black mothers, who tend to speak to their children as if they were adults (Heath, 1989).

Language development is further enhanced by parents reading to their toddler (Rice, 1989). Reading forms a link with written literacy that also begins emerging at about 5 years of age. While reading to the toddler is helpful in language acquisition, evidence suggests that a directive style which makes many demands on the child is correlated with a slower rate of acquisition (Nelson, 1973, cited in Rice, 1989). Consequently, a more indirect and relaxed approach to language development is necessary for optimal mastery.

A Systems Perspective of Language Development

A number of approaches address how children acquire language. Generative grammar theorists believe that syntax is an autonomous entity and does not depend on cognition or structure. On the other hand, cognitive linguists believe that language

■ *"Motherese," distinguished by frequent repetitive sentences, slow rate of speech, and frequent pauses between utterances, tends to characterize the speech pattern of white, middle-class mothers.*

acquisition is best explained in terms of cognition and communication. Developmental psychologists believe that children acquire language and other skills through a structured stepwise manner. See Tomasello (1992) for an in-depth discussion of these theories.

In contrast with approaches to language development that emphasize individual skills or needs of the child, the systems approach is concerned with the process of how the toddler becomes proficient with the use of language. The child becomes proficient in using language by interacting with the parents. According to a systems perspective, the term *acquisition of language* is not appropriate in the sense that a mutually interactive system is operative whereby the development of language is the by-product rather than the goal (Harris, 1975).

The system of interaction between parent and child is developed and maintained through the feedback system between parent and child. The system changes through interaction of various components of the system. The interactions of the child with

---

Box 5.1

■ ■ ■ ■ ■ ■ ■ ■ ■ ■

Language Acquisition

The exact route for the development of language is unknown. It is known, however, that teaching language to children may impede rather than enhance language development. Language development tends to emerge during the second and third years of life as a result of the child's interaction with parents. Although cognitive and social competencies are important in the development of language, they do not fully account for it.

Beyond the fact that children must hear language and experience some meaningful exchange with parents, little is known about how children learn to use language. Most efforts in understanding the development of language focus on description and patterns of acquisition in children. In a recently developed model of language acquisition, Rice (1989) has proposed that language development is not a linear progression but tends to be learned in rare events or isolated moments of understanding. As a result, stages in the acquisition of language may overlap and appear in an unequal or discontinuous process.

---

the parent and the environment are internalized and determine a structure for the continuing process. Neither child nor parent is most important in this interaction; rather, input from two distinct sources acts in the dual role of subject/object (Harris, 1975).

The interaction between parent and child involves giving and receiving both verbal and nonverbal messages. The verbal language is one among a number of ways parents and children communicate. Generally, two types of communication have been described in the literature, analog and digital (Harris, 1975). **Analog communication** is usually nonverbal, expressive, and emotional, whereas **digital communication** is more structured and precise. In the context of parent/child communication, the parent operates from an analog stance and the child operates from a digital stance.

The preverbal child communicates through emotional expression, gestures, and eye contact. The parent combines both analog and digital forms in a kind of mosaic to obtain a response from the child. The parent/child communication is **complementary**—that is, hierarchical—in that the parent sets the structure and frame for the interaction. Through analogic communicating, such as touching, holding, smiling, and similar behavior, the parent and child develop an open communication system. The child develops language by internalizing this interaction with the parent (Harris, 1975).

This interaction of analogic and digital styles of communicating results in the child being able to interpret the analog in digital terms. The child must be able to internalize this transition and respond to other shifts that take place between the parent and child in the continuing interaction. This continuing process is one in which the child increasingly masters the parent's style of communication. What may appear as imitation of the parent can better be described as the child shifting from the analogic to the digital style. In time the child will be equally competent in the use of both styles of communication. Baby talk can aptly be described as the parent shifting into the child's dominant style. The purpose of this shifting to the analogic is to be playful and facilitate the child's language development (Harris, 1975).

■ Play

For the toddler, most social interaction with same-age children appears in the form of play. Actually, what constitutes play has been questioned and only partially determined. A frequently used definition of **play** by Dearden (1967)—that is, a nonserious and self-contained activity—serves as a starting place for discussing play. Generally, play takes the form of providing excitement and enjoyment for the child and may vary from one setting to another.

In American society, play has evolved from the Puritan view that it was a "trifling" activity to the view that it is a significant necessity for normal child development. Puritan parents, for example, were greatly concerned about the amount of time children were involved in play activities. They were specifically concerned that the amount of play time would decrease time for more useful activities (Cohen, 1987). Not only did parents not engage in play with their children, they saw little use of play as a child activity. Gradually, parents have become more aware of the usefulness of play as part of the interaction with their child.

Although parents have gradually become partners with their children in play, little research has been done on the family at play (Cohen, 1987). For example, we know little about play in the family except as it relates to the development of cognitive and social skills. Play for sheer enjoyment or as an aid in directing, controlling, or initiating behaviors has been ignored. Observing families in their homes may be extremely important in answering some of these questions.

A few researchers in the past several decades have focused on the mother and infant in interaction, including the interaction of play. Most of these studies have been in the laboratory using questionable methodologies (Cohen, 1987). In these studies, infants are more involved in play when their mother is in view than when the mother is not in view (Corter, 1976, cited in Cohen, 1987). Likewise, as children age they also appear to be more responsive to different activities if their parents are engaged with them. For example, in an experiment with children 6 to 8 years old, children whose parents accompanied them to a museum were more interested in the exhibits than children who were part of a group of children (Henderson, Chalkesworth, & Gamradt, 1982, cited in Cohen, 1987).

In the 1980s, an emerging trend focused on the importance of play for the child. This trend was heavily influenced by the writings of David Elkind (1987), who warned of the dangers of the **hurried child.** Despite this trend in the general literature, there was little change in the curriculum for young children in day-care and preschool programs (Bloch & Choi, 1990). In fact, over this same period, play time in the curriculum of preschool programs has been reduced.

Historically, educators have seen play as an important aspect of learning. Early 20th-century pre-education programs included both supervised and unsupervised play activities. Reformers, referred to as progressives, wanted more free play introduced into the classroom. The free play resulted in near chaos and disorder in the classroom and caused some pre-education programs to attempt to return to academic subjects entirely (Bloch & Choi, 1990).

The present emphasis in preschool programs has been on a return to the basics—the academic subject matter of learning the alphabet—and on developing skills that are represented in standardized test scores which complement the early grade-school curriculum. This focus on academic success on test scores of preschool children may be detrimental to the long-term cognitive development of the child (Bloch & Choi, 1990).

Play and Cognitive Development

The current back to the basics in preschool education ignores much of the contribution of Piaget (1962). He believed that play was the mastery of activities for the sheer enjoyment of them without considering the outcome. As a result, play can be seen as the basis for all later **cognitive development.** In fact, educators have viewed play as equally important to the development of cognitive ability as physical, emotional, or social aspects of existence because it allows the toddler practice at gaining competency and mastery over the environment.

The case for the importance of play in the cognitive development of the child can be made with reference to the nature of symbolic representation. The use of symbols to represent an object is the basis for all learning. Similar to the way that sensorimotor intelligence of the child evolves from sensations and actions and the representational, play through its symbolic meaning moves from activity to representation (Atley, 1975).

This transition from the sensorimotor to mature adult thought takes place through play rather than language because language is mostly symbolic. Because play is mostly **assimilation,** a child views reality mainly through his/her imagination. In contrast to language, play is suitable for a transitional period because it is the way a child expresses needs and begins to understand reality (Atley, 1975).

Research findings support this view that play allows the toddler an opportunity to gain control and competency over the environment. For example, much of the toddler's play is symbolic. Researchers have found that toddlers engage in symbolic play for longer periods of time when the mother is present (Slade, 1987a). Other researchers have found that toddlers who participate actively in pretend play are more creative than those who do not in using ordinary objects in creative or symbolic ways (Dansky, 1980). Researchers have found that boy toddlers who are active explorers through play tend to be more competent in school than boys who are less involved in play. Likewise, girl toddlers who are inhibited and restricted in play tend to be both socially and cognitively impaired (Hutt & Bhavnani, 1972). The balance of research tends toward viewing play as an adaptive and functional activity for child development.

A number of researchers have addressed how parents, teachers, and other adults have enhanced play in the toddler. For example, if parents are actively involved with their toddlers in play, do toddlers play differently when parents are uninvolved with them? As playmates, parents can facilitate both the direction and the outcome of the play experience. In other words, what is the relationship between the social context and the ability to communicate and symbolize?

A systems perspective of play emphasizes the sharing of meaning that occurs between parent and child that leads to the ability to symbolize. This view of play means that symbolic and dyadic functions are merged together. **Symbolic play** is viewed as emerging within both an individual and an interpersonal context. The dyadic focus is in sharp contrast to approaches that emphasize only the individual changes. Researchers have found ample evidence of the link between the security in attachment to the caregiver and numerous social and economic competencies (Slade, 1987b).

In one study, Slade (1987b) attempted to determine the relationship between attachment and symbolic play and the differences in how mothers of anxious children and mothers of secure children use symbolic play. Subjects included 15 mother/infant dyads with the infants between 20 and 28 months old; eight of the infants were anxious and seven were secure. The researcher assessed the interactions between mother and child on a bimonthly basis.

Slade (1987b) found a positive relation between attachment and higher performance measured by duration of time and the level of symbolic activity. The findings for this study tend to support the assumption that secure children function at the optimal level of development whereas insecure children function at lower levels. Further, secure children engage in more creative and symbolic play than do insecure children. This research has much relevance because it attempts to include the mother's interaction with the child as a factor in the security status of the child and his/her competency. It could be that the relationship with the mother is of such magnitude that previous research will have to be reinterpreted in light of it.

In addition to mothers, fathers of infants and other family members are important aspects of the child's social interaction. In fact, the entire social system interacts with the frequency and duration of symbolic play, which suggests that the stranger test should be revised to reflect contextual methodology. This **contextual methodology** is based on the reciprocal nature of interpersonal relationships. For example, researchers have shown that when adults are active in imaginary play, toddlers gain the ability to direct the adult playmates in play activities (Eckerman & Didow, 1989).

Play as a Form of Social Competence

Play provides the toddler with the opportunity to learn about him/herself and the expectations of others, which is referred to as **social competence**. A toddler is free to try out new and different behaviors in a relatively safe setting. This safety in trying new behaviors means that the toddler can gain a feeling of competency before engaging in more serious pursuits of the same behavior.

■ *Children develop cognitive and social skills through play.*

Gradually, a more imaginative type of play, sometimes referred to as **fantasy play,** emerges during the second and third years (Piaget, 1970). This type of play serves the purpose of preventing loneliness and gives the toddler imaginary friends for practice relationships. Imaginary play, requiring few props, may be engaged in alone or with playmates. It declines sharply in the school-age years because, according to Piaget, the child can tell reality from fantasy. Researchers have found, however, that toddlers can tell the difference between a real object and what someone might pretend it to be (Flavell, Flavell, & Green, 1987).

In toddlerhood, fantasy play consists of four factors. First, toddlers string a sequence of actions together (Lucariello, 1987). The toddler may pretend to be a number of people in a series of actions. For example, in pretending to be cops and robbers, the toddler may be both the cop and the robber and change his/her action from chasing to capturing or from putting in jail to being in jail.

Second, because play involves a coordinated effort to take roles according to an overall plan, toddlers become more able to shift from themselves to others. Although toddlers may continue to play alone, they tend to prefer playing with others. But this play generally is characterized more as side-by-side than as actively engaged.

Third, fantasy play involves enacting the situations the child is familiar with; for example, the child attending day care pretends to be the teacher. Children may not need props in these pretend roles and may make elaborate use of what they have at hand. Gradually, these pretend characters become more complex and separated from the normal or common situation. For example, a child may pretend to be an astronaut, a fantasy not in his/her common experience.

Fourth, play becomes more organized. The efforts to organize play, no doubt, revolve around including more children in the play activity. Some children find the coordination of such fantasy to be quite satisfying. They may do a lot of planning and act as directors in acting out the fantasy. This type of play gives way to rules or games rather than free expression of a play activity.

A number of researchers have addressed the value of fantasy play. Piaget (1962) believed that fantasy play allows the child to master situations that in reality may be difficult to manage. In terms of social skills, toddlers who are advanced in fantasy play tend to be well liked by other children because their language and communication skills are well developed (Ladd, Price, & Hart, 1988). Play provides a first indicator of how socially competent a child is likely to be at a later time.

Play as a Form of Discipline

Although the importance of play has been delineated for cognitive and social development of children, it has never been developed as a significant parenting behavior for child management. Psychologists and social workers have used play as a form of therapy since the 1950s (Axline, 1947), but they have not applied play to parenting behavior. The application of play to changing or improving a child's behavior reflects a positive, or nonjudgmental, attitude toward the child in learning or therapeutic settings.

In contrast to viewing play as a normal, day-to-day activity, researchers have focused on play from a therapeutic point of view. Typically, the child engaging in play therapy is socially and psychologically impaired. The Freudian school of child therapy (Freud, 1965) applied classical psychoanalytic theory to play by attempting to improve the child's ego functioning. Freudian therapy opens new avenues of behavior designed to make the personality more adaptive. The therapist interprets and supports the child in guided play activities.

The play therapy of Axline (1947) is based on the work of Carl Rogers (1942). The underlying idea is to show acceptance and unconditional positive regard. The child is allowed unrestricted opportunity for play while the therapist interacts and makes appropriate comments that reflect the child's feelings. A nonjudgmental therapist who reflects the feelings that the child is unable to express verbally will facilitate positive growth and developmental normalcy.

Although **play therapy**—deliberate play aimed at helping the child work through problems—has been successful in the laboratory setting and applied to a number of situations, it has not been applied to normal families, except in a few cases, because a family does not lend itself to being studied in a laboratory (Guerney, 1969). It also seems plausible that the use and development of play in the family would be quite different from play in a therapeutic setting. For example, in normal families both children and adults initiate play, whereas in a therapeutic situation only the therapist initiates play. Furthermore, it is important to know how these different types of play affect the family and in what contexts the play appears.

A Systems Perspective of Play

As part of the interactive field within the family, a child's play must be understood within the family system in which it occurs. Because researchers have ignored the interaction within the family as a variable affecting the nature of play, there is little knowledge about the use of play in normal development. Changes in play over time might be an important starting place in understanding the significance of play in the family.

How parents use play to guide, direct, or discipline children has not been fully addressed in the literature. While the control function of play has received little attention in the research literature, there is no doubt that parents use play to control and direct behavior. Likewise, children use play to influence how parents respond to them. For example, sometimes parents make doing chores a playful activity.

Parents might be more successful in directing the behavior of children if they used play in a more deliberate manner. The limited research on parental influence on play suggests that the quality of play is related to the overall functioning of the parent—that is, the more competent the parent the more the parent expresses warmth and positive feelings toward the child (Mondell & Tyler, 1981). In this sense, play cannot be separated from the myriad of other interactions that occur within the recursive, or reciprocal, feedback system in the family.

Other research on the parental effect on play indicates that children play differently with parents than they play with other children (Stevenson, Leavitt, Thompson, & Roach, 1988). Play with other children usually takes an unstructured form or solitary side-by-side play. In contrast, when parents are involved, play is usually more interactive and structured. This research may signal the important role that parents have in the development of their children's play. Furthermore, it suggests that parents are more influential in the direction of play than usually believed.

In reflecting the major role that parents have in the development of their children's play, Kaye (1982, cited in Cohen, 1987) contends that the literature on the infant has exaggerated the infant's competencies. Kaye maintains that the mother takes both sides of the conversation with very young infants, but tends to act as if the infant is participating equally. Infants are taught to be sociable by their parents through a process that Kaye called **infant apprentices to social life.** Parents are motivated to take care of the infant on the false assumption of the infant's competence. The large number of verbalizations, gestures, and responses of the caregiver to the infant gives the infant a great deal to imitate. Consequently, the parent may be very instrumental in the kinds of activities the infant actually engages in.

In observing his own young children, Cohen (1987) reported that play tended to change over time and in reference to a number of other factors. Parents typically use

■ *Children play more structured games with parents than with their peers.*

very simple games initially, such as variations of "peek-a-boo," and increase the complexity as children learn more complex language. These games are repetitive and allow the child to learn the rules over a period of time.

As children age they are more capable of being active participants with the parent and of initiating as well as following the lead of the parent. For example, an interesting study by Ross and Lollis (1987) indicates that when parents do not take their turn in a play situation, the toddler will actively attempt to get the parent to participate by demonstrating and encouraging the parents to take their turn. This process of initiating the expected sequence in play suggests that children learn to take a more equal role in influencing the parents' behavior.

■
Individual and Social Development

By 20 months of age the typical toddler is able to recognize him/herself in a mirror and develop sentences that refer to the self (Smolak, 1986). They not only recognize themselves in videos and pictures but distinguish themselves from other

Table 5.2 ■ **The Toddler's View of Death**

- Seem curious about death
- Do not believe that death is permanent
- Believe that a dead person can be brought back to life
- Do not believe that death is universal
- Believe that death is caused by something external to the person

Source: Stambrook and Parker, 1987.

children, particularly on the basis of gender (Damon & Hart, 1982). They frequently refer to themselves as "me" and things belonging to them as "mine." These self-references can carry whole thought implications. For example, when the toddler says "mine," he/she most likely means "That toy is my toy."

Coupled with the recognition of the self is the belief about oneself in relationship with others, or the **self-concept.** Children learn and develop a self-concept in the second year through the socialization process in the family. The contact with parents and other intimates in the infancy and toddler periods forms the basis for the self-concept that is built on during the preschool years. Even the concept of death emerges as children interact with others and experience different situations (see Table 5.2).

Researchers generally have concluded that a number of correlates exist for the development of a positive self-concept. First, the behaviors of children are related to self-concept. For example, children with positive self-concepts tend to be happier and less anxious than other children. On the other hand, children with poor self-concepts tend to be unhappy, less popular, and more defensive than other children (McCandless, 1967).

Second, the quality of the **parent/child interaction** is an indication of how the child's self-concept might develop. Parents who show acceptance and warmth but still set firm and fair guidelines tend to raise children who have adequate self-concepts (Baumrind, 1967). A child whose parents maintain mutual respect with him/her tends to have high self-esteem.

In recent literature on the parent/child relationship, more attention has been given to the parents' cognitive beliefs about the child's behavior and the influence of these beliefs on the socialization of the child. These parental beliefs consist of social and interpersonal factors and events. The parental belief system about parenting, therefore, is the major context in which the child's social development takes place (Mills & Rubin, 1990).

To determine how parents react when children display maladaptive behavior, Mills and Rubin (1990) analyzed the emotional responses of parents to **aggression** and **social withdrawal.** First, based on other research, they speculated that the parental response to aggression and withdrawal would be anger. Second, researchers know little about the causes parents attribute to these maladaptive child behaviors and

■■■■■■■■■■

Box
5.2

The Impact of Social Relationships on Development

Researchers have only recently begun to consider the impact of social relationships on child development important enough to study. Some studies suggest that a child's effectiveness in social relationships is related to close intimate relationships. The amount of time spent with the parents and siblings may significantly affect how the child relates to others.

Two kinds of social relationships have been identified as integral to child development, vertical and horizontal. Parent/child relationships are considered vertical because the parent has more power and authority than the child. Parent/child relationships are complementary in that the interactional exchange consists mainly of parents controlling and directing the child while the child acts in a subordinate manner to elicit those parental behaviors. In the second year of life, children begin to be more concerned about horizontal relationships, or relationships with peers and siblings. Horizontal relationships are characterized by equal power and egalitarian exchanges.

The process of development occurs within a relationship of at least two individuals. Mother and father are experiencing developmental changes, although slowly, at the same time the child is developing relatively fast. Developmental change in the child affects developmental change in the parent and vice versa. The interaction between parent and child is geared so that the child's weakness is lessened by the parent's strength. Furthermore, children who are more attached to parents tend to be more popular and have more friends in nursery school and throughout life.

Friendships with peers begin developing in toddlerhood. These relationships are almost always with children of the same sex and are based on common interests and goals. Children with behavioral problems typically have poor relationships with peers. These difficulties with friends may be the outcome of poor social interaction from birth. Hartup's (1989) research findings give credence to the belief that aggressive and antisocial behaviors in children are related to coercive family interactions. The evidence tends to suggest that social failure is highly correlated with the familial interactive pattern.

whether parents differentiate between aggression and withdrawal in their children. Third, little is known about the strategies parents use in response to these child behaviors. Finally, gender differences may account for how parents respond to aggression and withdrawal in children. Mills and Rubin expected that parents would respond more negatively to aggression in girls than in boys because of traditional stereotypes.

This study incorporated systems concepts and ideas. For example, the researchers expected that the lack of personal and economic resources and decreased social support from family, friends, and spouse would increase the use of parental anger and power to control aggression in children. In addition, parents living under adverse educational and occupational conditions and dealing with an accumulation of negative life events will react to maladaptive behaviors in their children with a negative emotional response and a concomitant increase in power strategies.

In the same study, Mills and Rubin found that mothers and fathers reacted similarly to aggression and attributed like causes to these problematic behaviors. Aggression was associated with more negative parental behavior, and withdrawal was associated with uncertainty and less negative parental behavior. Mothers tended to place more confidence in information giving, or making statements to the child about specific behaviors, than in power strategies for controlling the aggression. This difference may result from the time differential in contact with children between mothers and fathers.

In addition, both fathers and mothers responded more intensely to aggression in girls than in boys. This study suggests that parents may accept deviant behavior in boys more than in girls. It also indicates that girls may be subjected to stronger socialization pressures to conform than boys, particularly in the early years.

In the Mills and Rubin study, mothers responded less to social withdrawal in their child than fathers did when they believed the withdrawal was caused by traits such as shyness. This finding may reflect that mothers have stronger beliefs about traits which are impervious to change. Or perhaps parents have less skill and knowledge about their child's social withdrawal, resulting in their greater passivity and fewer attempts to help the child become less withdrawn.

Finally, life circumstances and the ecological factors of occupation, education, and social support play a large role in the beliefs of parents and the particular strategies they use to control maladjusted behaviors in their children. As expected, lower occupational status was related to increased control strategies, particularly when social support was low.

■ Parent/Child Interaction

Child-development experts consider the quality of the parent/child interaction during toddlerhood and the preschool years as important as attachment of the infant to the parent in the development of normal children. The spectrum of positive or adaptive behaviors must be seen in broad terms rather than from a narrow perspective. Parental behaviors must be placed within the context of the social and cultural perspective in which they occur. Different parents may use quite different methods to control their children's behavior and be similarly effective. The tasks of parents during this period must be to set rules, monitor outcomes, and provide appropriate discipline for misbehavior.

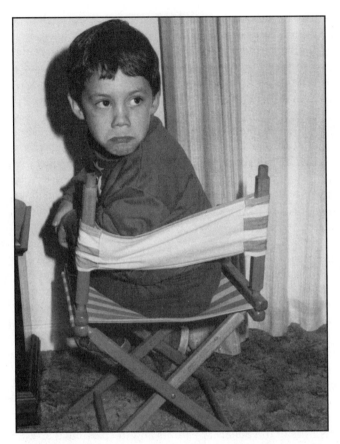

■ *Putting a child in time-out is a punitive method of discipline.*

Parental Attitudes Toward the Child

Bigner (1985) describes parental attitudes toward the child in terms of either nurturance or control. **Nurturance** includes a host of behaviors that refer to expressing warmth, acceptance, and understanding. Generally, children who have been treated with love and respect have the desire to communicate with their parents and maintain positive interactions. Children gain a degree of control over their own behavior when parents have created the pattern of sitting down and talking through problems. Whereas parental hostility has been related to poor compliance by children, warm and accepting parental behaviors have been related to increased self-reliance and greater learning.

Control refers to specific behaviors a parent engages in to influence the child to comply with certain rules and standards of behavior. Baumrind (1971) has related three types of parental behavior to control—authoritative, authoritarian, and permissive. **Authoritarian** parents impose strict rules and expect the child to have a high degree of compliance. If compliance does not follow, authoritarian parents resort to punishing the child without talking to him/her about the misbehavior and the reason for the punishment. Although the parent may gain momentary control through such means, the child may subvert the parent at every opportunity, or as sometimes may happen when parenting styles differ, the child may frequently avoid the punitive parent.

Authoritative parenting is similar to authoritarian parenting in that parents may set guidelines and rules and impose consequences for failure to comply. The two approaches differ in that authoritative parents consider the child's viewpoint and give the child a rationale for the restrictions. This reasoning with the child about the specific misbehavior is correlated with positive outcomes, whereas punishment without talking to the child, such as spanking, may actually increase the undesired behavior. Taking a firm hand with a child can be beneficial as long as it is not too restrictive.

Permissive parents allow the child excessive freedom of expression and rarely exert control. In providing little external control of the child's behavior, permissive parents fail to help their children gain the self-control and self-discipline they need in order to master their environment. Studies have shown that these children tend to get along poorly with peers and are bossy, aggressive, and rebellious (Baumrind, 1971). Of the three styles, the permissive style appears to be the least adaptive.

Researchers have attempted to determine the effects of using these styles of parenting on children. Baumrind followed her subjects until they were 8 to 9 years of age. She found that authoritative parenting resulted in children who were highly competent in both cognitive and social skills, authoritarian parenting resulted in children of average competencies, and permissive parenting resulted in children with low cognitive and social skills. More recent research indicates that these levels of child competencies related to the style of parenting continue throughout the school-age years and into adolescence (Dornbusch, Ritter, Leiderman, Roberts, & Fraleigh, 1987).

Strategies for Disciplining the Toddler

During the toddler period of development, parents attempt to gain control of the toddler's behavior through specific behaviors that are often referred to in the literature as strategies. The conflict between the parent and the toddler might be avoided if the parent has skill in gaining cooperation. Researchers have found that the toddler complies only about 50% of the time to direct maternal interventions. When mothers resort to punishment in order to gain compliance, the outcome is often poor. Punished children comply much less and are more likely to grasp breakable objects than children who are not punished (Power & Chapieski, 1986).

Although most parents feel the urge to physically restrain and/or punish a young child, the best method tends to be to divert the child to another activity. For example, when a toddler is exploring a dangerous environment, the parent might redirect him/her to a safe activity. When redirecting does not work, the parent should consider baby-proofing the home by removing furnishings or breakable objects that might interfere with the toddler's play.

As previously mentioned, the egocentrism of the toddler is a constant source of potential conflict with the parent. The true nature of discipline is not only to direct and structure but also to help the toddler gain self-control over his/her behavior. In fact, the goal in discipline should be to instill a sense of confidence in the toddler in his/her ability to impose self-limits on behavior in the absence of being overcontrolled and inhibited by the parent.

Researchers have categorized particular **strategies for discipline** in a number of ways. When parents use their authority to gain compliance—for example, threaten to take away privileges—they are resorting to a group of strategies defined as power assertions (Hoffmann, 1977). Generally, researchers have found that children respond to power assertions in like manner through an increase in aggressive behavior (Chwast, 1972). No doubt, the modeling of aggressive behavior by the parent is repeated by the child in similar interactional patterns with others. Parents with a temperamentally difficult child may feel inadequate and forced to use such behavior to control the child. Although parents may recognize that these tactics are not really working, they may believe that other strategies would be even less effective.

A second type of strategy used to describe the parents' attempts to intervene in influencing the toddler's behavior has been referred to as **love withdrawal.** Any activity whereby the parent withdraws from or isolates him/herself from the child can be considered withholding love. Researchers have found no positive relationship between withdrawing love and the development of moral behavior in the child (Newman & Newman, 1991).

A third general type of parenting strategy is the use of **induction,** or talking to the child explaining what he/she did wrong and attempting to gain cooperation. Researchers have found that when parents use inductions, it increases the child's empathy for others and improves communication, sociability, self-confidence and self-control (Newman & Newman, 1991).

A necessary parenting role in the toddler stage is the parent as protector. The mobile toddler does not know danger and has an insatiable curiosity. As a result, the attentive parent may find it tiring keeping up with the toddler. Early researchers believed that the period from 10 to 18 months was a sensitive period in the development of the child (White & Watts, 1973). They viewed this period as extremely important because of the relationship with the caregiver and the implications this relationship had for future relationships. Of particular importance was the social and intellectual development of the toddler. Later researchers have challenged this sensitive-period assumption (Banks, 1979). In analyzing mother/infant interaction patterns in the precrawl through walking stages, Banks found no relationship between levels of stress and the mother/infant relationship.

The most efficient way to protect the infant in this stage is to baby-proof the living areas. Valuables and especially breakable items should be put in a safe place. Furniture or items too large to change locale need to be addressed as "off-limits" so that the toddler is informed that some activities and surroundings are to be avoided. Generally, a "no-no!" followed by a redirection of the behavior will be a sufficient intervention.

The parent is probably tested more in this period by the toddler's **temper tantrum** than by any other defiant behavior. When thwarted in the desire to accomplish a task or an activity, the toddler will react with disgust for all to hear. Parents generally meet the temper tantrum with either giving in or showing force, neither of which is effective. Perhaps the parent engages both in giving in and in a power struggle for the same reason—namely, attempting to be a good parent. The good parent must keep control of the situation or the toddler will dominate and never be controllable, or so the argument goes. Parents who give in run the risk of increasing the undesired behavior because they show the toddler that this behavior has a pay-off. Parents who use force to control it, such as physically removing a child from a store where the child is demanding a candy bar, may create resentment and a repeating negative cycle in the parent/child relationship.

Parental Influences on Discipline

Typically, a number of factors influence and provide a background for the specific pattern of parental discipline.

Cognitive Structures of the Parent.   Recently, researchers have focused on the cognitive constructs of the parent. As discussed earlier, this new research is concerned with parental attitudes toward and beliefs about the physical development and cognitions of children (Goodnow, 1988). Rubin and Lollis (1988) have proposed a model suggesting that social competency in toddlers and older children is directly related to what parents believe about the development of social behavior. They view parental beliefs as affective and cognitive processes that influence the strategies parents might use to help their children develop social skills and to change undesired child behaviors.

These cognitive beliefs by parents must also be placed in their social context. For example, social and cultural environmental influences may directly influence the cognitive style of the parent. Viewing parental behavior in terms of both the affective and cognitive dimensions of the process is a drastic improvement over the usual tendency to focus on cognition at the exclusion of affect. As a result, the social competency of the child rests on a broader context than simply discussing parental cognitions as intrapsychic processes.

The dialectics of these considerations suggest that there are always competing factors in parents' cognitive beliefs. Different possibilities emerge constantly with respect to how the parent might approach a problem. For example, when should the parent use time-out rather than sitting down and explaining his/her reasons for insisting that the child stop misbehaving? The constant process of making decisions about intervening in the child's behavior takes place in a myriad of facts, emotions, and thoughts. The alternate components of this dialectic, however, are not opposites, but rather part of the same process. The family system contains the alternatives as part of the ecological environment brought about by a different thought, feeling, tension, stress, or other transient activity.

Parental Conflict. A second parental influence on discipline is parental conflict. Researchers have concluded that parental conflict has a detrimental effect on children, more on boys than girls (Hetherington, Cox, & Cox, 1978). Parental conflict seems to be exacerbated when the discipline is inconsistent. In addition, they may be so involved with the conflict that they either ignore the children or compete with each other to be considered the better parent. Unfortunately, often unaware of the effect their marital conflict has on their children, they ascribe other factors to the children's maladjusted behavior.

■ Frequent Problems in Toddlerhood

Some of the most frequent problems associated with toddlerhood are temper tantrums and lack of cooperation in dressing, toilet training, going to sleep, and other routines. How parents handle these common problems are correlated with feelings of success or failure in parenting (Minde & Minde, 1986). In contrast to "how to" books on parenting, the approach presented in this book would accept a wide range of possible parental responses.

When a child has a temper tantrum, parents and child must be viewed in the same context in which the tantrum occurred. For example, when Dreikurs and Soltz (1964) or Patterson (1976) suggest ignoring the tantrum by removing oneself from proximity with the toddler, they completely ignore the contextual underpinnings of the behavior. In effect, by removing the parent for the recursive cycle maintaining the child's behavior, the parent is not party to the tantrum in any way except to attempt to change or control it. The recurring feedback cycle between parent and child must be considered as equal dimensions of an ongoing process without end. The artificial compartmentalizing of breaking the interaction down to "correct" and "incorrect" parental responses to child misbehavior violates the cyclical nature of the interaction where a temper tantrum, or some other equally distressing child behavior, occurs.

From a systems perspective, the question of how a parent might best handle or respond to the child's misbehavior, such as the temper tantrum, is not the appropriate framework for viewing parent/child interactions. As discussed previously, parental behavior includes more than nurturance and control; namely, it also includes the parent/child ecosystem, or interactional system. Instead of beginning a discussion of the temper tantrum at the point of the child's acting out, it is more important to understand the total context in which the temper tantrum occurs. A tantrum has a history including a particular sequence or pattern in which parent and child act in certain ways leading to various outcomes. The tantrum itself is the outcome of a

■ *Toilet training should be an act of cooperation between parent and child.*

particular sequence of interaction. The most appropriate strategy of intervention, therefore, is a restructuring of the pattern or sequence leading to the undesired outcome.

Generally, other problems associated with the toddler mentioned earlier, such as lack of cooperation in dressing, sleeping, or toilet training, also represent particular sequences and a need for understanding the total context of the behavior. An unwillingness to go to sleep, for example, involves much more than simply a child who wants to stay up past bedtime. It may involve sleeping patterns during the day, the amount of stimulation during the evening, the parents' attitude toward the child, the amount of time spent with the child, or the conflict or degree of cooperation between the parents. When parent educators ignore these dimensions, the false and simplistic view that problematic child behaviors can be easily addressed by teaching parents how to respond to these behaviors in "correct" ways appears the most likely avenue.

Rather than teaching parents correct ways of responding to problematic child behaviors, parent educators might teach them to understand the sequence involving the undesired outcome. They could make parents aware of their own responses and attitudes to the child that contribute to the temper tantrum. In so doing, it might become more obvious how the child continues in the undesired behavior.

Parents have attempted to control aggressive and undesirable behavior through various means, including punitive ones such as physical and psychological punishment. Researchers have found that less punitive means of control have resulted in greater cooperation and more positive outcomes in parenting. The problem with punishment is the negative cycle that develops between parent and child and which continues regardless of the "problem." For example, if a child is spanked for having a temper tantrum, the child's negative feelings about the physical punishment do not merely disappear after the spanking, but become part of the ongoing sequence between parent and child, influencing future interactions.

The parent might consider discipline as the same process as learning. In this frame, the parent and child are mutually engaged in growth and development. Competent parents use novel parenting strategies, such as discipline through the use of play, without acknowledging them as such. Parenting strategies have always focused on deviant child behavior rather than what parents do naturally. Most strategies are concocted for certain targeted outcomes in contrast to the free flow of interaction between parent and child.

Family Portrait ■■■■■■■■■■

The Davis family consists of four family members. Bob Davis is a 35-year-old manager of a local company, who has been married to Linda, age 33, for about ten years. They have two children: Jenny, a daughter age 5, and an infant son, Chip. In many ways they are an ideal young family. Bob and Linda waited almost five years to have their first child, and almost five years again to have the second child. Pregnancy and childbirth was normal for both children. They have had tremendous support from family and friends. Both sets of grandparents live close by and visited often until Bob's father died suddenly of a heart attack.

The sudden loss of Bob's father and the subsequent changes in the family as a result have had some influence on current family tension. Bob's mother had never worked outside the home. To make ends meet she lived with Bob and Linda for several months at a time, sharing time also with Bob's older sister. At first, Linda did not object to the coming and going of Bob's mother in the home, but eventually it became extremely distressing. Linda believed it would be beneficial for Bob's mother to live alone and supplement her social security check with a part-time job.

Jenny appeared to be on schedule with social and individual development. She was toilet trained at age 3, and her language development was ahead of schedule. A few months ago, however, Jenny began having temper tantrums, especially at or just before the evening dinner. At first, neither Bob nor Linda appeared upset at Jenny's dawdling behavior. Bob's mother was noticeably upset that Jenny was noncompliant about mealtimes and seemed to compare her behavior unfavorably with that of the baby.

Various attempts were made to change Jenny's behavior. Bob noticed two things that correlated highly with Jenny's temper tantrums: one was the presence of Bob's mother, and the second was negative comparison with her baby brother. Bob and Linda gradually began to view the dinner temper tantrum as Jenny's way of expressing disapproval of her grandmother's interference in the family as a whole, and more specifically, disapproval of the pride expressed in her baby brother and not herself. Jenny was obviously not completely adjusted to having a younger sibling.

Bob and Linda worked out a plan whereby his mother would be less disruptive in the family and Jenny could more adequately adjust to having a baby brother. While Bob entertained Chip, Linda engaged Jenny in a game to set the table and prepare the meal. This "playful" discipline relieved any need to use a more punitive means of control.

Compare and Contrast

Dreikurs and Soltz (1964) would be concerned with Jenny's mistaken goal in the temper tantrum. For example, they would view her tantrums as an attempt to gain attention. Because the grandmother was frequently present and involved in the formation of the tantrum, they would assume that Jenny was jealous of the baby and vying for her grandmother's attention. Dreikurs and Soltz would pay little attention to the overall sequence of behavior or to the possibility that Jenny's behavior could be in response to and maintained by the system.

Two possible outcomes of this scenario exist from Dreikurs and Soltz's position. First, the parents might ignore Jenny's temper tantrum. When dinner was announced and Jenny dawdled, refusing to come to the table, instead of the grandmother or Bob and Linda engaging her in a struggle, the parents might simply ignore her and go about their meal. When they finished eating, they would put away the food and tell Jenny that if she didn't come to the table while food was out she would not be served. On the surface this intervention appears nonpunitive and likely to help Jenny develop a sense of responsibility. When viewed from a systems perspective, it appears quite punitive because the relational context is ignored. The context of the tantrum includes the grandmother's presence in the family and the birth of a new baby brother. The example depicts the use of play as a means of redirecting the behavior in a nonpunitive way.

Second, the logical consequence of Jenny not eating if she fails to come to the table would only exacerbate the situation. It is ludicrous to think that Jenny will automatically decide to come to the table next time because she has "learned" from the experience. Jenny will feel resentful and experience a decrease in self-esteem. What she most likely will learn is that her parents have proved to her that they prefer her baby brother even if she complies more willingly.

Behaviorists would focus on Jenny's tantrum as caused by accidental reinforcement (Patterson & Gullion, 1971). According to Patterson, a temper tantrum is never the result of bad parenting or of the parent not showing love. Rather, the misbehavior is the result of accidental learning where unwanted behavior was reinforced. The first step is to realize who does the reinforcement and when it occurs. Parents must also know how to observe their child and obtain a data baseline for the behavior. For example, Bob and Linda would observe Jenny's tantrums to determine what reinforces them and how often they occur. They would want to weaken the tantrum behavior while strengthening more socially acceptable behavior. Their parenting goal is to weaken the temper tantrum by allowing it to occur when there is no reinforcement present. To weaken Jenny's tantrum, Patterson recommends putting her in time-out every time she has a tantrum.

Along with the time-out procedure, Jenny would be socially trained in appropriate behavior by praise or rewards, such as toys or candy. If Jenny's behavior did not improve, the plan would be considered defective and a new plan would be implemented. Although this kind of plan may be effective in changing some child "behaviors," it completely ignores the underlying factors in maintaining misbehavior. The context of Jenny's misbehavior—that is, the grandmother's interference and Jenny's adjustment to the new baby—is completely ignored by the behavioral approach.

One final comment is the fact that Jenny is a girl and the oldest child. As discussed in the chapter, the parents' response to a child with a difficult temperament may be affected by the child's gender and sibling position. Because Jenny's temperament is somewhat difficult, Bob and Linda need to be patient and also to understand her behavior within the total context in which it occurs. Neither Dreikurs and Soltz nor Patterson mention these intervening factors.

Gordon (1975) would be interested in having Bob or Linda express an I-message to communicate their feeling about Jenny's not coming to the table. They might say, "I want you to come to the table when dinner is ready. I do not like it when you do not come." In addition, the parents would use active listening when Jenny responds to their I-message. They could also see the problem as Jenny's and use a strategy similar to the Adlerian strategy of letting her come to the table when food is prepared or go hungry until the next meal.

A systems perspective of this family would begin by looking at the family as a whole. The recent event of Jenny having a younger sibling is a life cycle event related to making new adjustments. When these events are mishandled, as might be the case when too much emphasis is placed on Jenny's misbehavior, a new set of negative interactions is put in motion. On the other hand, using a natural means of communicating to a child such as through play, rather than communicating about a problem, may have more beneficial consequences. Bob and Linda must orient themselves toward the family's adjustment to a new member rather than focus on Jenny's misbehavior.

■ ■ ■ ■ ■ ■ ■ ■ ■ ■ ■

Parenting Proposition

Parents who are most successful in parenting exhibit a variety of behaviors, most of which occur in a natural setting of interaction and play with the child. Parents who have the most difficulty with parenting rely on specific behaviors to gain specific outcomes in children.

Answers to "Test Your Knowledge"

1.	F	4.	F
2.	T	5.	F
3.	F	6.	F

Key Concepts

toddlerhood	symbolic play
socialization	contextual methodology
ossification	social competence
lateralization	fantasy play
self-help skills	play therapy
toilet training	infant apprentices to social life
language development	self-concept
phonology	parent/child interaction
semantics	aggression
morphology	social withdrawal
syntax	nurturance
motherese	control
analog communication	authoritarian parenting
digital communication	authoritative parenting
complementary communication	permissive parenting
play	strategies for discipline
hurried child	love withdrawal
cognitive development	induction
assimilation	temper tantrum

Study Questions

1 Discuss the history of play in preschool education. What do you speculate would be an appropriate direction for the future?

2 Describe a child's use of fantasy and symbolic play. How are these types of play related to cognitive and social development in the young child?

3 Discuss the development of self-help skills in the young child. How can parents help young children to develop self-help skills?

4 Discuss cognitive development in the young child.

5 Discuss a systems perspective of language development. How does it differ from other theories of language development?

6 Discuss the development of the self-concept in the young child. Why is the self-concept so important for social and intellectual development?

7 Discuss various styles of parenting. Which style appears more effective?

8 Discuss the difference in parenting the young child from a systems perspective and other approaches.

9 Discuss the concepts of nurturance and control in parenting the toddler.

10 Discuss the phrase "infant apprentices to social life."

References

Atley, I. (1975). Piaget, play, and problem solving. In D. Sponseller (Ed.), Play as a learning medium. Washington, DC: National Association for the Education of Young Children.

Axline, V. M. (1947). *Play therapy: The inner dynamics of childhood.* New York: Houghton Mifflin.

Banks, E. (1979). Mother–child interaction and competence in the first two years of life: Is there a critical period? *Child Study Journal, 9,* 93–107.

Bates, E., O'Connell, B., & Shore, C. (1987). Language and communication in infancy. In J. D. Osofsky (Ed.), *Handbook of infant development* (2nd ed.). New York: Wiley.

Baumrind, D. (1967). Child care practices anteceding three patterns of preschool behavior. *Genetic Psychology Monographs, 75,* 43–88.

Baumrind, D. (1971). Current patterns of parental authority. *Developmental Psychological Monographs, 4* (1, Pt.2).

Bell, R. W. (1968). A reinterpretation of the direction of efforts in studies of socialization. *Psychological Review, 75,* 81–85.

Best, C. T., McRoberts, G. W., & Sithole, N. M. (1988). Examination of perceptual reorganization for nonnative speech contrasts. Zulu click discrimination by English-speaking adults and infants. *Journal of Experimental Psychology: Human Perception and Performance, 14,* 345–360.

Bigner, J. J. (1985). *Parent–child relations: An introduction to parenting* (2nd ed.). New York: Macmillan.

Bloch, M. N., & Choi, S. (1990). Conceptions of play in the history of early childhood education. *Child & Youth Care Quarterly, 19,* 31–48.

Brazelton, T. B. (1974). *Toddlers and parents: A declaration of independence.* New York: Dell.

Chwast, J. (1972). Sociopathic behavior in children. In B. B. Wolman (Ed.), *Manual of child psychopathology.* New York: McGraw-Hill.

Cohen, D. (1987). *The development of play.* New York: New York University Press.

Corter, C. (1976). The nature of the mother's absence and the infant's response to brief separations. *Developmental Psychology, 12,* 428–434.

Cummings, J. S., Iannotti, R. J., & Zahn-Waxler, C. (1989). Aggression between peers in early childhood: Individual continuity and change. *Child Development, 60,* 887–895.

Damon, W., & Hart, D. (1982). The development of self-understanding from infancy through adolescence. *Child Development, 53, 841–864.*

Dansky, J. (1980). Make-believe: A mediator of the relationship between play and associative fluency. *Child Development, 51,* 576–579.

Dearden, R. F. (1967). The concept of play. In R. S. Peter (Ed.), *The concept of education.* London: Routledge.

Dornbusch, S. M., Ritter, P. L., Leiderman, P. H., Roberts, D., & Fraleigh, M. J. (1987). The relations of parenting style to adolescent school performance. *Child Development, 58,* 1244–1257.

Dreikurs, R., & Soltz, V. (1964). *Children: The challenge.* New York: Hawthorn.

Eckerman, C. O., & Didow, S. M. (1989). Toddler's social coordinations: Changing responses to another's invitation to play. *Developmental Psychology, 25,* 794–804.

Eichorn, D. H. (1979). Physical development: Current foci of research. In J. D. Osofsky (Ed.), *Handbook of infant development.* New York: Wiley.

Elkind, D. (1987, May). Super kids and super problems. *Psychology Today,* pp. 60–61.

Ferguson, C. (1989). Individual difference in language learning. In M. L. Rice & R. L. Schiefelbusch (Eds.), *Teachability of language.* Baltimore: Brookes.

Flavell, J. H., Flavell, E. R., & Green, F. L. (1987). Young children's knowledge about the apparent-real and pretend-real distinctions. *Developmental Psychology, 23,* 816–822.

Freud, A. (1965). *Normality and pathology in childhood.* New York: International Universities Press.

Goodnow, J. J. (1988). Parents' ideas, actions, and feelings: Models and methods from developmental and social psychology. *Child Development, 59,* 286–320.

Gordon, T. (1975). Parent effectiveness training. New York: Plume.

Guerney, B. G. (1969). *Psychotherapeutic agents: New roles for nonprofessionals, parents and teachers.* New York: Holt, Rinehart & Winston.

Harris, A. E. (1975). Social dialectics and language: Mother and child construct the discourse. *Human Development, 18,* 80–96.

Hartup, W. W. (1989). Social relationships and their developmental significance. *American Psychologist, 44,* 120–127.

Heath, S. B. (1989). Oral and literate traditions among black Americans living in poverty. *American Psychologist, 44,* 367–372.

Henderson, B. B., Chalkesworth, W. R., & Gamradt, J. (1982). Children's exploratory behavior in a novel field setting. *Ethnology and Sociobiology, 3,* 93–99.

Hetherington, E. M., Cox, M., & Cox, R. (1978). Family interaction and the social, emotional and cognitive development of children following divorce. Johnson and Johnson Conference on the Family, Washington D.C., May 1978.

Hoffmann, M. L. (1977). Moral internalization: Current theory and research. In J. Adelson (Ed.), *Advances in Experimental Social Psychology* (Vol. 10). New York: Academic Press.

Hughes, F. P. (1991). *Children, play, and development.* Boston: Allyn & Bacon.

Hutt, C., & Bhavnani, R. (1972). Predictions from play. *Nature, 237,* 171–172.

Jacklin, C. N. (1989). Females and males: Issues of gender. *American Psychologist, 44,* 127–133.

Kaye, K. (1982). *The mental and social life of babies.* Chicago: University of Chicago Press.

Kinsborne, M., & Hiscock, M. (1983). The normal and deviant development of functional lateralization of the brain. In M. M. Haith & T. T. Campos (Eds.), *Handbook of child psychology: Vol. 2. Infancy and developmental psychobiology* (4th ed.). New York: Wiley.

Kolb, B., & Wishaw, I. (1985). *Fundamentals of human neuropsychology* (2nd ed.). New York: Freeman.

Ladd, G. W., Price, J. M., & Hart, C. H. (1988). Predicting preschoolers' peer status from their playground behaviors. *Child Development, 59,* 986–992.

Lenneberg, E. H. (1967). *Biological foundations of language.* New York: Wiley.

Lucariello, J. (1987). Spinning fantasies: Themes, structure, and the knowledge base. *Child Development, 58,* 434–442.

McCandless, B. (1967). *Children: Behavior and development.* New York: Holt, Rinehart & Winston.

Mills, R. S. L., & Rubin, K. H. (1990). Parental beliefs about problematic social behaviors in early childhood. *Child Development, 61,* 138–151.

Minde, K., & Minde, R. (1986). *Infant psychiatry: An introductory textbook.* Beverly Hills, CA: Sage.

Mischel, W., Shoba, Y., & Rodriguez, M. L. (1989). Delay of gratification in children. *Science, 244,* 933–938.

Mondell, S., & Tyler, F. B. (1981). Parental competence and styles of problem-solving/play behavior with children. *Developmental Psychology, 17,* 73–78.

Nelson, K. (1973). Structure and strategy in learning to talk. *Monographs of the Society for Research in Child Development, 8* (1–2, Serial No. 149).

Newman, B. M., & Newman, P. R. (1991). *Development through life: A psychosocial approach* (5th ed.). Pacific Grove, CA: Brooks/Cole.

Patterson, G. R. (1976). *Living with children.* Champaign, IL: Research Press.

Patterson, G. R., & Guillion, M. E. (1971). *Living with children.* Champaign, IL: Research Press.

Piaget, J. (1962). *Play, dream, and imitation in childhood.* New York: Norton.

Piaget, J. (1970). Piaget's theory. In P. H. Mussen (Ed.), *Carmichael's Manual of Child Psychology* (3rd ed., vol. 1). New York: Wiley.

Power, T. G., & Chapieski, M. L. (1986). Childrearing and impulse control in toddlers: A naturalistic investigation. *Developmental Psychology, 22,* 271–275.

Ramsay, D. S. (1984). Onset of duplicated syllable babbling and unimanual handedness in infancy: Evidence for developmental change in hemispheric specialization? *Developmental Psychology, 20,* 318–324.

Rice, M. L. (1989). Children's language acquisition. *American Psychologist, 44,* 149–156.

Rice, M. L., & Woodsmall, L. (1988). Lessons from television: Children's word learning when viewing. *Child Development, 59,* 420–429.

Rogers, C. (1942). Counseling and psychotherapy. Boston: Houghton Mifflin.

Ross, H. S., & Lollis, S. P. (1987). Communication within infant social games. *Developmental Psychology, 23,* 241–248.

Rubin, K. H., & Lollis, S. (1988). Origins and consequences of social withdrawal. In J. Belsky (Ed.), *Clinical implications of infant attachment* (pp. 219–252). Hillsdale, NJ: Erlbaum.

Slade, A. (1987a). A longitudinal study of maternal involvement and symbolic play during the toddler period. *Child Development, 58,* 367–375.

Slade, A. (1987b). Quality of attachment and early symbolic play. *Developmental Psychology, 23,* 78–85.

Smolak, L. (1986). Infancy. Englewood Cliffs, NJ: Prentice-Hall.

Snow, C. E. (1984). Parent–child interaction and the development of communicative ability. In R. L. Schiefelbusch & J. Pickar (Eds.), *Communicative competence: Acquisition and intervention* (pp. 69–108). Baltimore: University Park Press.

Springer, S. (1989). Educating the two sides of the brain: Separating fact from speculation. *American Educator, 13,* 32–37.

Stambrook, M., & Parker, K. C. H. (1987). The development of the concept of death in childhood: A review of the literature. *Merrill-Palmer Quarterly, 33,* 133–157.

Stevenson, M. B., Leavitt, L. A., Thompson, R. H., & Roach, M. A. (1988). A social relations model of analysis of parent and child play. *Developmental Psychology, 24,* 101–107.

Tomassello, M. (1992). *First verbs: A case study of early grammatical development.* New York: Cambridge University Press.

Vaughn, B. E., Kopp, C. B., & Krakow, J. B. (1984). The emergence and consolidation of self-control from 18 months to 30 months of age: Normative trends and individual differences. *Child Development, 55,* 990–1004.

White, B., & Watts, J. (1973). *Experience and environment: Major influences on the development of the young child.* Englewood Cliffs, NJ: Prentice-Hall.

Chapter 6

Parenting the Preschool Child from 4 to 6 Years Old

Parenting Myth ■ Parents should always use direct, understandable, and concrete behaviors in relating to their child.

Test Your Knowledge ■ The following questions are designed to test your knowledge before reading the material in this chapter. Answers appear at the end of the chapter.

1 Between 3 and 5 years of age, children are beginning to categorize persons from youngest to oldest. True or false?

2 The 4- to 6-year-old child is less gender stereotyped than the 2- to 3-year-old child. True or false?

3 There is some evidence that preschool boys at times prefer playing with girls and wish that they were girls. True or false?

4 Preschool children generally feel competent and have high self-esteem. True or false?

5 A systems perspective of moral development in the preschool period emphasizes the continuing change rather than permanence as the basis for moral judgments. True or false?

6 Storytelling is an underdeveloped parenting behavior. True or false?

T he preschool years of 4 to 6 are both similar to and different from toddlerhood. Whereas the toddlerhood years kept the child close to home, the 4 to 6 years of age period may find him/her moving away from the home base and becoming more independent. For example, the preschool child may go to day care for the first time and at age 5 or 6 will go to kindergarten. While some families view these changes as challenging, others see them as quite problematic. In the preschool period, children grow in intellectual abilities and develop self-concepts which may remain intact through their lifetimes. Also during this period, with the increase of activity and independence comes greater probability for being victims of accidents (see Table 6.1).

■ Biological and Physical Development

After age 2, children progress fairly consistently in increasing height and weight until the onset of puberty. These changes usually amount to about 2½ inches in height and 6 pounds in weight annually (Eichorn, 1963). By age 6, the average height is about 3 feet 7 inches and the average weight is about 45 pounds. Compared with the infant, the 4- to 6-year-old child does not eat as much because of a slower overall growth rate.

Physical development and motor ability gradually improve as the child ages. The 4- to 6-year-old is capable of greater mobility and agility than the 2-year-old. As children age they are able to exert themselves more because of greater size, strength, and coordination (Haywood, 1986). By age 5, most children are able to demonstrate efficient and refined running ability. Other physical skills at this age include jumping a distance of 3 feet, hopping from eight to ten times on the same foot, hopping a distance of 50 feet in 11 seconds, and skipping. In addition, the typical 5-year-old is able to throw a ball by stepping with the same leg as the arm used in throwing and is able to repeat a pattern of kicking through the ball in playing soccer (Gallahue, 1982). In all of these physical skills there appears to be a pattern of progressing from simple to complex skills which tends to improve as a result of practice.

The increased coordination of physical skills parallels the increased competencies in self-help skills, such as dressing. Whereas the toddler has trouble putting on and buttoning a shirt, the 6-year-old child has little difficulty with dressing but may find learning to tie his shoelaces to be a challenging activity. Although toilet training has been discussed in a previous chapter and is usually accomplished by age 3, some children may have accidents until they are 5 or 6. Generally, if the accidents are common after age 5, there is a problem that needs the attention of a physician or other professional (Brazelton, 1979).

Although the aforementioned physical development and skills largely are automatic, there is some evidence that environmental and psychological influences are related to both positive and negative outcomes. For example, undernourished chil-

Table 6.1 ■ Injuries to Preschool Children

- Injuries are the leading cause of death of children from ages 1 to 14.
- Almost 8,000 children die every year in accidents.
- Most accidents are preventable.
- Motor vehicles are involved in about 50% of the injuries.
- For preschoolers, debilitating injuries include those due to fires, falls, choking, and drowning.
- The caregiver is absent or inattentive in more than 65% of the accidents.
- More focus on child safety is needed to protect children.

Source: National Safety Council, 1991.

dren have abnormal central nervous system development, which impairs brain growth (Lozoff, 1989). Skeletal development also may be stunted by undernourishment. Although undernourishment is a major factor in the physical development of children, social and psychological factors may compound the problem (Pollitt, Garza, & Liebel, 1984). Even adequately nourished children who lack love and acceptance may experience some developmental delays. The best scenario for optimal development appears to occur when children's physical, mental, and emotional needs are met and when they have an adequate diet.

■ Development of the Self-System

The development of the **self-system** is part of the individual's ongoing awareness of him/herself in interaction with others and the environment. Each period of development is related to particular tasks and expectations for behavior from the family and society. In the toddler, the self-concept centers around egocentrism and the ability to accomplish differentiation. After age 6, the self-concept is more related to the cultural expectations of that developmental level. For example, gender-role expectations play a major role in how 6-year-olds might view themselves.

Age and Self-Concept

Researchers have found that one of the first aspects of the **self-concept** to develop is an understanding of age differences (Edwards & Lewis, 1979). In fact, children age 3 to 5 can adequately place photographs of people into correct age categories from the lower end of "little boys or girls" to the upper end of "grandmothers and grandfathers." Preschool-age children are also able to distinguish themselves from others on the basis of age.

Gender and Self-Concept

Gender differences and gender identity are also categories that toddlers begin to discriminate between. For them, differences in others, such as mothers and fathers, are more pronounced than the toddler's own identity of him/herself. Three- to five-year old children believe that someone could change his/her gender by changing hair style or clothes (Marcus & Overton, 1978). Gradually, by the time children enter school, they not only know their own gender as being either boy or girl but also that their designation of boy or girl will never change (Williams, Bennett, & Best, 1975).

Not only do children develop their concept of gender identity early, they also subsequently develop **gender-role stereotypes,** expected behavior for being a boy or a girl. Researchers have found that toddlers between 2½ and 3½ already have concepts of how girls and boys differ. For example, they conclude that boys and girls play with different toys. Boys prefer playing with cars and helping their fathers, whereas girls prefer playing with dolls and helping their mothers prepare food (Kuhn, Nash, & Brucken, 1978).

Researchers have found that the belief that boys and girls should play with different toys and be interested in different activities tends to become more rigid from 4 to 7 years of age (Damon, 1977). For example, a toddler may believe that it is fine for a boy to play with a doll if he really wants to. This same child at 6 will believe that there is something wrong with a boy playing with girl toys. The belief is absolute and noncompromising. As a result, boys of this age will generally avoid another boy who persists in playing with girl toys. By 9 years of age, children are not as absolute and are more accepting of behavior that deviates from expected stereotypes.

Some researchers have attempted to determine why children are so stereotyped in their beliefs. For example, does this rigid stereotyping represent the process of socialization? Does it represent the intellectual development that characterizes cognitive development? The answer to these questions is not definitive but appears to be related to how children learn to distinguish between concepts in learning (Maccoby, 1980). For example, to learn a concept, a child must learn what something is as well as what it is not. In an either/or fashion, a child learns that he/she is a particular gender and plays with particular toys. For this concept to have meaning for the child, he/she must exaggerate it, or believe that it is always true. Gradually, as children are able to distinguish differences in meaning and to recognize that differences are not always clear-cut, they are less likely to be as stereotyped.

Concomitant with the development of gender identity is the preference for playmates of one's own gender. In other words, preschool-age boys prefer to play with other boys, and preschool-age girls prefer to play with other girls (LaFreniere, Strayer, & Gauthier, 1984). The reasons for the preference remain somewhat vague. The

■ *Girls sometimes wish they were boys and enjoy playing with them.*

attempt to answer this question is dated, and no research has been done in recent years. Jacklin and Maccoby (1978) did the major study of this question and concluded that boys interact socially more with boys and girls more with girls. In addition, when boys and girls play together, girls tend to withdraw from boys more than boys withdraw from girls. One plausible explanation is that boys play more aggressively than girls, resulting in girls feeling uncomfortable or scared playing with boys. Of course, children of the same sex identify with one another and, as discussed earlier, share similar stereotypes. The preference for playing with same-sex children may also be related to their more limited cognitive structures of what constitutes a boy or a girl.

Researchers have concluded that boys generally prefer being boys and never wish they were girls. On the other hand, girls sometimes wish they were boys (Goldman & Goldman, 1982). Why this difference exists is unclear, but it could be that boys have a greater variety of toys and engage in more stimulating activities than girls do. Boys may play in a more exciting way that is equally appealing to girls. Or perhaps girls learn early that the male role is more dominant and valued in American society.

Table 6.2 ■ Preschool Children and Depression

___

- A depressed child does not talk about being sad.
- The depression may be masked through aggressive behavior.
- Depression can develop as early as 3 years of age.
- Signs of depression may be:
  somatic complaints
  loss of interest in everyday events
  loss of appetite
- Although rare, some preschoolers may talk about and even attempt suicide.
- Depressive episodes recur during childhood and adolescence.

___

Source: Rutter, 1986.

The greater value placed on the male role in our society, however, may not be known by children of this age, but they may sense unconsciously that our society values males and females differently. Girls' preference for the male role tends to decline in middle childhood and has completely disappeared by adolescence. This change could be related to greater cognitive ability which would allow them to view their role more objectively, or to the fact that in adolescence girls become the main preoccupation of boys.

The self-concept in toddlers and preschoolers is concrete and described in physical characteristics. For example, when asked to describe themselves by filling in such statements as "I am a boy who _____," most 3- to 5-year-old boys say they have brown hair or wear a red shirt, or the like. These descriptions are always factual and are almost never descriptions of their psychological or mental characteristics (Damon & Hart, 1982).

Self-Esteem

The origins and process related to the development of self-esteem in children may be mysterious and only partly understood, but we can assume that part of the process must include the relationship with parents. In fact, researchers have found that when the parent/child relationship is positive and there is a high level of acceptance by the parents, parental self-esteem is usually reflected by high self-esteem in the child. In this regard, the child is simply reflecting what parents display toward the child (Isberg et al., 1989). Most likely low self-esteem in children reflects parenting that is negative or lacks understanding of the child. A negative parent/child relationship communicates to the child that he/she is inadequate and undeserving of love.

Self-esteem refers to the accumulation of the child's evaluation of him/herself over time in comparison with other children. It appears that as children mature, they assess their competencies in comparison with those of other children. Some children

---

<table>
<tr><td>**Box 6.1**</td><td>■ ■ ■ ■ ■ ■ ■ ■ ■ ■

Can Young Children Understand Changes in Their Mental States?</td></tr>
</table>

Researchers have established that children 3 years old and younger have difficulty remembering their false past beliefs whereas children 4 years old and older can make distinctions. In one study, Gopnik and Slaughter (1991) attempted to determine the relationship of beliefs and the representational character of belief. In other words, to be able to assess that our beliefs have changed we must be able to understand the representational process of how events are related to beliefs about those events. In a series of tasks, 3- and 4-year-old children were placed in different mental states, such as pretenses and beliefs, that state was changed, and they were asked to recall the first state. Three-year-old children were able to recall images, pretenses, and perceptions but were unable to recall beliefs. Four-year-old children were able to recall all states, including the belief state, equally well. Apparently, the nature of representation is extremely difficult for 3-year-olds to understand.

---

appear strong in one area but not in others. For example, some children are good students whereas others may be good athletes. Researchers have found that the child's self-assessment is generally accurate in that he/she realizes that excelling in one area may not carry over to another area. Young children, however, make more mistakes in accurately assessing their competencies (Harter & Pike, 1984).

Six-year-old children generally compare themselves in obvious ways such as in basic competencies like writing, spelling, or reading. Children who have high self-esteem compare themselves to others favorably in many situations. On the other hand, children who develop low self-esteem tend to compare themselves unfavorably with other children.

Erikson (1963) characterized the development of a sense of self by the 4- to 6-year-old child as **initiative versus guilt.** This goal of acquiring a sense of autonomy and competence in acting out fantasies and building or carrying through on various projects helps the child resolve this developmental task of taking a risk. Children who take initiative tend to engage in new and unexpected behavior, finding these activities enjoyable and satisfying. On the other hand, parents who punish children severely may contribute to a child's development of guilt, inhibiting his or her free exploration of the environment.

A child's total life experiences tend to be the basis on which the child determines his/her worthiness. Essential to a child's sense of self-worth is the feeling of being valued, loved, and supported by others. On the other hand, a child's low self-esteem may result from the experience of being unloved, ignored, or rejected. These early experiences may affect the child during childhood and into adolescence and adulthood because they form a repeated internal message (Pelham & Swann, 1989).

Although the family context takes precedence early as the barometer of self-esteem, after children begin day care, kindergarten, or first grade, extrafamilial experiences begin to affect the way they feel about themselves. A child may experience success and failure in different settings and, therefore, have various self-evaluations depending on the setting. Although positive experiences may lead to increased self-esteem, it may be that some children evaluate themselves negatively in some activity that they highly regard. This negative experience may lead to low self-esteem despite overwhelming successes in general. For example, in school a child may not run as fast as other children on the playground. This lack of running ability may lead to a negative self-image if the child highly values running despite success in other endeavors including spelling, writing, and reading.

In toddlerhood, children generally tend to feel competent and have high self-esteem. This feeling of high self-esteem is probably based on the self-centeredness of the toddler and the inability to distinguish between his/her own appraisal and reality. Researchers have found that children in the early grades, in contrast to toddlers, tend to have lower self-evaluations. In particular, girls tend to have lower self-esteem and less confidence in their competencies than boys do (Butler, 1990). When children enter the first grade, they are much more aware of their own competencies and actively compare themselves with others including peers, teachers, and older siblings (Butler, 1989). In terms of moral development, first-graders are beginning to distinguish behavior in terms of compliance to a set of rules, or codes, of conduct. Children who deviate from the moral standards of peers find themselves ignored and frequently isolated from their peers, resulting in reduced self-esteem.

■ ## Imaginary Playmates

It is not uncommon for preschool, especially first-born, children to invent **imaginary playmates.** Concerns about such behavior by child experts have been replaced by research evidence that children who have imaginary friends are quite creative and bright. These children tend to create imaginary friends because they lack playmates or because of their imaginative, creative, and initiative qualities. When a younger sibling is born, the child usually will give up the imaginary friend (Brooks, 1991).

By playing with their imaginary friend, children use their own resourcefulness in coping with life experiences. They may also be very clever in blaming things on their imaginary friend. For example, a 4-year-old boy named Pat had an imaginary playmate he called "Bully." He continued to play with his imaginary playmate for a while after his younger brother was born. During this transition period, when Pat was adjusting to his younger brother, his behavior became more noncompliant and aggressive, such as poking or pushing his younger brother. When caught in such behavior, he would often deny it by blaming it on Bully. His parents, exercising much patience and control, suggested he talk to Bully about such behavior and ask him to stop doing it. This parenting ploy worked shortly after when Pat announced that Bully would not bother the baby anymore because he was going to move away. Thereafter, Pat displayed a more playful and accepting attitude toward his younger brother.

■ Moral Development

Children develop the ability to distinguish among levels of behavior that govern specific actions. Current theories of the development of moral attitudes were discussed in a previous chapter. The following discussion focuses on how moral standards are internalized from a systems perspective.

A Systems Perspective of Moral Development

A systems perspective within a dialectical framework notes the process of continuing change in contrast to other theories that emphasize permanence. One can argue that the nature of reality is replete with contradictions which result in a need to posit constant change as the way to explain this reality. Even Piaget has been described in terms of contradiction, although his developmental approach emphasizes noncontradiction and a coherent thought process (Riegel, 1975). For example, Piaget arrived at his stages through a process of disequilibrium, or contradiction. Meacham (1975) has suggested that the stages described by Piaget are the process involved in dialectical thinking and reasoning. The stage is merely a synthesis arrived at through the process of two contradictory elements.

A **systems perspective of moral development** emphasizes the continuing nature of moral development. In contrast to other approaches, a systems perspective does not attempt to find stable traits that are related to moral development. Changes throughout the lifespan are viewed as more important effects on development than is the determination of permanent traits. Meacham (1975) considers this lifespan approach to be important because individuals are making decisions within the framework of a changing life situation.

One must view moral development within the spectrum of a broader view than merely the individual. Changes within the individual and changes within the social context are interdependent and part of the same process. Typically, approaches focus on processes either within the individual or external to the individual, such as in the environment, but fail to view the individual adequately within a social context (Meacham, 1975).

The literature usually distinguishes between moral behavior and altruism in assigning them different roles and attributes. For example, altruism is concerned with such behaviors as empathy, caring, and the welfare of others, whereas moral behavior generally refers to negative behavior. In contrast, a systems approach is concerned with both good and bad behavior as two developing aspects of the same process. The context in which the behavior occurs would determine its nature.

A systems approach is concerned with the interdependence of an individual's assessment of one's moral development. Most approaches do not consider the recursive nature of self-esteem and behavior. **Recursive causality,** or reciprocity of cause and effect, reflects a number of events that must be considered within the developing framework. When people evaluate each other, they are also evaluating themselves in relationship to the other (Meacham, 1975).

In sum, moral development depends on the synthesis of learned responses from one's social interactions and the self-concept, which is a composite of the recursive patterns of interactions with others. One may assume that mature moral development of the individual depends on the unity, or synthesis, of standards of behavior and self-esteem. On the other hand, immature moral development may be seen as the inability to promote a synthesis of the standards of behavior and the self-concept. As a result, the individual is guided more by the demands of the self-concept than by the demands of standards. The individual would be in constant need to shore up the self-concept by manipulating the standards to his/her own liking (Meacham, 1975).

From a systems perspective, compromise is viewed as essential. Moral decisions are based on the ability to differentiate between contradictions and conflicts. A number of factors may be important in determining how well a particular individual resolves this contradiction. This view of moral development suggests that the process of resolving this contradiction continues throughout the life course rather than representing a specific sequence in the individual's development. The interdependence of moral development and self-esteem suggests that changes in the self-concept may alter one's ability to make even minor moral decisions (Meacham, 1975).

Because the individual is embedded within a family that is likewise embedded within a particular society, the structure of a society is as important as other factors, such as cognitive reasoning. The influence of the society on the individual and the influence of the individual on the society determine and are determined by the same process (Meacham, 1975). For example, the individual who appears to have escaped the clutches of society and opposes the standards of society is, in fact, part of the same process. His/her opposition may be explained in terms of an internalized self-esteem that influences the decision-making process.

■ The Parent/Child Relationship

The **parent/child relationship** during the preschool period continues along the same general pattern as during toddlerhood; namely, parents must have an understanding of the developing child, provide structure, and increase the complexity of the rules. Whereas in the toddler period parents provided very simple and easy-to-master rules, such as appropriate mealtime behavior and how to dress oneself, the rules for the 4- to 6-year old must be more complex because the child is involved in a social network outside the home. For example, a 5-year-old may be expected to sit quietly in the sanctuary during the morning worship rather than being allowed to go to the nursery. Because children tend to rehearse behaviors as they master them, it is advisable for parents to present one rule at a time.

Presumably, parent and child during the 4- to 6-year-old period will have more equal interaction in that the parent does not constitute the majority of the interaction. The child will be shifting his/her pattern of communication from analog, or nonverbal, to digital. This more verbal ability means that the child can more directly influence the administration of rules. Although children have more input, clearly the parents are in charge and must not give up their parental responsibilities.

Many **routines** have generally been set by this age, although some require further development. A toddler may be expected to sit at the table during a meal and feed him/herself without much regard for being messy, but a 5-year-old is expected to have better manners. Other routines such as bedtime, dressing, and taking a bath are all fairly established in toddlerhood but must be further developed during the preschool period.

Although a bedtime routine generally is established in toddlerhood, around age 5 the child may begin to experience some reticence in going to bed. This may be in the form of a fear of the dark or of some unpleasant thoughts. When a child has a bad dream or is afraid to go to sleep alone, the tendency is to disrupt the routine, reinforcing the child's fears and making the initial fear even more disturbing. Some assurance and firm control help children realize that the fears are not real.

A child's fear of going to bed or intense fear during the night probably are triggered by some interactional dynamic. Ferber (1985) has suggested that the child's fear of going to bed may be expressed in his/her less cognitive control at night. Because there is less structure in thinking patterns as the child attempts to go to sleep, the child may feel overwhelmed by his/her thoughts and not be able to consciously control them. Frightening thoughts that the child kept under control during the day may be difficult to control at night.

Effects of the Parent/Child Relationship on Sibling Relationships

A child's relationship with a brother or a sister is referred to as a **sibling relationship.** It is a common occurrence in American society for a child 4 to 6 years of age to have a sibling who is a toddler. Researchers have found that preschoolers tend to change their digital communication with toddler siblings to a simpler form in the same way that parents change their communication patterns with a young child. In a sense, the preschool child parallels the way the parents interact with the younger child. The preschooler may also play with the younger sibling in a rough and tumble way characteristic of parent/child play (Dunn & Munn, 1985).

The literature suggests that the arrival of a newborn can be a stressful experience for the family, especially for the first-born child. The first-born often begins showing some regressive behaviors, such as bed wetting or temper tantrums. When the parents misunderstand these behaviors and do not view them as a normal adjustment to the birth of a sibling, the older child is well on the way to becoming a problem child.

Researchers have found that the older child's relationship with the parents prior to and after the birth of the baby is an important variable in how well he/she adjusts to the new baby's presence. Generally, the older child's positive relationship with the parents is related to a positive adjustment to the new sibling (Dunn & Kendrick, 1982). Researchers have also found that a good marital relationship is related to positive relationships among siblings (MacKinnon, 1989).

From a systems perspective, the birth of a new baby is an interruption in the family process to which family members must adjust. Just as the birth of a first child affects the marital relationship, the birth of subsequent children tends to affect family relationships. The adjustment task for the family is to maintain the bonds among members while including the new member within the family boundary. When considered a normal part of family development, the regressive or hostile behaviors of the older child in reaction to the birth of a sibling do not threaten family relationships.

Parents should prepare the older preschool child for the arrival of a new baby in the family by involving him/her in many of the details of the arrival and some of the care after birth. Parents who have a positive relationship with their older child will be motivated to continue having time for him/her after the arrival of a baby. A balance between time for the new baby and time for the older child enhances the adjustment process.

Researchers have found that the relationship between siblings is a mixed experience as they grow up together. Although siblings acknowledge that their relationships with each other are often conflictual in comparison with relationships with others, they also tend to place greater importance on sibling relationships (Abramovich, Corter, Pepler, & Stanhope, 1986). No doubt, this importance attached to sibling relationships rests on a number of valuable reciprocal roles. For example, siblings can provide support for each other in their relationships with others, including relationships with parents. Clinicians have found this supportive relationship between siblings to be particularly helpful when parents are too stressed to provide adequate parenting (Minuchin, 1974).

Sibling relationships tend to benefit one another in that younger siblings learn from older siblings and older siblings, in rehearsing behaviors, tend to learn by teaching their younger siblings. A favorite pastime of children in day care is to rehearse the things they did during the day with parents and younger siblings at night. Researchers have found that this teaching behavior is common among siblings and benefits both the older and the younger sibling (Paulhus & Shaffer, 1981). Older siblings tend to perform better on scholastic tests when they have taught younger siblings.

Effects of the Marital Relationship
on the Parent/Child Relationship

A systems perspective of parenting must include the marital relationship and how the marital relationship affects the behavior of the child. As addressed in other chapters, the marital relationship of parents is a key component of the child's problem in misbehaving. When the marital relationship is mutually supportive, chronic behavior problems in children are less likely to occur. On the other hand, when behavioral problems do occur and become a regular pattern in the family, it is likely that there is marital conflict.

Clinicians focus on the marital relationship as one of the major forces that govern family interaction. The interest in the marital relationship stems from the belief that this relationship is the primordial relationship in the family on which other relationships are based. For example, in the life-cycle concept of the family, the marital relationship not only predates all relationships but also needs time to be established before an introduction of children occurs in the family. Functional families have been described as those with a strong marital bond prior to the birth of the first child (Carter & McGoldrick, 1980).

When the marital bond is weak or lacks intensity, a number of problems can occur. First, the family may become child-focused (Bowen, 1978). A **child-focused family** has placed the child in the head of the family position or executive position in the hierarchy, and the parents tend to defer to the child in crucial issues. In order to gain the child's love or support to deal with the other spouse, one or both spouses may make overt overtures to the child inappropriately. For example, one parent may tell the child a secret that is inappropriate for the child to know.

In a child-focused family, neither parent is effective in discipline. Rather, each tends to cancel the other out. The child realizes that he/she has the power in the family and may make outlandish demands on both parents. This reversal of power may not be recognized by either parent, since the child's happiness is most important to both parents. From a systems perspective, the pattern of the child functioning as the executive in the family is the issue that must be addressed.

A systems perspective of parenting is not concerned with momentary behaviors or isolated acting out by children. The focus is on repeated patterns that appear to be related to an ongoing sequence. This sequence is thought of as both cause and effect of the misbehavior. According to a systems perspective, any particular behavior is a recursive link with other behaviors within the social network and continues regardless of the efforts to change it. When children have been elevated to the executive role in the family through the interactional patterns within the family, the parents most likely are dissatisfied but feel helpless to do anything about it. Much more is needed to change the behavior than a narrow focus on the child's behavior. A picture of the family emerges that shows the recursive nature of the behavior.

The recursive cycle in every problem regarding the child involves much more than the intrapsychic aspects of the child. In contrast to other approaches, it also involves much more than the dyadic relationship between the child and one parent.

Behavior within the family must be understood as a function of at least three persons. When the child has a chronic behavioral problem, it can be assumed that the process involves triangulation into the marital relationship.

The preschool years are prone to triangulation because of the child's need to attach to parents and the parents' need to attach to the child. These natural forces that initiate triangulation, however, can go awry in families, such as when one or both spouses become closer to the child than to each other. This type of triangulation is referred to as **cross-generational coalition.** A cross-generational coalition violates normal family hierarchy where both parents are in the executive position and the child or children are in the subordinate position. Clinicians have stated that covert cross-generational coalitions are more dangerous to the family than overt coalitions (Hoffman, 1981).

When a child develops a symptom, a pattern of behavior that is disruptive or manipulative, one parent is usually more involved with the child than the other is. This overinvolvement with the child means that parents are not mutually supporting each other. From a systems perspective, the child's behavior might be improved by involving the distant parent, which would realign the hierarchy in the family so that the child is no longer in a favored position with one of the parents (Haley, 1976).

A systems perspective views the family as a self-regulating system that operates to correct itself through feedback from the environment. When families fail to change in response to feedback, they are prone to develop multiple problems. A child's misbehavior may be one type of problem a particular family may experience. A chronic misbehavior problem in a child, whether expressed at school or at home, signifies that this family has poor monitoring of the family rules in responding to additional input.

As discussed elsewhere, family rules are patterns of repetitive behavior that family members can alter in response to feedback from the environment. Because this feedback loop is constantly in motion, flexibility is a key aspect of functional families. A systems perspective proposes that families responding poorly to changes and failing to adapt to new input do not have a rule for responding to changes (Haley, 1976).

Placing a child in a position of scapegoat in the family in which misbehavior becomes the focal point can damage the child's self-esteem and feeling of competence. For example, when a rigid family, convinced that the only problem in the family is a temperamentally difficult child, is faced with the input that suggests the father and the mother have a conflictual marriage, the parents may redouble the efforts to control Johnny's behavior. The more they attempt to solve Johnny's problem, the more difficulty they have solving it.

Focusing on Johnny's problem, as all parenting strategies except a systems approach would do, would preserve the system as it is and ensure that the problems underneath, such as the marital difficulties, would never be addressed. The mother and the father would try even harder to control Johnny's behavior. Johnny would be more convinced that he was problematic and needed different treatment from other children.

The tendency of parents to increase their efforts to control the symptom amounts to what some family researchers refer to as **misguided solutions** (Watzlawick, Weakland, & Fisch, 1974). Because they view the initial problem as the family's attempt to maintain homeostasis in the family, any change—for example, even the recognition that Johnny's parents have severe marital discord—would be resisted. If Johnny were to become more compliant, the parents would have to focus more directly on the behavior that was not yet compliant in order to maintain homeostasis. In other words, to acknowledge improvement would be to dramatically alter the family stability.

A systems perspective of parenting, especially for the preschool child, involves a number of characteristics, including the family influence, as discussed in this chapter. In considering the family influence, we must remember that the larger social network also has reciprocal influence in the family. A later chapter discusses the larger network in detail.

In summary, parenting the 4- to 6-year-old preschool child is much like parenting the toddler. The tasks are to educate the child toward expected behavior, set rules and guidelines for behavior, cooperate with one's spouse, and be able to change rules as they apply to changing circumstances. Most parenting strategies used to address chronic behavioral problems, such as noncompliant behavior or aggressiveness, assume that the child has a problem and that either the parent is a reinforcing agent or the child is temperamentally difficult or has some other intrapsychic problem.

One way to view a child problem is to assume that the misbehavior may be the result of stress or conflict which the child experienced in his/her social interactions. The parents may begin to see this behavior as a problem and then attempt to stop or control the unwanted behavior. As efforts to control the problem intensify, a vicious cycle is initiated in that these efforts actually the problem to develop further. Parents get feedback that the child's behavior is not changing, but the family lacks a rule for change, negating any new or different behavior. The initial innocuous behavior of the child becomes, in the end, a severe, unrelenting behavioral problem that maintains the family homeostasis (Amatea, 1989).

■ The Use of Storytelling

Storytelling in Parent/Child Interaction and Implications for Use as a Disciplinary Technique

Discipline of the preschool child from 4 to 6 years of age differs little from that of the toddler. To avoid redundancy, this chapter will not discuss in detail what has already been discussed. It is necessary, however, to restate that a systems perspective of parenting is based on the belief that when parents have adequate knowledge of child development across the life span, have a mutually supportive relationship, and can adapt to changes in the life course, they will tend to have minor problems with parenting.

Chapter 5 discussed some unique or novel uses of techniques for parenting, such as the use of play. Another unique parenting technique that has a number of untapped applications is **storytelling.** Toddlers, preschoolers, and even lower-grade school-children are highly influenced by stories. Many parents use stories to get the child to bed at night or as a special treat. There are many wonderful books that help children understand and develop various skills. Some of children's favorite authors tend to write about situations children have some concerns about, such as having a new baby sitter, going to the doctor, and being small in a big person's world. Some stories help in the transition to using the potty or in getting them to go to sleep by themselves in their own room.

Children tend to commit to memory favorite stories and books and correct parents when they have made a mistake in reading. This identification with characters in stories and books makes moving from one learning skill to another easy and less stressful for both children and parents. As children master new skills they tend to have greater interest in stories that are related to the skills not yet mastered.

Although stories and books on many subjects, as well as those for fun and entertainment, are commonly used by middle- and upper-class parents, there has been little attention to the creative use of stories in the ongoing interaction between parents and children. For example, the application of stories to correcting behavior, gaining compliance, or using discipline has lacked extensive development in the literature. By creatively telling a story that allows the child to unconsciously associate with the character, the child may gain more control over the problem than he/she would gain through rewards and punishments or logical and natural consequences.

Storytelling in Therapy with Children

Clinicians have been making some use of stories and storytelling in therapy with children in order to change their behavior. The use of stories, analogies, and metaphors was one of the significant contributions to the development of therapy by Milton Erickson (1964a, 1964b, 1965, 1975). Erickson used a unique blend of hypnotherapy, direct and indirect inductions, to bring about change in his clients. His success in therapy was based on the response of the client to his communication with them, which took the form of stories and metaphors. He relied very little on the use of specific maneuvers to improve the child's behavior (Dolan, 1985).

A **metaphor** is something that stands for something else. A process metaphor is one that accurately addresses the dynamics of the person's relationship patterns with others. It may not be readily apparent what the message being communicated means on a conscious level, but there is a resultant change in behavior or in the interactive pattern with others. The telling of the story in therapy should be done in an atmosphere of rapport and comfort; otherwise, the effect is lost. If the client appears uncomfortable or asks why the therapist is telling the story, the effect may be lost. For example, the following is a metaphor told to a man who had been unable to get out of a particular behavioral pattern:

> My friend visited a Chinese restaurant called The Dragon, and after dinner we were served fortune cookies. HE broke open his fortune cookie, and it said,

JERRY (client's name) YOU WILL NOW BEGIN TO FIND A SOLUTION TO YOUR PRESENT PROBLEM. My friend laughed heartily at the message. He was surprised when he returned home from his business trip to find that some interesting changes had occurred, and yet he retained his skepticism. He and his wife enjoyed a good laugh about that (Dolan, 1985, p. 121).

Telling a story in this manner in therapy where rapport and caring are expressed in the relationship can induce an altered state of consciousness, such as hypnosis. In fact, hypnosis is described as a natural state where a person is in a deep level of concentration. A spellbinding story, with its intense emotional component, can easily induce hypnotic-like states. The favorite bedtime story, which acts to induce deep relaxation in the child, for example, is a natural hypnotic state (Dolan, 1985).

Richard Gardner (1971) developed the therapeutic application of storytelling with children. Gardner believed that **mutual storytelling** was a natural form of communicating for the child and would help the child to improve his/her behavior without the use of more traditional psychoanalytic techniques, such as developing insight. In a very playful way as a make-believe TV host of a storytelling program, Gardner engages the child in a game of telling a story. There are a number of rules, such as the story has to be made up and not some story the child has been told, a TV program, or a movie. The therapist guides the child along in a nonthreatening manner, providing some of the basic structure of the story and engaging the child in filling in the content. After hearing the child's story and the moral or lesson implied from the story, the therapist takes some time to construct a story of his/her own. The therapist attempts to retell the same or similar story as the child but with greater adaptive resources and alternatives. The goal is to aid the child in determining that there is more than one choice available (Gardner, 1971).

The following is an example of Gardner's technique with a boy who was referred because of poor social skills and poor school performance. Here is the boy's story:

> Once upon a time there was a bear. He was trying to get some honey from a beehive. He got it from the beehive. He went home with it. The bear ate the honey (Gardner, 1971, p. 39).

Gardner interpreted this story to mean that the boy was having a great problem getting the love (honey) from his mother (beehive). He believed the child's relationship with his mother was bittersweet and to get her love the child must also experience his anger and possibly her rejection. Because the mother refused to participate in the therapy, Gardner believed that she probably would not improve significantly. He told the following story in response to the child's story:

> Once upon a time there was a bear. This bear loved honey very much. There was a beehive nearby but he knew that the bees were not always willing to let him have some. Sometimes they were friendly and then they would give him a little

bit. Other times they were not, and he knew then that it was wise to stay away from them or else he would go to another part of the forest where there were maple trees which dripped sweet maple syrup. When the bees were friendly, he would go to them for honey (Gardner, 1971, p. 40).

In his retelling of the story, Gardner attempted to help the boy realize that his mother was unreliable but sometimes could give him the love he needed. His best tack with her was to accept it when she offered it but have other sources available as well. He might seek the alternate sources to compensate for the mother's lack of love and support.

Not all first stories have therapeutic value as the one discussed here. Gardner expects that a number of sessions may be needed for the child to feel comfortable enough to tell a story that reveals his/her inner feelings. The therapist can use these opportunities to prime the child for therapeutic work as the process continues.

This process of therapy involves a number of stages. The first stage involves breaking down resistance so that therapy can occur in the later stages. The middle stages of therapy consist of the child becoming more trusting of the therapist and revealing more of his/her inner conflicts. Many of the stories in this stage may have violent themes and be repetitive in nature. If the child is resolving the conflicts that led to therapy, there will be a gradual decline in the repetitive stories. The content of the stories will change as the child develops greater resources to deal with his/her problems. In the late stages of treatment, the child will tell stories that indicate he/she has worked through the problem area sufficiently.

Although the specific techniques used by Gardner and the psychodynamic interpretations he made are interesting, following the model as he developed it is not suggested here. The importance of Gardner's method is to illustrate how the forgotten or undeveloped parenting interaction of storytelling can be effective in intervening in a child's unwanted or unruly behavior. In addition, this method is an appropriate alternative to the use of punitive behavior.

Research regarding the effectiveness of the mutual storytelling technique is scarce. Some research tends to validate its use combined with play therapy for children who are experiencing severe problems (Stilles & Kottman, 1990). The mutual storytelling technique is recommended for children over 5 years of age who have developed language necessary to communicate in some detail.

Stilles and Kottman (1990) applied the mutual storytelling technique to a boy who was referred for therapy because of temper tantrums at school and crying spells. Three years prior, he had been playing with his sister when she fell, breaking her neck, and died instantly. The boy talked about wanting to join his sister in heaven. Treatment consisted of combining play therapy and mutual storytelling. Gradually over the course of treatment, the boy was able to shift his play and stories away from burial and rescue to more appropriate play for his age and cognitive ability. Gardner believed that the more adaptive outcome was enhanced by the use of storytelling, which provided an avenue for the child's creative imagination to work for him.

Improving Learning Through Storytelling

A number of authors and educators have begun emphasizing the need to use storytelling to improve learning (Baker & Greene, 1977; Barton, 1986; Dailey, 1985; Geisler, 1988; Greene & Shannon, 1986; Griffin, 1989; Hamilton & Weiss, 1988; Kinghorn & Pelton, 1991; Livo & Rietz, 1987; Pellowski, 1987). The storytelling tradition in education in general, aside from the written tradition of stories, has not had a significant impact on improving learning (Pellowski, 1990). Storytelling, in contrast to written stories, represents an oral tradition that lacks the scholarship and creativity of the written tradition. Recently, educators have begun to see the possibilities of using storytelling for enhancing thinking and creativity.

The move in education toward the use of storytelling is to make the child aware of environmental and emotional experiences that affect daily events. These experiences, in addition to being fun and enjoyable, can be linked to a series of perceptions about the nature of life and reality. Creative storytelling involves the child developing awareness of both the five senses and academic skills. When storytelling is combined with visual aids, the child's cognitive and academic abilities are enhanced (Pellowski, 1990).

Educators have used a number of techniques to increase children's comfort level in telling stories. One technique is to list the five senses on the board and have the children use words or phrases to describe them. The teacher might ask students to respond to sentences that describe a person, place, or thing. Students could also be asked to add dialogue or description to favorite written stories, such as "Little Red Riding Hood" and "The Three Little Pigs." In addition, students might also be given pictures and asked to write a description of what they see in terms of the five senses. After practice with these exercises, students could be expected to begin developing an original story (Kinghorn & Pelton, 1991).

Recent Research on the Use of Storytelling and Metaphor

Although there is limited research on storytelling, some recent research tends to support and validate the significance of it for improving children's behavior and enhancing their relationships. In an interesting study, Dent and Rosenberg (1990) investigated visual and verbal metaphors. A **visual metaphor** is a metaphor expressed in pictures. Children's books, for example, are illustrated with pictures that could be described as metaphors. A bloodhound may be dressed as a detective because of its tracking ability regardless of its role in the story. In the "Peanuts" comic strip, Snoopy walks upright rather than on all four legs like his master Charlie Brown to show that he is a companion.

A **verbal metaphor** contains a number of components that must be present in order to call it a metaphor. The literature defines the components of a metaphor as having a topic; a vehicle, which refers simultaneously to the topic and another object that is altogether different; and a ground, or the similarity between the topic and the vehicle. For example, if a child observing snow falling calls it sugar, he/she is using a metaphor. The topic would be the snow, the vehicle would be sugar, and the ground would be the similarity between the two (Dent & Rosenberg, 1990).

The visual metaphor is analogous to the verbal metaphor in that it takes a similar form and structure, although no words are used. That structure would be to reveal one thing (topic) in terms of a different thing (vehicle) which is very close in appearance to the first thing (ground). In the visual metaphor, the ground is emphasized and the topic–vehicle is explicit (Dent & Rosenberg, 1990).

In their study to investigate the comprehension of visual metaphors through the use of verbal metaphors, Dent and Rosenberg (1990) found that metaphoric comprehension increases with age. They compared three-dimensional visual metaphors with similar, but standard, objects; for example, a leaping deer was combined with a dancer in tights wearing a skirt. Half of the three-dimensional and half of the standard objects were movable so that the researchers could test the effects of motion on children's use and comprehension of metaphors. Thirty subjects in each of four age groups, including 5-, 7-, and 10-year-old children and college students, participated in the study. The three-dimensional compound objects and the standard objects were arranged in pairs with half of the subjects describing one set of objects and the other half describing the other set. Of the three-dimensional compound objects, half were moving and half were stationary. Subjects were asked to describe the objects both literally and in a new and different way.

Dent and Rosenberg (1990) found that all subjects could explain the objects literally and that they could relate moving objects to more metaphor descriptions than they could standard objects. For standard objects, adults used more metaphors in their new and different descriptions, followed by 10-year-olds, 7-year-olds, and 5-year-olds. For compound objects, the 7- and 10-year-old groups used more metaphors than the 5-year-old group or adults. An increase in metaphors occurred between ages 5 and 7 and between age 10 and adult subjects. This study is important because it provides evidence that visual metaphors are powerful communication tools at every age level. Although the metaphor descriptions varied according to age and cognitive development, even 5-year-olds were able to communicate effectively and retain information provided in stories and metaphors.

The Effect of Storytelling on Parent/Child Interaction

The preceding development of storytelling and metaphors in therapy and education can be directly applied to parenting. The use of stories and metaphors, like applying the concept of play to the parent/child relationship, does not require higher intelligence or the mother staying home with the child. It does require a change in focus to a systems/dialectical process model of parenting. The **systems/dialectical process model** describes the ongoing interaction between parent and child, which is ever changing, and the change itself becomes a new part of the relationship. How the child uses and incorporates the "hidden message" in a story is related to the individual's freedom in selecting and disregarding information.

■ *Storytelling can serve many purposes for parents, such as providing information, entertaining the child, and guiding the child's behavior.*

While the research described earlier gives credibility to the use of stories and metaphors in improving children's ability to communicate, there has been little application of stories and metaphors, aside from children's books, to parent/child interaction. No doubt there are a number of reasons for this lack of application. First, teaching parents to use metaphors or tell stories would require a formal structure, such as through a didactic educational model of parent education. In one sense, however, models of parent education do use specific training modules to aid parents in "mastering" the time-out procedure or in constructing logical consequences. It would seem that teaching parents how to use stories to influence a child's behavior could be an integral part of a model for parenting in the same way that teaching parents to use time-out is taught.

Second, teaching a communication method would require parents to be patient and less directive in discipline. They would have to revise the common view that the two major goals of parenting are nurturance and control. As discussed previously, a new component of parenting would be introduced—the interactive process—which would function to control the differential power between parent and child. The interactive process is not a linear pattern as exhibited by other models. Rather, it is viewed as part of the process whereby children mature in cognitive and relationship matters through interaction with parents and their social network. The use of storytelling to help generate alternatives for children remains true to a circular view of causality in that parents are providing feedback so that children may view their situation in a unique way. The story or metaphor would not itself carry a directive that the child must follow, as in a linear model, but would furnish new information that the child could interpret in various ways.

Storytelling and using metaphors are not suggested to become the modus operandi of parent/child relationships. Like any specific parenting behavior, storytelling should not be overused but should be a strategy for a few special situations. The primary use of stories would be to help a child resolve a conflict brought about by a transition from one stage to another or to help a child deal with a crisis in his/her interaction with the family. Storytelling could help the child increase his/her response repertoire by providing options in story or metaphor form that were outside the child's cognizance.

The following is a story told by a grandfather to his 4-year-old granddaughter shortly after the stillbirth of the grandchild's younger sibling. The granddaughter had been looking forward to the birth of her younger sibling and was quite distraught when the sibling was born dead. She had difficulty sleeping and told her parents she wanted to die too so that she could be with the baby. She was extremely disturbed that the baby was buried in the ground. Her grandfather, who was very close to the granddaughter, told her the following story:

> Many, many years ago there was a large forest of many different kinds of trees. There were big trees, little trees, tall ones, all shapes and sizes. There were trees of all shades of colors. Some were bright, some were subdued, but they all blended to make a beautiful forest.
>
> On the north side of the forest was a very attractive tree. It was perfectly shaped as a tree and it was colorful. During the different times of the year, there would be different colors. The tree grew well with a certain hardness in the warm sunshine of the summer and the soft snows of the winter.
>
> In the southwestern part of the forest was another tree. It was tall, stately, and strong. In spite of its early bad beginnings, it survived the drought. It responded to soft rain and sunshine. Like the tree to the north, its limbs were strong and birds built nests in its branches and animals rested in its shade.
>
> The interesting thing about these trees was their ability to move to different places in the forest and yet put their roots down to moist rich soil. They both moved to a beautiful valley. And on the same bank of a small stream, they put their roots down. It wasn't long until they became aware of each other and developed a strong bond and affection for each other. Neither stood in the shadow of the other. Both were distinct and strong—but there was touching in the gentle breeze—as they were open to each other.
>
> Not long after a small tree began to grow. The tall stately tree and the round symmetrical tree were joyful because this was their little tree. All the trees in the valley felt their sense of joy. The little tree did not stay long. In spite of the sunshine and the soft rains, the little tree withered and died. There was quite a sadness between the two trees and all the other trees in the forest. The trees in the valley leaned toward these two trees and spread their strong and warm branches to provide comfort, love, and support.

That night there was a terrible storm. The clouds were dark and heavy. The lightning cracked as it darted and zigzagged toward the valley. The thunder was loud as it rolled up and down the valley. The whole ground whistled and shook. It was a long, long night but eventually it became quiet. Somewhere in the distance there was the sound of a nightingale, followed by the response of a mockingbird. In the east the sun's rays began to reach their long fingers over the jagged purple mountain ridges and bring light to the valley. As the sun rose, it brought warmth to the trees and the rays glistened in the rain drops on the leaves. The ground felt moist and the green grass felt soft and fluffy.

The tall stately tree and the round symmetrical tree in their sadness were looking down and they saw a very small seed where their little tree had grown. It was not there yesterday, but somehow the rain uncovered the seed during the terrible storm. The seed was cherished and protected.

Then one day the two trees decided to plant the seed. The place they chose was a special place where there was much solitude and quietness. As the sun shown and the gentle rains nourished the seed, it grew and grew into a large, strong, and beautiful tree. Birds and animals would come to the tree and find calmness in the shade from the sun. And here were feelings of peace and joy for it was a restful place to go.

When the tall stately tree and the round symmetrical tree were in the forest, they could always see this special tree. When this special tree swayed in the wind, the sun reflected different colors of light and even in the storms there was always a rainbow nearby. When the two trees looked at this special tree, they could see a long way because it was very clear and they heard the gentle sounds of the swaying branches. The coolness of the breezes let them know that this was the way and it was wonderful to be near it (Crews, 1985).

The Relationship Between Storytelling and Culture

Although storytelling has been viewed as important for the development of a healthy society, there has been little overall research on the process of how storytelling is related to healthy outcomes in a society (Pellowski, 1990). In addition, the relationship between the impact of culture and the preservation of oral traditions passed on to future generations has not been fully determined. For example, researchers have not yet determined the relationship between storytelling as a means to preserve a cultural tradition on the one hand and the role storytelling plays in the acculturation of a subgroup into the dominant culture. There is some research evidence, however, that immigrants change the context of their traditional oral stories to fit the new context, resulting in a change to the original story. This finding suggests that storytelling has served to integrate subgroups into the larger society.

It is likely that storytelling has served to preserve a view of reality within a particular context. As that context changes, so does the storytelling. With reference to families, it might be that the oral tradition and use of storytelling have decreased in a society that uses other means to create a sense of reality for its members, such as mass media including television and movies. It can also be assumed that storytelling could assist in both the formation of a feeling of cohesion, or bonding, and the adaptation to change. In families, shared rituals and meanings are important for giving members a sense of belonging. A vehicle for how members feel bonded could be through storytelling. To help members adapt to change, the content of the story could change to be more accommodating to a changing context.

Family Portrait   ■■■■■■■■■■

Dan and Jody Baker, married for 12 years, have two children, Lisa age 5 and Ty age 1. Dan and Jody co-managed a restaurant for a number of years before Lisa was born. After Lisa's birth, Jody stayed home for the first year and thereafter worked part-time. Dan's parents, who were retired, cared for Lisa during the days that Jody worked. After Ty was born, Jody again stayed home to be with Lisa and Ty. Lisa is now attending kindergarten and Jody is working three days a week. The grandparents take care of Ty and pick Lisa up from kindergarten on days Jody works. Dan works very long hours and is not at home enough to be actively involved in the day-to-day management of the household or the care and discipline of the children. Jody has felt overburdened at times with child responsibilities and has complained to Dan, who appears unaffected by her concerns.

Although Jody has felt support from Dan's parents in that they take care of the children while she works, Jody often complains to Dan that his parents have used this help as a way to control them on other matters, such as where they live, or what car they drive. In discussing his parents with Jody, Dan usually takes the position that Jody is too sensitive to his parents and should not be bothered by their attempts to control their lives. Rather, she should stay calm, accept their genuine concern for their well-being, thank them politely, and then go about her business doing what she wishes to do.

Lisa's behavior during the past few months since she started kindergarten has been a concern to Jody. At first, Jody thought being around other children for long periods of time was the main cause of the change in Lisa's behavior. Before starting kindergarten, Lisa had always been either at home or at the grandparents' house during the day, so, presumably, going to kindergarten had to be somewhat problematic for her. The problems at home center around eating, getting to bed on time, and some obvious sibling rivalry. Lisa has always been a good but picky eater, but for the past few months she has been making mealtime extremely difficult. She sometimes refuses to come to the table, leaves in disgust after coming to the table if the meal is not to her liking, or leaves the table early without eating very much because she is "full." Jody is usually preoccupied with feeding or tending to Ty to notice Lisa's needs very much. Typically, this behavior occurs before Dan gets home since he is seldom there for the evening meal. Sometimes, Jody takes the children to a restaurant for dinner. On these occasions, Lisa eats well and presents no other problems.

Another problem that has emerged over the past few months is Lisa's being afraid to go to sleep alone in her room. Ty's crib is in the parents' bedroom, although they intended to move it out months earlier. Jody noticed that Lisa became afraid to go to sleep alone in her room the night after watching a UFO documentary on TV with her parents. She asked many questions during the program about aliens and was especially bothered by the descriptions of aliens having "insect-like eyes" and pale white skin with only a slit for a mouth reported by persons who claimed to have been taken aboard UFOs. Once asleep, however, Lisa remains asleep for the night. No amount of convincing Lisa that aliens do not exist has helped her combat this fear.

Perhaps the problem that concerns Jody most is Lisa's reactions to Ty. Lisa sometimes plays very well with Ty, but if she becomes frustrated, which she does often, she takes toys away from him, pushes him down, or complains frequently to Jody about his behavior. Jody wants these behaviors to stop and frequently punishes Lisa by placing her in time-out. The effect of such punishment on changing Lisa's behavior appears negligible.

In kindergarten, Lisa is sometimes noncompliant and aggressive. Particularly during play time, Lisa becomes frustrated and grabs a toy away from another child and refuses to share, or directly refuses to do something the teacher has asked the children to do. These episodes are followed by Lisa crying very loudly, which is disruptive to the teacher. The teacher thinks of Lisa as a very bright girl and highly praises her for her work, which is generally superior to that of her peers.

Compare and Contrast

Parenting strategies such as PET and behavioral techniques would attempt first of all to decide which problem should be the focus of the intervention. Recognizing that all problems cannot be handled at once, family specialists using PET would determine a plan that focused on one behavior at a time. For example, in applying PET to Lisa's eating problem, Gordon would emphasize that her parents use active listening and problem-solving skills in helping Lisa resolve her eating difficulties (Gordon, 1975). The parents would engage Lisa in a conversation about the problem and encourage her to discuss her feelings about eating. In addition, Lisa's parents would want to discuss some specific alternatives to help resolve the problem. A likely explanation for Lisa's eating difficulty may be a desire to gain attention in that Jody's time is being taken up feeding and caring for Ty. From the standpoint of PET, once Lisa is able to talk about her problem and her parents listen and give feedback, she will improve.

Dreikurs and Soltz (1964), on the other hand, would structure Lisa to eat at mealtimes by letting her know that if she did not come to the table at the dinner time, she would miss out on food for that meal. She would not be allowed to eat snacks or between-meal treats. If the parents can keep to this schedule for two or three days, Lisa will get the message that she must eat at mealtime. Dreikurs noted that many parents are reluctant to let their child go to bed hungry.

The behaviorists (Patterson, 1976) would be concerned with both how to extinguish the negative behavior and how to replace it with good or desirable behavior. The behaviorists would be more concerned with every aspect of this problem than the other approaches would be. Knowing the frequency of Lisa's refusal to eat and her coming to the table and leaving before finishing would be absolutely necessary. Jody may also be encouraged to reward the appropriate behavior, such as rewarding her when she comes to the table on time or eats an appropriate amount of food.

From a systems perspective, the eating problem would be seen as part of the interactive dynamic of parent and child. The focus on Lisa's behavior as problematic, while denying the interactive aspects of that behavior, falsely blames Lisa and makes her totally responsible for the behavior. The context in which Lisa's eating is considered problematic is the addition of a new brother who takes most of Jody's time. The interactive sequence between Jody and Lisa leads to Lisa finding a way to get the attention from Jody, negative though it is, that she feels she is not getting. The structure of this interactive sequence between Jody and Lisa would be a focus of change from the systems perspective. Jody could think of Lisa's eating difficulty as a transition, or adjustment, to sharing time and possessions with a younger sibling. She could use a playful way to involve Lisa in caring for or feeding the baby. She could also tell Lisa a story that would communicate to her in metaphor form. An example of a story appears at the end of this section.

Lisa's problem of not wanting to go to bed would be handled differently by the three perspectives. Dreikurs and Soltz (1964) would want Lisa to take responsibility for her own behavior by having the parents reassure Lisa that there is no danger, but otherwise the parents would not pay attention to the fear. He believed that parents create a greater problem by attempting to solve the problem by such behaviors as staying in the child's room until he/she falls asleep or allowing the child to remain in the parents' room until falling asleep. If Lisa comes to the parents' room because she is afraid to sleep in her own bed, Dan and Jody should escort her back to her room and reassure her that there is no danger from her fear of aliens. A prolonged discussion about her fear of aliens or staying in their room would only make her fears greater.

Patterson (1976) also would pay little attention to the fear as such. He would want to know what the parents are doing to reinforce this unwanted behavior and how often it occurs. Dan and Jody would need to reward Lisa's attempt to control this fear without their help. Patterson would assume that Dan and Lisa have somehow reinforced behavior that they say they do not want.

Gordon (1975) would suggest that Dan and Jody talk with Lisa about her fears and use active listening and reflective responding to help her reduce her fears. Talking to Lisa might also include determining a plan to correct this behavior that all could agree with. A number of alternative solutions could be proposed, such as Lisa going to bed earlier, having a night light, or not watching frightening programs on television, among others.

A systems perspective would view the preceding suggestions as window dressing but not addressing the issue. Lisa's fear of going to sleep would be viewed as normal and expected behavior. It may become a problem depending on the way Dan and Jody focus on it and whether it serves another purpose in the family. The context of Lisa's fear of aliens must be determined in order not to focus simply on her behavior.

A number of questions would have to be raised about the context. For example, do Dan and Jody allow Lisa too much freedom to watch programs that are inappropriate for her age level? Is Lisa's behavior related in some way to Ty still sleeping in the room with Dan and Jody? Is Lisa simply unable to control her thoughts when she is trying to go to sleep? Is it an interaction of all of these factors?

In Lisa's case, the context seems to be the result of a number of factors. Lisa is bothered by the attention given to Ty, who still does not sleep through the night and requires feeding during the night. Lisa is sometimes awakened by his crying. Her sleeping problem may reflect "regressed" behavior meant to compete with Ty. It also may be influenced by her developing cognitive ability, which cannot control her imaginative processes. The severity of the problem may also reflect that Dan and Jody have created a problem by their level of frustration and reaction.

Whether Lisa's sleeping difficulty is sibling rivalry or not, it is real to her and her parents should address it as a real issue. In contrast to Dreikurs, openly talking to Lisa about her fears and displaying concerns for her would not be considered making the problem worse. Instead of punishing Lisa for her sleeping difficulty, Dan and Jody should discuss the situation with her. At the same time, they should make changes in the context, such as limiting certain television programs, moving Ty into his own bedroom, and not allowing Lisa to sleep with them. They should practice patience and self-control in not trying to solve the sleeping problem in one night.

Lisa's problem of being too aggressive with Ty would also be addressed differently from the standpoint of each of the three approaches. Dreikurs and Soltz (1964) believed that children have a purpose, or goal, for their behavior that is more important than the specific behavior. The purpose of Lisa's aggressive behavior toward Ty seems to be attention getting. Dreikurs and Soltz would encourage Dan and Jody to give Lisa attention when she was not demanding it and to structure her in her play with Ty. Dan and Lisa also would be encouraged not to "police" Lisa and Ty at play, but to let them work out their own differences.

The behaviorist (Patterson, 1976) would approach Lisa's aggressive behavior by rewarding appropriate behavior and setting consequences for aggressive behavior. Time-out is commonly used for aggressive children (Clark, 1985). In Lisa's case, it would involve placing her in a dull or boring room for a specific amount of time when she became aggressive with Ty. Using time-out for a behavior that in the Adlerian approach represents an attempt to get attention would seem to be a mistake.

Gordon (1975) would encourage the parents to use active listening when talking with Lisa about her behavior. They might also use "I-messages" to tell Lisa what they expect from her. Depending on the success of these techniques, the parents may need to sit down with Lisa and attempt to problem-solve.

A systems perspective would consider the context as just discussed. This context would include both Dan's and Jody's relationship with Lisa. Whereas other approaches would not be concerned with how each parent interacts with Lisa, a systems perspective would consider the imbalance in Dan's and Jody's parenting time one of the major issues related to Lisa's behavior problems. Involving Dan in handling some of these problem areas would bring a new perspective and change the established triangles. By involving Dan more directly in parenting, Jody would be relieved of some of the over-responsibility and, at the same time, the established patterns that maintain Lisa's problem behavior would be disrupted.

Lisa's problem in kindergarten would be of little consequence for Dreikurs and Soltz (1964). The problem should be handled by the kindergarten teacher with little or no attention given to it by Dan and Jody. Lisa will learn that aggressive behavior in kindergarten does not get her what she wants from others. The behaviorists would work more in concert with the parents and the kindergarten teacher to reinforce the same behavior. Gordon would suggest that the parents talk with Lisa and find out her feeling about the school problem. The parents may also need to generate options for changing the behavior.

From a systems approach, the aggressive behavior in kindergarten could be seen as triangulation; that is, Lisa acts out an implicit conflict with her mother explicitly in kindergarten. Having Lisa's mother work with the kindergarten teacher would tend to maintain the same triangle in that there would still be two parties who were close and in major conflict with a third party. To make the father more active in Lisa's kindergarten problem, however, breaks up the triangle in that Lisa is not conflicted with him. At the same time, Dan could be encouraged to have special time with Lisa.

In using a systems approach, Dan and Jody could incorporate play in their efforts to gain Lisa's cooperation. For example, in behaviors such as eating or sleeping difficulties, they could use play activities in the form of games. A game such as "Who can get to bed first?" could be played with the winner getting a prize of his/her choice.

In addition to play, Dan and Jody could make up a story to tell Lisa that is constructed around one particular problem. Multiple stories could be told over a period of time to help Lisa work through this transition phase of having a younger brother who gets most of the attention from the mother. Although a number of stories could be told, the following story illustrates the kind of story a parent could construct to help a child with his/her problem.

Once upon a time there was a mother and father pig who had a precious little girl pig whom they named "Piggie." She was adored by everyone in the barnyard, especially by Goose and Charley Horse. She went to Goose's house almost daily when mother pig had work to do in the barnyard. She loved Goose very much and liked to play at her house.

One day it was time for her to go to the special school that all barnyard animals had to attend. There were many things to learn and many things to play with. There were other pigs, horses, goats, geese, chickens, dogs, cows, and other animals too numerous to mention. Piggie's favorite playmate was a frog, named "Froggle." They played in the pond and both learned the ABCs together.

One day when she returned home, her mother showed her a special gift that was wrapped in a special blanket. The gift was a little boy pig named "Piglet." Piglet was very tiny and didn't know any of the things that Piggie knew. He couldn't talk or walk or even eat food. Mother pig explained that she must teach Piglet how to do everything for himself just like Piggie. She said that it would take a lot of her time to teach Piglet, but it would take less time if she had help. Everyone had to think of something that she or he could do to help Piglet learn. Goose was very fond of Piglet too, and also wanted to help. One day, if they all helped, he would be as strong, smart, and as good a playmate as Froggle.

Parenting Proposition

In the natural interaction between parent and child, both conscious and unconscious factors affect the process of interaction. Storytelling is a natural way of affecting this process through indirect and unconscious means.

Answers to "Test Your Knowledge"

1. T   4. T
2. F   5. T
3. F   6. T

Key Concepts

self-system

self-concept

age and self-concept

gender and self-concept

gender-role stereotyping

self-esteem

initiative versus guilt

imaginary playmate

systems perspective of
  moral development

recursive causality

parent/child relationship

routines

sibling relationship

child-focused family

cross-generational coalition

misguided solutions

storytelling

metaphor

mutual storytelling

visual metaphor

verbal metaphor

systems/dialectical process model
  of parenting

Study Questions

1 Describe the development of the self-system in preschool children. How are age and gender related to self-concept?

2 Discuss the development of gender-role stereotyping in the preschool child. Why are toddlers generally more gender-role stereotyped than their parents?

3 Discuss the development of self-esteem in preschool children. How is Erickson's concept of initiative versus guilt related to self-esteem?

4 Why do children have imaginary playmates? Does having an imaginary playmate have a positive or negative effect on the child?

5 Discuss a systems perspective of moral development in the preschool child.

6 Discuss the development of routines. Why are routines so important for development to preschoolers?

7 What enhances the acceptance of the birth of a sibling by the preschool child?

8 Why are child-focused families problematic? Why are families with a cross-generational coalition between a parent and child problematic?

9 Discuss storytelling as a technique of parenting. Under what conditions should parents consider using stories to enhance parental influence on the child?

10 Compare and contrast a systems perspective of parenting with other approaches to parenting.

References

Abramovich, R., Corter, C., Pepler, D. J., & Stanhope, L. (1986). Sibling and peer interaction: A final follow-up and a comparison. *Child Development, 57,* 217–229.

Amatea, E. S. (1989). *Brief strategic intervention for school behavioral problems.* San Francisco: Jossey-Bass.

Baker, A., & Greene, E. (1977). *Storytelling: Art and technique.* New York: Bowker.

Barton, B. (1986). *Tell me another.* Markham, Ontario: Pembroke.

Bowen, M. (1978). *Family therapy in clinical practice.* New York: Jason Aronson.

Brazelton, T. B. (1979). Behavioral competence of the newborn infant. *Seminars in Perinatology, 3,* 35–44.

Brooks, J. (1991). *The process of parenting* (3rd ed.). Mountain View, CA: Mayfield.

Butler, R. (1989). Mastery versus ability appraisal: A developmental study of children's observations of peers' work. *Child Development, 60,* 1350–1361.

Butler, R. (1990). The effects of mastery and competitive conditions on self-assessment at different ages. *Child Development, 61,* 201–210.

Carter, E. A., & McGoldrick, M. (1980). The family life cycle and family therapy: An overview. In E. A. Carter & M. McGoldrick (Eds.), *The family life cycle: A framework for family therapy* (pp. 237–252). New York: Gardner Press.

Clark, L. (1985). *SOS! Help for parents.* Bowling Green, KY: Parents Press.

Crews, L. W. (1985). *Two trees in the forest.* Unpublished manuscript.

Dailey, S. (1985). *Storytelling: A creative teaching strategy.* Mt. Pleasant, MI: Author.

Damon, W. (1977). *The social world of the child.* San Francisco: Jossey-Bass.

Damon, W., & Hart, D. (1982). The development of self-understanding from infancy through adolescence. *Child Development, 53,* 841–864.

Dent, C., & Rosenberg, L. (1990). Visual and verbal metaphors: Developmental interactions. *Child Development, 61,* 983–994.

Dolan, Y. M. (1985). *A path with a heart: Ericksonian utilization with resistant and chronic clients.* New York: Brunner/Mazel.

Dreikurs, R., & Soltz, V. (1964). *Children: The challenge.* New York: Hawthorn.

Dunn, J., & Kendrick, C. (1982). *Siblings: Love, envy and understanding.* Cambridge, MA: Harvard University Press.

Dunn, J., & Munn, P. (1985). Becoming a family member: Family conflict and the development of social understanding in the second year. *Child Development, 56,* 480–492.

Edwards, C. P., & Lewis, M. (1979). Young children's concepts of social relations: Social functions and social relations. In M. Lewis & L. A. Rosenblum (Eds.), *Genesis of behavior: Vol. 2. The child and its family.* New York: Plenum Press.

Eichorn, D. H. (1963). Biological correlates of development. *Yearbook of the National Society for the Study of Education, 62,* 4–61.

Erickson, M. H. (1964a). "The surprise" and "My friend John" techniques of hypnosis: Minimal cues and natural field experimentation. *American Journal of Clinical Hypnosis, 6,* 293–307.

Erickson, M. H. (1964b). An hypnotic technique for resistant patients: The patient, the technique, its rationale, and field experiments. *American Journal of Clinical Hypnosis, 7,* 8.

Erickson, M. H. (1965). The use of symptoms as an integral part of therapy. *American Journal of Clinical Hypnosis, 8,* 57–65.

Erickson, M. H. (1975). The varieties of double bind. *American Journal of Clinical Hypnosis, 18,* 143–155.

Erikson, E. H. (1963). *Childhood and society* (2nd ed.). New York: Norton.

Ferber, R. (1985). *Solve your child's sleep problems.* New York: Simon & Schuster.

Gallahue, D. (1982). *Developmental experiences for children.* New York: Wiley.

Gardner, R. A. (1971). *Therapeutic communication with children: The mutual storytelling technique.* New York: Science House.

Geisler, H. (1988). *The best of the story bag.* San Diego: Geisler.

Goldman, R., & Goldman, J. (1982). *Children's sexual thinking: A comparative study of children aged 5 to 15 years in Australia, North America, Britain and Sweden.* London: Routledge & Kegan Paul.

Gopnik, A., & Slaughter, V. (1991). Young children's understanding of changes in their mental states. *Child Development, 62,* 98–110.

Gordon, T. (1975). *P.E.T.: Parent effectiveness training.* New York: New American Library.

Greene, E., & Shannon, G. (1986). *Storytelling: A selected annotated bibliography.* New York: Garland.

Griffin, B. (1989). *Students as storytellers: The long and short of learning a story* (4th ed.). Medford, OR: Griffin.

Haley, J. (1976). *Problem-solving therapy.* San Francisco: Jossey-Bass.

Hamilton, M., & Weiss, M. (1988). *Children tell stories: A guide for teachers.* Ithaca, NY: Tandem.

Harter, S., & Pike, R. (1984). The pictorial scale of perceived competence and social acceptance of young children, *Child Development, 55,* 1969–1982.

Haywood, K. M. (1986). *Life span motor development.* Champaign, IL: Human Kinetics Publishers.

Hoffman, L. (1981). *Foundations of family therapy.* New York: Basic Books.

Isberg, R. S., Hauser, S. T., Jacobson, A. M., Powers, S. I., Noam, G., Weiss-Perry, B., & Follansbee, D. (1989). Parental contexts of adolescent self-esteem: A developmental perspective. *Journal of Youth and Adolescence, 18,* 1–23.

Jacklin, C. N., & Maccoby, E. E. (1978). Social behavior at 33 months in same-sex and mixed-sex dyads. *Child Development, 49,* 557–569.

Kinghorn, H. R., & Pelton, M. H. (1991). *Every child a story teller: A handbook of ideas.* Englewood, CO: Teachers Ideas Press.

Kuhn, D., Nash, S. C., & Brucken, L. (1978). Sex-role concepts of two- and three-year-olds. *Child Development, 49,* 445–451.

LaFreniere, P., Strayer, F. F., & Gauthier, R. (1984). The emergence of same-sex affiliative preferences among preschool peers: A developmental ethological perspective. *Child Development, 55,* 1958–1965.

Livo, N. J., & Rietz, S. A. (1987). *Storytelling activities.* Littleton, CO: Libraries Unlimited.

Lozoff, B. (1989). Nutrition and behavior. *American Psychologist, 44,* 231–236.

Maccoby, E. E. (1980). *Social development.* New York: Harcourt Brace Jovanovich.

MacKinnon, C. E. (1989). An observational investigation of sibling interactions in marital and divorced families. *Developmental Psychology, 25,* 36–44.

Marcus, D. E., & Overton, W. F. (1978). The development of cognitive gender constancy and sex-role preferences. *Child Development, 49,* 334–344.

Meacham, J. A. (1975). A dialectical approach to moral judgement and self-esteem. *Human Development, 18,* 159–170.

Minuchin, S. (1974). *Families and family therapy.* Cambridge, MA: Harvard University Press.

National Safety Council. (1991). *Injury fact book.* Chicago: Author.

Patterson, G. (1976). *Living with children* (rev. ed.). Champaign, IL: Research Press.

Paulhus, D., & Shaffer, D. R. (1981). Sex differences in the impact of number of older siblings and number of younger siblings on scholastic aptitude. *Social Psychology Quarterly, 44,* 363–368.

Pelham, B. W., & Swann, W. B., Jr. (1989). From self-concepts to self-worth: On the sources and structure of global self-esteem. *Journal of Personality and Social Psychology, 57,* 672–680.

Pellowski, A. (1987). *The family storytelling handbook.* New York: Macmillan.

Pellowski, A. (1990). *The world of storytelling.* New York: H. W. Wilson.

Pollitt, E., Garza, C., & Liebel, R. (1984). Nutrition and public policy. In H. W. Stevenson & A. E. Siegel (Eds.), *Child development research and social policy* (Vol. 1, pp. 321–470). Chicago: University of Chicago Press.

Riegel, K. F. (1975). Subject-object alienation in psychological experimentation and testing. *Human Development, 18,* 135–147.

Rutter, M. (1986). The developmental psychopathology of depression issues and perspectives. In M. Rutter, C. E. Izard, & P. B. Read (Eds.), *Depression in young people: Developmental and Clinical Perspectives.* New York: Guilford Press.

Stilles, K., & Kottman, T. (1990). Mutual storytelling: An intervention for depressed and suicidal children. *The School Counselor, 37,* 337–342.

Watzlawick, P., Weakland, J., & Fisch, R. (1974) *Change: Principles of problem formation and problem resolution.* New York: Norton.

Williams, J. E., Bennett, S. M., & Best, D. L. (1975). Awareness and expression of sex stereotypes in young children. *Developmental Psychology, 11,* 635–642.

Chapter 7

Parenting the School-Age Child
from 6 to 12 Years Old

Parenting Myth ■ Misbehavior in the school-age child must be handled in a way that allows the parent to maintain control. Physical punishment is sometimes needed to take control of a misbehaving child.

Test Your Knowledge ■ The following questions are designed to test your knowledge before reading the material in this chapter. Answers appear at the end of the chapter.

1 Children who are successful in any activity carry over some of that success to other activities. True or false?

2 At entry into the school system, there is little difference in the competency levels of minority and majority children. True or false?

3 Children have higher self-esteem when teachers attribute their success to effort rather than ability. True or false?

4 Researchers have concluded that the best way to maintain compliance in schools is to have a strict policy of corporal punishment. True or false?

5 A peer group is defined as same-age children. True or false?

6 Researchers have concluded that television watching helps children understand appropriate sex roles. True or false?

T he elementary school years have been referred to in the literature as the middle years of parenting. In the past there was not much interest in this period, but recently a wave of interest has occurred. For parents, the elementary school years are vastly contrasted with infancy, toddlerhood, and preschool in their relative ease. The basic skills of eating, dressing, language development, and toilet training have passed, and the child is able to do many things independently. In place of these skills, 6- to 12-year-old children are acquiring intellectual skills of reading, writing, mathematics, science, music, and any subject of interest. They are also learning about the society in which they live and taking on roles for later successful adventures.

During the elementary school years, children learn to compete with peers and master social skills. They become one of the gang with peers and develop appropriate hierarchical relationships with parents. Children who develop strong intimate ties with parents and peers tend to be rewarded in numerous ways, such as in academic performance and social acceptance. On the other hand, some children fail to adjust adequately in this period, resulting in discouragement, withdrawn behavior, and discipline problems. For these children, adolescence and adulthood loom ominously on the horizon.

■ Biological and Physical Development

Physical development in the school-age child is characterized by gradual growth. The gradual rate of growth will dramatically increase at the end of this period, or the beginning of puberty. Children differ in their physical development in height and weight during this period. Some children may be obese while others are underweight. Some school-age children may have health problems because of being obese and having poor exercise habits (Reif, 1985).

During the school-age years, the child is losing the chubby appearance of toddlerhood and the skeleton is becoming more adult-like. These changes are not uniform in all children in that there is a wide variety of physical types. Not uncommonly, children of the same age differ greatly in height or weight. The rate of growth for a particular child depends on a number of factors including nutrition, emotional experiences, and genetic makeup (Tanner, 1970).

The majority of school-age children are physically more active than at any other period of life. They engage in many different types of sports or play activities that require both gross and fine motor coordination. At the same time they are learning to play baseball, they may also be learning to play the piano. Building on basic skills learned in toddlerhood and the preschool period, the school-age child may learn more complex physical skills such as swimming and dancing. The ongoing frequent participation in these physical activities gives the school-age child a sense of mastery.

Physical differences during the school-age period between girls and boys are minimal (Hall & Lee, 1984). Boys have greater strength, and girls have some advantage in

■ *In the early school-age years, children develop attitudes toward work.*

coordination. The ability to participate in baseball, soccer, or other sports appears fairly equal during this period. Both age of the child and the amount of time spent in practice are more important factors than gender.

There is some evidence that present generations are taller and weigh more than past generations (Roche, 1979). In addition, both girls and boys are sexually maturing at earlier ages than in the past. The early age of menarche for females is related to earlier sexual contacts and a younger age at first birth (Ventura & Lewis, 1990). As a later chapter will discuss, these changes significantly impact family life.

Although there is great variety in normal physical development in children, the psychological impact of one's physical appearance may affect children differently. Children whose physical appearance differs significantly from that of their peers may experience more psychological distress than others. A boy who does not keep up with his peers in physical changes, for example, may develop a poor self-image that interferes with his socialization (Cash & Pruzinski, 1990).

■
Intellectual Development

The elementary school years have been described as very important for **intellectual development,** growth in thinking, perceiving, and reasoning. Much of Piaget's work (Piaget & Inhelder, 1969) revolves around the development of thinking and

Table 7.1 ■ **The School-Age Child and Humor**

- In contrast to the preschool child, who has not mastered concrete operational thought, the school-age child enjoys jokes in which there is a pun or a play on words.

- The change in humor occurs about age 11 when children are no longer challenged by riddles and puns.

- Children seem to appreciate jokes that coincide with their level of cognitive development.

Source: McGhee, 1979.

mental operations. Piaget used the term *operation* to define an action taken on an "object." "Mental operations" were transactions in thoughts rather than behaviors.

Two major strides in intellectual development are reached during the elementary school years. The first, the intuitive stage of the preoperational period, occurs from age 4 to 7. During this period, the child learns through resolving issues in the present rather than through some set of principles or operations. The second, from age 7 to about 12, is the period of concrete operations.

During this period, children are able to solve problems in a more logical and orderly manner than they could during their previous level of mental operations. They are less egocentric, able to take a more objective position, and appreciate humor (see Table 7.1). Children attempt to organize and understand the mechanisms whereby principles are operational. This shift in their intellectual ability allows for greater understanding of the physical world.

Conservation

One principle learned by children during the concrete operations period is that of conservation. The term **conservation** refers to the knowledge that physical matter does not change in quantity regardless of its shape. When children are able to conserve, they are able to determine that two pieces of playdough containing the same quantity of material are the same regardless of the form they take. For example, if a child is presented with two identical pieces of playdough in the shape of balls and one ball is flattened, he or she will still believe that they are equal in quantity.

In making this discrimination, the child may be basing this belief on the concept of *identity*. For example, the child recognizes that no new playdough has been added and that the only change is the shape. Another way the child may become aware that the two materials are the same is through the concept of *reversibility*, or the knowledge that the playdough could be changed back at any time. Finally, the child may notice that the pancake is larger around but the ball is thicker. When the child is able to relate two dimensions such as circumference and thickness, he or she is discriminating by using the concept of *reciprocity*. Researchers have found that children learn to conserve more easily when they are presented with familiar objects (Gulko, Doyle, Serbin, & White, 1988).

Researchers have reported that children can be taught to conserve at earlier ages than the ages reported by Piaget. Preschool and kindergarten children have been found to conceptualize the world in terms of conservation (Brainerd, 1977). The question could be raised regarding the efficacy of teaching conservation to children. Generally, researchers have concluded that teaching children to conserve earlier than their normal development does not pose negative consequences.

Self-Concept During the Elementary School Years

Researchers tend to view *self-concept* as a continuation of the preschool period in which *development* was defined in certain categorical ways, such as one's description of gender or hair color (Montemayor & Eisen, 1977). Younger children tend to think of themselves in certain categories that describe "who they are." Being a boy may be the most significant fact related to most males' self-identity. As the child moves into the later stages of this period, self-concept shifts to being based on acceptance into the peer group, competence in school subjects, competence in sports, and a solid sexual identity (Harter, 1982). For the most part, these descriptions of self-identity are thought of as enduring or permanent.

There seems to be some evidence that children who not only believe in their abilities but also overestimate them achieve more than children who have accurate self-assessments. Children who underestimate their abilities may tend to give up, or otherwise not show the effort needed for success. They become more easily discouraged than children who overestimate their performance. Although the toddler's tendency to overestimate his or her ability declines when advancing into the school-age period, there is some evidence that school-age children who overestimate their abilities are more competent (Connell & Ilardi, 1987). This overestimating of their abilities may be related to the fact that they have greater perseverance and determination than their peers who have a more realistic view of their abilities.

Being able to distinguish between one's **private self** (the inner world of thoughts not shared with others) and **public self** (the part that one shares with others) appears to be related to both maturation and a change in self-concept. Prior to age 6, children do not seem to distinguish between private and public selves. In the elementary school years, children do become aware that their actions and emotions may be incongruent. The difference in the private and the public selves becomes more pronounced and abstract as the child moves into the adolescent years (Selman, 1980).

Developmental Tasks

Erikson (1963) postulated that the elementary school years are important because children establish basic attitudes toward work and a competitive spirit that drives them to succeed. Although all children do not compete on the same level, children develop **self-evaluation,** comparing their abilities with those of others, which is extremely important for analyzing the outcome. Erikson defined the concept of **industry** to mean the degree to which the child is motivated toward profitable work. The motivation for the acquisition of skills and knowledge makes this period highly exciting for children and parents.

Although children may involve themselves in a number of tasks that differ greatly from one another, the feeling of accomplishment and success at organizing and mastering a task is the essential element. This psychosocial stage differs from the previous one in that children's efforts are evaluated more stringently and objectively. The school-age child must accomplish goals that are commonly acquired by all persons during this period (Erikson, 1963).

The basic challenge is for the school-age child to develop a sense of identity that includes working with others. Many of the skills to be mastered during the school-age period require that children cooperate with others. For example, they must learn to get along with same-age children and learn appropriate masculine or feminine social roles. They must develop attitudes that lead not only to group participation but also to greater personal independence. Furthermore, school-age children must develop a sense of conscience and morality to guide their social interactions.

Typically, school-age children are optimistic about the world and their ability to accomplish goals. They believe that there is an indeterminant amount of time to accomplish a task and that eventually they will master the task. Increased interaction with a large number of people gives school-age children feedback about how they come across to others. Although this feedback may not be completely objective, it can help with an internal dialogue that is necessary for self-evaluation.

The family still remains the center of the child's life during the elementary school years. Toward the end of this period, the peer group takes on more importance through questioning of adult authority. The school-age child begins to be somewhat critical of parents, teachers, and others who represent authority. Although there may be some antagonisms, adult role models are still important to the school-age child.

Although most children advance through this period by gaining mastery in learning and acquiring new skills, some children do not progress as well. These children, hampered by lack of success, develop a feeling and mode of behaving defined as **an inferiority complex.** While no child can proceed through this stage without failure in some aspect of development, the cumulative effect for most children is positive. In addition, children tend to evaluate themselves higher when they succeed in activities that are highly valued by society. When children are successful in activities that carry little prestige, there may be little carryover in their self-esteem (Holloway, 1988).

Children can fall into a pattern of failure that continues despite all attempts to bolster self-confidence. They are aware of how they compare with others. Subsequent failures may lead to lack of motivation to pursue a particular activity in the future. This burdensome problem of the child's withdrawal and refusal to compete is apparent in school problems. Children with poor school performance internalize the experience and are less willing to participate in future situations. Because the school is representative of the larger society, children who fail to compete in school may have difficulty in performing their social functions later in life. This basic sense of inferiority persists into adulthood and may represent a lifelong inability to compete and perform in society.

Researchers have described the success or failure in the school-age years from different perspectives. A brief look at several of the theories demonstrates the complexity of understanding this process. First, the concept of "learned helplessness" has been offered as an explanation why some children fail to perform in school. **Learned helplessness** is the withdrawing from competition even though the child has in the past performed at high levels. Researchers have found that about a fifth of first-graders experience helplessness and give up making an effort because they perceive that they are deficient and inadequate to complete the tasks (Phillips, 1984).

Researchers emphasize that the way teachers give feedback to students about their work is the major factor affecting students' self-evaluation (Dweck, Davidson, Nelson, & Enna, 1978). For example, if teachers give feedback in a way that attributes success to high effort and failure to low ability, children tend to develop learned helplessness. On the other hand, students learn to value their performance when teachers praise successful activities as high ability and failure as lack of effort. It could be argued that the principle of learned helplessness is based on a linear model and does not sufficiently include what the child brings to the situation.

Second, **attribution theory** posits that children make sense of their experiences by analyzing the situation and finding a plausible explanation for the success or failure of a given activity (Weiner, 1986). There are four possible explanations for the success or failure of a particular behavior: a person's ability, his/her effort, the difficulty of the activity, and luck. Ability and the difficulty of the task are considered stable dimensions that do not change, whereas the amount of effort and luck are considered to vary with the activity. When the child succeeds at a task and attributes a stable cause to it, he/she is likely to have success in the future. Conversely, when the child attributes success to unstable causes, such as to effort or luck, future success may not be as predictable. On the other hand, when failure is attributed to a stable cause, such as ability, the child may experience failure in similar situations in the future. Likewise, when the child attributes failure to unstable causes, he or she would be expected to have success in the future in the same endeavors.

■
Performance in School

The elementary school years are related to many competencies the child must acquire. For example, intellectual and social development are two endeavors the child is constantly involved in. The literature documents the effects of the school experience on children and their development of basic skills. For example, students perform at a higher level and the dropout rate is lower when class size is small

---

■ ■ ■ ■ ■ ■ ■ ■ ■ ■ ■

Box 7.1

Is Maternal Employment Related to Children's Poor School Competence?

Researchers have found that the effects of maternal employment on time with children are negligible (Moorehouse, 1989). Evidence suggests that employed mothers may compensate for the possible negative effects of their employment by increasing their contact and activities with their child. Studies also have revealed that school-age children of employed mothers are as well adjusted as children whose mothers are not employed. In general, girls whose mothers are employed do as well in cognitive development as girls whose mothers are not employed. Boys, on the other hand, sometimes experience some negative effects associated with maternal employment. Some studies also have found that changes in the mother's employment are associated with changes in the attachment status of the child.

In a recent study meant to answer some of the questions related to change and stability in maternal employment, researchers attempted to determine whether patterns of stable full-time employment or shifts to full-time employment are associated with poor outcomes in school except when parent and child participate frequently in shared activities. Researchers found that when frequent activities occur between parent and child, there are no differences in outcomes between children whose mothers are employed and those whose mothers aren't employed. When activities are infrequent, however, children whose mothers are employed have lower scores in school than children whose mothers are not employed. The key to children's success at school is the amount of activities the parent and child share.

(Linnery & Seidman, 1989). In addition, students tend to perform better when a feeling of cooperation is established rather than the competitiveness that has characterized schools in the past.

The evaluation of parents has been found to be extremely important to the self-image of preschool children. After first grade, however, the self-image appears to be related to factors other than appraisals by parents (Phillips, 1984). Children begin to evaluate their abilities similarly to teachers and peers after first grade.

In the early school years, teachers generally view boys as more problematic in school than girls. It is not surprising when viewed from the perspective of the structure of the classroom. While boys tend to be more productive in a situation that emphasizes activity, the typical classroom is organized with a high degree of verbal

Table 7.2 ■ **Effective Schools**

Factors that are not related to effective schools:
- Amount of money budgeted per student
- Number of volumes in library
- Teachers' salaries
- Teachers' academic credentials
- Average class size
- Grouping students according to ability

Factors that are related to effective schools:
- Intellectually capable students
- Teachers who strongly emphasize academics
- Flexible, relaxed atmosphere
- Effective management of discipline problems
- Cooperative relations among school faculty
- Good fit between classroom and environment

Source: Rutter, 1983.

input in which sticking to the task is essential. The high verbal content tends to favor the strengths of girls (Weinstein, Marshall, Sharp, & Botkin, 1987).

Because schools are multicultural, there is a need to consider the role that culture plays in children's performance and mastery of skills. One would expect that minority students would have more difficulty acquiring skills in a school in which the faculty and most of the students were of the majority race. The exception might be Asian students, who tend to outperform majority students even where the faculty are majority. For the most part, the tendency has been to label black students in a majority school setting as disinterested. Researchers have suggested that much of this labeling of black school performance as inadequate may be a cultural bias. The structure of majority schools is much more formal than many of these children are accustomed to. Consequently, the label is applied more for the cultural differences than other presumed reasons (Hale-Benson, 1986).

Some researchers have found that black and majority students are virtually comparable at entry into the first grade on such subjects as math, but differences appear after beginning school (Entwisle & Alexander, 1990). These differences are puzzling to researchers because black mothers have been found to be as concerned or more concerned as majority mothers about education. In fact, the high dropout rate for black students is not predicted from the performance evaluations through the fifth grade (Hale-Benson, 1986).

A systems perspective of the process of learning through school participation provides opportunities for the school to be aware of and include contextual components in the curriculum. Table 7.2 lists specific factors related to effective and ineffective schools. Educators should tailor the school experience to fit the particular needs of children by engaging them in activities that foster growth and development. Teachers should include cultural diversity in their lesson plans so that children can identify with the presented material. This process of validation may improve the participation of minority students who historically have felt alienated from the educational experience.

The School as a System

The school is an organized structure composed of interrelated parts in the same way the family is a system. The **school system** is maintained by patterns of communication and feedback loops. Like a family, the school is made up of subsystems that operate according to a set of rules and through affiliation or nonaffiliation among its members. It has a particular style of communication and problem solving between members and subsystems. The permeability of the boundaries determines the degree of flexibility within the system and between the system and other social systems (Okum, 1984).

When children begin attending school, they move from an evolving family system in which all members participate in the system's evolution to an established system in which they have no input. The child is assigned to a classroom subsystem that lasts for one year, dissolves, and is reorganized the following year. In addition, the child may become a member of other subsystems such as the Cub Scouts, sports teams, or specific activity groups. Each of these subsystems may demand different behaviors from the child and create a sense of confusion (Okum, 1984).

A child whose family has a particular style of interacting may become a member of a school subsystem that operates according to a contrasting style. The inability to adjust to a new subsystem may cause the child to be labeled a problem. Unfortunately for the child, this label may be very difficult to dispel, even after moving to a different subsystem. It can be assumed that a good many school problems could be more adequately described as children's failure to adapt to different subsystems (Okum, 1984).

A child's behavior may not be the same in all subsystems, however, because behavior is viewed as context dependent. For example, a child may act differently at home than at school, or different in one classroom than in another. The relationship with one teacher may not be the same as with another teacher. A child's conduct problems in the second grade may reflect the particular relationship with the teacher rather than the internal or permanent traits of the child.

The clash of family and school value systems and differences in the family system and the school may make it difficult for the child to adjust. The family influences may pull the child in one direction while the school system may pull the child in another direction. The **dialectical process** may not necessarily be negative in the sense that the resolution of the clash in values is unique for different children (Okum, 1984).

Family developmental changes may directly influence the child's school performance or interaction. Changes in parent/child relationships as the family moves from

■ ■ ■ ■ ■ ■ ■ ■ ■ ■ ■

Box 7.2

Is Mother/Child Attachment Related to School Competency in 6-Year-Old Children?

Researchers have found that the social competence of a child is related to the parent/child relationship (Cohn, 1990). Studies show that secure attachment to the mother is related to a number of positive outcomes in children. Recently, researchers concluded that securely attached 6-year-old first-grade boys are liked more by teachers and peers, are less aggressive, have fewer behavior problems, and are more competent than their less secure counterparts.

The preceding association is not true for girls, whose attachment to the mother is not related to social competence. The researchers concluded that this finding is consistent with other research on attachment where girls from lower-income families rather than from middle-income families have behavior and temperament similar to those of boys. Insecurely attached middle-class girls generally do not have behavior problems. Consequently, their peer relationships and teacher evaluations do not deviate substantially from those of securely attached girls.

---

one stage to another in the family life cycle may have ripple effects in the child's relationships within the school system. In addition, nondevelopmental changes affecting the family may create crises that the child exhibits in the school context. The effects of divorce on children's behavior and school performance, for example, are well documented. Changes in the teacher's life, both developmental and nondevelopmental, influence the school context and, consequently, the teacher/child relationship (Okum, 1984).

A significant point is that a problem the child has in the school system must include the other systems in which the child is involved. The coordination of these systems has been poorly orchestrated with one system blaming the other for the problem. The more finger pointing that occurs, the less attention is placed on appropriate action that would improve the child's behavior.

From a systems perspective, the school system should be more willing to involve the family and professionals in addressing the needs of children who have problems in school. The teacher's relationship with the child is also an important variable in understanding the child's behavior. School administrators must be more willing to view the school as a contributor to the child's behavioral problem. The school system may benefit by increasing counseling services for families to include family therapists.

School Phobia

School phobia is typically a problem associated with going to school for the first time or during the first few months. It may also develop in response to other changes during the elementary school years or later. Although a number of theories exist about the etiology of school phobia, a systems perspective offers a unique and novel way of conceptualizing this phenomenon.

A typical scenario in the clinical literature related to the development of school phobia is the concept of **enmeshment**, which refers to family boundaries that are too rigid. Members lack the ability to differentiate themselves from one another, leading to overindulgent or overprotective behavior. Enmeshed families are wonderful for babies, who thrive on the attention. But as children grow up, the attention and over-protectiveness tend to prevent separation and individuation. Parents who continue to indulge their child may find that he/she resents authority and has very poor self-control. These children are not able to negotiate the moves from the family to school or to other environments and activities. If children have problems initially adjusting to school, their "understanding parents" may actually prevent them from working through the impasse by making it easy for them to stay home from school. In terms of a dialectical process, the parents have prevented the child from resolving the conflict by taking away one side of the opposing dialectic, namely, the school environment (see Minuchin, 1974).

Even if the child goes to school, the lack of boundaries with the parents will signal a problem at some point in the future. Such a child probably will not get along well with playmates or will have difficulty making friends. Furthermore, compliance with school rules and with codes of conduct would be particularly difficult for a child who is enmeshed with his/her parents.

Another way of looking at school phobia from a systems perspective is to consider the communicative aspects. For example, a child who is afraid to go to school may be communicating a message that something dreadful in the family may occur if the child attends school. School phobia from this perspective may be protective in that as long as the child has the problem, the parents do not have to address it themselves. In protecting the parents, the child has become the problem, preventing the parents from dealing with the underlying problem (see Haley, 1976).

Triangulation

Triangulation, as discussed earlier, refers to the tendency to include a third party in the conflict within a dyad, or two-person, system. Although most discussion of triangulation has concerned an intrusion within the marital dyad, other forms of triangles occur as well. The school is often triangulated into the family because of frequent contact between the two systems.

The school can be triangulated into the family conflict in a number of ways. First, the child can displace conflict with a parent into the school arena. For example, a 10-year-old boy is enmeshed with his mother and distant from his father. When his parents argue, or when his mother becomes emotionally upset, he has become acculturated to come to his mother's aid by giving her support. This support of the mother to some degree deflects the conflict between the parents to the father/son relationship and reduces the conflict between mother and father.

A variation on this theme occurs when the child has problems at school because the relationship with the teacher is very similar to the relationship with the estranged parent. In this case the conflict with the parent is being deflected through the teacher. As long as the conflict with the parent is hidden, the problem with the teacher will continue.

Another scenario occurs when the parent has a problem with the school system that is deflected through the child. In other words, the parent has a hidden or concealed problem with the school system, such as a disagreement about school policies or a personality conflict with a teacher, but the child embodies it through noncompliant behavior. Focusing on the child as the problem, which is the common way to address a child acting out in school, would do little to improve the situation. In fact, focusing on the child probably would create a longstanding problem between the child and the school system. In this way the child is protecting the parent from having to deal with the school system directly.

Another type of parent/school problem could be the parent's academic or social problems recurring through the child. No doubt, parents have given the child messages regarding their own competencies in school and influenced the child in the mastery of these competencies. When the parents are incompetent in either the social or the academic area, they may focus inappropriately on the child's minor social or academic issues, creating a problem for the child. When the child identifies with the parents' projection of their problem on the child, no appropriate resolution can take place.

Schools and Discipline

When teachers **discipline** a child's noncompliance at school, many parents may have concerns. The issue from the school's point of view is to control noncompliant behavior so that the process of education is not disrupted. Although this goal is accepted as needed and one that should be enforced, parents often question the way schools go about maintaining order. The most common context in which discipline is used is punitive. If the child's noncompliant behavior at school represents triangulation or a displaced family problem, as systems theory would contend, punishment would be certain to create a greater problem than the one being addressed.

Discipline in school occurs under the rubric of **loco parentis,** that is, "in place of the parent." This premise derived from old English law in which the father delegated part of his head of the household authority to the schoolmaster to restrain and correct children under his tutelage (Zirkel & Reichner, 1987). Initially, the idea was that the teacher in direct contact with the student was acting in loco parentis and had the right to restrain an unruly child within reasonable limits. Generally, these limits referred to two factors: the child had to deserve being punished and permanent bodily harm could not be inflicted.

By the beginning of the 20th century, the courts were also using other standards to judge the use of **corporal punishment.** Instead of looking only at the punishment as causing permanent damage or resulting from malice, the courts began to rule that the "reasonableness" of the punishment could be determined as a matter of fact by a jury. In recent years, the courts have allowed the doctrine of loco parentis to be applied based on multiple dimensions, including the type of punishment given, the child's behavior, and age (Zirkel & Reichner, 1987). In the only case ever to go before the Supreme Court, loco parentis was broadened to include the domain of the state. In other cases before the Court, such as those involving school rules, the use of loco parentis has been confirmed as the school's right.

The prevalence of corporal punishment in schools today is mostly unknown, although a few studies conclude that its use is widespread both at home and in school (Crayan, 1987). Not only is corporal punishment used widely, researchers have found that it is not effective in producing positive change in children. The net effect of corporal punishment in schools is the high correlation with the child's destructive behavior toward teachers and property.

Perhaps the most damning finding is the negative relation between corporal punishment and academic learning and achievement. Rosenshine and Furst (1971) did the classic study on this relation. They concluded that teacher criticism of a child's school performance is negatively related to school performance. In a more recent study supporting the findings of Rosenshine and Furst, Lamberth (1979, cited in Crayan, 1987) found that excessive punishment is related to diminished learning.

Corporal punishment of children in schools and at home is related to increased aggression in children, deviousness, sexual aberrations, poor learning, and low self-esteem. It is not advocated by child experts, and many organizations have developed position papers against the use of corporal punishment. Although abuse and spanking may be different behaviors, there is concern that children experience a humiliating experience even by the most innocuous form of hitting.

While corporal punishment is the popular form of discipline in the United States, some other societies do not advocate it. In 1979, for example, the Swedish government passed a law to ban the use of physical punishment in schools and families. The main thrust for this law was for the government not to take over the role of parenting Swedish children, but rather to adequately address the problem of child abuse. A primary issue in the Swedish law is the belief that children have a right to protection from assault. Although a child is legally dependent on his parents, physical assault in the form of corporal punishment does not help create a mutually respectful relationship (Ziegert, 1983).

Because of the tensions involved in rearing children and establishing a career at the same time, young parents are more vulnerable to behaving abusively to their children than are older parents. These parents see corporal punishment of children as an easy way to control a child's noncompliant behavior. Changing the trend to use corporal punishment in American society would require a massive parent-education effort. In order to expedite the transition from the use of corporal punishment to other alternatives, the Swedish government made pamphlets and training sessions available to parents and educators (Ziegert, 1983).

Although corporal punishment has been used for some time both in schools and at home, the time has come to reexamine its use in controlling children's behavior. Instead of blaming either children or their parents for the child's noncompliant or aggressive behavior, a systems perspective focuses on the child's behavior as representing a larger network, which also may include the school system. Laws are needed that not only protect the rights of children but also make it possible to address the child's behavior within the context in which it develops. For example, teachers dealing with a child misbehaving in school should familiarize themselves with the familial context and include the parents and siblings in assessing the situation. This involvement of the family should help school personnel to find alternative solutions to the use of corporal punishment.

Child Care for School-Age Children

The rapid increase in the number of mothers with young children who are now in the work force has profoundly changed **child care** both within and outside the home. Over the past decade, there has been a substantial increase in the use of day-care centers for taking care of young children and a decrease in children being taken care of by the family and friends (Satran, 1988). The use of group day-care facilities for young children has occurred in greater numbers because of a number of factors, including the family structure and resources, the cost of substitute care, the perceived quality, and consumer preferences and tastes (Camasso & Roche, 1991).

The cost of day care is viewed as the single most important variable in making a particular choice (Hofferth & Wissoker, 1990). At the same time, research has also demonstrated that family resources, such as family income, are not significantly related to choice of a group day-care facility (Hofferth & Wissoker, 1990). Some differences have been found, however, with respect to the income of mothers and fathers. For example, the incomes of working mothers have been found to be positively related to choice of a group day care, whereas the incomes of fathers have shown no relation to choice of a group day care (Hofferth & Wissoker, 1990).

A number of recent studies have focused on the relation of the structure of the family to the choice of group day care. Researchers have found the age of the child to be significantly related to the choice of group day care. Generally, as the child ages, the possibility for group day care increases (Hofferth & Wissoker, 1990). For preschool children, this greater involvement in group day care has been believed to be related to the parent's educational level. For school-age children, however, researchers have not found a relation between the parent's educational level and the choice of group day care (Cain & Hofferth, 1989).

One would expect that the quality of the group day-care facility would be important in choosing a facility. However, few researchers have actually considered quality in their research designs. When quality has been included as a factor in the design, it has been a measure of the ratio of teacher to student. As this ratio of student to teacher increases, a negative relation with child-care choice has been found (Hofferth & Wissoker, 1990).

In a recent study that intended to build on prior research findings, researchers emphasized aspects of family characteristics that might be related to choosing group day care. Some of these characteristics included family structure, cost, and quality (Camasso & Roche, 1991). The quality factor was specifically designed to be multidimensional and to tap the willingness to change to a group day-care arrangement.

The sample for Camasso and Roche's (1991) study was drawn from a large survey of all New Jersey state employees in 1988. Respondents were asked to comment on the child-care arrangements, cost, quality considerations, and preferences for each of their children. Findings indicated that with the increase in the number of children there is a decrease in the willingness to change to group day care. The findings supported the research of Hofferth and Wissoker (1990) that there is a greater willingness to use group day care as children get older. No evidence was found to support that single-parent families may be more likely to change from individual day-care arrangements, such as a relative providing the care, to group day care than are two-parent families.

For school-age children the family income was not found to be a factor in the willingness to change to group day care. In fact, the higher the income, the more likely the child was to be taken care of at home by relatives or a baby sitter. The cost variable reflected that for the school-age child, parents' willingness to change to group day care depended on how much more it would cost than the current child-care arrangement. For example, if the rate of increase was expected to be handled within the current family budget, change to a group day-care arrangement would be more likely (Camasso & Roche, 1991).

One of the major issues in Camasso and Roche's (1991) study was to determine how quality was a factor in the change from informal to group day-care arrangements. For the school-age child, a few factors were significant. For example, physical exercise, structured play, and listening to stories were considered positively related to a decision to change child-care arrangements to group day care. In addition, parents who value self-respect, respect for others, and honesty in their child's socialization were more likely to change to group day-care arrangements.

Before- and **after-school programs** have been created to meet the needs of working mothers. These programs generally begin at 7 A.M. and continue after school until

- *Latchkey children without adult supervision may be at high risk for problematic behavior.*

6 P.M. These programs may have some educational benefits but tend primarily toward playground or group activities. Although the school may offer these programs for additional fees, the use of facilities and additional personnel is problematic.

Within the past several decades, a new phenomenon has appeared: latchkey children. **Latchkey children** return home before their parents and must be home alone for some time before the parents arrive home from work. The general assumption is that latchkey children are at higher risks for problems than other children. Some researchers have confirmed this perception, concluding that latchkey children are lonely and face greater stress (Long & Long, 1983), whereas other researchers have found no differences between latchkey children and the general population (Steinberg, 1986). One study of middle-class suburban children found no significant differences between latchkey children and other children in terms of school performance or standardized test results (Vandell & Corasaniti, 1988).

A number of factors are related to outcome in latchkey studies. First, not all situations are the same. For example, some children may report to a parent by the telephone periodically or a neighbor may look in on the child. The age of the child is also an important factor. Generally, the older the child, the more positive the latchkey situation is. One would expect a fifth-grader to be more responsible in self-help skills than a first-grader. Second, living in inner cities may be riskier than living in a suburban or rural area. Presumably, living in the city may be related to less supervision and more distractions leading to possibly dangerous situations (Robinson, Coleman, & Rowland, 1986).

■ Social Development

The development of friendship is an essential aspect of the school-age years. Although friendships may have some of the same characteristics of attachment to family members, middle school children tend to describe them in terms of someone much like themselves (Ainsworth, 1989). This identification with someone like themselves displays much the same structure as attachment and is practice for living and working as a cooperative member of society in the future.

Many factors contribute to the sociability of children, not the least of which is the family background. Researchers have suggested that attachment to the mother in infancy may be linked to the ability to form friendships with other children. For example, children who have a secure attachment with their parents are more likely to be successful in forming friendships in school (Park & Waters, 1989).

Parent/child interactions influence the child in making and keeping friends. A child may model his/her pattern of interaction with parents in friendship relationships. When the parent/child relationship is marred by conflict and stress, children tend to mirror those same relationships with peers. Children who have received harsh parenting may have severe limitations in interacting with others in that either they may be shy and socially withdrawn or they may be aggressive and have poor impulse control (Hart, Ladd, & Burleson, 1990). Obviously the children who have the best results in interacting with others are those who have much family support and feel positive about themselves.

Contrary to a popular belief that the **peer group** represents the child's same age group, researchers have found that the peer group may be more adequately defined as social equals, but not necessarily the same age (Ellis, Rogoff, & Cromer, 1981). In studying neighborhood patterns of play, researchers found that children tend to play more with children who vary more than a year from their own age. Children who share the same interest, such as playing in a tree house or collecting stamps, may spend more time together even if their ages differ by several years.

During the early school-age period, the child shifts from an emphasis on what "the friend can do for me" to a more realistic appraisal that the friend may have different beliefs and values. Toward the end of the school-age period, children begin to see a friend as someone who shares a reciprocal relationship (Selman, 1980). Both children view the relationship as mutual and are equally respectful of the other's thoughts and ideas. Because of the mutual basis of the friendship, relationships in the late school-age period tend to last longer than those in early childhood.

Interacting with friends is beneficial to children for a number of reasons. Children recognize peers as being equals and are better able to strike bargains and compromises in peer relationships than in parent/child relationships. Researchers have found that children who are successful in peer relationships have **social/ cognitive abilities** that tend to be related to positive peer relationships. In other words, a circular or recursive pattern exists between social/cognitive skills and friendships (Downey & Walker, 1989). Researchers have found that children who are accomplished at **role-taking,** behaving in similar ways as the other person, tend to have more friends (Gnepp, 1989). Children skilled in role-taking are better able to respond to the nonverbal dimensions of relationships and anticipate the needs of others. What is set in motion is a cycle whereby socially competent children are on one path toward greater growth and satisfaction in interpersonal relationships and incompetent children are set in motion on a downward spiral of relationship formation and poor skill development.

School-age children who are more competent, particularly those with greater social/cognitive and role-taking skills, tend to be more popular with their peers. In addition to these competencies, other factors may be related to popularity. Attractiveness may be a type of unconscious stereotype that children learn very early and act out through subtle prompting from others. Attractive children learn that they are more desirable in many ways than are unattractive children, who also act out the part of undesirable behavior and traits (Langlois, 1986). A type of self-fulfilling prophecy tends to be operative for both the attractive child and the unattractive child.

Other factors related to **popularity,** such as name and how children initiate play with other children, may also set up certain future cyclical expectations and patterns of behavior. For example, children with more common and accepted names tend to be more popular than children with unusual or odd-sounding names (Langlois, 1986). In addition, socially competent and popular children tend to initiate play with other children in a way that fits in with or complements their play. On the other hand, unpopular children seem to be insensitive to other children's style of play and often are seen as too aggressive (Putallaz & Wasserman, 1989).

As the child moves through the school years, the relationship with the teacher becomes less important and the relationship with peers becomes more important. Researchers have found that peer pressure to conform to standards of behavior that were different from one's own standards increases in the elementary school years as the need to be accepted by the peer group increases (Gavin & Furman, 1989). Researchers have found that school friends tend to be similar on many of the same factors that characterize adolescent and adult relationships including social class, intelligence, and attractiveness (Clark & Ayers, 1988).

An important aspect of social interaction during the elementary school years is **team play,** or sports. In team play, children learn to subordinate their own desires for the benefit of the team. Team play allows children to view the impact of their actions on others and, reciprocally, the actions of others on themselves. The lesson learned from team involvement is that one's actions are interdependent with actions of others. In addition, children learn to cooperate and to do their share while allowing others to do their share. In soccer, for example, a girl who may not run well but can kick well may learn that her contribution on defense is as valuable as the best runner's ability is on offense. In systems terms, the child has learned that the whole is greater than the sum of the parts. Although individual competition may motivate some children to be recognized as the best, cooperation is necessary in order to win.

In such endeavors as team play, children gain a sense of belonging to a common group and view the opponent as a common enemy. Winning is important because it represents a successful cohesive group activity. Not only is competition with the other team encouraged, but one must be devoted to one's team even if a best friend is on the other team.

Researchers have addressed the question of sex differences in the formation of friendships. Boys tend to have more friends outside of school than girls and initiate more unreciprocated friendships than girls (Clark & Ayers, 1988). On the other hand, girls tend to have more friends in school and more reciprocal friends than boys. Both boys and girls prefer same-sex friendships and often are somewhat reluctant to initiate friendships with the other sex.

This preference for same-sex friends appears in young children so that by age 2 children already have very strong preferences. As children age, the preference becomes more pronounced. Although the tendency may be more pronounced in American society than in other societies, gender preference is closely associated with increasing age and role expectations (Whiting & Edwards, 1988).

Television and the Family

Television has become a major influence on the family during all periods of child development. The school-age child is influenced by **television viewing** because it competes with time spent on other endeavors, particularly schoolwork. In the past three decades, television has become almost universal in American homes (Parke & Slaby, 1983). Television is watched on average about four hours a day in most homes, which accounts for the most time spent in one activity other than sleeping (Singer, 1983). By the time a child graduates from high school, he or she has spent more time watching television than in the classroom.

■ *Limiting television watching and guarding against inappropriate programming can be a very difficult task for parents.*

The effects of television on children and family members are ambiguous and unclear. Some researchers believe, however, that the impact of television on child development is equivalent to the impact on development of the family, the school, and society (Fabes, Wilson, & Christopher, 1989). Some researchers have found a negative impact of television watching on reading fluency and creativity (Williams & Handford, 1986). The more school-age children watch television the lower their reading fluency.

Television includes many different types of programming, but the most prominent theme is violence. It is estimated that by the time a child is 18 years of age he or she has witnessed 13,000 murders and numerous muggings, robberies, assaults, wife batterings, obscene and vulgar language, rapes, and explicit sexual encounters. Researchers have found that children who watch a great deal of television tend to be indifferent to violence, whereas children who do not watch television are more concerned when the two groups are shown a film with explicit violence (Drabman & Thomas, 1976).

Research on television has mainly been limited to a few studies focusing on the effects of frequent viewing on children. Other issues, such as the effects on family relationships, have not been studied to any extent (Fabes, Wilson, & Christopher, 1989). Perhaps one of the reasons that research regarding television and the family has lagged behind is the view that television is a type of family entertainment that eventually will be replaced by some other activity. On the contrary, television continues to be a major form of family entertainment involving both parents and children.

The effect of increased television viewing on the family appears to be related to the quality and quantity of interaction (Fabes, Wilson, & Christopher, 1989). When family members engage in television viewing, there is a change in family interaction. The most obvious change is the reduction in interaction since family members are preoccupied. The experience of watching television is mainly private and isolating, even when family members are sitting side by side.

Recently, a number of researchers have challenged the trivializing of the effects of television on the socializing of the family. In summarizing this recent research, Fabes, Wilson, and Christopher (1989) found that there is ample evidence demonstrating that television watching has a socializing effect on family relationships. Contrary to the accepted assumption that television watchers distinguish between fantasy and the real world, recent research evidence supports the view that watching television tends to shape how one views the world.

Television families tend to be middle class, intelligent, witty, physically attractive, and able to meet any challenge. Seldom are working-class families portrayed as the major characters, except for perhaps the sitcom *Roseanne*. Watching resourceful middle-class intact or single-parent families solve an array of problems while remaining calm and collected may not connect with a working-class single-parent family. Consequently, many families that watch sitcom families on television may evaluate their own lives more harshly in comparison.

Researchers have found that parents tend to lose control of their children's television watching during the late school-age period. During the adolescent period, parents exert little or no direct control over television watching nor are they even aware of the type or frequency of their children's television viewing. In addition, researchers have found that parents tend to underestimate the effects of horror movies or scary programs on their children (Fabes, Wilson, & Christopher, 1989).

Some guidelines have been developed to assess the relation of television watching to the quality of family life (Fabes, Wilson, & Christopher, 1989; Osborne, 1988). Having family members fill out a checklist not only of the frequency of television viewing but also of the effects of watching television on family relationships, such as time spent in common activities, may give the family some idea about how the television influences family interaction. Some researchers suggest limiting the amount of time and the type of programming that children are allowed to watch (Osborne,

1988). Placing the television in a strategic place and using a video recorder may be ways to limit viewing time and provide a time when all members can be together to watch a recorded program.

■ Parent/Child Relationships

In the middle years, parent/child relationships emphasize different aspects of parenting than in the toddler or preschool periods. For example, parents are less involved in the daily routines of their children, although they continue to approximate their respective activities with children; that is, mothers are more involved in care taking and fathers are more involved in play (Russell & Russell, 1987). In recent years, fathers have been more involved with children, but the mother's work role and other responsibilities are generally related to increased father participation.

Parenting Tasks

A major reason for the difference in parent/child relationships in this period is the change in **parenting tasks.** Whereas the parent was more involved in the toddler and preschool periods, the tasks for the elementary school years are centered outside the home. The major parenting tasks in this period are establishing flexible but firm rules, maintaining proper hierarchy, understanding differential authority, and allowing the child to establish relationships outside the family (Roberts, 1991). Because of school the child is in contact with peers more than with parents. This separation from the parent means that parents must be willing to increase the boundaries to the family sufficiently to include school and peer relationships while maintaining the integrity of the family boundary. At the same time, the family boundaries must not become so permeable that one cannot distinguish family members from outsiders.

The parenting task of establishing **differential authority** refers to the differences in hierarchy in the family. From a systems perspective, parents and children must be viewed as not sharing equal power. In contrast with Adlerian theory, a systems perspective does not view the family as a democracy as depicted by Dreikurs & Soltz (1964). Rather, children are viewed as belonging to a subordinate subsystem where the end goal of parenting is to elevate them to being able to assume the executive position of authority when they establish their own differentiated homes.

In this regard, a systems theory also contrasts with PET (Gordon, 1970). In the PET model, defiant children are believed to be reacting against parental authority. Instead of exerting authority, parents are encouraged to be understanding of their children by using "active listening" and making "I-statements" when they expect certain responses from their children. Parents would never be encouraged to invoke rules or judgments that children did not want (Roberts, 1991).

The question of differential authority never surfaces from a behavioral perspective. Parents are simply assumed to have the power in the family. For example, parents are viewed as reinforcers of the child's behavior. The parent can change the child's behavior through reinforcing certain desired behaviors. If the desired change in the child does not occur, the parent did not have the appropriate plan (Roberts, 1991).

Another important parenting task in the school-age period is establishing firm and flexible rules. Many of these rules revolve around school participation. In contrast to the Adlerian perspective, which would attempt to put the child in charge of problems with the school system, a systems perspective would consider the sequence or pattern of behavior to be inseparable from the behavior itself. For example, when a child finds it difficult to get up in the morning and is frequently late for school, a systems perspective would view resolving the problem as more complex than merely buying the child an alarm clock as the Adlerians would do (Roberts, 1991).

It is not unusual for the child in the elementary school years to feel some conflict between what parents expect and what the peer group expects. Whereas parents place importance on making good grades, having a neat appearance, and being responsible, the peer group may openly show disdain for these behaviors by confronting the parents. Although the school-age child is influenced by peer group behaviors, a recent study reveals that parents are more important than peers in matters of long-term significance (Thompson, 1985). When a conflict between the peer group and the family does occur, the school-age child may overalign with one over the other. This imbalance may lead directly to problematic behavior in that the child will be reprimanded by one and overidentified with the other.

The use of discipline changes during the school-age years as well. Prior to this period the parent was involved with the child more as a teacher than as a disciplinarian. During this period the parent is concerned not only about consequences for particular behavior but also about how the family functions as a unit. Family cohesiveness and the ability to adapt to change are two family dimensions that researchers have related to healthy or dysfunctional family patterns (Olson, Russell, & Sprenkle, 1983).

Approaches to parenting typically describe particular behavior problems that parents could have in this phase of parenting and make suggestions for how they might handle these problems. Although it is necessary for parents to set consequences for their children's behavior, their own behaviors might be considered either appropriate or inappropriate. The perspective presented here, as stated previously, is that parenting must not resort to a "cookbook" approach whereby parents apply certain actions in response to particular child behaviors.

Parents should be viewed as having a mixture of behaviors, some of which could be considered problematic, based on their particular problem-solving ability and the family and social structure of which they are a part. The systems perspective considers the daily interactions of parent and child to be of great significance in understanding parenting behavior. Parenting behaviors seem to be motivated by the ongoing interactions with a changing child, which produce conflicts and crises. The resolution of these conflicts occurs spontaneously through the parent's ongoing interaction with the child.

■
A Systems/Dialectical Process Model of Parenting the School-Age Child

In 1988 Holden and Ritchie advanced a model of flexible parenting behavior based on dialectical theory. They noted two types of parenting dialectics: outer dialectics, defined as conflicts with other people or situations, and inner dialectics, debates within the individual. Outer dialectics refer to any conflict between the parent and the child or the school, or between parents. These frequently occur when the needs of one person conflict with the needs of another person. Inner dialectics exist inside the parent's cognitive processes and are concerned with how appropriate the parent believes the parenting behavior to be.

A systems perspective of parenting takes a dialectical stance in that parents are viewed as needing to be flexible in responding to changing behaviors of the child. Researchers have concluded that parenting behaviors that emphasize nurturance, responsiveness, and stimulation without rigidity or excessive controlling produce children who have better success in school and greater intellectual development (Belsky, Lerner, & Spanier, 1984; cited in Holden & Ritchie, 1988).

The dialectical process in parenting involves conflicts between different elements, but these elements are not viewed as polar opposites. Rather, they are viewed as similar elements within the same process, contributing to the whole or combinations of elements (Holden & Ritchie, 1988). Viewing the various elements of the dialectic as part of the same process means that there are no given points of resolution to any of the conflicts. This conclusion challenges the current view that parent education offers the parent with a blueprint for solving particular child behaviors. On the contrary, parents must alter their behavior to meet the changes in themselves, their child, and the larger social network. They must see their parenting behavior as having multiple dimensions that must be understood before they assess the appropriateness of the behavior.

A **systems process model of parenting** focuses on how parents make decisions and resolve the conflicts that arise. How problems are resolved must be viewed as equally important as what those decisions are. The parenting literature generally ignores the process of how parents come to particular decisions. Rather, the focus tends to be on imparting particular "skills" through learning parenting behaviors that control or manipulate the child's behavior. If parents paid more attention to the process involved in strategies they imposed on their children, more efficient problem solving probably would take place.

In relying on particular strategies for parenting behavior, parents do not have to think or be concerned with how they arrived at their decisions. For example, in relying on a particular method of handling a child's temper tantrum, the parent may not be aware of the many influences on the temper tantrum. Consequently, the parent may not be aware of his/her contribution to the problem, and the attempted solution may not contribute overall to positive parent/child interactions. Successful parenting means that parents will not have ready-made answers but must struggle for answers through the dialectical process (Holden & Ritchie, 1988).

Family Portrait ■■■■■■■■■■

Bill and Jane Bailey have been married for 15 years and have three children, Billy 10, Joey 8, and Kara 3. During the past three years, Billy has gradually developed problems both at home and at school. As a young child Billy was placed in a day-care facility because both parents worked. Billy's father frequently was away from home for several days at a time. Generally, Billy was not picked up at day care until 6 P.M., and his mother noted that he was fussy for some period after getting home. When Billy was 2 years old his younger brother, Joey, was born. Although Billy and Joey eventually became fairly close playmates, Billy was initially jealous and displayed some regressive behavior. Jane always felt some guilt about the fact that she worked, and attempted to make up for it by giving the children treats and being lenient with discipline. Bill, on the other hand, was not as involved with the children and thought Jane too lenient. They had frequent arguments about family rules and discipline of children, which often occurred in front of the children. Generally, an array of misbehavior, particularly by Billy, followed these parental arguments. Billy would frequently become noncompliant, watch both parents become frustrated, then skillfully manipulate them into an argument that resulted in him getting what he wanted. One of his most annoying behaviors was to dawdle, making him late for school and delaying the family whenever they had planned an outing. Joey and Kara were described as perfect children except when prompted by Billy's misbehavior.

The marital relationship has been shaky for a number of years, but the conflict has increased in the past year. Bill moved out for a short time twice in the past year, but both times reconciliation followed. Billy's behavior was exaggerated during the separation, and Jane appealed to Bill for help with Billy. Shortly after Bill returned home, the same familial pattern continued, with the parents arguing over Billy's behavior.

Although the behavior in the family was problematic at times, neither parent felt the need to consult outside help. At school Billy's behavior was inconsistent both in academic subjects and in conduct. In fact, Billy's teacher thought he was "disturbed" and responsible for much of the disruption in the classroom. When Billy's parents were asked to come to school recently for a conference, only Jane attended the conference because Bill was too exacerbated with what he considered to be Jane's incompetence as a parent and her unwillingness to allow him to exert more direct control over Billy. The teacher interpreted Bill's absence as his disinterest in Billy and believed even more that the family was to blame for Billy's behavior.

In the classroom, Billy often did not complete assignments because he did not listen well enough to the teacher. He talked inappropriately and, at times, appeared withdrawn, which also got the teacher's attention. It was clear that Billy was the focal point for any disruption in the classroom, although his behavior was not much different from that of other students.

One final consideration that other approaches would overlook is the teacher's own personal situation that might influence her interaction with Billy. The teacher's son, two years younger than Billy, recently has displayed some unpleasant behavior. She is currently separated from her husband, although no plans for a divorce have been made. She is concerned that her son's behavior may be a reaction to the marital problem and worries about the long-term effects that a divorce would have on him.

Compare and Contrast

An Adlerian would not need all the information presented in this case to devise a strategy to work with Billy. The mistaken goal of Billy's behavior is obviously an attempt to gain power in the family. His attempts to gain power generally have been successful at home but have failed in the school setting. Specific behaviors that might be addressed are dawdling and the school problem. Although Dreikurs and Soltz (1964) do not address a case as complex as this one, it would be assumed that Billy's problem of being late for school would be handled by making Billy take responsibility for his waking up and getting to school on time. He would have his own alarm clock and would be informed what time to be ready for the school bus or the ride to school with his father. If Billy continued to dawdle, the logical consequence would be that he would miss his ride. His getting to school late would then be a problem between Billy and the school that Billy would have to take responsibility for.

The problem of making the family late for family outings would be handled by informing Billy that they were leaving at a certain time. If Billy was not ready, he would have to get dressed in the car. In this way, Billy would be forced to take responsibility for his own actions by experiencing the logical consequences of his behavior.

The marital problem would be addressed in the sense that Bill and Jane would be asked to come to a consensus on their parenting beliefs. An Adlerian family expert would present the idea of a democratic family to Bill and Jane during weekly family meetings. Everyone would have an equal voice in the meetings. A more cooperative problem-solving method would improve this family's overall functioning and Billy's misbehavior.

Behaviorists would take a somewhat different approach in that the background information would be important to determine how specific behaviors were reinforced (Patterson, 1976). For example, when Billy dawdles at home and fails to be ready to go on time, it would be necessary to determine the frequency and extenuating circumstances in order to devise a plan to correct them. It might be the case that the parents have not prepared Billy in taking appropriate steps in dressing. When they announce that it is time to leave, he may be expected to be fully ready to go. Another possible scenario is that Bill and Jane inadvertently reinforced Billy's dawdling.

After determining the parameters of Billy's problem, a behaviorist would devise a plan of action. The principle of rewarding appropriate behavior and punishing or ignoring negative behavior would be used. Typically, one problem is attacked at a time. Certain privileges would be made contingent on an improvement in Billy's behavior. For example, by being on time for the school bus, he would earn tokens. An accumulation of tokens would result in his being able to receive certain privileges. Bill and Jane might praise Billy as his behavior improved, but they would direct the praise to the specific behavior.

Once the dawdling behavior was addressed and improvement made, the behaviorist could develop a plan for improving Billy's behavior at school. Cooperation with the teacher would be necessary in order to improve the school situation. Again, a token system could be used to reinforce Billy's positive behavior and punishment could be used to weaken the negative behavior. Some punishment, such as time-out, would not be appropriate for improving his academic performance.

Each problem would be addressed in this fashion until all problems were improved. The behaviorist would ask Bill and Jane to cooperate to determine what reinforcers to use and work together in implementing them. In addition, a primary emphasis would be direct, open communication between the parents and between them and Billy.

A practitioner from the PET approach (Gordon, 1970) would not be particularly interested in all the information given about this case. The primary focus would be to determine who had the problem and how to problem-solve to find a solution. Active listening and communicating would be extremely important from the outset. It would be assumed that Billy needs to be able to talk about his problem to his parents without their attempting to solve it or criticizing him for having it.

Bill and Jane would be instructed how to give I-messages to communicate their expectations to Billy. They would not try to force or coerce him to act differently. They would attempt to problem-solve by coming to an agreement that would satisfy everyone. According to the PET approach, active listening, making I-statements, and cooperative problem solving would eliminate the problem.

A systems/dialectical perspective would be concerned with all the information presented in the case history. This approach would replace the simplicity of the other approaches with a thorough understanding of the interaction of the various systems and subsystems involved in the problem. For example, one of the most significant facts is the marital relationship. The fact that Bill and Jane differ about how to structure Billy is not so much the problem as how they disagree. Undermining one another does not lead to a positive outcome. They need to learn not only how to structure Billy in a more cooperative way but also how to resolve the issue related to their separations. A systems specialist could help them in keeping their parental and marital subsystems separated.

In the case presented, two systems intersect—the family and the school. Each blames the other for Billy's problem. Neither is willing to assume responsibility for the part of the problem that it contributes to. From a systems perspective, both systems must be transformed and restructured to be more functional.

■■■■■■■■■■

Parenting Proposition

How parents arrive at decisions regarding a specific response to a child's behavior is as important as the response itself. For example, physical punishment of the child tends to be the result of the parent being out of control rather than being in a defensible position.

Answers to "Test Your Knowledge"

1. F
2. T
3. F

4. F
5. F
6. F

Key Concepts

intellectual development

conservation

private self

public self

self-evaluation

industry

inferiority complex

learned helplessness

attribution theory

the school as a system

dialectical process

school phobia

enmeshment

triangulation

discipline in school

loco parentis

corporal punishment

child care

before-school programs

after-school programs

latchkey children

peer group

social/cognitive abilities

role-taking

popularity

team play

television viewing

parenting tasks

differential authority

systems process model of parenting

Study Questions

1. Discuss Erikson's concept of industry

2. What does self-evaluation refer to? How does the school-age child evaluate his/her efforts in school? Explain how an inferiority complex develops in the school-age child.

3. Explain the concept of learned helplessness. How does the school-age child develop learned helplessness?

4 What is attribution theory? How does the school-age child develop a feeling of self-esteem and competence?

5 Discuss the school as a system by using such terms as *enmeshment* and *triangulation*. How can school phobia be understood in terms of systems theory?

6 What does the term *loco parentis* refer to? Discuss loco parentis regarding the use of corporal punishment in schools.

7 Discuss child-care issues for the school-age child including before- and after-school programs and latchkey kids. Are latchkey kids at greater risks for problematic behavior?

8 What is the peer group? How does it help a child's adjustment? Discuss the importance of team play and friendships during the school-age period.

9 Discuss the impact of television watching on the school-age child. How does television watching affect the process of socialization?

10 Compare and contrast a systems perspective of parenting with other approaches to parenting.

References

Ainsworth, M. D. (1989). Attachment beyond infancy. *American Psychologist, 44,* 709–716.

Belsky, J., Lerner, R. M., & Spanier, G. B. (1984). *The child in the family.* Reading, MA: Addison-Wesley.

Brainerd, C. J. (1977). Cognitive development and concept learning: An interpretive review. *Psychological Bulletin, 84,* 919–939.

Cain, V. S., & Hofferth, S. L. (1989). Parental choice of self-care for school-age children. *Journal of Marriage and the Family, 51,* 65–77.

Camasso, M. J., & Roche, S. E. (1991). Parental considerations of cost and quality in child care arrangements. *Journal of Marriage and the Family, 53,* 1071–1082.

Cash, T., & Pruzinski, T. (1990). *Body images.* Guilford, CT: Guilford Press.

Clark, M. L., & Ayers, M. (1988). The role of reciprocity and proximity in junior high friendships. *Journal of Youth and Adolescence, 17,* 403–411.

Cohn, D. A. (1990). Child-mother attachment of six-year-olds and the social competence at school. *Child Development, 61,* 152–162.

Connell, J. P., & Ilardi, B. C. (1987). Self-system concomitants of discrepancies between children's and teachers' evaluations of academic competence. *Child Development, 58,* 1297–1307.

Crayan, J. R. (1987, February). The banning of corporal punishment. *Childhood Education, 146–153.*

Downey, G., & Walker, E. (1989). Social cognition and adjustment in children at risk for psychotherapy. *Developmental Psychology, 25,* 835–845.

Drabman, R. S., & Thomas, M. H. (1976). Does watching violence on television cause apathy? *Pediatrics, 37,* 329–331.

Dreikurs, R., & Soltz, V. (1964). *Children: The challenge.* New York: Hawthorn/Dutton.

Dweck, C. W., Davidson, W., Nelson, S., & Enna, B. (1978). Sex differences in learned helplessness: II. The contingencies of evaluative feedback in the classroom, and III. An experimental analysis. *Developmental Psychology, 14,* 268–276.

Ellis, S., Rogoff, B., & Cromer, C. C. (1981). Age segregation in children's social interactions. *Developmental Psychology, 17,* 399–407.

Entwisle, D. R., & Alexander, K. L. (1990). Beginning math competence: Minority and majority comparisons. *Child Development, 61,* 454–471.

Erikson, E. H. (1963). *Childhood and society* (2nd ed.). New York: Norton.

Fabes, R. A., Wilson, P., & Christopher, F. S. (1989). A time to reexamine the role of television in family life. *Family Relations, 38,* 337–341.

Gavin, L. A., & Furman, W. (1989). Age differences in adolescents' perceptions of their peer groups. *Developmental Psychology, 25,* 827–834.

Gnepp, J. (1989). Personalized inferences of emotion and appraisals: Component processes and correlates. *Developmental Psychology, 25,* 277–298.

Gordon, T. (1970). *P.E.T.: Parent Effectiveness Training.* New York: New American Library.

Gulko, J., Doyle, A., Serbin, L. A., & White, D. R. (1988). Conservation skills: A replicated study of order of acquisition across tasks. *Journal of Genetic Psychology, 149,* 425–439.

Hale-Benson, J. E. (1986). *Black children: Their roots, culture, and learning styles* (rev. ed.). Baltimore: Johns Hopkins University Press.

Haley, J. (1976). *Problem-solving therapy.* San Francisco: Jossey-Bass.

Hall, E. G., & Lee, A. M. (1984). Sex differences in motor performing in young children: Fact or fiction? *Sex Roles, 10,* 217–230.

Hart, C. H., Ladd, G. W., & Burleson, B. R. (1990). Children's expectations of the outcomes of social strategies: Relations with sociometric status and maternal disciplinary styles. *Child Development, 61,* 127–137.

Harter, S. (1982). The perceived competence scale for children. *Child Development, 53,* 87–97.

Hofferth, S. L., & Wissoker, D. A. (1990). *Quality, price, and income in child care choice.* Washington, DC: Urban Institute.

Holden, G. W., & Ritchie, K. L. (1988). Child rearing and the dialectics of parental intelligence. In J. Valsiner (Ed.), *Child development within culturally structured environments* (Vol. 1.). Norwood, N.J.: Ablex.

Holloway, S. D (1988). Concepts of ability and effort in Japan and the United States. *Review of Educational Research, 58,* 327–345.

Lamberth, J. (1979). The effects of punishment on academic achievement: A review of recent research. In I. A. Hyman & J. A. Wise (Eds.), *Corporal punishment in American education.* Philadelphia: Temple University Press.

Langlois, J. H. (1986). From the eye of the beholder to behavioral reality: Development of social behaviors and social relations as a function of physical attractiveness. In C. P. Herman, M. P. Zanna, & E. T. Higgins (Eds.), *Physical appearance, stigma, and social behavior: The Ontario Symposium (Vol. 3.).* Hillsdale, NJ: Erlbaum.

Linnery, J. A., & Seidman, E. (1989). The future of schooling. *American Psychologist, 44,* 336–340.

Long, T. J., & Long, L. (1983). *The handbook of latchkey children and their parents.* New York: Arbor House.

McGhee, P. E. (1979). *Humor: Its origin and development.* New York: Freeman.

Minuchin, S. (1974). *Families and family therapy.* Cambridge, MA: Harvard University Press.

Montemayor, R., & Eisen, M. (1977). The developments of self-concepts from childhood to adolescence. *Developmental Psychology, 13,* 317–327.

Moorehouse, M. J. (1989). Linking maternal employment patterns to mother-child activities and children's competencies. *Developmental Psychology, 27,* 295–303.

Okum, B. F. (1984). Family therapy and the schools. In J. C. Hansen, (Ed.), B. F. Okum (Vol. Ed.), *Family therapy with school-related problems* (pp. 1–12). Rockville, MD.: Aspen.

Olson, D. H., Russell, C., & Sprenkle, D. (1983). Circumplex model of marital and family systems: VI. Theoretical update. *Family Process, 22,* 69–83.

Osborne, P. (1988). *Parenting for the '90s.* Intercourse, PA.: Good Books.

Park, K. A., & Waters, E. (1989). Security of attachment and preschool friendships. *Child Development, 60,* 1076–1081.

Parke, R. D., & Slaby, R. G. (1983). The development of aggression. In E. M. Hetherington (Ed.), P. H. Mussen (Series Ed.), *Handbook of child psychology: Vol 4. Socialization, personality, and social development* (pp. 547–641). New York: Wiley.

Patterson, G. R. (1976). *Living with children.* Champaign, IL: Research Press.

Phillips, D. A. (1984). The illusion of incompetence among academically competent children. *Child Development, 55,* 2000–2016.

Piaget, J., & Inhelder, B. (1969). *The psychology of the child.* New York: Basic Books.

Putallaz, M., & Wasserman, A. (1989). Children's naturalistic entry behavior and sociometric status: A developmental perspective. *Developmental Psychology, 25,* 297–305.

Reif, G. (1985). *Fitness for youth.* Unpublished report. Ann Arbor: Department of Physical Education, University of Michigan.

Roberts, T. W. (1991). A systems perspective of parenting: The family's responsibility in misbehavior. *Family Science Review, 2,* 1–13.

Robinson, B. E., Coleman, M., & Rowland, B. H. (1986). The after-school ecologies of latchkey children. *Children's Environments Quarterly, 3,* 4–8.

Roche, A. F. (1979). Secular trends in human development, maturation, and development. *Monographs of the Society for Research in Child Development, 44,* 3–4.

Rosenshine, B., & Furst, N. (1971). Research in performance criteria. In B. O. Smith (Ed.), *Research in teacher education* (pp. 37–72). Englewood Cliffs, NJ: Prentice-Hall.

Russell, G., & Russell, A. (1987). Mother-child and father-child relationships in middle childhood. *Child Development, 58,* 1573–1588.

Rutter, M. (1983). School effects on pupil progress: Research findings and policy implications. *Child Development, 54,* 1–27.

Satran, P. R. (1988, April). Who shares the care? *Working Mother,* 55–57.

Selman, R. L. (1980). *The growth of interpersonal understanding.* Orlando, FL: Academic Press.

Singer, D. G. (1983). A time to reexamine the role of television in our lives. *American Psychologist, 38,* 815–816.

Steinberg, L. (1986). Latchkey children and susceptibility to peer pressure: An ecological analysis. *Developmental Psychology, 22,* 433–439.

Tanner, J. M. (1970). *Education and physical growth.* New York: International Universities Press.

Thompson, D. (1985). Parent-peer compliance in a group of preadolescent youth. *Adolescence, 25,* 501–508.

Vandell, D. L., & Corasaniti, V. A. (1988). The relation between third-graders' after-school care and social, academic, and emotional functioning. *Child Development, 59,* 868–875.

Ventura, S., & Lewis, C. (1990). Report on teen birth statistics. Washington, DC: National Center for Health Statistics.

Weiner, B. (1986). *An attributional theory of motivation and achievement.* New York: Springer-Verlag.

Weinstein, R. S., Marshall, H. H., Sharp, L., & Botkin, M. (1987). Pygmalion and the student: Age and classroom differences in children's awareness of teacher expectations. *Child Development, 58,* 1079–1093.

Whiting, B. B., & Edwards, C. P. (1988). *Children of different worlds: The formation of social behavior.* Cambridge, MA: Harvard University Press.

Williams, T. H., & Handford, A. G. (1986). Television and other leisure activities. In T. H. Williams (Ed.), *The impact of television: A natural experiment in the community* (pp. 143–213). Orlando, FL: Academic Press.

Ziegert, K. A. (1983). The Swedish prohibition of corporal punishment: A preliminary report. *Journal of Marriage and the Family, 46,* 917–926.

Zirkel, P. A., & Reichner, H. E. (1987). Is loco parentis dead? *Phi Delta Kappan, 69,* 466–469.

Chapter 8

Parenting the Adolescent

Parenting Myth ■ Parenting the adolescent does not differ greatly from parenting the toddler or preschool child. The adolescent still needs the parent to provide the nurturance and control functions of parenting.

Test Your Knowledge ■ The following questions are designed to test your knowledge before reading the material in this chapter. Answers appear at the end of the chapter.

1 The age at which menstruation begins has gone unchanged in our society for decades. True or false?

2 Early-maturing adolescent males and females have clear advantages over late-maturing adolescents. True or false?

3 Researchers have found that boys were more peer oriented in the 1970s and girls were more peer oriented in the 1980s. True or false?

4 The double standard has broken down to the extent that female adolescents in committed relationships are expected to have sexual relationships. True or false?

5 A systems/dialectical process model of identity suggests that identity crises continue throughout one's lifetime rather than being an adolescent phenomenon. True or false?

6 American teenagers are more sexually active than European adolescents. True or false?

A dolescence is usually thought of as a period of development in which conflict with parents is the predominant image of the parent/child relationship. This view may not be consistent with recent research, which suggests that adolescents have similar value systems as their parents and good communications with and positive feelings about their relationships with their parents (Sebald, 1986). One can assume, however, that changes in adolescents relative to biological and social dimensions influence parenting in many ways. Flexible parents are able to change in reference to new situations and can deal with increasing complexity in the parent/child relationship.

The adolescent period appears to be broad and uneven, representing more than one dimension. For example, Erikson's (1963) psychosocial stage of development, **identity versus role confusion,** does not seem to characterize the first part of adolescent development. This heterogeneity has caused some researchers to suggest that there are two distinct divisions of adolescence: early adolescence, beginning at puberty and ending at about 18; and late adolescence, beginning at 18 and ending at 22 (Newman & Newman, 1991). These two periods are distinct and have different developmental tasks.

■ Early Adolescence (12–17)

When adolescence is viewed from the perspective of issues related to these two periods, it seems to be consistent with the biological and social changes during this period to group them according to Newman and Newman's suggestions. **Early adolescence** is dominated by the physical changes caused by the increase in sex hormones (Rice, 1989). The brain signals the pituitary glands to increase production of the female hormone estrogen and the male hormone androgen, which are present in both girls and boys. Boys produce more androgen and girls produce more estrogen, resulting in different developmental pathways.

Biological and Physical Development

One of the earliest observable aspects of early adolescence is the **growth spurt** that runs its course in about four years. Prior to the growth spurt in **puberty**—physical and sexual maturation between 10 and 14 years of age—boys and girls have comparable heights and weights. Girls reach puberty about two years before boys, beginning at about age 10, peaking at 11, and ending at about age 14. Boys, on the other hand, begin in their 11th year, peak at 13, and level off at about 15 years of age (Rice, 1989).

For girls, sexual maturation appears concomitantly with the growth spurt. For example, at about 9, light pubic hair appears, followed in the next year by changes in the size of the sex organs. The breast buds begin developing and are well formed by **menarche,** the first menstrual period. Researchers have found that although menarche is generally addressed in the mother/daughter relationship, girls receive preparation for hygiene but are not informed of the full meaning of the role of menstruation in sexual behavior (Logan, 1980). Menstruation seems to be a mixed bag for most girls. Because it occurs earlier than sexual development occurs in male peers, many females may have difficulty accepting it. Girls adjust better to menarche when they have been prepared both physically and mentally (Ruble & Brooks-Gunn, 1982).

Other physical changes in girls, such as increased body weight and the growth of hair on arms and legs, may present some concerns about body image. Of particular concern is weight. Many adolescent girls diet in an attempt to control what they fear is a weight problem. Their self-esteem may suffer as a result of not understanding normal body change (Ruble & Brooks-Gunn, 1982).

Maturation of girls, particularly menarche and the accompanying physical changes, appears to be occurring at younger ages in American society (Tanner, 1981). Researchers have found that early-maturing girls are at significant disadvantages in education and social relationships (Silbereisen, Petersen, Albrecht, & Kracke, 1989). They tend to score lower on standardized tests and make lower grades in school. Because they are more similar to older adolescents, they shun their own age groups and may be involved with deviant and antisocial behavior.

The growth spurt affects girls' bodies by broadening hip bones while shoulders tend to be the focal point in boys. Boys develop deeper voices and more muscle mass. Their height peak is reached, however, before their muscle mass peaks, leaving males prone to an awkward and gawky period, which is usually uncomfortable for them and may result in some loss of self-esteem (Carron & Bailey, 1974). Internal organs grow during early adolescence, resulting in greater physical capability for both sexes, but more pronounced in boys.

Boys, like girls, usually are not prepared for the changes occurring in the sexual organs. They may not have adequate information about their changing bodies. Parents tend to be an unreliable source of sex information, and the adequacy of sex education in schools depends on a number of other variables, such as who teaches it, how much is covered, and whether students are able to have discussion groups. In fact, anxiety tends to characterize the first experiences of ejaculation in boys (Marsiglio, 1988).

Other changes in boys may cause a variety of feelings. Voice change may give boys a sense of their growing masculinity in addition to the growth of hair on the legs, arms, and face. Boys may use shaving as a type of ritual to confirm their masculinity and to provide solid evidence for bragging about their appearance in general. Boys who develop ahead of schedule tend to be more popular and have higher self-esteem than those who develop more slowly (Carron & Bailey, 1974). Late-maturing boys, on the other hand, have the disadvantage of not portraying the masculine ideal at a time when one's appearance tends to be of elevated significance. Not only do these late-maturing boys have the disadvantage of not living up to an internal ideal, but peers may respond to them as if they were actually younger, giving objective credibility to their diminished status.

Researchers have attempted to determine if the impact of these differences in sexual development continues into adulthood. Generally, whether or not the advantages of early sexual development continue into adulthood depends on the circumstances. For example, some researchers have found that, in their 30s, early-maturing males are still more confident and sociable than their later-maturing counterparts. On the other hand, later-maturing males are more innovative and creative in dealing with adversity than are early-maturing males. In addition, early-maturing females who have a more difficult time adjusting during adolescence appear more self-directed in their 30s when compared with late-developing females. These findings suggest that the individual may contribute to his/her situation by adapting to an undesirable environmental situation (Sigelman & Shaffer, 1991). According to a systems perspective, the dialectic between the components of the individual's experience would be seen as more important than any one component of that experience, such as viewing biology as the most important.

Social Development

Peer Groups.   Adolescents tend to rely more on advice and companionship of a **peer group** than on a relationship with parents. Although friendships have been important since the early school-age period, in adolescence friendships take on a group quality. Those with similar interests tend to associate together. One's peer group may say much about particular attitudes about school, authority, parents, and other emerging social issues, such as the feminist movement or relationships with minorities. Frequent contact seems important to maintain one's status and association with the group. Loyalty to the group is viewed as a primary duty of the members of a particular peer group (Tedesco & Gaier, 1988).

In a longitudinal study of peer relationships in adolescent boys and girls, Sebald (1986) found that whereas boys were more peer oriented in the 1970s, girls surpassed boys in preference of peers over parents in the 1980s. Peer groups seem especially influential in certain areas, such as fashions and dating relationships, but not as influential in career or financial planning. This finding suggests that adolescents may value the peer group but also turn to other sources for appropriate guidance when needed. Successful adolescents are able to discriminate among their needs and use various sources to meet them rather than relying simply on the peer group. In turn, their parents are more available to them, making contact less stressful (Condry & Simans, 1974). Adolescents who feel rejected or abandoned by their parents develop low self-esteem and suffer depression (Robertson & Simons, 1989).

Dating and Sexual Relationships.   **Dating** and sexual relationships are important in the adolescent period. In early adolescence, dating may be related to anxiety and fear, which dissipates as a function of time and greater experience. Becoming sexually active may represent a number of discrete factors for adolescents. For example, sexual activity typically represents the maturing of sexual organs and the increase of sex hormones. Researchers, however, have found other factors important in the develop-

■ *Adolescents tend to prefer those who are similar to themselves in much the same way adults prefer to interact with others of similar social class, background, and interests.*

ment of sexual activity in adolescent girls and boys (Brooks-Gunn & Furstenberg, 1989). Parental attitudes and influence on social relationships and educational expectations are an important factor in whether or not adolescents initiate sexual behavior.

Although the term *sexual behavior* may have a variety of meanings, it is generally used to refer to sexual intercourse, or coitus. Necking or heavy petting may be practiced by many adolescents, but only a small group of adolescents have sexual intercourse on a regular basis. Research suggests that sexually active adolescents are less religious and attend church services infrequently or not at all (Thornton & Camburn, 1989).

Over the past several decades, adolescents have changed their attitudes about sexual activities. For example, they tend to believe that if there is affection in the

■ *The age at first sexual intercourse has been declining in recent years.*

relationship, sex is acceptable (Dreyer, 1982). This greater acceptance of sexual behavior within an affectionate relationship means that sexual activity as part of the relationship is expected. Consequently, today's adolescents tend not to believe in the old **double standard** that males can have multiple sex partners but females cannot. Although a promiscuous female may be judged more harshly than a promiscuous male, there is general acceptance that a female can and should have sexual relations within an intimate relationship. Her past sexual relationships are not generally a point of contention within the relationship. There is evidence, however, that much confusion still exists in the sexual behavior of adolescents.

Researchers have found that adolescents are involved at earlier ages in intimate sexual behavior than a few decades ago (Dreyer, 1982). Adolescents tend to progress through a sequence of sexual behaviors starting with kissing and ending with oral/genital contact. Researchers have found that first intercourse occurs at an earlier age for both males and females, although the change is greater for females than for males. By 1979 early-adolescent females were experiencing first sexual intercourse in record numbers.

Intellectual Development

Piaget (1972) characterized intellectual development of the early adolescent as **formal operations,** or when the individual begins to think more logically and rationally. Although younger children can reason in a concrete sense when the object is at hand, they are not able to think abstractly when the object is not directly observable. For example, adolescents can reason out a solution to a problem and select a course of action from a number of possible solutions. They can hypothesize about a problem, analyze possible solutions, foresee consequences, and determine a specific course of action based on this mental processing, which allows them to make more realistic educational and occupational plans for the future (Gillies, 1989).

This ability to perform formal operations does not develop all at once. Rather, there is evidence that over a period of a number of years the adolescent is developing these skills. Furthermore, particular abilities may not develop uniformly, but at various speeds and under different circumstances (Neimark, 1975). Although the early adolescent is capable of more logical and realistic thinking, he or she may be surprised, shocked, or angered that others have a different opinion. This egocentrism, however, begins to give way to an understanding that others may not share the same views. Accepting others' points of view and being able to adapt one's own view to accommodate others represents a mature development of formal operations (Piaget, 1972). This struggle about how one's own view of the world is similar to or varies from others' perceptions of the world and the response of others to one's views is an endeavor that continues into adulthood.

Newman and Newman (1991) discuss a number of factors that facilitate formal operations. First, different role relationships enhance formal operations and decrease egocentrism. An adolescent experiences various roles, which may necessitate taking different perspectives about the same situation. They may also learn the valuable lesson that what works in one situation may not work in another. Second, changing from middle school to high school may give adolescents a broader view of cultural differences and an appreciation that persons do not have to be alike. Third, the school curriculum exposes the adolescent to deductive forms of logic through a variety of courses.

Some **intellectual abilities** appear to be related to the timing of puberty in early adolescence. Females begin outperforming males on verbal tests while males begin outperforming females on visual/spatial abilities. Researchers have debated the reasons for such differences for some time. An interesting explanation has been proposed by Waber (1977), who concluded the early development of females may affect the process of specialization which takes place later. Early-maturing females would have less time for the brain to develop the specializations required for spatial performance. Waber found that late-maturing adolescents tend to have greater specialization of both sides of the brain than early-maturing adolescents. In addition, she found that both late-maturing males and females outperformed early-maturing females on various measurements of visual/spatial ability. Sanders and Soares (1986) found that these differences continue into late adolescence and early adulthood.

Intellectual ability measured by IQ tests tends to become more consistent, although some variability continues, in the adolescent years. Children who did well in grade school tend to continue doing well in middle school and high school. Adolescents with higher IQs tend to go to college in greater numbers than do those with lower IQs (Brody & Brody, 1976).

Late Adolescence (18–22)

Late adolescence is marked by physical and sexual maturity and the identity crisis described by Erikson (1963). The changes in American society over the past several decades tend to be most represented by the attitudes of adolescents and young adults. For example, the incidence of **premarital intercourse** has been increasing among female adolescents of higher socioeconomic and educational status (Zelnick & Kantner, 1980). Of 16-year-old females and males in 1979, the incidence of premarital intercourse was 38% and 69% respectively. This statistic for premarital intercourse tends to be increasing among younger adolescents so that the age of first intercourse is declining each year.

Psychosocial Development: Identity Versus Role Confusion

Erikson's (1963, 1968) theory held that adolescence was a period when the individual must come to terms with a consistent self-concept, or the integration of one's attitudes, beliefs, and behaviors. This search for a consistent view of oneself may involve questioning social conventions, determining a career choice, and solidifying one's religious, ethical, or moral beliefs. Although a gradual process is involved in developing one's identity, there is evidence that the search for identity is a painful experience for many adolescents.

The adolescent experiences the identity crisis because of a number of interlocking factors. For example, the rapid changes in physical and sexual development may affect the self-image. The change in physical functioning combined with the change in cognitive skills and abilities is closely associated with both the questioning of and the coming to resolution of one's identity. The adolescent is further immersed in identity issues by societal pressures to separate from the family of origin. This differentiation

■ *Identity issues are extremely important in adolescence.*

from the family is equivalent to forming an autonomous personality. In recent years, leaving home to go to college has aided the older adolescent in separating from the family. College can provide a place for adolescents to experiment with various roles and behaviors in resolving the identity crisis.

A number of studies have focused on the process of achieving identity. Marcia (1980) conducted the classic study on identity. In using a survey format, Marcia attempted to determine the degree to which the adolescent experiences a crisis or struggle in forming a resolution or commitment. He determined four categories of adolescence: identity achievement, a crisis has been experienced and a resolution achieved; foreclosure, no crisis experienced but the adolescent appears to have achieved a sense of commitment to particular beliefs similar to that of parents; moratorium, a crisis is being experienced without a resolution; and identity confusion, there may or may not be a crisis, but no commitment is demonstrated.

Researchers have found that older adolescents tend to be moving toward the moratorium category, whereas younger adolescents are not (Meilman, 1979). In fact, only 40% of college students and about 50% of 24-year-old young adults have reached identity achievement status. Other researchers have suggested that this process of identity formation is uneven and hardly a uniform occurrence (Kroger & Haslett, 1988). These findings suggest that this period may better be addressed in a systems/dialectical model than in a stage model. In turn, this suggests that one can view identity as a changing process related to a number of interdependent variables. The dialectical process would suggest that individuals at all ages may, in fact, question their identities and form new resolutions. Less attention is given to the later periods of identity crises because individuals are less prone to question basic premises, such as the meaning of life. Adults also generally support themselves through independent living and relate to others in a consistent manner. One could argue that divorce, extramarital affairs, change of jobs or careers, having children, and numerous other events in middle life result from a crisis in identity.

The systems/dialectical process also emphasizes the social embedment of the family in a particular culture. For example, an adolescent in an impoverished inner-city neighborhood may have a different identity process than an adolescent in an affluent suburb. One may represent an exaggerated attempt to belong characterized by gang membership, whereas the other may represent a period of crisis followed by a decision to enter a particular career.

The resolution to the identity crisis has a number of possibilities—some positive, others negative. Erikson (1959) referred to this negative outcome as **negative identity.** The goal of the resolution is not necessarily to arrive at a specific outcome but to resolve the crisis and uncertainty that one feels. The career criminal's identity may develop in the same way a future Nobel Prize winner's identity forms. The process is the same regardless of the outcome.

Identity confusion is somewhat more difficult to define. For example, the typical description of an individual in a state of identity confusion is that he/she cannot resolve the identity in a consistent manner. The adolescent is in a state of confusion in which a functional sense of self may not exist. A systems perspective of this dilemma is that the dialectical process of the resolution to the crisis is constantly taking place. Confusion is as legitimate an outcome as identity; neither would be viewed as the end product of the continuum. Contrary to the developmental process that would view a movement from foreclosure to confusion as regression (Waterman, 1982), a systems/dialectical process would view that, given the context of the individual, any outcome makes sense and is developmentally significant. Change the context, and one changes the outcome.

Differentiation from the Family of Origin

Differentiation from the family of origin is a developmental task of the adolescent family. Murray Bowen (1978) defined **differentiation** as the emotional state of not being controlled or affected by one's family. From Bowen's perspective, remaining in close contact with one's family of origin is essential. Only fully differentiated persons can be considered autonomous in their behaviors. When a person moves away or is not in close contact with the family of origin, this is an **emotional cutoff.** This attempt at differentiation by physical distance does not address the fact that differentiation is a psychological process. According to Bowen, emotional differentiation is the ability to remain in the eye of the hurricane without being emotionally affected.

Differentiation and Family Relationships.   The view of the family as an organism is an important feature of a systems perspective. A family, like an organism, has a distinct boundary that identifies it. In adolescence this boundary must be permeable enough to allow the adolescent to establish independence. Adolescents need understanding and room to develop their autonomy. Open and direct communication that leads to clear and direct expectations is related to positive outcomes in adolescent development (Kamptner, 1988).

Bonds with parents generally continue through this differentiation period. Differentiated adolescents are able to distinguish between their own and their parents' perspectives without feeling intruded on or neglected by parents. Adolescents are also engaged in creating relationships with other people, who can be viewed as surrogate family members. Many of these new relationships have a bonding and attachment similar to that in family relationships.

Adolescents who are able to successfully create a sense of self while remaining in close contact with family members have adequately differentiated from their family. Although many adolescents separate successfully, there are many adolescents for whom separation is quite a struggle. This other end of the continuum of separation–individuation may lead to pathological or maladjusted behavior. It is frequently characterized by hostile, defiant behavior, including alcohol and drug abuse, sexual promiscuity, a rejection of family and social norms for behavior, and in some cases, suicide.

Leaving home tends to be the major event when adolescents begin to function more autonomously. Going to college, joining the military, or getting a job and moving into an apartment seem to be important events related to living separately from the family. Parents have viewed leaving home as more closely associated with getting married than adolescents have, and stepfamilies view moving out as a sign of developing independence (Goldscheider & Goldscheider, 1989).

Early Leaving Home and Family Structure.   Leaving home appears to be related to a number of interrelated factors. Recently, researchers have found that the family structure may be an important component of the leaving-home phenomenon, particularly the specific timing of the event (White and Booth, 1985). Children in single-parent families and remarried families tend to leave home at an earlier age than children in intact families. These children have reported having to grow up so fast they missed out on childhood (Wallerstein, 1985). The major problem for adolescents occurs when there is a blurring of the boundaries between themselves and their custodial parent. In the single-parent family, these boundaries often become blurred because the custodial parent may use the adolescent as a confidant or support person.

Some researchers have suggested that separation–individuation of the adolescent is impaired in the single-parent family because of the lack of traditional division of labor (Smollar & Youniss, 1985). The father's traditional instrumental role sets standards for accomplishments, and the mother's expressive role offers acceptance and nurturance. After divorce or widowhood the mother is forced to play both her traditional role and the role of the absent father. The result is an overburdened mother who may be unable to meet either role adequately. Without a father, the adolescent must focus attention on the mother only for the process of individuation.

Although the timing of leaving home has been correlated with single-parent and remarried families, researchers have not adequately described the other forms of childhood living arrangements or other familial circumstances that occur (Aquilino, 1991). It is virtually unknown what effects the particular family form has on the leaving-home phenomenon.

Aquilino's (1991) review of the literature concluded that children growing up in stepfamilies, especially girls, would be more susceptible to leaving home early. Single-parent families, particularly those formed after a harsh divorce, would also produce children who would leave home early, more so for boys than girls. Likewise, Aquilino predicted living apart from both parents during the childhood years to be correlated with leaving home early. In addition, living in a relative's household, low socioeconomic status, and living situations in which a parent or relative wasn't present were predicted to be correlated with leaving home early.

The results of Aquilino's (1991) study, which included 5,322 subjects who participated in the National Survey of Families and Households (NSFH; Sweet, Bumpass, & Call, 1988) generally confirmed the predictions. For example, living in a stepfamily greatly increased the probability of leaving home early, more so for girls than boys. More than two-thirds of girls 19 years of age or younger from stepfamilies, compared to 50% of girls in intact families, left home prior to 19 years of age. Living in a single-parent family following divorce increased the probability for leaving home early, whereas living in a single-parent family from birth did not increase the probability. In addition, adoption, living with a nonparent, living in a relative's home, and low socioeconomic status were correlated positively with leaving home early.

The specific pathways out of the home for nonintact structures compared to intact structures was much increased (Aquilino, 1991). "Living in a single-parent family after marital disruption, a stepfamily, adopted family, or a nonparental living situation significantly increased the likelihood of choosing residential independence as the pathway for first home-leaving" (p. 1006). Generally, family structure had little influence on leaving home for marriage, joining the military, or going to school, except for living in stepfamilies, which was higher in all family forms associated with leaving home early.

The results of Aquilino's (1991) study have implications for gender. Males were much more likely to leave home early to go to college or join the military, whereas females were more likely to leave home early for marriage or residential independence. In addition, living with parents in a relative's home and nonparental living arrangements were associated with leaving home early.

In a remarried family, a reason for the adolescent's early home leaving may be explained from the standpoint that the developmental process in the remarried family is to form cohesion and unity while the adolescent is attempting to separate and live more autonomously. The adolescent may also be unwilling to relinquish any of the ascribed parental roles to the stepparent, thus decreasing the likelihood of a smooth transition to the stepparent status. To some degree the adolescent may continue to grieve about the loss of the family and the noncustodial parent. The loyalty to the biological noncustodial parent may take on a particularly attractive appearance. At the same time, the stepparent may exert more pressure in an attempt to increase bonding in the stepfamily. This scenario may be one of many leading to negative outcomes in the adolescent's differentiation from the family.

Researchers have found that other variables may also affect the time of leaving home for adolescents. For example, parents' educational level, birth order, and geographic location are other variables related to early leaving home for adolescents (Bianchi, 1987). Girls typically leave home sooner than boys in most familial situations. Furthermore, a subtle pressure is exerted within the family on members at certain points, suggesting that leaving home is expected at this time. Researchers have also argued that living near or in an urban area may affect early leaving home of adolescents because these areas generally are centers for educational and occupational opportunities (Young, 1987).

A Canadian study attempted to determine factors related to early leaving home (Mitchell, Wister, & Burch, 1989). Like other recent studies, the style or type of family form was considered a major emphasis. In addition, the study was concerned with the number of children in the family, the region in which the family resided, the family's socioeconomic level, and the sex of the adolescent. The researchers concluded that family form, intact versus single parent or remarried, was a significant factor in predicting the early departure of the adolescent from the home. Other findings that support earlier studies include a significant finding for sex in that females were found to leave home significantly earlier than boys. Furthermore, urban regions were found to be more associated with early leaving home than were rural regions. The researchers speculated that the urban regions offered greater opportunities for education and alternate living arrangements. Neither the educational level of the parents nor the socioeconomic level of the family appeared to be related to early leaving home.

In another study on early-leaving-home patterns of adolescents, Goldscheider and Goldscheider (1989) were particularly interested in the intergenerational transmission of leaving home early. Using data from the High School and Beyond (HSB) senior cohort collected in 1980, these researchers concluded that families tend to push boys out of the home first rather than girls—a finding that contrasts with what

■ *For many, the lesson of leaving home is part of the process of differentiation from the family of origin.*

other researchers have found. In stepfamilies, adolescents reporting few religious beliefs tend to have the highest incidences of early home leaving. Early leaving home in stepfamilies was believed to be related to encouragement to marry at the traditional age and to less intergenerational closeness.

Moral Development

Kohlberg's (1964) theory of moral development has been discussed earlier but needs to be reemphasized in reference to adolescent development. Kohlberg contended that moral development in adolescence is qualitatively different from the previous periods of development. The conventional level of moral reasoning, roughly the early adolescent period from ages 10 to 18, is defined as the adherence to the rule structure and respect for authority. The postconventional stage of moral reasoning, which does not appear until after age 18, represents reasoning at the highest level. It includes both the acknowledgment of relativism and the adherence to a belief system of moral principles.

Researchers have found that the moral reasoning of an individual tends to occur in a stage-type sequence in which a particular stage is dominant and the individual reasons at that stage or below rather than at a higher stage (Walker, 1982). Although different cultures tend to follow a sequence in moral reasoning in that parents reason at higher levels than children do (Colby & Kohlberg, 1987), it also appears that in some nonindustrial cultures individuals do not attain the same level as in industrial cultures.

The level of moral reasoning appears to be directly related to educational attainment. For example, with each additional year of education researchers have found that moral reasoning has increased (Rest & Thoma, 1985). Compared to those who do not attend college and those who drop out, college graduates have higher levels of moral reasoning. A systems perspective emphasizes continuing exposure to complex and stimulating ideas and the dialectical nature of integrating these ideas and experiences. The process of arriving at resolutions to the continual set of propositions moves one toward greater complexity in reasoning and thinking.

Sex and the Adolescent

It is clear from research findings that sexual behavior among adolescents not only has increased but also has become more problematic. Family relationships appear to be an important factor predicting early irresponsible sexual behavior. Religious middle-class adolescents who were reared in a stable family environment and who received adequate sex education tend to engage in responsible sexual behavior (Forste & Heaton, 1988). Some researchers have found that boys and girls are affected differently by familial relationships. For example, boys who experience the divorce of parents in adolescence tend to be more sexually active than those from intact families, whereas the more sexually active girls tend to be those who were raised by single mothers rather than those affected by family disruption per se (Newcomer & Udry, 1987).

Family Communication and Sexual Attitudes/Behaviors of Adolescents.   In recent years, a number of articles have been published that investigate the relation between family communication and sexual attitudes and behaviors of adolescents. Moore, Peterson, and Furstenberg (1986) found that when the family had traditional attitudes and discussed sexuality with their adolescents, only girls had lower incidences of sexual activity. On the other hand, in families with traditional attitudes, family communication about sexual behavior tended to increase sexual behavior for adolescent boys. These researchers concluded that family attitudes and gender are significant factors in the sexual behavior of adolescents.

In another study, the researcher concluded that parental attitudes about sexual behavior are an important variable in analyzing adolescent sexual behavior (Fisher, 1989). Parents who held liberal attitudes about sexual behavior and talked to their adolescents about sexual behavior tended to influence their daughters' increased sexual activity but not their sons'. Because a lack of consensus appears to exist between parents and their children regarding the actual information transmitted between them, Fisher (1989) recommends that data be collected from both parents and adolescents.

Religious beliefs and affiliation have been found in a substantial number of studies to be correlated with lower sexual activity among adolescents. Most researchers have assumed that the direction of the influence was the effects of religious beliefs on the adolescent rather than a reciprocal effect (Thornton & Camburn, 1989).

Although a variety of religious beliefs exist concerning sexual behavior, most denominations prohibit indiscreet sexual behavior, including premarital intercourse and extramarital affairs (Thornton & Camburn, 1989). Some churches require youths to abstain from sexual relationships before marriage, whereas others emphasize the need to make mature and rational judgments. Catholic and fundamental Protestant denominations tend to have more prohibition against sexual activity than do nonfundamental churches. Adolescents who attend services often and value Christian doctrines may be less likely to engage in sexual intercourse than adolescents who do not value religious attitudes.

A study by Thornton and Camburn (1989) attempted to develop a causal model to estimate the reciprocal effects of religious beliefs on the adolescent and the adolescent's effect on religious expression. These researchers concluded that as expected religious beliefs influence sexual behavior: the more religious adolescents have more conservative attitudes and participate less in sexual activity. A strong **intergenerational effect,** particularly expressed in the mother's religious and sexual beliefs, was influential in the adolescent's religious and sexual beliefs. Furthermore, the adolescent's religious participation has a greater effect on determining sexual attitudes than does religious affiliation. It appears that the religious content of all churches insulates adolescents from premarital sexual activity. If adolescents change their beliefs about religion, it becomes clear that they modify their relationship with their church. Finally, Thornton and Camburn explored a generation gap because they had found differences between religious attitudes and sexual beliefs of mothers and their adolescent children, both boys and girls. Mothers were much more likely to attend church and value religious beliefs and believe in sexual abstinence than either their sons or daughters. This generational gap probably reinforces and is reinforced by religious beliefs.

Researchers have found that teenage girls from single-parent families are more likely to have sexual experiences prior to marriage. Researchers have also found that adolescent girls with older brothers have earlier sexual contact (Rodgers, 1983). A study by Miller and Bingham (1989) found that adolescent girls from single-parent families were more likely to have sexual intercourse than girls from intact families. This effect was diminished when race, social class, age, and religion were taken into account. The effect was still found to be significant when placed into a regression analysis. This study found no significant effect for early sexual experience for adolescent girls with younger brothers.

Adolescents and Unmarried Pregnancy.   In the United States about 1 million teenage girls become pregnant each year (see Table 8.1). As a statistic, the number of births to unmarried teenage girls is alarming. Social support programs to aid such

Table 8.1 ■ **Adolescents and Unmarried Pregnancy**

- In 1960, 224,000 births were to unwed mothers.

- In 1986, 879,000 births were to unwed mothers.

- In 1987, adolescents accounted for 1,101,588 pregnancies. Of those:
  121,128 were miscarriages
  469,409 (43%) were aborted
  511,505 were born alive
  281,000 were born to unwed mothers
  In that same year, 230,050 pregnant adolescents married hastily before the birth.

Source: U.S. Bureau of the Census, 1989.

families are expensive and draining to the taxpayer. The problem to society created by irresponsible sexual behavior, although serious, is not the most difficult. The most serious problem is that many of the children reared by teenage mothers, especially boys, will have difficulty in school and in relating to others (Furstenberg, Brooks-Gunn, & Chase-Lansdale, 1989). These negative outcomes can be reduced somewhat if the mother is provided with adequate prenatal care, child care, parent education, and job training.

Some researchers have uncovered interesting data about teenage pregnancies in America. American teenagers are no more sexually active than European teenagers but appear to differ on the use of contraception (Furstenberg, Brooks-Gunn, & Chase-Lansdale, 1989). Cultural and racial differences exist in incidences of premarital pregnancies. For example, about 50% of all black female teenagers become pregnant out of wedlock (Conger, 1988). In addition, some evidence suggests that some adolescent females may desire pregnancy to serve basic psychological rather than sexual needs (Stark, 1986). The pregnancy may give these teenagers attention from others, or help them feel worthwhile or loved. When this behavior is accepted within a culture, there may be a type of unspoken cultural imperative to engage in such behavior.

Little research has been conducted on teenage fathers. Generally, researchers have found that the father does not marry the mother but does tend to have frequent contact after the baby is born (Robinson & Barret, 1985). Teenage fathers also have unrealistic expectations about having a child and the resultant changes in their lives. Consequently, the more problems encountered by these fathers, the more likely they are to disappear and withdraw even cursory support.

A Systems Perspective of Teenage Pregnancy. A systems perspective of teenage pregnancy using a dialectical model begins with an understanding of the relationship between the partners. The adolescents in question must be viewed as getting some type of "reward" for having a child out of marriage. The pregnancy must be viewed as an outcome in a particular relationship that emerged over time, being shaped by both partners (Sigelman & Shaffer, 1991).

In addition to the interpersonal dimension of the relationship, the social and cultural influences cannot be ignored. For example, there are many variables to consider in discussing teenage pregnancy. Adolescents in contemporary society are inundated with sexual messages implicit in the music they listen to, the clothes they buy, and the relationships with their peers. While having greater societal sexual pressure, adolescents are supervised less today than in the past. Both parents are typically involved in the work force leaving adolescents at home alone (Sigelman & Shaffer, 1991).

Another factor affecting today's adolescents is early sexual maturity. Teenagers have better diets and health than a few decades ago, resulting in a biological determination to early sexual maturity. Those who have poor diets or are affected by some disorders, such as anorexia nervosa, mature later. Undernourished girls reach menarche later and may cease menstruation after they have begun, and undernourished boys may produce less healthy sperm than their well-fed peers (Frisch & McArthur, 1974). Early maturity coupled with increased messages to engage in sexual activity greatly increases the possibility for pregnancy. On the other hand, most of these teenagers are not emotionally mature enough to parent a child or even to be engaged in a protracted sexual relationship (Sigelman & Shaffer, 1991).

These social, personal, and biological dimensions of development create conflicts within the individual. Adolescents will attempt to reduce the conflict by engaging in some behavior. They may resolve the issue by engaging in risky sexual behavior to convince themselves that they are mature enough to handle a pregnancy. Other adolescents may resolve the conflict in a quite different way, namely, by using contraception. Adolescents who postpone pregnancy may be resolving the conflict through consideration of long-term goals, such as careers, which might be compromised through irresponsible sexual behavior (Sigelman & Shaffer, 1991).

On the other hand, poor or disadvantaged youths in inner-city areas may not have the option of a career waiting for them. Many face unemployment, lower health standards, and poor education. Although the desire for a better way of life may be present, having children at an earlier age may be the best option. The typical adolescent girl in the inner city will have familial support for child care, which will make it possible for her to get a job or return to school. Adolescents who give birth may in fact be using an adaptive skill to deal with a difficult environment (Sigelman & Shaffer, 1991).

Another problem correlated with adolescents is **sexually transmitted diseases.** Of particular concern is the contracting and spreading of Acquired Immune Deficiency Syndrome (AIDS). Some researchers have found that adolescents know few basic facts about AIDS, such as who is more likely to contract it (Price, Desmond, & Kukulka, 1985), while other researchers have found that the knowledge about AIDS is inconsistent (DiClemente, Zorn, & Temoshok, 1986). In the latter study, only 60% of the respondents knew that the risk in contracting AIDS could be decreased by using a condom. In another study, only 15% of the sexually active respondents reported that they had changed their sexual behavior because of AIDS. Of those who had changed their behavior, the majority reported that they had become more selective of sexual partners.

This apparent lack of behavioral change in response to the AIDS epidemic may be related to the adolescent's view of indestructibility. They are not ready to take responsibility for their sexual activity and, consequently, deny the risk involved in indiscriminate sexual behavior (Keeling, 1988). There is some evidence, however, that adolescents may be subconsciously influenced by AIDS to establish long-term relationships (Hirschorn, 1986). The benefit might be that while they are still sexually active, they may engage in sex with fewer partners, thus reducing their chance of acquiring the disease.

■
Parent/Child Relationship

The parent/child relationship in adolescence has received little attention in the literature relative to the attention given to the infant and childhood periods (Grinder, 1982). To further complicate this issue, the extant literature has focused on behavior problems rather than normal development of the adolescent. Although this period can be problematic, researchers have found that the relationship between adolescents and parents is generally good and supportive (Offer & Offer, 1974).

Parenting Tasks

Parents may find that relationship issues in this phase of parenting are quite different from those in previous periods. The increased physical maturity of the adolescent, coupled with intellectual development and social competence, makes parenting a much different activity. In contrast to parenting the school-age child, when the major task was to provide adequate rules and expectations for behavior, the adolescent period demands a shift in **parenting tasks,** specific parenting behaviors, that can be summed up as the need to let the adolescent leave home appropriately. All parental concerns about peer relationships, grades, chores, and communication can be viewed as an effort to let the child learn to function independently. Of course, some parents have difficulty allowing children to leave home, which will be discussed in detail later in the chapter.

Today's teenager must confront many different choices regarding friends, the use of alcohol and drugs, and sexual behavior. In the 1940s and 1950s, adolescents had social models of accepted behavior and choices were more straightforward. Incidences of premarital sex were much lower than today, and such consequences as teenage pregnancies were minimal. In three decades, the situation of adolescents has changed to the degree that no clear-cut choices exist for any decision. In the need to try out new roles, many adolescents engage in behaviors that their parents find disturbing because parents do not perceive these new behaviors leading to greater responsibility and maturity. Consequently, parent/child relationships may be strained with constant turmoil and conflict.

Consultant.   The major parenting task is that of consultant. A consultant may provide suggestions and options but not decisions. Some parents find the role of consultant too narrowly defined and leaving too much room for the adolescent to make faulty decisions. These parents are not concerned about decisions their children make so long as those decisions are similar to their own thinking and beliefs.

Substance abuse is a major concern for most parents. About 50% of adolescents report regular alcohol use. Drug abuse, affecting far fewer adolescents, has been correlated with one's peer group and with the style of discipline the parent employs (Coombs & Landsverk, 1988). Other family variables associated with drug use are the degree of parental affection, involvement, and concern about the adolescent (Hundleby & Mercer, 1987). Researchers have found that the occasional use of drugs reflects peer-group pressure, whereas heavy use and abuse of drugs reflects an emotional problem (Newcomb & Bentler, 1989).

Although some parents feel less concerned about the use of alcohol, adolescent use of alcohol can be potentially more problematic than illegal drugs. Researchers have found, however, that drinking patterns of adolescents tend to represent similar drinking patterns of parents (Barnes, Farrell, & Cairns, 1986). Moderate use of alcohol by parents tends to be correlated with appropriate alcohol use by adolescents, whereas either abstinence or heavy drinking tends to be related to alcohol abuse in adolescents.

Anticipatory Guidance.   While it was noted earlier that parents would do a better job of parenting if they knew about developmental issues and expectations at each stage of development of the child, it must not be forgotten that adolescents need special attention regarding developmental issues. Whether theirs is a traditional or nontraditional family, parents should be informed about the adolescent period of development. They could benefit from getting together with other parents in skill-development groups and discussing how to improve problem-solving and family communication skills (Daniels, 1990). Self-help groups may be one way to disseminate information to parents of adolescents. Other ways include community lecture series, programs at churches, and school newsletters.

Making information available to different family structures, including single-parent families and stepfamilies, may help these families make better adjustments. The normative changes affecting adolescent development, though somewhat hidden in traditional families, may be completely obscured in nontraditional families. When parents do not know what to expect in this life-cycle stage, the myth of turbulence and chaos may be the only path expected by parents.

▪ Problematic Adolescent Behavior

As mentioned earlier, a major problem in adolescence can be substance abuse, particularly alcohol abuse. Researchers have connected family dynamics with the growing problems of adolescent alcohol and drug abuse (Spotts & Shontz, 1985). An adolescent with an alcohol or drug problem has been described as coming from a family with rigid and enmeshed boundaries (Cleveland, 1981). These rigid families prevent the normal separation/differentiation that is necessary for the adolescent.

Separation/differentiation, as discussed earlier, is the key developmental issue for adolescents. The adolescent must separate from the family while maintaining attachment. Likewise, the parent/adolescent relationship must change to accommodate this increased independence in the adolescent. Adolescent development, like child development, is a process in which individual and family systems change and mutually affect each other. The family system must be viewed as an important part of individual development (Bartle & Sabatelli, 1989).

The family systems literature describes a continuum with well-differentiated families at one end and enmeshed families at the other end (Bowen, 1978). In **well-differentiated** families, interpersonal distance is regulated in such a way that members are enhanced in the dual endeavors of establishing autonomy and connectedness. In this way, the adolescent's development is enhanced through both behavior that leads to greater autonomy and self-sufficiency and behavior that leads to greater connectedness with others. On the other hand, families that require separateness at the expense of togetherness, or vice versa, are considered **enmeshed** in the clinical literature. These families typically have members who are not functional, such as alcohol or drug abusers.

Conflict in the marital relationship is often related to the development of adolescent problems (Haley, 1980). Marital conflict may be related to different philosophies of parenting. One parent may be lenient to offset the perceived rigidity of the other. A repetitive cycle is set in motion with an ongoing power struggle to gain an insider position with the adolescent.

Even after divorce, the increased drug and alcohol use make the adolescent the center of attention in symbolically keeping the parents involved in his/her behavior. The drug or alcohol problem may serve the purpose of getting the parents to discuss the problem, which they otherwise would never have done. Although containing the substance problem is the first thing that must be done, it is necessary to reorganize the family structure so that the underlying problems can be addressed (Quinn, Kuehl, Thomas, Joanning, & Newfield, 1989).

Bartle and Sabatelli (1989) attempted to find a relationship between the level of functioning of the family and the level of differentiation of the adolescent. They hypothesized that, in well-differentiated families, adolescents would be able to handle the peer pressure to abuse alcohol or drugs. They concluded that the level of differentiation in the family tends to mediate individual development. Specifically, the best predictor of individual identity is the level of differentiation of the opposite-sex parent in both males and females.

**Box
8.1**

■■■■■■■■■■

Do Adolescents in Single-Parent and Remarried Families Have Greater Difficulty in Differentiating Than Adolescents in Intact Families?

Adolescents from single-parent families display a maturity not found in adolescents from intact families (Daniels, 1990). Generally, adolescents view this early adult responsibility as positive. The key factor for the adolescent in single-parent families is to receive nurturance and support from an available parent. The process of differentiation is enhanced in single-parent families when the noncustodial parent is available and active in parenting. Without the involvement of the noncustodial parent, the custodial parent may develop a relationship that is too close to the adolescent, compromising the hierarchical structure in the family.

In remarried families or stepfamilies, opposite forces tend to pull on the adolescent simultaneously. For example, concomitant with differentiation is the opposite force to bond together and form a **cohesive** unit. A typical scenario is a closer bond with the biological parent and some distance from or conflict with the stepparent. Barriers, such as lack of closely defined roles or the inability to form a close bond with the stepchild, may increase family disharmony. Likewise, these barriers that prevent closeness may also inhibit appropriate differentiation. Differentiation may be hampered by displaced anger at and conflict with the stepparent regarding the process of separating from the family.

Some gender differences were found in the preceding study. For example, males' attitudes toward drinking and actual drinking behavior appear less related to the level of family differentiation than do those of females. Females were found to experience more negative consequences to drinking both when they perceived their parents' relationship to be less differentiated and when their reciprocal relationship with their mother was less differentiated (Bartle & Sabatelli, 1989).

Much adolescent problematic behavior appears to be related to drug and alcohol use, which in turn tends to be related to a number of factors specifically identified with the family. For example, the consequences of divorce have been delineated for children in a number of research studies, but the specific impact of divorce on adolescent drug or alcohol abuse has not been thoroughly researched.

In a longitudinal study of the effects of divorce on adolescent drug and alcohol abuse, researchers found that substance use among adolescents from divorced families increased more during the five-year period of the study than it did among adolescents from intact families (Needle, Su, & Doherty, 1990). In comparing adolescents and preadolescents, or children, the researchers found that overall drug use was greater for the adolescent group from divorced families than for the child group from divorced families, although the difference was not significant. The researchers concluded that adolescents whose parents are divorced experience greater propensity for substance abuse than do children whose parents are divorced. The adolescent's use of alcohol and drugs may be one way to cope with the trauma of divorce and the reduced relationship resources available.

Other findings included a significant difference in gender. Both adolescent boys and younger boys were found to increase drug and alcohol use as a consequence of divorce, whereas girls' substance use was not affected by divorce. Girls' drug and alcohol use increased, however, when their custodial parent remarried. On the other hand, remarriage appeared to have a positive effect on boys in that adolescent boys whose mothers remarried reported fewer substance-use problems than boys whose mothers remained unmarried (Needle, Su, & Doherty, 1990).

The literature in the past decade suggests that emerging midlife issues for parents may affect the parent/child relationship as much as the changing adolescent (Galinsky, 1980; Nachman, 1979; Peters, 1985). This period of life has been referred to as **middlescence,** that period of time in adulthood when the real and the ideal confront one another. It is the last-ditch effort for the individual to achieve idealized goals before a forced resignation to the fact that he/she must give up the childhood dreams of success. At the same time parents are dealing with the uncertainty in the lives of their adolescents, they are also having to deal with uncertainty in their own lives. These issues, the adolescent acting-out behavior and the parents' uncertainty about their own future, are confounded by being merged together. When the parent explodes to the adolescent about coming home too late, the real issue may be the worry over recognizing his/her own limitations.

■ **Adolescent Depression**

Although not always considered a problem, **adolescent depression** has emerged as a major problem in the past few years (Simons & Murphy, 1985). Until quite recently, depression was considered normal for the adolescent period because of the adolescent's identity confusion and groping for adult status. Recent researchers have found not only that adolescents become depressed but also that they tend to continue into adulthood with major depressive episodes (Kandel & Davies, 1986). This link of depressive symptoms beginning in adolescence and continuing into adulthood may help open the door for future research into the familial aspects of depression.

Table 8.2 ■ Adolescents and Suicide

- About one-half million adolescents attempt suicide every year.
- About 6,000 adolescents succeed in killing themselves each year.
- Boys succeed at much higher rates, but girls are three times more likely to attempt it.
- Fourteen percent of all adolescents have attempted suicide.
- Suicide of white adolescents is up in recent years.
- Ninety percent of adolescents who attempt suicide have known someone else who attempted.

Source: National Center for Health Statistics, 1988.

Adolescent suicide has been researched in recent years. In the past decade, adolescent suicide accounted for 14% of all female suicides and 20% of all male suicides (U.S. Department of Health and Human Services, 1983). These figures compare with an overall adolescent suicide rate of about 5% in the 1960s. The reasons for this increase in the adolescent suicide rates in the United States are now being studied by more researchers (see Table 8.2).

Initially, most research on adolescent depression used a cognitive model, assuming that depressive symptoms resulted from a distorted view of the self or of the world. Most researchers found that only feelings of low self-esteem are related to adolescent depression, not a distorted view of the world (Robertson & Simons, 1989). Generally, researchers have connected depressive symptoms to familial relationships or traumatic childhood events. Although most studies have been retrospective, a recent prospective study found that parental loss or rejection during adolescence is related to depression at 19 years of age (Lefkowitz & Tesing, 1984, cited in Robertson & Simons, 1989).

Studies of depression in children corroborate the findings of adolescent research (Robertson & Simons, 1989). Specifically, it has been found that depressed children have rejecting and uncaring parents. Researchers have suggested that the connection between depression and parental rejection is mediated through feelings of self-esteem and self-worth. When the **self-esteem** variable is controlled for, the link between depression and suicide is eliminated.

The relationship with parents may be one of the most significant relationships for the elimination or containment of depressive symptoms in adolescents. When adolescents do not have parents to confide in, they may be much more susceptible to depression. Parental rejection may not be as important a variable affecting depression in adolescents as not having a parent as a confidant.

A study by Robertson and Simons (1989) attempted to develop a model for adolescent depression. The first part of the model assumed that parental rejection was correlated with depression. A number of family variables were related to adolescent depression, including high parental control and family conflict. Once controls were introduced, only parental rejection was significantly related to adolescent depression. The relation between self-esteem and depression was not as strong as predicted. In fact, self-esteem did not predict future depression. The researchers concluded that while self-esteem and depression are related, self-esteem seems to be related to particular events in the present and, as such, is not an enduring trait; rather, self-esteem varies over time from high to low, depending on the circumstances. In the face of some crisis or depression, self-esteem would be expected to reflect the present circumstance. A reduction in self-esteem would be correlated with depressive symptoms.

Family Portrait   ■■■■■■■■■■

B ob and Lisa Smith have been married for almost 20 years. They have two children, a 16-year-old boy and a daughter 10 years of age. During the past year the son, Rob, has developed problems at school and has become increasingly noncompliant at home. He has worked some evenings and weekends at a drugstore where he is able to make spending money.

The major parenting issues have been Rob's frequent curfew violations and his lack of respect for rules and regulations at home. Rob has begun wearing his hair too long for his parents' liking, playing loud music even at night, and refusing to accompany the family to church. In school, his performance declined from a straight "A" student to failing most of his subjects. This change in Rob's behavior seemed sudden and unexplainable by his parents, who were at a complete loss for what to do.

A crisis occurred when Rob wanted to go to a rock concert in a different city and afterwards spend the weekend with a friend. The parents objected to his spending the weekend away from home because they suspected the friend was using drugs. Although they had never caught Rob with drugs, the father had found empty beer cans and the butt of a hand-rolled cigarette in his car. Rob perceived that his parents were intruding in his life and threatened to leave home if they continued to harass him.

Although most clinicians or child experts would stop at this point in gathering information, other family information is useful in understanding Rob's behavior. For example, Bob admitted to a drinking problem early in the marriage that was severe enough for Lisa to take the children and leave until Bob got help. After a three-month separation and joining Alcoholics Anonymous, Bob and Lisa reconciled and Bob has never touched alcohol again. Soon after the reconciliation, Bob joined a fundamentalist church and has been very involved in church work. Although Lisa joined the church with Bob, she has never been very involved and frequently has stayed home while he forced the children to attend church with him.

Over the past year, Lisa has been unhappy in the marriage and has considered divorce. She reported a brief affair during the past year with her work supervisor. Bob claims to have no anger at Lisa about the affair and says that he prayed about it and forgave her. He also disclosed to her that he had an affair during the time when he was drinking heavily. Lisa does not believe he has forgiven her because he has brought it up in arguments about Rob.

Bob and Lisa frequently argue about differences in parenting. Lisa thinks Bob is too rigid and harsh, while Bob thinks Lisa is too lenient. Each has tried to make up for the other's perceived failure in parenting with the result that Bob has become more demanding while Lisa has become more permissive. These differences are exaggerated because Bob frequently works at night and Lisa works during the day. The work schedule places Lisa in more direct contact with Rob to control his behavior, specifically when he is wanting to go out or do something he is not allowed to do. Bob sets certain limits on Rob's behavior but is not there to enforce them. On the other hand, Lisa is there with Rob but also feels the limits are too strict and gives in to Rob's demands. Bob blames Lisa for allowing Rob to "run all over her." Lisa attacks Bob for not being at home and accuses him of not really caring for the family. Rob attempts to avoid his father by waiting until he is at work and asking Lisa for permission to do forbidden activities.

Compare and Contrast

Addressing this case from the four perspectives would find some differences and some similarities. Patterson (1976), for example, using the behavioral perspective, would not be particularly interested in the history of the marital relationship or the family dynamics, except in devising a strategy to control Rob's behavior. In terms of Rob's choice of friends, letting the behavior run its own course would be suggested. Patterson would point out to Bob and Lisa that Rob had a right to select his own friends. In fact, he had a right to do poorly in school or drop out if he desired. Instead of forbidding certain relationships from occurring, Bob and Lisa might be encouraged to invite the friend into the home for meals and time with the family. This exposure could have a number of different outcomes, but a behaviorist would view all outcomes as more positive than the negative consequences of forbidding the friendship.

A behaviorist would see the school problem as ultimately a problem that Rob would have to face himself. The parents might place some contingencies on the use of the automobile or his outside work for spending money if his grades fell below a certain point. They would also be encouraged to discuss the problem openly with Rob and be clear in their communication.

An Adlerian perspective would focus on letting Rob know how the parents felt about his friends while not directly interfering in his relationship with them (Dreikurs & Soltz, 1964). The parents would do nothing to encourage the friendship, such as have the friend over for dinner, and would want Rob to come to the conclusion on his own that the friend is a loser and drug abuser. The school problem would be handled by letting Rob know their wishes for him but not trying to control or force him to stay in school. Since Rob is old enough to drop out of school legally, the parents should let him take responsibility for his own behavior.

Thomas Gordon (1970), who developed Parent Effectiveness Training (PET), would be concerned with who should take responsibility for the problem. How Rob performs in school and the long-range effect of not performing well would be Rob's responsibility, not the parents'. Bob should talk to Rob and attempt to come to a solution in which they could all agree. Bob would be encouraged to turn some of the decisions over to Rob and not make them himself. Both parents would be instructed on sending I-messages and using active listening.

A systems perspective of this family would vary from the other perspectives in a number of ways. For example, it would consider highly relevant the fact that Bob and Lisa are unhappy in their marriage. This conflict has appeared in a number of circumstances in parenting Rob. Their undermining of each other's parenting has not contributed to a successful outcome in controlling Rob's behavior. Furthermore, they must deal with Lisa's recent affair and Bob's obvious anger in order to function better as parents. Another bit of relevant information is Bob's former alcohol abuse and his plunge into a religious belief system that seems as addictive and dysfunctional as the alcohol addiction. It can be assumed that the issues surrounding the separation subsequent to the reconciliation have not been completely resolved.

A systems specialist might conclude that boundaries in the family are confused in that Lisa and Rob have a closer relationship than Lisa and Bob. When Lisa sides with Rob, she is guilty of forming a cross-generational alliance with Rob. Family rules perpetuate the family dynamics by making it very difficult for Lisa or Bob to act differently. The family functions in a state of homeostasis whereby Rob's behavior maintains the things the way they are.

Other considerations must also be addressed, such as Bob's work schedule. He has blamed Lisa for Rob's behavior getting out of hand but is never at home to be involved himself. Perhaps the work schedule is a way for Bob and Lisa to avoid intimacy in the marriage. Rob's behavior may be a misguided way for Bob and Lisa to maintain a relationship without dealing with the loss of intimacy and betrayal they both must feel in the relationship.

A systems perspective would focus initially on the marital dyad. Getting Bob and Lisa to come to a consensus about their parenting, or at least not interfering with each other's parenting, would be important. Bob's own addictive tendencies would need to be explored, specifically in how these tendencies contribute to his rigid response to Rob's alcohol behavior. Getting Bob to respond more directly to these issues may prevent some of the blurring of boundaries noted in this family.

■■■■■■■■■■■

Parenting Proposition

Parenting the adolescent should be done with regard to the reciprocal influences of peer relationships, cultural influences, the parents' changing environment, and the adolescent's developing awareness of taking responsibility.

Answers to "Test Your Knowledge"

1. F　　4. T
2. F　　5. T
3. T　　6. F

Key Concepts

identity versus role confusion

early adolescence

growth spurt

puberty

menarche

peer group

dating

double standard

formal operations

gender differences in
   intellectual ability

late adolescence

premarital intercourse

negative identity

differentiation

emotional cutoff

leaving home

intergenerational effect

systems perspective of
   teenage pregnancy

sexually transmitted diseases

parenting tasks

substance abuse

well-differentiated families

enmeshed families

family cohesion

middlescence

adolescent depression

self-esteem

Study Questions

1 Discuss the growth spurt in early adolescence in both males and females. How is the growth spurt related to personal and social development?

2 Discuss the onset of menarche in adolescent girls. What factors contribute to adjustment for girls during this time?

3 Discuss the consequences of early and late sexual maturing in adolescents. How does it affect peer relationships and dating?

4 Discuss the development of formal operations in adolescents. What are the differences in intellectual functioning in adolescent girls and boys?

5 Discuss the concept of identity versus role confusion.

6 Explain the concept of differentiation. What characterizes mature differentiation? What does the concept of emotional cutoff refer to?

7 What does the concept of intergenerational effect refer to?

8 Describe the prevalence of drug and alcohol use among adolescents. How do drug and alcohol use among adolescents affect family relations?

9 Describe the problem of teenage pregnancy. What insight does a systems approach add to a discussion on teenage pregnancy?

10 Discuss adolescent suicide. What factors contribute to suicide among adolescents? How is self-esteem related to the likelihood of suicide?

References

Aquilino, W. S. (1991). Family structure and leaving home: A further specification of the relationship. *Journal of Marriage and the Family, 53,* 999–1010.

Barnes, G., Farrell, M., & Cairns, P. (1986). Parental socialization factors and adolescent drinking behaviors. *Journal of Marriage and the Family, 48,* 27–35.

Bartle, S. E., & Sabatelli, R. M. (1989). Family system dynamics, identity development, and adolescent alcohol use: Implications for family treatment. *Family Relations, 38,* 258–265.

Bianchi, S. M. (1987). *Living at home: Young adults' living arrangements in the 1980s.* Paper presented at the annual meeting of the American Sociological Association, Chicago (August).

Bowen, M. (1978). *Family therapy in clinical practice.* New York: Jason Aronson.

Brody, E. B., & Brody, N. (1976). *Intelligence: Nature, determinants, and consequence.* Orlando, FL: Academic Press.

Brooks-Gunn, J., & Furstenberg, F. F., Jr. (1989). Adolescent sexual behavior. *American Psychologist, 44,* 249–257.

Carron, A. V., & Bailey, O. A. (1974). Strength development in boys from 10 through 16 years. *Monographs of the Society for Research in Child Development, 39*(4).

Cleveland, M. (1981). Families and adolescent drug abuse: Structural analysis of children's roles. *Family Process, 20,* 295–304.

Colby, A., & Kohlberg, L. (1987). *The measurement of moral judgement: Vol.1. The theoretical foundations and research validation.* Cambridge, England: Cambridge University Press.

Condry, J., & Simans, M. L. (1974). Characteristics of peer and adult children. *Journal of Marriage and the Family, 36,* 543–554.

Conger, J. J. (1988). Hostages to fortune: Youth, values, and the public interest. *American Psychologist, 43,* 291–300.

Coombs, R. H., & Landsverk, J. (1988). Parenting styles and substance abuse in childhood and adolescence. *Journal of Marriage and the Family, 50,* 473–482.

Daniels, J. A. (1990). Adolescent separation-individuation and family transitions. *Adolescence, 25,* 105–116.

DiClemente, R. J., Zorn, J., & Temoshok, L. (1986). Adolescents and AIDS: A survey of knowledge, attitudes, and beliefs about AIDS in San Francisco. *American Journal of Public Health, 76,* 1443–1445.

Dreikurs, R., & Soltz, V. (1964). *Children: The challenge.* New York: Hawthorn.

Dreyer, P. H. (1982). Sexuality during adolescence. In B. B. Wolman (Ed.), *Handbook of developmental psychology* (pp. 245–269). New York: Wiley.

Erikson, E. H. (1959). The problem of ego identity. *Psychological Issues, 1,* 101–164.

Erikson, E. H. (1963). *Childhood and society.* New York: Norton.

Erikson, E. H. (1968). *Identity, youth, and crisis.* New York: Norton.

Fisher, T. D. (1989). Family sexual communication and adolescent sexual behavior. *Journal of Marriage and the Family, 51,* 637–639.

Forste, R. T., & Heaton, T. B. (1988). Initiation of sexual activity among female adolescents. *Youth and Society, 19,* 250–268.

Frisch, R. E., & McArthur, J. W. (1974). Menstrual cycles: Fatness as determinant of minimum weight for height necessary for their maintenance and onset. *Science, 185,* 949–951.

Furstenberg, F. F., Brooks-Gunn, J., & Chase-Lansdale, L. (1989). Teenage pregnancy and childbearing. *American Psychologist, 44,* 313–320.

Galinsky, E. (1980). *Between generations,* New York: Times Book.

Gillies, P. (1989). A longitudinal study of the hopes and worries of adolescents. *Journal of Adolescents, 12,* 69–81.

Goldscheider, C., & Goldscheider, F. (1989). Family structure and conflict: Nest-leaving expectations of young adults and their parents. *Journal of Marriage and the Family, 51,* 87–97.

Gordon, T. (1970). *Parent effectiveness training.* New York: Peter H. Wyden.

Grinder, R. E. (1982). Isolationism in adolescent research. *Human Development, 25,* 223–232.

Haley, J. (1980). *Leaving home: The therapy of disturbed young people.* New York: McGraw-Hill.

Hirschorn, M. W. (1986, April 29). AIDS is not seen as a major threat by many heterosexuals on campus. *Chronicle of Higher Education,* pp. 32–34.

Hundleby, J., & Mercer, G. (1987). Family and friends as social environments and their relationships to young adolescents' use of alcohol, tobacco, and marijuana. *Journal of Marriage and the Family, 49,* 151–164.

Kamptner, N. L. (1988). Identity development in late adolescence: Causal modeling of social and familial influences. *Journal of Youth and Adolescence, 17,* 493–514.

Kandel, D., & Davies, M. (1986). Adult sequelae of adolescent symptoms. *Archives of General Psychiatry, 43,* 255–262.

Keeling, R. P. (1988). Effective response to AIDS in higher education. *NEA Higher Education Journal, 4,* 5–22.

Kohlberg, L. (1964). Development of moral character and moral ideology. In M. L. Hoffman & L. W. Hoffman (Eds.), *Review of child development research* (Vol. 1). New York: Russell Sage Foundation.

Kroger, J., & Haslett, S. J. (1988). Separation-individuation and ego identity status in late adolescence. A two-year longitudinal study. *Journal of Youth and Adolescence, 17,* 59–80.

Lefkowitz, M. M., & Tesing, E. (1984). Rejection and depression: Prospective and contemporary analysis. *Developmental Psychology, 20,* 776–785.

Logan, D. D. (1980). The menarche experience in 23 foreign countries. *Adolescence, 15,* 247–256.

Marcia, J. E. (1980). Identity in adolescence. In J. Adelson (Ed.), *Handbook of adolescent psychology* (pp. 159–187). New York: Wiley.

Marsiglio, W. (1988). Adolescent male sexuality and heterosexual masculinity: A conceptual model and review. *Journal of Adolescent Research, 3,* 285–303.

Meilman, P. A. (1979). Cross-sectional age changes in ego identity status during adolescence. *Developmental Psychology, 15,* 230–231.

Miller, B. C., & Bingham, C. R. (1989). Family configuration and sexual behavior of female adolescents. *Journal of Marriage and the Family, 51,* 499–506.

Mitchell, B. A., Wister, A. V., & Burch, T. K. (1989). The family environment and leaving the parental home. *Journal of Marriage and the Family, 51,* 605–614.

Moore, K. A., Peterson, J. L., & Furstenberg, F. F. (1986). Parental attitudes and the occurrence of early sexual activity. *Journal of Marriage and the Family, 48,* 777–782.

Nachman, G. (1979). The menopause that refreshes. In P. Rose (Ed.), *Socialization and the life cycle* (pp. 279–293). New York: St. Martin's.

National Center for Health Statistics. (1988). *Vital Statistics of the United States, 1986: Vol. 2. Mortality, Part A* (DHHS Publication No. PHS 88-122). Washington, DC: U.S. Government Printing Office.

Needle, R. H., Su, S. S., & Doherty, W. J. (1990). Divorce, remarriage, and substance use. *Journal of Marriage and the Family, 52,* 157–170.

Neimark, E. D. (1975). Longitudinal development of formal operations thought. *Genetic Psychology Monographs, 91,* 175–225.

Newcomb, M. D., & Bentler, P. M. (1989). Substance use and abuse among teenagers. *American Psychologist, 44,* 242–248.

Newcomer, S., & Udry, J. R. (1987). Parental marital status effects on adolescent sexual behavior. *Journal of Marriage and the Family, 49,* 235–240.

Newman, B. M., & Newman, P. R. (1991). *Development through life: A psychosocial approach.* Pacific Grove, CA: Brooks/Cole.

Offer, D., & Offer, J. (1974). Normal adolescent males: The high school and college years. *Journal of American College Health Association, 22,* 209–215.

Patterson, G. R. (1976). *Living with children* (rev. ed.). Champaign, IL: Research Press.

Peters, J. (1985). Adolescents as socialization agents to parents. *Adolescence, 20,* 921–931.

Piaget, J. (1972). Intellectual evolution from adolescence to adulthood. *Human Development, 15,* 1–12.

Price, J. H., Desmond, S., & Kukulka, G. (1985). High school students' perceptions and misconceptions of AIDS. *Journal of School Health, 55,* 107–109.

Quinn, W. H., Kuehl, B. P., Thomas, F. N., Joanning, H., & Newfield, N. A. (1989). Family treatment of adolescent drug abuse: Transitions and maintenance of drug-free behavior. *American Journal of Family Therapy, 17,* 229–242.

Rest, J. R., & Thoma, S. J. (1985). Relation of moral judgement development to formal education. *Developmental Psychology, 21,* 709–714.

Rice, F. P. (1989) *Human sexuality.* Dubuque, IA: William C. Brown.

Robertson, J. F., & Simons, R. L. (1989). Family factors, self-esteem, and adolescent depression. *Journal of Marriage and the Family, 51,* 125-138.

Robinson, B., & Barret, R. (1985, December). Teenage fathers: Many care about their babies. *Psychology Today, 66,* 66–70.

Rodgers, J. A. (1983). Family configuration and adolescent behavior. *Population and Environment, 6,* 73–83.

Ruble, D. N., & Brooks-Gunn, J. (1982). The experience of menarche. *Child Development, 53,* 1537–1556.

Sanders, B., & Soares, M. P. (1986). Sexual maturation and spatial ability in college students. *Developmental Psychology, 22,* 199–203.

Sebald, H. (1986). Adolescents' shifting orientation toward parents and peers. *Journal of Marriage and the Family, 48,* 5–13.

Sigelman, C. K., & Shaffer, D. R. (1991). *Life-span human development.* Pacific Grove, CA: Brooks/Cole.

Silbereisen, R. K., Petersen, A. C., Albrecht, H. T., & Kracke, B. (1989). Maturational timing and the development of problem behavior: Longitudinal studies in adolescence. *Journal of Early Adolescence, 9,* 247–268.

Simons, R. L., & Murphy, P. I. (1985). Sex differences in the causes of adolescent suicide ideation. *Journal of Youth and Adolescence, 14,* 423–434.

Smollar, J., & Youniss, J. (1985). Parent-adolescent relationship: Adolescents whose parents are divorced. *Journal of Early Adolescence, 5,* 129–144.

Spotts, J. V., & Shontz, F. C. (1985). A theory of adolescent substance abuse. In D. W. Brook, J. S. Brook, D. J. Lettieri, & B. Stimmel (Eds.), *Advances in alcohol and substance, 4,* 117–138.

Stark, E. (1986). A grandmother at 27. *Psychology Today, 20,* 18.

Sweet, J. A., Bumpass, L. L., & Call, V. (1988). *The design and content of the National Survey of Families and Households* (Working Paper NSFH-1). Madison: University of Wisconsin, Center for Demography and Ecology.

Tanner, J. M. (1981). *A history of the study of human growth.* Cambridge, England: Cambridge University Press.

Tedesco, L. A., & Gaier, E. L. (1988). Friendship bonds in adolescence. *Adolescence, 23,* 127–136.

Thornton, A., & Camburn, D. (1989). Religious participation and adolescent sexual behavior. *Journal of Marriage and the Family, 51,* 641–654.

U.S. Bureau of the Census. (1989). *Statistical Abstracts of the United States, 1989* (109th ed.). Washington, DC: U.S. Government Printing Office.

U.S. Department of Health and Human Services. (1983). *Vital Statistics of the United States.* Washington, DC: National Center for Health Statistics.

Waber, D. P. (1977). Sex differences in mental abilities, hemispheric lateralization, and rate of physical growth at adolescence. *Developmental Psychology, 13,* 29–38.

Walker, L. J. (1982). The sequentiality of Kohlberg's stages of moral development. *Child Development, 53,* 1330–1336.

Wallerstein, J. S. (1985). Children of divorce: A preliminary report of a ten-year follow-up of older children and adolescents. *Journal of Child Psychiatry, 24,* 545–553.

Waterman, A. S. (1982). Identity development from adolescence to adulthood: An extension of theory and a review of research. *Developmental Psychology, 18,* 341–358.

White, L. K., & Booth, A. (1985). The quality and stability of remarriages: The role of stepchildren. *American Sociological Review, 50,* 689–698.

Young, C. M. (1987). *Young people leaving home in Australia* (Australian Family Information Project, Monograph No. 9). Melbourne: Australian Institute of Family Studies.

Zelnick, M., & Kantner, J. F. (1980). Sexual activity, contraceptive use, and pregnancy among metropolitan area teenagers: 1971–1979. *Family Planning Perspectives, 12,* 23–237.

Chapter 9

Parenting in Single-Parent and Remarried Families

Parenting Myth ■ Single-parent families and stepfamilies are at greater risk for problems than two-parent biological families because the former are inherently flawed family forms.

Test Your Knowledge ■ The following questions are designed to test your knowledge before reading the material in this chapter. The answers appear at the end of the chapter.

1 Single-parent families make up a homogenous group. True or false?

2 The majority of research on divorce supports the belief that divorce has negative effects on children. True or false?

3 The single-parent experience makes children susceptible to lower educational and occupational achievements. True or false?

4 The term *binuclear* was coined to refer to families after remarriage. True or false?

5 Typically, discipline is not an issue in remarried families. True or false?

6 The best custody arrangement for the child's adjustment is believed to be sole custody by the mother. True or false?

■ Parenting in Single-Parent Families

Single-parent families have greatly increased in American society in the past three decades. A number of factors have led to this increase. Since the 1960s, the rising divorce rate and the increase in the number of births to unwed mothers have resulted in more single-parent homes. The single-parent family, however, appears to be a dynamic versus a static family form in that families classified as single-parent represent a **transition** from one family form to another. For example, while about one-fourth of all American families are classified as single-parent, it is predicted that two-thirds of today's toddlers will live in a single-parent family before age 18 (Brophy, 1986). Although a large number of families may be classified as single-parent at some point in their development, it remains true that this designation is usually of short duration (Bumpass, 1984).

Not only is the single-parent family a transition to other types of families, it may also represent a variety of different family experiences. For example, a 16-year-old mother of an unplanned infant represents a different family unit than a 30-year-old manager of a company who decided to become pregnant because she wanted a child. Both of these women would be considered the head of a single-parent household, but the resulting family style and roles may be very dissimilar. Likewise, the divorced mother of three small children who must rely on welfare may have very little in common with an employed divorced father who has custody of two young sons. It seems clear that using the generic term *single-parent family* when discussing all families with one parent does not adequately explain the myriad differences in the composition of these families (Norton & Glick, 1986).

Generally, the majority of single-parent families are female headed. The occurrence of single-parent families is much higher for minorities, especially blacks, than for whites. For example, the majority of black children are born to single mothers and the divorce rate is much higher for blacks (U.S. Bureau of the Census, 1989). About 12% of single-parent families are now headed by men, but these families appear to have some clear advantages over female-headed families. These advantages are noted in greater economic stability and other resources available to these families (Greif, 1985).

A major problem in single-parent families is financial instability. Many female-headed households have incomes that fall below the poverty line (U.S. Bureau of the Census, 1989). This problem is incurred partly because female-headed households have about 50% of the income of male-headed households. About 60% of children whose mothers have sole custody are living in poverty (Moore, Peterson, & Zill, 1985). Never-married women with children have the highest rate of poverty, about 81%. In addition, many noncustodial fathers, although legally liable, do not help support the family after divorce (U.S. Bureau of the Census, 1987). Only 50% of women who are awarded child support actually receive it.

Fletcher (1989) compared male-headed households who pay child support and female-headed households who receive child-support payments. The study found

■ *Single mothers have fewer resources available to help them in parenting than mothers in two-parent families have.*

vast discrepancies in the income, expenditures, and the amount of child-support payments reported by nonresident fathers and single-parent mothers. Nonresident fathers reported expenditures for child support that were 47% greater than child support reported received by single-parent mothers. These child-support expenditures amounted to about 9.5% of the nonresident father's income. On the other hand, single-parent mothers reported that the nonresident fathers gave only 6.5% of their income. In addition, mothers who are in the greatest need for support receive the least support, and fathers who have the least income contribute the least to child support.

Another problem that single-parent families must deal with is inadequate **child care.** Because the typical single mother must work to support the family, she must place the children in day care, receive help from nonrelatives, or have help from relatives in a home setting. Single-parent mothers may have to decide on the kind of child care on the basis of resources rather than other concerns. A good day-care center may cost more than single mothers can afford, especially if they have a number of children. A study by Quinn and Allen (1989) concluded that the single-parent mothers who are concerned most about child care have fewer resources than mothers who are not concerned about child care.

The Effects of Single-Parent Families on Children

Being reared in a single-parent home may have certain effects on children, all of which may not be known. For example, it might be relatively easy to document the effects of divorce on a 10-year-old boy who is very close to his father but difficult to determine the effects on the same boy if his parents had not divorced and continued the marital conflict. Nevertheless, researchers have determined that divorce can have profound initial effects on children (Wallerstein & Blakeslee, 1989). Children of divorce lose the security of the home and regular contact with at least one of their parents, usually the father. They may abruptly develop problems at school and at home through noncompliant or aggressive behavior. They may be subjected to reduced resources in that the family income is usually much less after divorce, even in middle-class homes.

The classic study of the effects of divorce on children was conducted by Judith Wallerstein and Joan Kelly (1980). This study, conducted at the time of divorce and followed at one, two, five, ten, and fifteen years after divorce, interviewed all members of 60 families. The findings indicated that children were still not doing well one year after the divorce. Generally, by two years after the divorce, the family had stabilized and the children seemed to have improved. At the five-year follow-up, most children appeared to have adjusted well to divorce. There were, however, a significant number of children who were unhappy and reacting through angry and hostile behavior. Although at the ten-year follow-up most of these children were psychologically healthy individuals, there was evidence that some had not adjusted well. Overall, the children were viewed as having some psychological distress related to the loss of the family and loss of regular contact with their father.

The effects of divorce on children may also be a consequence of age and the developmental level of children at the time of divorce. Preschool children may feel that they are to blame for the divorce because they have been bad. Regressive behavior in the form of bed-wetting or temper tantrums may follow a separation and divorce. Although disturbing, these behaviors generally will eventually end if the parent handles them appropriately. Parents who talk openly to their children about the divorce and are equally accessible to them will help the children make a better adjustment than parents who continue to argue and restrict each other's access to the children (Wallerstein & Kelly, 1980).

There is ample evidence that children who adjust better after divorce have good relationships with both parents. Noncustodial fathers have to be sensitive to the needs of their children and be available to them. The continuing conflict with the former spouse prevents many fathers from becoming as involved with their children as they would like to be following divorce (Hetherington & Camara, 1984).

Children between 5 and 7 years old may have particular difficulties because they understand the situation better than younger children do but do not have the cognitive skills to cope with it. Sadness and a sense of loss are the most common emotions these children experience. Children in the early school grades may experience depression and the inability to concentrate in school. Because children often do not verbally express their feelings about the divorce, some increased acting out in school and home may be an initial response. Adolescents may be better able to handle the divorce of parents because of their involvement outside the family with their peer group. No doubt, adolescents have been exposed to divorce through their friends. Adolescents still may be vulnerable to the negative side effects of divorce, which are expressed through sexual promiscuity and drug experimentation and abuse (Wallerstein & Kelly, 1980).

A troubling finding related to girls who appeared to be adjusted well at earlier follow-ups but did not seem to fare as well at the ten-year follow-up. A significant number were afraid of marriage and family commitment and expressed anxiety over long-term relationships. Their parents' divorce loomed as the number one influence in their distrust of protracted relationships (Wallerstein & Blakeslee, 1989).

Another aspect of the single-parent family that Wallerstein and Blakeslee reported was the negative effects on the children's social life. For example, it was not uncommon for children in single-parent families to report refraining from participation in activities outside the family in order to complete household responsibilities or take care of the parent. This type of role reversal in these families was viewed as potentially damaging to the children because it put too much responsibility on them for the operation of the family.

In reviewing single-parent families, Stephen Nock (1988) found that two factors were present in all the published literature, namely, children of single-parent families have lower educational and occupational attainment than those who were reared in two-parent families. The lower educational level on average is about two years, and the occupational level differs according to both income and professional status.

Nock (1988) pointed out that the popular argument that social class and income of the family account for these differences cannot be verified. In fact, he found no differences between two-parent families and single-parent families in the educational or occupational level of children based on social class alone. In addition, the importance of education in the family was not found to contribute positively to increased educational attainment of children. In other words, there was no difference in educational attainment between single-parent families that valued education and encouraged children to perform and single-parent families that did not appear to value education. He also found that the length of time a child spends in a single-parent family is not a factor in his/her educational and occupational attainment. These findings led Nock to conclude that merely being exposed to a single-parent family is detrimental to children's educational and occupational performance.

Wallerstein and Blakeslee (1989) in the ten-year follow-up on families of divorce found that educational attainment was lower for children whose parents had divorced. Fathers who valued education were found to be only marginally financially supportive of their children's college education. Many fathers apparently do not feel obligated to help their noncustodial children after age 18. Furthermore, there is evidence that fathers are supportive of the college education of their sons but not their daughters. The reason for this difference is unclear, but one could argue that fathers have more empathy with sons and generally support the idea of greater educational need for sons over daughters. Because fathers maintain more contact with sons during the divorce and single-parent period, it is only logical that they would be more financially supportive of their sons' college education.

Although custody generally goes to the mother, there is growing evidence that children may adjust better when the parent of the same sex is given custody of them (Santrock & Warshak, 1986). Fathers have frequently taken care of children, especially sons, who were awarded custody to the mother. Typically this informal shift of living arrangement for sons to their fathers occurs because single-parent mothers have greater difficulty with the noncompliance and independence of sons than with that of daughters (Mullis, Mullis, & Markstrom, 1987). It could be that identity issues are better met in a single-parent situation when the parent is of the same sex as the child.

Other researchers have generally found that single parenting produces differences in adjustment in children (Amato & Keith, 1990). Although these differences have been found, it appears that in the long run a number of other factors may be equally influential in the outcome affecting adjustment. One could view the single-parent family as predisposing the child toward factors that would adversely affect adjustment but could be modified anyplace in the adjustment process.

A number of researchers have found strengths in single-parent families (see Table 9.1). For example, Hanson (1986) found that the mental health of single-parent mothers and their children is generally good. A number of factors are related to the mental health of mothers and children in single-parent families. For example, custody arrangements—especially joint custody, open communications, and availability of resources—tend to be related to improved adjustment and mental health of mothers and children.

Weiss (1979) found that single-parent families may have an advantage over two-parent families in the development of **independence** in children. This development of independence means that children participate more in the day-to-day operation of the family, have input in decision making, and are less dependent on the family in general. These findings are in marked contrast to most findings studying single-parent families, especially Wallerstein's findings.

Single-Parent Mothers

As previously mentioned, most single-parent families are headed by females. The general comments about single-parent families previously mentioned refer mostly to female-headed households. Many single-parent mothers have low educational levels

Table 9.1 ■ Strengths of Children in Single-Parent Families

- Exposure to variant life situations early in life
- Greater independence than children raised in two-parent families
- Early maturing
- More decisive in decision making

Source: Weiss, 1979.

and when they are employed, the jobs are typically low paying. Burden (1986) has found single-parent mothers to have low satisfaction and motivation for work when compared to married women. This lack of motivation further decreases the process of adjusting to the single-parent family.

Researchers have recently found that women who were dominant in their marriages before divorce were better able to adjust to the single-parent role than women who were less dominant and more traditional in roles (Fassinger, 1989). Women who were more traditional in values generally were less invested in their jobs both before and after divorce. The actual divorce was much more traumatic to these traditional women in terms of economic and other resources.

Courts generally provide for the care and financial maintenance of children by requiring the noncustodial parent to make **child-support payments.** Although the majority of women receive some child support, less than 50% actually receive the amount decreed in the divorce settlement. As mentioned earlier, the lower the socioeconomic status of the woman, the less chance she has of receiving support (Greif, 1985). The women who need the support the most are the least likely to receive it.

Another problem single-parent mothers face is **role overload.** They must play both roles of breadwinner and homemaker, leaving little time (and energy) to spend with their children. Children can feel that they have lost both parents, one because of the custody arrangement and the other because of the reduced amount of time and contact (Coleman, 1988).

Some researchers have found that the time spent with the custodial parent and with the noncustodial parent differ. For example, time spent with the noncustodial parent may involve activities and recreation, whereas time spent with the custodial parent involves day-to-day activities, such as schoolwork (Goldzband, 1985, cited in Asmussen & Larson, 1991). These different roles may suggest that in single-parent families the custodial and the noncustodial parents take on different, but equally important, styles of parenting.

In their study, Asmussen and Larson (1991) found that adolescents in single-parent families, when including time spent with extended kinfolk, and in two-parent families did not differ in the amount of time they spent with other family members. In addition, they found that adolescents in single-parent and in two-parent families did not differ in the amount of time spent in activities such as housework. This research also suggests that single-parent mothers do not spend more time in housework than

■ ■ ■ ■ ■ ■ ■ ■ ■ ■

Box 9.1

Women Who Remain Above the Poverty Line After Divorce

The economic decline of women after divorce has been the focus of much research and debate. On the other hand, the literature has ignored women who have not fallen below the poverty level and women who have increased their standard of living following divorce.

Teresa Mauldin (1990) conducted a study that focused primarily on women who remained above the poverty level after divorce. She drew data from the National Longitudinal Survey of Work Experience of young women interviewed by the U.S. Bureau of the Census 11 times between 1968 and 1982.

The sample was comprised of women who had experienced divorce between 1960 and 1980, who had not been previously divorced, and who were still divorced or separated. Of the original 5,159 women, only 620 met all of these criteria.

Results support the contention that health and job training are significant factors affecting the improved status of women following divorce. Furthermore, greater education and being white versus black differentiated the women who had improved status after divorce versus those who fell below the poverty level.

their married counterparts, although it may be assumed that some maintenance-type household activities are left undone in single-parent families. This study failed to support earlier studies that indicated adolescents have poorer relationships with single-parent mothers than with married mothers.

Many single-parent mothers express problems with parenting issues, especially in the area of **discipline.** To some degree, the typical arrangement of father as disciplinarian in the two-parent family predisposes the single-parent mother to have difficulty with parenting. Role overload may also have a significant impact on the family because mothers have to let some things go; they may not be able to take their children to Little League games or other activities, for example. In such a family, the mother may be as absent as the noncustodial father (Amato, 1987). Furthermore, children of female single-parent families are much more likely to be the victims of child abuse than children of two-parent biological families. However, one must keep in mind that a number of variables affect the ability of single mothers to parent effectively, including age, educational background, and beliefs about parenting (Luster & Rhoades, 1989).

Researchers have found that single-parent mothers initially tend to become more punitive and restrictive when compared to other parents (Amato, 1987). Over a number of years, however, single mothers tend to decrease the authoritarian style of parenting and return to a more authoritative model. The authoritative model has been linked with competency in children, whereas the authoritarian model has been linked with aggressive and noncompliant behavior.

Many single-parent mothers are lonely and isolated from social contacts, particularly when they are employed. Although the job may improve their financial condition, it also takes time and energy away from involvement with the community. It is not uncommon for single-parent mothers to feel trapped in a situation they cannot change. The social isolation may further limit the single mother's ability to adjust to changes and provide consistent behavioral modeling for children (Wallerstein, 1986).

Single-Parent Fathers

Most of the literature on single-parent families has been on female-headed households. There is reason to believe, however, that single-parent households headed by fathers may represent a unique style of family. Although there are a number of similarities in female-headed and male-headed households, researchers have noted a number of differences. First, single fathers tend to have higher remarriage rates than single mothers. The single-parent period tends to be a shorter transition from one family type to another for single fathers (Greif, 1985).

Researchers have found that the onset of single parenthood for fathers is a stressful experience. Typically, single fathers are divorced, although some become single parents as the result of the death of the spouse. Very rarely is single fatherhood inaugurated by adoption, although it does occur (Hanson, 1986). This crisis related to parenting means that single-parent fathers must adjust to the new situation of sole parent, which involves being able to add the caretaker role to the breadwinner role they usually carry.

A second difference is that single-parent fathers have a more secure economic situation than single-parent mothers. Fathers are in a better financial position partly because they begin at a different point. For the most part, single-parent fathers are working prior to and during the divorce. They are better educated than their female counterparts and have higher paying jobs (Greif, 1985). Researchers have given this superior financial position as the major reason for the success rate of single-parent fathers versus single-parent mothers.

Third, single fathers report more difficulty in managing the household than single mothers do. For example, few men shared housework equally with their wives before the divorce. As a single parent of young children, the father must take full responsibility for cooking, cleaning house, and getting children to and from events. Many of these activities require time and energy that compete with work. The single father finds that he is unable to work late or attend a weekend seminar that would help him be promoted. In fact, he must compromise his occupational goals for the sake of the children. This experience of housekeeping has increased the empathy and sensitivity that the single-parent father has for the traditional homemaker role (Greif, 1985).

Developing intimate relationships after divorce may be problematic because single fathers tend to be concerned that dating might interfere with child-rearing responsibilities. As a general rule, single fathers do not cohabitate before remarriage, which to some degree puts their family life and social life in conflict (Greif, 1985).

Single-parent fathers report some difficulty in parenting, especially in parenting girls (Schlesinger, 1978). The admitted bias in parenting boys over girls may be the lack of comfort in dealing with sexual issues with daughters. More research is needed to determine the parenting effectiveness of single-parent fathers related to the gender of children.

In general, single-parent fathers tend to reorganize their lives to accommodate their children (Amato, 1987; Greif, 1985). When single fathers are able to satisfactorily juggle the different roles required to be the sole parent, they feel the overall experience is positive. Researchers have corroborated this finding of a generally positive outcome in better adjustment of children in father-headed single-parent families than in female-headed single-parent families (Greif, 1985). In fact, children may feel somewhat special in these families and actually prefer this arrangement.

Parent/Child Relationships in Single-Parent Families

Single-parent families have the potential for undermining the security of the parent/child relationship. The process of divorce has the potential for long-term effects of distress and sadness on the child. These emotions are frequently translated into misbehavior on the part of the child. Some researchers have suggested that the misbehavior of children following divorce in single-parent families may actually represent the parent's depression or helplessness. From this point of view, the child's misbehavior may be seen as an empowering of the parent to mobilize him/her to deal with the child's problem. The child's misbehavior is a protective device to prevent the parent from experiencing depression (Fulmer, 1983).

In general, single-parent families are correlated with increased levels of children's noncompliant and resistive behavior, especially in boys (Hetherington, Hagan, & Anderson, 1989). One explanation, offered by researchers, is that boys are more often exposed to conflict and aggression in the family. In addition, boys reared in female-headed single-parent homes have more difficulty in self-control and in the development of a masculine image. A significant number of boys will have to receive counseling as a result of the adjustment to their parents' divorce and to living in a single-parent family. However, the vast majority of boys in single-parent families do not need counseling as a result of divorce and living in a single-parent family (Emery, 1988).

Researchers have found that parenting style is related to positive outcomes in child behaviors. For example, authoritative parenting by single parents is related to desirable outcomes in children whereas permissive parenting is related to the undesirable scenario in parenting (Santrock & Warshak, 1979). Authoritarian parenting is also related to negative outcomes in parenting, but it tends to be correlated with fewer problems with children overall than permissive parenting.

A systems perspective of parenting assumes that the parent/child relationship is reciprocal; that is, parents affect children and children affect parents. The following factors appear to be interactive in forming the child's total ecosystem: the child's temperament, intelligence, and self-esteem; the parent's socioeconomic status, gender, and mental well-being.

In general, the higher the socioeconomic level of the single-parent family, the higher the level of adjustment of the children. An exception to this rule would be the single-parent mother who must work long hours to bring in additional income. Although the greater family income may be desirable, the positive effects are offset by the reduced availability of the mother to the children. This reduced contact between children and mother as a consequence of the mother's employment tends to affect boys more than girls and to be related to greater problems with boys (Hetherington, Hagan, & Anderson, 1989).

The more social support for the single-parent family, the better the parent/child relationship. When support is missing, which is often the case, the parent/child relationship suffers because single parents have greater difficulty parenting under such circumstances. These findings tend to be the same regardless of the parent's gender or race (Hetherington, Hagan, & Anderson, 1989).

Family cohesion tends to be related to family functioning (Olson, Sprenkle, & Russell, 1979). Researchers have postulated that a balanced level of **cohesion,** or togetherness, is related to adequate family functioning and too much or too little cohesion is related to dysfunctional family relationships. In single-parent families, the custodial parent may become too close to a child or children. This **cross-generational alliance** may interfere in the child's normal development. When the noncustodial parent, typically the father, remains equally accessible to the child after divorce, the child tends to have a better relationship with both parents (Wallerstein & Blakeslee, 1989).

When the custodial mother and noncustodial father are unable to agree on issues related to the child's welfare, the child will typically show more problems getting along with both parents. Children can be easily **triangulated** into the marital conflict by parents who continue their conflict after divorce. The battle over custody is just one way the war continues after divorce. Each parent may attempt to "win the child over" through gifts or promises and permissive parenting. In the long run, neither parent is parenting effectively because the family hierarchy has been altered.

A Systems Perspective of Parenting in the Single-Parent Family

A **systems perspective of parenting in the single-parent family** concerns boundaries, hierarchy, roles, and functions. Adequate parenting means that these dimensions of the family function in accord with the developmental needs of the child. A child's dysfunction or misbehavior would be viewed as representing a system that prevented differentiation and optimal functioning of the child. For example, a systems perspective would raise the question of how adequate the family boundaries are to protect the child from negative forces outside the family.

Role responsibilities include such behaviors as a division of labor to perform household tasks and child care, providing for the family's economic stability, and ensuring a certain level of intimacy in the family. Single-parent families are somewhat at a disadvantage in meeting these roles because of fewer resources and persons to carry them out. Consequently, performing these roles may mean adjusting the allocation of time and responsibilities. Roles typically performed by parents may be reassigned to children in the reorganization of the family.

Although this reassigning of roles may have some positive aspects for children in that they develop independence, as previously mentioned, a number of negative outcomes may occur. For example, inappropriately assigned roles to children in single-parent families may result in a relaxing of the generational boundaries between parents and children. Minuchin (1974) has referred to the child to whom adult roles have been assigned as the **parentified child.** This child may give the appearance of being more mature than siblings, but pays a great price in the loss of the childhood years.

As this parentified child becomes an adult, the loss of the adolescent years will begin to play a major role in certain behavioral patterns. For example, depression and anxiety may be common emotions that affect his/her adjustment. Regressive behavior, such as irresponsibility or sexual promiscuity, may also characterize adult behavior.

Researchers have found that, instead of relying on a child or children to carry out adult roles, single-parent families should consider **external familial resources** as the best alternative to decreased role functioning. The use of external resources is not without the potential for some problems, however. For example, when a single-parent family turns to the family of origin for support, problems may develop if boundaries are blurred and unclear. Old unresolved issues may resurface and need to be addressed. The single-parent family hierarchy may be undermined because parents may find it very difficult to be involved dispassionately in the life of their children and grandchildren. The tendency to want to solve the problem for their adult children may place the parents (grandparents) in the executive position of decision making in the family.

Social support in the form of baby sitting by friends may relieve some of the pressure caused by the constraints of time and energy, but it may also open the family up to the possibility of neglect or abuse. Children appear much more vulnerable to neglect and abuse from noninstitutional day-care facilities. Researchers have found that single-parent fathers use social support more than single-parent mothers do and that such support tends to benefit moderately distressed single mothers more than severely distressed mothers (Hetherington, 1989).

It could be that severely distressed single mothers misuse social support so that the final outcome is detrimental rather than helpful. For example, when a single mother relies on economic resources such as welfare for financial support, the long-term effect might be that she will rely less on her own initiative and ability to solve her own problems. One of the main focuses of future research with single-parent families will be to help the most distressed utilize the resources that are available without decreasing their own initiative.

The changing roles, boundaries, and hierarchy associated with the single-parent family moving through time are referred to in the literature as the **family life cycle.** A systems perspective utilizes a life-cycle approach because of the interaction of the family with its environment as it moves through time. With each new stage, the family must reorganize itself in terms of new roles and expectations (Carter & McGoldrick, 1989).

Initially, researchers applied the family life cycle only to intact families based on the child's birth, attending school, reaching adolescence, and leaving home. Over the past three decades that image of the family has given way to a view that includes divorce, single-parent families, and remarriage. The simultaneous stages of the life-cycle imposed on families because of divorce increase the complexity and difficulty in adjustment. In single-parent families, the timing and duration of the stage may be protracted. As a result, the transition from one stage to another may be more difficult to master. For example, if divorce occurs during the adolescent period, the single parent may have more problems with the child in regard to such issues as dating, alcohol and drug use, and schoolwork. This additional stress may make this period much more difficult than it would have been if the family had stayed intact (Hill, 1986).

The divorce of an intact family creates the **binuclear family,** or two separate bio-logical families (Ahrons & Wallisch, 1987). Binuclear families must adjust to multiple ecological systems that may not always be working cooperatively together. This link-ing together of various subsystems of the single-parent family system may be one of the major sources of problems. One can expect that the links between the various subsystems would experience the greatest amount of stress.

Family hierarchy—the family's power structure—is a major issue and potential source of problems in single-parent families. In problematic families, children have been promoted to an emotional status in the family equal to that of the single parent (Haley, 1987; Minuchin, 1974). Emotional closeness between a child and the single parent may give the child a special feeling of belonging, but this bond may ultimately lead to family dysfunction.

Nock (1988) hypothesized that the breakdown in family hierarchy noted in all the research he reviewed is the cause of the lower levels of educational and occupa-tional attainment by children in single-parent families. He ruled out other factors that have been accepted as the cause, such as the family's social status or attitudes about education and occupation. According to Nock, the organizational structure of both educational and occupational systems presupposes a hierarchical arrangement where a select few make decisions and pass them down to others to implement. Be-cause single-parent families tend to lack a functional hierarchy, children from such families may be at a disadvantage in educational and occupational systems because these systems are organized hierarchically. Although this hypothesis has not been tested in research, it is a logical deduction of the literature.

■ Parenting in Remarried Families

A number of terms have been used to describe families in which at least one partner was previously married. **Remarried** and **reconstituted** are the most common. Where children are involved in remarriage a number of other, more specific terms have been used, including **stepfamily** and **blended** family. In stepfamilies, members must work very hard to blend the family unit into a cohesive and adaptive unit (Visher & Visher, 1978). Table 9.2 lists the many types of remarried families.

The rates of remarriage are very high for divorced persons, almost as high as the rates for first marriage. About 46% of all marriages today are remarriages (National Center for Health Statistics, 1990). The result of the large number of remarriages means that many children are being reared by at least one nonbiological parent. Although a trend has begun for fathers to get custody of children and take them into a remarried situation, most children in remarried families are in homes with biological mothers and stepfathers (Ambert, 1985). This fact presents some predictable problems in remarried families that will be addressed later in the chapter.

The Roles of Stepparenting

Researchers have found that neither the role of stepfather nor the role of stepmother is easy to perform. Researchers have found that stepparents report more unhappiness and dissatisfaction in family life than parents in first-married families report (White & Booth, 1985). In fact, until quite recently the literature tended to describe the stepfamily as lacking in role definitions (Cherlin, 1978). Because these roles were ill defined, stepparents not only were on their own in defining them but also were confused and frustrated. For example, stepfathers have little idea what role they should play in the discipline of their stepchildren. In stepfamilies, roles are not typically assigned on the basis of position. A stepparent may assume the position of parent, but not be given the authority to parent.

Roles in stepparenting tend to be worked out by trial and error (Walker & Messinger, 1979). For example, a stepfather may find it easier to be accepted as the parent when he takes time to become a friend of the stepchild than when he tries to take over discipline immediately. Typically, the mother assumes the responsibility for child care and discipline of her children initially and gradually allows the stepfather to assume more responsibility as he becomes more accepted in the parenting role (Dahl, Cowgill, & Asmundsson, 1987). In **instant families,** in which the woman was previously married and divorced with young children and the stepfather had never been married, women describe themselves as teachers for their inexperienced husbands (Roberts & Price, 1987).

Not only do societal proscriptions prohibit remarried stepfathers from taking a more active role in parenting of stepchildren, there are few legal precedents for defining the limits of stepparenting. For example, legal questions regarding survival rights for property tend to be unclear and vary from state to state. Such issues as visitation

Table 9.2 ■ Types of Remarried Families

Couples in which only one spouse was previously married:
• Remarriages with no children

• Remarriages with children born after remarriage

• Stepfather families

• Stepmother families

• Natural children plus stepfather

• Natural children plus stepmother

• Two stepparent families (one had a child out of wedlock)

Both spouses were previously married:
• Remarriages with no children

• Common children after remarriage

• Stepfather families

• Stepmother families

• Natural parent plus stepfather

• Natural parent plus stepmother

• Two stepparents

• Natural parents plus two stepparents

• Custodial children of mother plus father's noncustodial children

• Custodial children of father plus mother's noncustodial children

Source: Rice, 1990.

and child-support rights after divorce for the stepparent and custody rights for step-parents after the death of the biological parent are not clarified. Incest issues, the marriage of stepparents and stepchildren or of stepsiblings, also raise questions without definitive answers (Ramsey, 1986).

The two major issues researchers have found that affect happiness in remarriage are children and finances. As mentioned previously, the stepparent role creates much stress because of the lack of defined roles. Although the presence of stepchildren is related to marital distress, researchers have found that children in remarriages differ little in adjustment from children in other types of marriages, such as intact (Pasley & Ihinger-Tallman, 1988).

Researchers have found that boys benefit more from the remarriage of their mother than girls do (Hetherington, 1987; Zaslow, 1989). The main reason for the advantage is related to the addition of a role model for the boy to emulate. Girls, on the other hand, have more difficulty in both remarriages where there is a stepfather and remarriages where there is a stepmother. This difficulty is probably related to the

---

Box 9.2

Unique Features of Stepfamilies

S tepfamilies share a number of characteristics. First, because some parents and children predate the present marriage, the preexisting bonds between some family members may prevent another member from fulfilling his/her role. For example, a mother with children from a previous marriage has a much longer and more meaningful relationship with her children than with her new spouse. Consequently, the mother/child bond may prevent the stepfather from exerting authority in matters of discipline.

Second, spouses in a stepfamily may not have adequate time to bond because children are present from the beginning. The tasks for beginning families—for example, marital bonding—may not take place because the marital relationship is preempted by parental responsibilities.

Third, the majority of remarriages occur and stepfamilies form because a previous marriage failed. This experience of a failed marriage can act either to create a sense of determination to make the remarriage work or to create a feeling of continued failure.

---

typical close relationship between mothers and daughters, which can lead to the daughter competing with the stepfather for the mother's attention and does not allow the stepmother to assume the role of substitute mother (Hetherington, 1987).

The Stepfather Role

As mentioned earlier, boys respond better to the stepfather than girls do, but in general stepfathers rate their performance as lower than they would like (Bohannan & Erickson, 1978). In general, stepfathers are more numerous and more accepted in society than stepmothers. This social acceptance assumes a positive image for the role and does not carry the negative myth of the wicked stepmother so prominent in children's literature. In addition, research implies that stepfathers, particularly instant fathers, make a concerted effort to do a good job (Roberts & Price, 1987). This tendency to want to do the best job, however, can work against them in the sense that they may attempt to take over the father role by limiting the children's access to the biological father. Attempting to do the best job may also be related to the tendency to come across as rigid and role defined.

Although stepfathers do not have as equal a role in discipline as the biological mother, there seems to be some evidence that children adjust better when the biological father continues as the "father" role and the stepfather functions as the supporter or friend. The literature indicates that these two roles are quite different and that attempting to merge them may cause greater problems. To have a good relationship with the biological father and the stepfather is the ideal in stepfamilies (Wallerstein & Blakeslee, 1989).

Researchers have found that children, primarily girls, have reported distance in the relationship with the stepfather (Ganong & Coleman, 1987). Stepfathers, on the other hand, may also experience distance from stepchildren because of a number of factors. A major factor may be a sense of guilt about the circumstances under which he became part of this family. For example, he and the children's mother may have had an affair prior to the divorce, or he might have guilt feelings about taking their father's place. Many stepfathers are also financially supporting children from previous marriages and have visitation rights. This conflict between the former and the present family may be related to ambiguous feelings and confused behavior on the part of the stepfather.

This continuing relationship with the children and the spouse from the former family may make it difficult for the stepfather to become fully integrated into the new family. He must deal with his own children about financial matters, discipline, and sometimes a change in custody. The new spouse and stepchildren may resent his continued efforts in the former family. The stepfather may find himself in a position of decreased efficiency in all of his roles. Conflicts arising out of these relationships may lead to a feeling of disappointment and, ultimately, despair.

The quality of the remarried father's relationship with his former wife may be a significant factor affecting the remarriage. Researchers have found that when the relationship with the former spouse is good or at least tolerable, a remarried father is more likely to maintain contact with his biological children (Wallerstein & Kelly, 1980). Researchers have found that continued conflict with the former spouse who has custody of the children is the major factor in how often divorced and remarried fathers see their biological children (Wright & Price, 1986). A study has found that the stepfather's relationship with his former spouse is related to increased stress in the remarriage (Guisinger, Cowan, & Schuldberg, 1989). In addition, the more discrepancy between the remarried father's view about children from the first marriage and his current wife's view about his children, the greater the potential for problems in the remarriage.

When rapport between the stepfather and the stepchildren is built quickly, the relationship may not always work out in the long run. The positive early relationship may have been based on unrealistic expectations that the stepfather would be the perfect father and make up for the biological father's deficiencies. The stepfather also may have seen himself as the "rescuer" for the family. After a short period of time, it may become clear to all family members that the stepfather is not able to deliver. This disappointment could be extremely damaging to the stepfather's long-term efforts to build a good relationship with his stepchildren.

The Stepmother Role

Although there are fewer stepmothers in society than stepfathers, stepmothers have not been ignored in the literature. In fact, the stepmother myth has been written about for centuries. Generally, the stepmother has been portrayed in a negative light

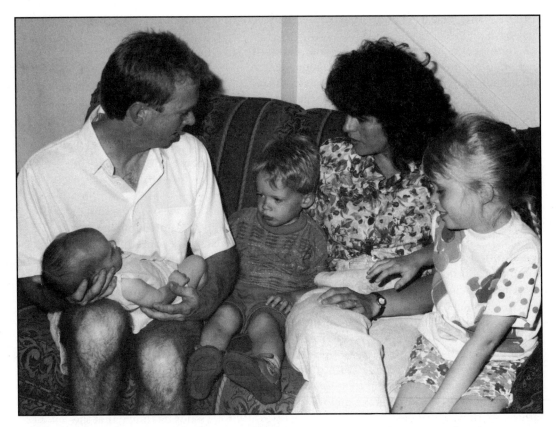

■ *The child born to the couple after remarriage becomes a symbol for the new family.*

in children's books and stories. In reality, the stepmother fares only slightly better in the research literature (Duberman, 1975). The stepmother is expected to enter the family as the nurturer and caretaker of children and to love the stepchildren as if they were her own. These expectations placed on the stepmother role require superhuman efforts, and when the stepmother falls short of them, the myth of the "evil" stepmother is strengthened and preserved.

One reason why stepmothers are viewed as having more problems with stepchildren may be because of the greater amount of time spent with children. The stepmother role predisposes children to be in close personal contact which, paradoxically, increases the opportunity for conflict. If stepfathers had as much contact with stepchildren as stepmothers have, they probably would have as difficult a time with stepchildren as stepmothers do.

When the stepmother resides in the same household with the stepchildren, there is the possibility of a close relationship developing between them *gradually*. This relationship could be hampered, however, because of the stepchildren's frequent contact with their biological mother, particularly if a conflict exists between the biological mother and the stepmother (Clingempeel & Segal, 1986).

Another reason why stepmothers may find the role difficult is because society generally assigns the mother role as more important than the father role. Children are expected to have a good relationship with the mother regardless of their relationship with the father, and they are expected to want to live with the mother after divorce. Women who voluntarily give up custody of children to their husbands are viewed as uncaring and rejecting, whereas fathers are rarely expected to pursue custody. In the recent past, awarding fathers custody of children was based on the mother being declared an "unfit mother" in a court of law. Not having custody was a type of scarlet letter that the woman had to wear.

In American society, the most common type of stepmother role is part-time—the weekend stepmother for the children of her present husband. The part-time stepmother role may be more difficult because stepchildren are in the home only twice a month and live with the biological mother the remainder of the time. This arrangement would favor the biological mother in that the stepmother would be compared negatively to her. It may also be that during the visitations the stepmother would actually spend more time with the stepchildren than the biological father spends with them. Consequently, she may have to discipline or structure them more, running the risk of conflict or causing resentment on the part of the stepchildren.

Some researchers have found that the gender and age of the stepchild play a role in the outcome. For example, the younger the child, the easier the stepmother has of relating positively. Stepmothers, as would be expected, have more difficulty relating to stepdaughters than to stepsons (Dahl, Cowgill, & Asmundsson, 1987). On the other hand, other researchers have found little difference in how stepmothers and mothers in intact and single-parent families relate to the children (Amato, 1987; Ganong & Coleman, 1987).

A Systems Perspective of Parenting in the Remarried Family

A systems perspective offers a unique way to view the remarried family. Important issues from a systems perspective are: family structure, interactional patterns, family boundaries, triangulation, feedback loops, and homeostasis. From a systems perspective, parent/child relationships would be expected to represent how the family system adjusts to the transitions in roles, the addition and subtraction of members, and the ongoing dialogue with former members (Roberts & Price, 1985).

The Factors Involved. An adequate understanding of a systems perspective of parenting in stepfamilies is enhanced by a number of factors. First, viewing the stepfamily as a process that is moving through time where change is considered normal may illustrate the interrelationship among various segments of the family. One must look upon remarriage as a process that begins with the first marriage and continues into the future. Too often stepfamilies are discussed without reference to the developmental processes, which include: the courtship period, the first marriage, divorce, the single-parent family, courtship after divorce, and remarriage (Roberts & Price, 1985). Not seeing the overall process has resulted in research that has focused on segments, such as divorce, without viewing divorce as a temporary part of a continually changing family through time.

Not only must stepfamilies be viewed as a process involving transitions through time, but, secondly, they must be seen as comprising different types corresponding to unique family relationships (Katz & Stein, 1983). For example, in one type of stepfamily the husband was previously married and has children from that marriage and his wife had not been married before. A reverse of this situation constitutes a second type, namely, the wife was previously married, has children from that marriage, and marries a man who had never been married. In a third type of stepfamily, both spouses were previously married and have children from those marriages. A fourth type is a single parent whose former spouse remarries.

Family Roles and Boundaries.   Two dimensions that describe the complexity of stepfamilies are establishing family roles and family boundaries (Walker & Messinger, 1979). **Family roles** refer to the reciprocal rights and obligations of family members, and **family boundaries** refer to the definition of a family as a unique group. Family roles include such things as the division of labor and the spousal, parental, and sibling subsystems. For example, someone takes the role of breadwinner in the family while another member takes the role of homemaker. The mother and the father usually take the parental role, although another family member may perform it.

In first marriages, the roles are more clearly defined than in second marriages, where less is assumed about the performance of roles. As previously stated, when divorced persons get remarried they must work out the family roles in a trial-and-error manner. Roles are less prescribed according to a prearranged plan. Generally, the family member who is most competent or the person who has the most interest in the outcome will perform the task.

Because of the lack of defined roles, tasks can be inappropriately performed. For example, a 10-year-old girl may take on the parental role for a younger sibling in the afternoons before both parents arrive home from work. Such an arrangement may have occurred innocently initially but over time may result in the teenager assuming greater parental responsibility and a role reversal with the stepparent.

The problem of discipline of stepchildren by stepparents has already been mentioned. To further develop this point from a systems perspective, it seems plausible to discuss the discipline issue in remarried families as a problem in family hierarchy. In other words, the biological parent is able to perform the parenting task, but the stepparent is not. The premise that both adults perform their parenting tasks equally, as would be expected in first-married families, does not apply to remarriages.

In stepfamilies, where the stepparent is usually not allowed to completely assume the parenting role, the question arises regarding the actual role the stepparent performs. For example, in a stepfamily in which the mother is the biological parent and the father is the stepparent, roles established during the single-parent period prevail. The stepfather enters an established system that is governed by rules established by the mother and her children. His addition to the family has come after the system has been firmly established. For the stepfather to fit into the family, he must make a gradual transition into different roles and behaviors.

This transition of the family into new behavioral patterns may create a period of instability and uncertainty in the family. For example, if the stepfather begins to exert parental influence during periods of time when he is home alone with his stepchildren, they may show marked responses to his new behavior. Initially, they may respond by reminding him that he is not their parent and complain to their mother when she returns.

A key factor in legitimizing the stepfather's role is the mother's support for his attempts at disciplining of the children. If she sides with the children against her husband, she elevates the children to her level in the hierarchy and demotes the stepfather to a child's role, further undermining his authority. If she supports the husband, she may initially be met with more acting-out behavior of the children because of their loss of power in the family. Over time, however, the children probably would adjust to a change in the hierarchical structure allowing a more equal parenting role for the stepparent.

Cohesion in Stepfamilies.   In addition to hierarchy in stepfamilies there is the issue of **cohesion,** or the bonding and attachment among members. Cohesion is problematic in stepfamilies because they are formed with part of the family being biologically related and having an existing history predating the marriage. For example, a divorced woman with children from a previous marriage who marries a divorced man with children from a previous marriage may find that biological members tend to be bonded and nonbiological members are not. Attempting to force cohesion may actually hamper rather than promote a sense of belonging because members may try even harder to maintain their bonding with certain members.

The cohesion concept can be described in terms of **separateness versus connectedness,** which means that either extreme is related to the development of problems. Family relationships that are too distant create families that are disengaged, and those that are too close create families that are enmeshed (Minuchin, 1974). The single-parent family as part of the process related to the formation of stepfamilies is typically a time when the parent and children are enmeshed. They may be prone to develop a rigid boundary around the relationship which, after remarriage, prevents the stepparent from penetrating. After remarriage the new family is characterized by the parent/children subsystem being too close and the stepparent/stepchildren subsystem being too distant.

The exclusion of some family members from full participation in the family leads to increased stress and ambiguity. The result of **role ambiguity** is lack of clarity about the internal and external transitions affecting members. While the stepfather may be excluded from certain significant roles, others outside the boundary of the family, such as former spouses and in-laws, may exert an enormous influence. The net effect of such ambiguity is the increase in uncertainty and confusion that members experience.

Because family boundaries may be selective in that some members are included and others excluded, it is possible for members to feel cohesive with some members, but not with all (Roberts & Price, 1985). For example, a stepfather may form immediate rapport with a stepson but not be accepted by the stepdaughter. The stepson may find that he and the stepfather have many things in common. It may be easy to relate to the stepfather as a surrogate father. The stepdaughter may resist his authority or, on the other hand, feel some split in loyalty by liking the stepfather.

Adaptability in Stepfamilies.   In addition to cohesion, **adaptability** is a family dimension that researchers believe is related to adequate adjustment in family outcomes (Olson, Sprenkle, & Russell,1979). A middle range or balance between too much and too little adaptability is desired. For example, a family that adapts to everything would be considered chaotic whereas a family that adapts to almost nothing would be considered rigid. Functional families maintain stability by adapting to some changes and resisting other changes. A stepfamily's ability to adapt to changes would be expected to differ from that of a first-married family because adaptation requires flexibility.

Cynthia Pill (1990) conducted a study to determine the relation between the stepfamily and cohesion and adaptability dimensions of family functioning. She noted that most studies to date fail to provide a theoretical base applicable to stepfamilies. The sample consisted of 29 nonclinical families composed of 58 adults and 65 stepchildren living together. One of the major goals of the study was to clarify how cohesion plays a role in the level of satisfaction in the stepfamily. Pill found that the majority of the families were on the separated end of the cohesion dimension. In interviews with family members, Pill noted that members deliberately widened the context of family events to include a greater number of the extended kinfolk network. Vacation and other activities to which members invited friends were considered more successful than outings that only the stepfamily members attended. Generally, family activities were not considered as important as activities that included a number of people outside the family.

On the adaptability dimension in the study, Pill found that stepfamilies tended to be in the upper levels of adaptability. Individual marital satisfaction scores were not related to either cohesion or adaptability, but family satisfaction scores were significantly related to high levels of cohesion. This study emphasizes a major difference in stepfamilies and two-parent biological nuclear families. In contrast to two-parent biological families, which tend to be high on the cohesion scale, the most satisfying stepfamily relationships tend to be on the low end of the cohesion dimension. Stepfamilies must be seen as a unique family form that may not conform to expectations consistent with two-parent biological nuclear families.

Another important issue in stepfamilies is **reorganization,** or changes in structure from one family form to another. The purpose of family homeostasis is to keep the family in a steady state. Changes brought about by divorce, the formation of the single-parent family, and the establishment of the stepfamily create stress that may be very difficult for children to handle. The change in structure from a single-parent family to a two-parent family demands that members are flexible enough to take on different roles, open their boundaries, and renegotiate their hierarchies. Problematic behavior, especially in children, may be considered a failure to adjust to the changing structure. For example, one could expect that a misbehaving 10-year-old boy who had always done very well in school until his parents divorced would be acting out family stress resulting from the divorce of his parents.

The misbehavior in the child may become the focal point around which the family interacts. Consequently, the child's misbehavior functions to maintain the stability of the family. When the child's behavior becomes central to the family functioning in this way, it is extremely difficult to change because all members behave in a way to perpetuate it. A change in the child's behavior would unbalance the family again and force it to reorganize around other behavior.

Family Portrait ▪▪▪▪▪▪▪▪▪▪

T he Bensons, Ben and Betty, have been married for ten months. The marriage, the second for each, has been plagued by problems since the beginning. Ben was married for 15 years to his high school sweetheart and had three children, Ben, Jr., age 13, Mary age 11, and Kelly age 8. He has been divorced from his first wife, Marla, for almost four years. Betty, married for almost 12 years to David, had two children in that marriage, Brandy 12 and Jerry 8. She has been divorced for three years.

Prior to the remarriage, Ben had regular visits with his children. During the summer, all three children lived with Ben. The summer before the remarriage, Ben, Jr., was seriously considering moving in with his dad. Ben's relationship with Marla was fairly amiable until Ben's marriage to Betty.

Ben and Betty met at a party sponsored by a local single-parent organization. Although Ben did not have custody of his three children, they frequently stayed with him and he attended parenting classes and meetings with other single parents. Both Ben and Betty were immediately attracted to each other. Betty described their meeting as a fantasy come true. As she passed a group of people at the party on her way to the ladies' room, her eyes met Ben's as he was talking to someone and she fell immediately in love. Ben acknowledged the rush when he saw her as well. After a whirlwind romance of a few months they got married. Neither thought very much about the children and believed it would just work out. Although they were together almost all the time before marriage, they did not cohabitate because they were concerned with how it would affect the children.

After marriage to Betty, Ben's contact with his own children decreased partly because Betty had difficulty relating to them and partly because Ben was making an effort to accommodate Betty and her children. Ben made a number of attempts to reduce the tension between Betty and his children by supporting Betty and attempting to get them to relate to her in positive ways, but to no avail. He believed that they needed time to adjust to the quick marriage. Betty came to the conclusion that they resented her and that nothing would help.

Furthermore, Betty's children had problems accepting Ben. Ben had moved into their apartment with the intention of buying a house as soon as they could. A number of financial setbacks and sporadic child-support payments from Betty's former husband doomed their immediate efforts to find a house. Brandy seemed to have more of a problem relating to Ben than her brother, Jerry, had because during the divorce she had comforted her mother and, at times, slept in her room. She greatly resented Ben for taking her mother away from her. In addition, the new marriage had interrupted the contact with extended kin and in-law relationships. Before the remarriage Betty's children spent a large part of each summer at her former husband's parents' home.

Brandy had also developed some problems at school. She was a very bright girl but did not like to study or do homework. During the single-parent period, Betty spent countless hours with Brandy in such activities as doing homework. Since the remarriage, Betty had not been as available to Brandy and her grades were evidence of it. In school, Brandy had moved to the back of the room and frequently talked out loud while the teacher was talking. She did not pay attention and many times did not know of homework assignments. The teacher sent several notes home to Betty and had a number of parent/teacher conferences. Brandy would be extremely compliant immediately after the conferences but would resort back to noncompliant behavior shortly after these meetings.

Betty set a rigid schedule in the evening to help Brandy structure herself so that she would be able to do the homework. Ben attempted to reinforce this schedule when Betty was away in the evening, but found Brandy unwilling to do anything to improve the situation. A number of strategies had been tried, such as grounding, not talking on the phone to friends until homework was completed, and taking away privileges. None of these strategies improved the situation.

To complicate the situation, Ben and Betty began to disagree about how to handle Brandy. Ben believed that Betty was too lenient and inconsistent. According to Ben, Betty would fail to carry through on a particular strategy because she felt sorry for Brandy or because Brandy would complain to Betty that it was Ben's fault. Ben was angry that his own children were not welcomed in the home and felt he had given up a great deal for very little in return. To complicate matters, Ben's former wife was angry about his remarriage and threatened to reduce his visitation rights. This renewed conflict with the former wife made Ben reluctant to contact her even when the situation demanded it.

Compare and Contrast

Parenting approaches dealing with this situation from PET, Adlerian, and behavioral perspectives would not be concerned with the description just given. In fact, aside from the targeted behavior, the behavioral approach would disregard any other information as not needed. The focus in all three would be on changing the unwanted behavior as if it occurred in isolation rather than in the specific context mentioned earlier.

PET (Gordon, 1975) would focus on the parent/child relationship, in this case Brandy and her mother. Betty would be helped in giving reflective and understanding responses to Brandy in an attempt to show that she cares. The goal would be that

Brandy would tell her mother her concerns, feel accepted, and be able to solve her problems at school herself. Betty would be taught how to use I-messages to tell Brandy specifically what she expected of her. Problem solving with Brandy might also help her make decisions about how to improve her behavior.

Although the PET (Gordon, 1975) approach emphasizes the importance of communication, it does not address the structural issues in this family. While Betty might be advised how to communicate better with Brandy, the coalition between Betty and Brandy is not addressed. This coalition tends to prevent Betty from being able not only to effectively communicate with Brandy but also to effectively structure her.

The Adlerian approach (Dreikurs & Soltz, 1964) would acknowledge the familial situation as being important in Brandy's problems but would not make structural changes in the family system. For example, Adlerians might be aware that Betty's brief courtship and remarriage may be related to Brandy's behavior, but they would be more concerned about Brandy being reared in an atmosphere where she learned to take responsibility for her own behavior.

Betty would be helped in letting Brandy suffer the consequences of her own behavior in her schoolwork and in setting logical consequences for her misbehavior around the home. Brandy's relationship with Ben, her stepsiblings, and her grandparents would be of little significance to Adlerians.

Behaviorists (Patterson, 1976) would be interested in setting a goal or targeting specific behavior to focus on. Brandy's noncompliant behavior at home might be the first behavior to change. She would be rewarded for positive behavior, and some punishment might occur for negative behavior. The long-range goal would be for her to complete her homework assignments, pay attention in school, and improve her relationship with Ben. Goals would be worked on separately as if they were independent. The structural dimensions of the problem, how it is related to the homeostasis of the family, would not be a focus of intervention.

Although a systems perspective would have similar goals in changing Brandy's behavior, the main focus of intervention would be the family and the social network. The family structure would need to be reorganized, particularly in terms of boundaries and roles. For example, the boundaries of the family do not fully include Ben, and Brandy has an enmeshed boundary with her mother, preventing her from establishing her own identity. This boundary between Brandy and Betty prevents Betty and Ben from forming a firm marital bond. Betty is unable to break the bond or coalition with Brandy because of her guilt feelings about the divorce from Brandy's father.

This history, important as it is, must also be utilized in its present context. In other words, effective change must involve the family members in the strategy to change Brandy's behavior. The focus would not be on the problem per se, but rather on how the problem is maintained. For example, the systems specialist would be interested in how Brandy's poor academic and social behavior is maintained at home and in the school context. The home, or the school, or a combination of the two contexts could become the focus for change. In this case, the home appears to be the context that supports and maintains Brandy's misconduct.

The first intervention in this family would be to reframe Brandy's behavior. This reframing would be necessary because Betty is convinced that everything has been tried and nothing has worked. Reframing Brandy's misbehavior into something different would open up possibilities for trying new behavior. Reframing Brandy's behavior as her lack of adjusting to her mother's remarriage would pose the problem in a different mode and allow for a possible solution.

Another important issue at home would be to prevent Brandy from intruding in the marital relationship between Betty and Ben. Brandy's position of closeness to Betty places her in a position of power over Ben and relegates his role as co-executive with Betty in the family configuration. Brandy has also been able to maintain power over the school system because her parents have not responded conjointly to the school's concern about her behavior.

The developmental level of the family also is a significant fact that needs some attention. For example, Brandy is entering puberty, or the adolescence stage in the family life cycle. While the family is at the adolescent stage according to the ages of children, it is also merely in the beginning family stage in terms of adjustment. Betty and Ben are still working through the coupling that takes place in the beginning family stage. The Benson family has been responding rigidly to this life-cycle transition.

Brandy's poor performance in school is an attempt to maintain a special place with her mother. Betty's response to protect Brandy from suffering the consequences of the punishment devised to change her behavior has undermined her marriage and alliance with her husband. A systems specialist would encourage Brandy to do some activities with Ben alone, such as play tennis together, which they both enjoy. Betty and Ben need to spend time together and make decisions about how they as a couple will handle the discipline of their children. One of these decisions may be how they will work together with the school system. Another might be how to reopen the family boundaries to the extended family, including former in-laws.

■ ■ ■ ■ ■ ■ ■ ■ ■ ■ ■

Parenting Proposition

Single-parent families and stepfamilies are at higher risk for problems than are two-parent biological families because of difficulties with boundaries, roles, family hierarchy, feedback loops, triangulation, and cross-generational coalitions.

Answers to "Test Your Knowledge"

1. F   4. F
2. T   5. F
3. T   6. F

Key Concepts

single-parent families   child care

transition   custody

custodial parent

noncustodial parent

independence

single-parent mothers

child-support payments

role overload

discipline

single-parent father

family cohesion

cross-generational alliance

systems perspective of parenting
  in single-parent family

role responsibilities

parentified child

external familial resources

family life cycle

binuclear family

family hierarchy

authoritative parenting

triangulation

remarried family

reconstituted family

stepfamily

blended family

stepparenting

instant families

stepfather

stepmother

family roles

family boundaries

cohesion

separateness versus connectedness

role ambiguity

adaptability

family reorganization

Study Questions

1 Describe different types of single-parent families. Why is it important to have knowledge of different types of single-parent families? Discuss the concept of transition in terms of single-parent families. How do various factors, such as race and resources, affect the formation and maintenance of single-parent families?

2 Discuss the effects of divorce on children. What factors are related to good adjustment, and what factors are related to poor adjustment in single-parent families?

3 What factors are related to custody arrangements? Discuss the plight of the noncustodial parent. Are there ways to safeguard children in custody disputes?

4 Discuss factors related to the stepfather role. What are the special problems that stepfathers must address? Discuss factors that improve the stepfather's chance of being accepted as a parent figure.

5 Why is the stepmother role considered harder to master than the stepfather role?

6 What is the parentified child? Why is this role detrimental to the child? What dynamic best describes this situation?

7 Discuss the following systems terms as they apply to the single-parent family: triangulation, cross-generational alliance, family life cycle, and family cohesion. Discuss these terms in reference to remarried families.

8 What are the unique features of remarried families?

9 Discuss separateness versus connectedness in remarried families.

10 Discuss similarities and differences in female- and male-headed single-parent homes.

References

Ahrons, C., & Wallisch, L. (1987). Parenting in the binuclear family: Relationships between biological and stepparents. In E. Hetherington & J. Aratesh (Eds.), *Impact of divorce, single-parenting, and stepparenting on children* (pp. 225–256). Hillsdale, NJ: Erlbaum.

Amato, P. (1987). Family processes in one-parent, stepparent, and intact families: The child's point of view. *Journal of Marriage and the Family, 49,* 327–337.

Amato, P., & Keith, B. (1990, April). Consequences of divorce for the well-being of children: A meta-analysis. Paper presented at the Midwest Sociological Society, Chicago.

Ambert, A. (1985). Custodial parents: Review and longitudinal study. In B. Schlesinger (Ed.), *The one-parent family in the 1980s: Perspective and annotated bibliography, 1978–1984* (pp. 13–34). Toronto: University of Toronto.

Asmussen, L., & Larson, R. (1991). The quality of family time among young adolescents in single-parent and married-parent families. *Journal of Marriage and the Family, 53,* 1021–1030.

Bohannan, P., & Erickson, P. (1978, January). Stepping in. *Psychology Today,* pp. 53–59.

Brophy, B. (1986, October 27). Children under stress. *U.S. News and World Report,* pp. 58–63.

Bumpass, L. L. (1984). Children and marital disruption: A replication and update. *Demography, 21,* 7–82.

Burden, D. (1986). Single parents and the work setting: The impact of multiple job and homelife responsibilities. *Family Relations, 35,* 37–43.

Carter, E. A., & McGoldrick, M. (1989). *The changing family life cycle* (2nd ed.). Boston: Allyn & Bacon.

Cherlin, A. (1978). Remarriage as an incomplete institution. *American Journal of Sociology, 84,* 634–648.

Clingempeel, W. G., & Segal, S. (1986). Stepparent–stepchild relationships and the psychological adjustment of children in stepmother and stepfather families. *Child Development, 57,* 474–484.

Coleman, J. S. (1988). Social capital in the creation of human capital. *American Journal of Sociology, 94,* 95–120.

Dahl, A., Cowgill, K., & Asmundsson, R. (1987). Life in remarried families. *Social Work, 32,* 40–44.

Dreikurs, R., & Soltz, V. (1964). *Children: The challenge.* New York: Hawthorn.

Duberman, L. (1975). *The reconstituted family: A study of remarried couples and their children.* Chicago: Nelson-Hall.

Emery, R. E. (1988). *Marriage, divorce, and children's adjustment.* Newbury Park, CA: Sage.

Fassinger, P. A. (1989). Becoming the breadwinner: Single mothers' reaction to changes in their paid work lives. *Family Relations, 38,* 404–411.

Fletcher, C. N. (1989). A comparison of income and expenditures of male-headed households paying child support and female-headed households receiving child support. *Family Relations, 38,* 412–417.

Fulmer, R. (1983). A structural approach to unresolved mourning in single-parent family systems. *Journal of Marital and Family Therapy, 9,* 259–269.

Ganong, L., & Coleman, M. (1987). Stepchildren's perceptions of their parents. *Journal of Genetic Psychology, 148,* 5–17.

Gordon, T. (1975). *Parent effectiveness training.* New York: Peter H. Wyden.

Goldzband, M. G. (1985). *Quality time.* New York: McGraw-Hill.

Greif, G. (1985). *Single fathers.* Lexington, MA: Heath.

Guisinger, S., Cowan, P., & Schuldberg, D. (1989). Changing parent and spouse relations in the first years of remarriage of divorced fathers. *Journal of Marriage and the Family, 51,* 445–456.

Haley, J. (1987). *Problem-solving therapy.* San Francisco: Jossey-Bass.

Hanson, S. (1986). Healthy single families. *Family Relations, 35,* 125–132.

Hetherington, E. M. (1987). Family relationships six years after divorce. In K. Pasley & M. Ihinger-Tallman (Eds.), *Remarriage and stepparenting: Current research and theory* (pp. 185–205). New York: Guilford Press.

Hetherington, E. M. (1989). Coping with family transitions: Winners, losers, and survivors. *Child Development, 60,* 114–131.

Hetherington, E. M., & Camara, K. (1984). Families in transition: The process of dissolution and reconstruction. In R. Parke (Ed.), *Review of child development research 7: The family* (pp. 398–431). Chicago: University of Chicago Press.

Hetherington, E. M., Hagan, M., & Anderson, E. (1989). Marital transitions: A child's perspective. *American Psychologist, 44,* 303–312.

Hill, R. (1986). Life-cycle stages for types of single-parent families. *Family Relations, 35,* 29–39.

Katz, L., & Stein, S. (1983). Treating stepfamilies. In B. Wolman & G. Streicker (Eds.), *Handbook of marital and family therapy.* New York: Plenum Press.

Luster, T., & Rhoades, K. (1989). The relations between child-rearing beliefs and the home environments in a sample of adolescent mothers. *Family Relations, 38,* 317–322.

Mauldin, T. A. (1990). Women who remain above the poverty level in divorce: Implications for family policy. *Family Relations, 39,* 141–146.

Minuchin, S. (1974). *Families and family therapy.* Cambridge, MA: Harvard University Press.

Moore, K. A., Peterson, J. L., & Zill, N. (1985). *Social and economic correlates of family structures: A portrait of U.S. children in 1983* (Child Trends Working Paper No. 85-01). Washington, DC: Child Trends.

Mullis, R. L., Mullis, A. K., & Markstrom, C. (1987). Reports of child behavior by single mothers and married mothers. *Child Study Journal, 17,* 211–225.

National Center for Health Statistics. (1990, July 26). Annual summary of births, marriages, divorces, and deaths: United States, 1988. *Monthly Vital Statistics Report, 34.*

Nock, S. L. (1988). The family and hierarchy. *Journal of Marriage and the Family, 50,* 957–966.

Norton, A. J., & Glick, P. G. (1986). One-person families: A social and economic profile. *Family Relations, 35,* 9–13.

Olson, D. H., Sprenkle, D., & Russell, C. (1979). Circumplex model of marital and family systems: 1. Cohesion and adaptability dimensions, family types, and clinical applications. *Family Relations, 18,* 5–28.

Pasley, K., & Ihinger-Tallman, M. (1988). Remarriage and stepfamilies. In C. Chilman, E. Nunnally, & F. Cox (Eds.), *Variant family forms.* Newbury Park, CA: Sage.

Patterson, G. R. (1976). *Living with children* (rev. ed.). Champaign, IL: Research Press.

Pill, C. (1990). Stepfamilies: Redefining the family. *Family Relations, 39,* 186–193.

Quinn, P., & Allen, K. R. (1989). Facing challenges and making compromises: How single mothers endure. *Family Relations, 38,* 390–395.

Ramsey, S. (1986). Stepparent support for stepchildren: The changing legal context and the need of empirical policy research. *Family Relations, 35,* 363–369.

Rice, F. P. (1990). Intimate relationships, marriages, and families. Mountain View, CA: Mayfield.

Roberts, T. W., & Price, S. J. (1985). A systems analysis of the remarriage process: Implications for the clinician. *Journal of Divorce, 9,* 1–25.

Roberts, T. W., & Price, S. J. (1987). Instant families: Divorced mothers marry never-married men. *Journal of Divorce, 11,* 71–92.

Santrock, J. W., & Warshak, R. A. (1979). Father custody and social development in boys and girls. *Journal of Social Issues, 35,* 112–124.

Santrock, J. W., & Warshak, R. A. (1986). Development, relationship, and legal/clinical considerations in father-custody families. In M. E. Lamb (Ed.), *The father's role: Applied perspectives.* New York: Wiley.

Schlesinger, B. (1978, May/June). Single parents: A research review. *Children Today, 12,* 18–22.

U.S. Bureau of the Census. (1987). Child support and alimony: 1985. *Current Population Surveys Special Studies* (Series P-23, No. 152). Washington, DC: U.S. Government Printing Office.

U.S. Bureau of the Census. (1989). Fertility in American women: June 1988. *Current Population Reports* (Population Characteristics Series, P-20, No. 436). Issued May, 1989.

Visher, E., & Visher, J. (1978). Common problems of stepparents and their spouses. *American Journal of Orthopsychiatry, 48,* 252–262.

Walker, K., & Messinger, L. (1979). Remarriage after divorce: Dissolution and reconstruction of family boundaries. *Family Process, 18,* 185–192.

Wallerstein, J. S. (1986). Women after divorce: Preliminary report from a ten-year follow-up. *American Journal of Orthopsychiatry, 56,* 65–76.

Wallerstein, J. S., & Blakeslee, S. (1989). *Second chances: Men, women, and children a decade after divorce.* New York: Ticknor & Fields.

Wallerstein, J. S., & Kelly, J. B. (1980). *Surviving the breakup.* New York: Basic Books.

Weiss, R. S. (1979). Growing up a little faster: The experience of growing up in a single-parent household. *Journal of Social Issues, 35,* 97–111.

White, L. K., & Booth, A. (1985). The quality and stability of remarriages: The role of stepchildren. *American Sociological Review, 50,* 689–698.

Wright, D., & Price, S. J. (1986). Court-ordered child support payment: The effect of the former-spouse relationship on compliance. *Journal of Marriage and the Family, 48,* 869–874.

Zaslow, M. J. (1989). Sex differences in children's response to parental divorce: Two samples, variables, ages, and sources. *American Journal of Orthopsychology, 59,* 118–141.

Chapter 10

A Cross-Cultural Perspective of Parenting

Parenting Myth ■ The cultural differences in parenting cause different outcomes in children.

Test Your Knowledge ■ The following questions are designed to test your knowledge before reading the material in the chapter. Answers appear at the end of the chapter.

1 Black parents spend more time racially socializing their children than do white parents. True or false?

2 White parents use more coercive means to control a child than do black parents, who talk more to their children. True or false?

3 Hispanic parenting emphasizes the process of differentiation in contrast to group affiliation. True or false?

4 Asian-American students do better in academic subjects and on standardized tests than majority students even though they may not be as conversant in the English language. True or false?

5 Black children are much more likely to be physically abused than white children. True or false?

6 Teachers tend to be biased against children who continue to exhibit language patterns that represent a cultural heritage. True or false?

As discussed in an earlier chapter, development across the life cycle can best be explained in a **systems/dialectical model,** which posits that the individual is both a system and a subsystem in a larger **ecosystem.** This ecosystem is constantly in process so that acquiring and maintaining an equilibrium is more appearance that actual. Changes in a part of the ecosystem lead to changes in all parts, including the ecosystem itself. A significant aspect of the ecosystem is the cultural dimension. As part of the ecosystem, culture is viewed as changing and never static. Cultural influences change unevenly in that some segments of society appear unchanged whereas other segments have lost much of their cultural uniqueness. Each new generation tends to pass on the cultural heritage to their offspring and slightly modify it in the process.

The ecosystem approach to the study of families means that the debate of the primacy of any one function over another is moot. The old debate of the primacy of nature over nurture is a pointless argument when both biological and social factors are viewed within an ecological perspective. The interaction and reciprocal influence of these systems within the ecosystem change both the system and the ecosystem itself.

While some developmental issues may be considered consistent across different cultures, there is some evidence that in American culture, racial and ethnic subcultures do exist and explain some of the differences in children and families. Some of these differences may be related to beliefs about parenting, gender roles, appropriate expression of emotion, and treatment of the elderly that tend to be transmitted via the complex patterns of socialization.

The purpose of this chapter is to be sensitive to the total ecosystem, or context, in which the child is developing. The cultural context is viewed as extremely important to the developing ecosystem and can help explain how people sharing the same general influences may have similar belief systems and similar behavioral patterns. In order to limit this discussion while providing a framework for understanding cultural influences, three racial groups will be discussed: the black family, the Hispanic family, and the Asian family.

■ The Black Family

It is not unusual for different images to emerge when discussing the black family. One of the first to emerge is that of the single black mother who is receiving welfare and has little or no support from the father of the child. A less common but just as descriptive image of the typical black household is two working adults with children who are equally competitive with their peers. In fact, researchers have generally found that there is little difference between what black and white parents want for their children (Peters, 1988). Studies indicate that the black middle-class family varies little from the white middle-class family in emphasizing the importance of the parenting experience (McAdoo, 1988; Peters, 1988).

Table 10.1 ■ Sexual Attitudes in Different Cultures

- Children's attitudes about sexual behavior appear to be the product of the particular culture in which they are reared.

- In restrictive cultures such as New Guinea, sexual relations may not occur until after marriage.

- Permissive cultures, such as Sweden's, permit openness about sexuality. Children learn about sex at an early age and are permitted to openly engage in sexual behavior in adolescence.

- The American culture appears to be a "semi-restrictive" culture in that, although children are learning about sex, many parents still attempt to restrict such knowledge.

Source: Gagnon, 1985.

Socialization in Black Families

The extent to which **socialization,** the process by which society influences members through the development of certain attitudes and beliefs, may be a unique experience in the black family is just now beginning to emerge in the literature. Some researchers suggest that black parents have the dual role of socializing their children to function in the larger society while identifying themselves as members of the black subculture (Peters & Massey, 1983).

Black parents socialize their children through verbal means, modeling, and artifacts. This type of socialization includes an emphasis on both individual and intergroup identity. Researchers have differed overall in findings regarding the **racial socialization** of black children. For example, some researchers have found that some black parents have emphasized racial socialization while other parents have not. Black parents who focus on the racial socialization of their children believe that it is important not only to rear an American but also to rear a black American. Black parents who do not racially socialize their children generally feel that there may be negative effects in doing so (Thornton, Chatters, Taylor, & Allen, 1990). For example, they may not develop adaptive attitudes to fit in with the majority culture.

In racially socializing their children, black parents generally do not teach specific facts about black culture or heritage. Rather, they focus on teaching them the experience of being a minority in a majority culture. Helping their children maintain self-respect and deal with prejudice tends to comprise the content of such socialization (Thornton et al., 1990).

Another group of black parents believe that it is more important to instill certain human values in their children that are not race specific. For example, certain human values, such as respect and ambition, transcend race and are seen as more important for success in living than identity in a racial group. One would expect that, in acquiring certain generic life skills, black children would be more competitive with white children than if they received instruction only in their black identity (Thornton et al., 1990).

■ *Black youths gain identity through shared activities.*

In a survey of racial socialization, researchers found that most black parents do engage in some form of racial socialization. Subjects most likely to racially socialize their children were older, resided in the north, and were married versus being a single parent. The age variable was correlated with formal education for women but not for men so that the higher the education and the older a respondent the more likely racial socialization occurred (Thornton et al., 1990).

Although the preceding discussion adds some knowledge to how black parents racially socialize their children, a systemic orientation might give greater clarity to how parents teach their children about racial identity. Furthermore, the larger social network might provide important input in how racial identity is transmitted to the child and from the child to the parent. The impact of memberships in certain activities, such as gangs versus sports or cultural events, might also provide valuable information about the process involved in racial socialization.

Identity Processes Among Black Children

The racial and ethnic factors related to child and adolescent development have seldom been addressed adequately in the literature (Gibbs & Huang, 1989). It is reasonable to assume, however, that children of color are subjected to more prejudicial behavior by majority children in contact at schools. Parents of children of color have a difficult task not only to be helpful to their children in expected development but also to protect their children from prejudice (Spencer & Markstrom-Adams, 1990).

Although race and ethnicity may overlap, the two terms refer to different concepts. *Ethnicity* provides the participant a shared or common heritage and a sense of belonging to a particular group. Ethnic group membership provides the individual with a schema by which to process the world. *Racial identity,* while referring to a particular self-consciousness, appears more stable across time and is deeper than ethnic characteristics (Spencer & Markstrom-Adams, 1990).

Researchers have found that minority children have shown a marked **white bias,** or preference for white identity and attitudes. The reasons for such biases are not known, but some researchers suggest that minority children must operate in the macrosystem level of white dominance. Black children may be expected to develop a white bias in a system where they are bombarded with white culture at every turn (Spencer & Markstrom-Adams, 1990).

In an earlier chapter, identity formation in adolescence was delineated according to Erikson. These identity issues for minority adolescents have not been systematically explored. Researchers have generally found that black children tend to be higher in foreclosure—that is, prematurely closing off exploration of identity—than white children. Although researchers have attempted to match adolescents in terms of social class, they have not controlled for single-parent households. Other researchers have found that black adolescents have a better sense of the meaning of prejudice and their identity within their own culture than do white adolescents. This finding suggests that the experience of prejudice might increase the need for understanding one's own culture (Spencer & Markstrom-Adams, 1990).

The Black Family and Poverty

Black families have been overrepresented in lower socioeconomic and poverty status, referred to as **black poverty.** Although blacks improved relative to whites during the

1970s, there has been a reversal of the trend since 1979. In fact, by the mid-1980s black poverty was at an all-time high (Billingsley, 1988). About half of all black children now reside in poverty (Children's Defense Fund, 1985). A major factor related to poverty in black children is the high incidence of teenage pregnancy and female-headed households. The divorce rate is higher for blacks than for whites, and divorces typically occur at younger ages (Norton, 1983). This disadvantage in the way families are formed and structured may predispose black children toward particular outcomes, such as lower educational and occupational attainment.

This view of the black family as residing in poverty has been a major theme since the 1960s with the publication of Senator Patrick Moynihan's report "The Negro Family: The Case for National Alarm" in 1965. This report essentially described the black family as disorganized, lacking in certain basic resources, matriarchal, and suffering from the aftershocks of slavery and discrimination. It suggested that the black family had been destroyed by slavery and never regained status because it was matriarchal.

Since Moynihan's report was published, there has been much criticism and some rethinking and rewriting of the condition of the black family. Researchers have concluded that Moynihan's conclusions were based on faulty reasoning. For example, during slavery there is evidence from slave owners' records that the black family remained intact with both parents present (Steckel, 1980). Researchers have also demonstrated that in 1965, when Moynihan's report was published, the majority of black families contained two parents (Staples, 1985).

Despite the tendency to view all black families similarly, there is evidence that black families, like white families, represent diversity. Some researchers, for example, have noted that black families are represented in all social strata (Willie, 1981). Others have noted that diversity in black families includes differences in values, religious orientation, customs, and family socioeconomic status (Billingsley, 1988). Although black heritage continues to be a source of influence, black families in America are exposed to the predominating Euro-American culture. This exposure over time means that the black experience tends to be somewhat diluted by the dominant culture and, as such, is a kind of smorgasbord of cultural influences.

Strengths in Black Families

While much has been written about the problems in the black family, there is also evidence that black families have many unique strengths. The fact that the black family could survive the hardships of slavery, poverty, segregation, and discrimination speaks for its inherent strength and resilience. No other type of family in American society has endured as much stress and economic hardship as the black family.

A major source of strength in the black family has been a strong religious heritage. No doubt, the experience of oppression led blacks to rely on divine grace and otherworldly involvement. The church also functioned as a forum for political and social activism, which redefined the black experience not only for blacks but also for the larger society.

Researchers have found that family ties are strong among members in the black family. For example, black families tend to be more extended than white families, and it is common for black families of origin to offer support to offspring in the formation of nuclear and single-parent families. Furthermore, black families tend to help with child care and provide many unpaid services for members. Children are highly regarded and valued in black families (Taylor, 1986).

Family roles tend to be more flexible and less rigid in black families. The father role may be assumed by an uncle, a grandfather, or an older brother. Marital roles in black families tend to be more egalitarian than marital roles in the majority culture in which both husband and wife share in the household division of labor. This ability to share roles has been linked to less stress in two-parent families (Gary, Beatty, Berry, & Price, 1986).

Black Culture and Parenting

Black children and white children tend to vary on a number of issues related to family and parenting variables. On average black children tend to be more active from birth than white children. Their advanced motor skills may have developed because of a number of factors. For example, black mothers tend to hold and handle young children more than white mothers do. The mother's behavior may stimulate more physical activity on the part of the black child. This maternal behavior, in addition to the high noise and activity level in black homes, may account for more stimulation and, consequently, more physical activity on the part of the child (Hale-Benson, 1986).

Specific parenting behaviors tend to differ in black and white families. For example, black parents tend to believe in and use physical punishment more than white parents. Typically, this use of physical punishment is related to a belief in the need to control behavior and gain the child's respect for authority. Black parents, in marked contrast with white parents, tend to encourage their children to fight back when in confrontation with others (Hale-Benson, 1986).

The emphasis on physical punishment may also reflect a reduced capacity to parent in a supportive and resourceful manner. The overuse of physical punishment is usually related to a lack of resources and alternatives for resolving a parent/child conflict regardless of the race of the parent (Patterson, DeBarsyshe, & Ramsey, 1989). The increase in stress and psychological distress in mothers has been related to punitive and aversive child-rearing techniques. For some black families, the level of family stress related to certain factors, such as poverty and discrimination, might make them at high risk for using excessive physical punishment.

In a number of ways, blacks seem more vulnerable to stress than whites. First, researchers have found that there is a higher incidence of mental or emotional problems for persons in the lower socioeconomic class (McAdoo, 1986). Because a higher proportion of blacks than whites are below the poverty line, it seems that blacks would be more vulnerable to stress than whites. Researchers have found that black men who are concerned about job loss and have fewer financial resources experience more psychological distress than black males who are confident about the future (Bowman, 1988).

Second, the higher incidence of female-headed households predisposes black families for problems (McAdoo, 1986). Much of the distress in black female-headed households is related to being overburdened with the total care of the household and parenting. Researchers have found that female-headed households are much more likely to experience unemployment, change of residence, illness or death of a child, and change in household composition (Belle, 1984).

Third, blacks who live in poverty are predisposed to experience more unfavorable psychological and physical conditions than middle-class blacks or whites. Poverty seems to be the conduit whereby other equally problematic and debilitating conditions occur. Researchers have found that when economic conditions are not confounded by other stressful events, there is no difference between blacks who live in poverty and middle-class blacks and whites (Kessler, Turner, & House, 1987).

Researchers have found that poverty is related to the following specific parenting behaviors: power assertion, less support given to children, expectation of value compliance rather than creativity from children, physical punishment, and nonverbal behaviors, such as pointing. Overall, there appears to be an impoverished parent/child relationship in the black family (Peterson & Peters, 1985). Behaviors normally associated with functional parenting, such as listening, empathy, and patience, are in short supply when the parent is overstressed and overburdened. Reduced efficiency in parenting appears to be correlated even to relatively minor stresses (Patterson, 1988).

Discipline in Black Families

As mentioned earlier, black children are more likely to be physically punished than white children. In addition, researchers have found that black children are three times more likely to be abused than white children (Children's Defense Fund, 1985). Black parents use coercive and punitive means of obtaining compliance (Allen, 1985) and use fewer strategies meant to create a sense of internal control for behavior than do white parents (Durrett, O'Bryant, & Pennebaker, 1975).

Although a number of factors, perhaps related to black heritage, may account for some of the differences between blacks and whites, a plausible explanation is the difference in resources in black and white families, even those of the same social class. Researchers have found that black and white families of the same social class may experience different levels of psychological stress (Kessler & Neighbors, 1986). In addition, the tendency of black women to have more children spaced only a few years apart may change the pattern of parenting significantly. Increased anxiety, psychological stress, and economic hardship appear highly correlated with reduced ability to parent. These factors mean that the black mother is more likely to use punitive and coercive methods of parenting than a more understanding and empathic approach.

Some limited research supports the contention that when disadvantaged black mothers emulate white parenting strategies of increased support and verbal exchanges with their children, they improve their parenting effectiveness (Blau, 1981). Apparently, when there is interracial contact, the black parent is better able to prepare the child for interaction within the mainstream society. Conversely, other researchers have found that when blacks live in an integrated neighborhood where they are the minority, they have more psychological distress and presumably more problems with parenting than when they live in a racially consistent neighborhood (McAdoo, 1982).

Researchers have found that the black family has a large support system which provides help in such areas of parenting as discipline (Cotterell, 1986). Black grandmothers tend to be very active in parenting when the mother is unmarried. This type of joint child care may provide the inexperienced mother not only with information about how to care for a child but also with appropriate modeling of parenting behavior. Because grandmothers have been found to engage with grandchildren in less punitive means than teenage mothers, it would be expected that teenage mothers whose mothers are jointly involved in parenting would be able to parent more effectively (Wilson, 1986).

When black grandmothers are co-residents in an offspring's family, particularly a single-mother household, her employment status determines her child-care responsibilities (Pearson, Hunter, Ensminger, & Kellam, 1990). The grandmother is much more likely to have the sole responsibility for parenting when she is unemployed. On the other hand, if the grandmother contributes to the family income, she may also exert considerable influence in household decisions and child rearing. Generally, studies have found that co-residing black grandmothers are more involved in parenting than their nonresiding counterparts.

Peer-Group Relationships in Black Families

In all cultures, peer-group relationships take on an important role in late childhood and early adolescence. How black children relate in peer groups both reflects and also differs from majority society. For example, among blacks the peer-group experience is more pronounced for males than females. Certain games whereby the black male gains competency in relating to other males and gains control over his own emotions predominate in the peer group. These games tend to be a kind of rite of passage, or testing of one's skill that is correlated with success in the peer-group experience (Hale-Benson, 1986).

Although the peer group takes a different focus for black girls, there is some evidence that it is very important. To some extent, social norms for adult male–female relationships appear to be greatly influenced by the adolescent's peer group. However, because females tend to be involved in household responsibilities and taking care of younger siblings, the impact of the peer group is somewhat limited for black females (Hale-Benson, 1986).

Box 10.1

■■■■■■■■■■■

Multigenerational Households: The Role of the Black Grandmother

Pearson, Hunter, Ensminger, and Kellam (1990) attempted to determine the family structure where black grandmothers and grandchildren reside in the same household, the degree to which grandmothers participate and influence parenting decisions in the family, and the effects of the grandmother's employment status on parenting. Subjects included cohorts of first-graders and their families from the 1966–1967 statistics of the Woodlawn community in Chicago, a predominantly black community characterized by poverty and overcrowding. The Mental Health Assessment and Evaluation Unit assessed 1,391 children and interviewed their mothers or mother surrogates, generally grandmothers, on such issues as the child's functioning, family household characteristics, and interaction with community organizations. Families with grandmother co-residents in the home, comprising about 10% of the families, were the focus of this research. Family size ranged from 2 to 18 with 68% of the families having mothers. Families that included grandmothers typically did not have grandfathers. In the families that included a grandmother but no mother, the majority had no father or grandfather present. Only three families, excluded from the study, included a father and a grandmother in the same household. Parents or parent surrogates, such as grandmothers, provided the information in the study. Questions such as who reads the child stories, sets the rules, or provides punishment were asked of all parent surrogates.

Sixty-three percent of the families were at or below the poverty line. When the family was headed by the grandmother alone or by the mother/grandmother, the poverty index was about 69%. Of the grandmothers in the study, 35% were married, 39% were widowed, 20% were separated, and 7% were divorced. Mothers were the most active in child rearing when they were present, including reading stories, setting bedtime routines, and providing discipline. Fathers were much more active than grandfathers but were generally not present at bedtime. Grandmothers who were involved in parenting were more likely to be active when the mother was not present in the family. Employment of grandmothers had little correlation with the type of family. The evidence appears to support the contention that black grandmothers are more likely to reside in the daughter's or son's family and are more involved in the operation of that family than are grandmothers in other cultures.

Researchers have attempted to investigate the tendency for children to become members of cross-cultural peer groups in school settings (Gottman & Mettetal, 1986; Hallinan & Teixera, 1987). Recently, researchers found that in the third grade of an ethnically mixed school, children were forming cross-ethnic friendships without regard to social status variables (Howe & Wu, 1990). This finding was at variance with previous studies that found cross-ethnic friendships were strongly influenced by social status in that students of similar social statuses tended to form relationships regardless of ethnicity.

The Black Family and Education

In the United States, blacks have always been at a disadvantage in equal access to economic, political, social, and educational endeavors (Comer, 1985). To some degree, blacks have functioned at two levels, the "haves" and the "have nots." The **haves** occupy leadership positions in the community and church and interact with the white community. The **have nots** tend to gravitate to the lowest level of society and make up the large, poor **underclass,** which is least prepared to take advantage of the resources that are available in the black communities.

There is some evidence that school personnel view black children entering the school system as deficient because of obvious cultural differences, such as speaking in a black dialect (Coalition of Advocates for Students, 1985). Teachers tend to expect less of students who appear culturally different and reinforce their lower self-esteem and sense of failure. Furthermore, researchers have found that teachers value black males least among their students, and it is black males who have the lowest achievement (Hale-Benson, 1986).

Although black children and white children tend to start out on equal ground in the first grade, blacks tend to lose ground during the school-age years and during adolescence. The high school dropout rate of blacks is twice the rate of whites, and the school suspension rate is three times the rate of white students (Children's Defense Fund, 1985). Only 20% of black high school graduates go on to college, and only about 4% will ever complete a graduate program (Hale-Benson, 1986).

Over the past several decades, the tendency has been for school districts to become resegregated. About 80% of black children are educated in about 4% of the national school districts. Where schools do represent diversity in student backgrounds, students tend to be from the same social class background (Coalition of Advocates for Students, 1985).

■
The Hispanic Family

The Hispanic population is made up of various Spanish-speaking persons from Mexico, Puerto Rico, Cuba, and South American countries. During the 1980s the Hispanic population rate in the United States grew faster than the rate of all other racial and ethnic groups combined. During this period the Hispanic population grew from 14.6 million in 1980 to 18.8 million in 1987, while the non-Hispanic population grew from 212 million to 220 million, or an increase of just 6% (U.S. Bureau of the Census, 1986). By the year 2025, Hispanics will be the largest minority if current population rates continue (Weeks, 1989).

Hispanics and Education

In grade school, Hispanic students tend to have **educational deficits,** including lower reading and math competency levels. Hispanics tend to have lower educational attainments than non-Hispanics in completing high school and college. Mexican-Americans, who make up the majority of the Hispanic group, tend to have lower rates than other Hispanics (Education of Hispanics Sets Record, 1988). About 17% of Hispanics from 17 to 24 years of age were enrolled in college in 1981 (U.S. Bureau of the Census, 1983). There is some evidence that Hispanics prefer to attend two-year colleges rather than four-year colleges.

In grade school, Hispanic students tend to be relegated to special classes more often than the general population. Typically, this need for special education for Hispanic students is because of a reading deficit of about two years compared to non-Hispanic students. Whether this deficit is real or the result of biases is debatable, but it is clear that Hispanic students are disadvantaged in the educational arena (Hoffer, 1983). Researchers have found that when Hispanic students are proficient in English, their success rates in school approximate those of Anglos. The use of English as the standard for Hispanic success in schools has been a debatable issue because Hispanics must give up a native language and become proficient in English, the dominant language (Fligstein & Fernandez, 1982). Anglos and non-Hispanic minorities do not have this additional burden in school achievement.

As would be expected of Hispanics and is true of comparison groups, Hispanics from middle-class families tend to fare better in all aspects of education than those living in poverty. On the whole, Hispanic family income, although higher for Hispanics than for blacks, tends to be significantly lower than Anglo family income (U.S. Bureau of the Census, 1986).

Buenning and Tollefson (1987) found that both high-achieving Hispanic and non-Hispanic students in the fifth through the eighth grades held nontraditional views about authority and displayed more field independence than low-achieving students. Other researchers have found that students with an internal locus of control tend to be higher achievers than students with an external locus of control (Sherris & Kahle, 1984).

Identity and Self-Concept

Hispanic culture is passed on to children through the process of socialization. The specific term that applies to socialization is **enculturation.** Although increasingly children of different minority groups are educated together, evidence suggests that there are differences in behavior based on race or ethnicity. Typically, as ethnic minority children move from the early grades to the higher grades, they become more aware of their ethnic status (Aboud, 1987).

As ethnic minority children become aware of their **group affiliation,** the identification with that group is associated with an understanding of their own identity. Researchers have found that when high school students have a sense of their own ethnicity, they have higher self-esteem than those students who are not aware of their ethnicity (Phinney, 1989).

Rotheram-Borus and Phinney (1990) attempted to determine individual, group, and age-related differences in social expectations of children of black and Hispanic backgrounds. They selected subjects from an equal number of Hispanic and black children recruited from the inner-city area of Los Angeles. The Hispanic group was primarily comprised of Mexican-born children. The methodology consisted of recording the responses of children observing videotape presentations of children in common situations occurring at school.

The videotaped segments included the following: "a student asking a peer for a loan, a peer who is disliked by a child asks the child for a loan, a student is scolded by a teacher who is disappointed, a student is scolded by a teacher who is angry, a child is corrected by a classmate, a child is rejected for a school team, a child has to respond to two peers fighting, and a child needs to borrow a crayon from a classmate" (Rotheram-Borus & Phinney, 1990, p. 544).

Raters of the children's responses included six male psychologists—two black, two Mexican-American, and two white. Children were removed from the classroom and tested together with about six of their same ethnic group. After completing a self-esteem inventory, students were shown the videotapes and asked to write a response to them.

The results revealed some significant differences according to ethnicity. For example, Mexican-American children were much more likely to loan money than black children. In the scene where the disliked child had no money for lunch and requested money for lunch, Mexican-American children were much more likely to give the money to this child than were black children. In the scene with the teacher scolding the child by expressing disappointment, the Mexican-American children were more likely to feel anger and the black children were more likely to apologize or say they were sorry (Rotheram-Borus & Phinney, 1990).

Parenting in Hispanic Families

Little research has been conducted on the parenting styles of Hispanic parents. The view of Hispanics that permeated the literature until quite recently was the view that the husband dominated the family and that the wife and children had to be submissive or they were subjected to abuse and maltreatment by the father. Fathers were generally not involved a great deal in the day-to-day operation of the household. Wives tolerated infidelity if the husbands did not flaunt the affairs openly. Researchers found discipline of children to be harsh, including intimidation and physical punishment to control behavior. As a result, children were viewed as lacking initiative and being dependent on parents (Mirande, 1979).

More recently, researchers have revised some of the earlier conclusions about Hispanic families. In general, these researchers have concluded that Hispanic parents appear to be more supportive and protective of their children than either white or black parents (Bartz & Levine, 1978). One study has found that Hispanic mothers differ little from Anglo mothers in parenting styles (Martinez, 1988). In addition, Hispanic fathers are viewed as warm and supportive of their children, spending much time with their children and engaging in mutual activities with them (Burrows, 1980).

A major motif in the Hispanic family is the central role of family relationships, including parenting. The process of socialization in Hispanic families tends to teach the importance of family roles and customs (Ramirez & Castaneda, 1974). In fact, the dominance of the father role is no longer viewed as a negative but as a unique way of maintaining family order and stability. If the father abuses his privileged role in the family, it would be expected that he would also lose it.

Hispanic Family Relationships

Researchers have found mixed results in studying Hispanic families. Some have found differences in Mexican-American families and Anglos on such dimensions as cognitive styles and intimate interpersonal relationships. For example, Mexican-Americans have consistently been found to be more cooperative and less competitive than Anglos (Knight & Kagan, 1977). Other researchers have found that Hispanics tend to be more dependent on others than Anglos are (Ramirez & Price-Williams, 1974).

On the other hand, a number of researchers have found no significant differences in Anglos and Hispanics on the cohesion and adaptability dimensions of the family (Vega, Kolody, & Valle, 1986). Whether this lack of difference on these family dimensions means that Hispanic families do not differ significantly in the role and importance of the family is debatable. More research is needed to answer this question.

Researchers have found that Hispanic families tend to be large and have frequent contact with extended family members. In studying Mexican-American families, Vega, Kolody, and Valle (1986) found that the support from one generation to another tends to increase. This strong family support system means that Mexican-American families can provide many services for their members that families of other ethnicities do not receive. The family system is typically larger than the nuclear family. When studying Mexican-American families, it becomes clear that the boundaries of the family must also include the extended kinship network.

Parent/child Relationships in Hispanic Families

Parenting in the Hispanic culture places much focus on the maternal role of nurturance and support. Perhaps the traditional roles as housewife and mother support and perpetuate this view. Researchers have found that education plays a major role in the

Box 10.2	■■■■■■■■■■ **Is Maternal Socialization Related to Obesity in Mexican-Americans?**

Mexican-Americans have more difficulty with obesity than other Americans. Researchers have found that children of obese parents have a greater probability of being obese than other children. Olvera-Ezzell, Power, and Cousins (1990) conducted a study to examine the socializing strategies Mexican-American mothers use to influence their child's eating habits, the relation between maternal strategies and the child's food consumption, and the impact of maternal education and the child's age and gender on maternal behavior toward the child.

The researchers recruited mothers, ranging from 20% to 100% overweight, from churches to participate in a weight-loss program. They randomly assigned subjects to three treatment groups. At the completion of one year in the program, families were observed at mealtime in their homes and interviewed about their socialization styles. The researchers distinguished live coding and audiotape coding according to healthy and unhealthy eating habits. These rates were based on guidelines of the American

Heart Association and the American Dietetic Association. A second coding sheet analyzed all verbal interaction between parent and child. These interactions were coded according to the time it occurred, persons involved, parental control behavior, and the child's response. The mother was interviewed at the end of the meal to determine the strategies used to encourage or to discourage the child's eating practices.

The results revealed that the average meal was 19 minutes. During the meal mothers encouraged eating predominantly through both direct and indirect means and they almost never discouraged eating. Maternal education correlated positively with healthy eating habits and negatively with forced compliance. Mothers encouraged boys to eat more than girls. This result may be explained by the mother's concern for the daughter's weight. It can be assumed that these mothers take an active role in restraining their daughters' eating habits. These obese Mexican-American mothers tend to use a high degree of control in getting their children to follow directives about eating.

style of parenting, particularly in the use of punitive means of control. Educated Hispanic mothers, as would be expected, use corporal punishment much less than other forms of discipline.

In some regards, the Hispanic parent/child relationship reflects the patterns of Anglos. For example, mothers are closer to daughters than sons and fathers are somewhat more distant from both children, particularly as children age (Buriel & Cardoza,

■ *Hispanic families are very cohesive social units.*

1988). Hispanic fathers, however, appear to have a strong sense of family commitment. The loyalty issues caused by the strong family ties may well be the major factor differentiating Hispanic families from Anglo families.

■ The Asian-American Family

The phrase *Asian-American* refers to a number of different groups in the United States including persons of Japanese, Chinese, Korean, Philippine, Vietnamese, Cambodian, and Hawaiian origins. Although these groups share some characteristics in general, it would be a mistake to consider them a homogenous group. Different backgrounds and customs separate them in much the same way that European ethnic groups differ. In addition, length of time in America may be a significant factor affecting the differences noted in these groups.

Chinese immigrants began coming to America in the 1800s, primarily as laborers in building the railroads connecting the West. Although Chinese workers were exemplary in work, they were subjected to intense prejudice, which led to Congress passing the Chinese Exclusion Act of 1882. This act remained in force until World

War II when the government repealed it because of China's alliance during the war (Lai, 1980).

Asian-Americans, although traditionally targeted for discrimination, have fared much better than comparable groups. Statistical data reveal the advantage that Asian-Americans, particularly Chinese, who account for the largest Asian subgroup, have over other minority groups and also over the majority, or Anglo, population. For example, Asian per capita income, educational attainment, and employment rates are all higher than those for the general population in the United States (U.S. Bureau of the Census, 1989).

Researchers view Chinese-Americans as the ideal minority group because of their high educational attainment, low divorce rate, and high income status. Chinese-Americans are more likely than the general population to have children under 18 years of age in the household. More Chinese-American families have two parents present in the family. Among Chinese-Americans, there are fewer single-parent households, and where they do exist, they typically have fewer children than single-parent households among other groups (U.S. Bureau of the Census, 1989). Chinese-Americans place a high value on the two-parent family and take family responsibilities, such as parenting, very seriously.

Parent/Child Relationships in Asian-American Families

The typical Asian-American family has very strong family ties and a traditional view of gender roles. The sense of family pride and loyalty to the family is more important than individual accomplishments. If family and individual needs clash, the family's needs take precedence (Lott, 1976).

Parenting in Chinese-American families tends to emphasize the traditional values of parental authority. Parents are viewed as authoritarian and use punishment to gain compliance. Chinese-Americans view the misbehavior of a child as bringing shame on the family. The concept of "losing face" also applies to Chinese parenting. Behavior that does not support the family or the social order is followed by the person losing support from other members. Shame is, consequently, a primary means of acquiring cooperation from all members of society, but especially children (Ho, 1987).

Asian-American parents often encourage their children to perform adequately rather than attempt to be perfect. This tendency appears more in interpersonal relationships where a **stoic emotional style** pervades. This characteristic to be stoic in the face of emotionally charged issues may make the Asian-American appear lacking in aggression. Unfortunately, traditional American values are at variance with this belief and may lead to mislabeling and misunderstanding Asian-American behavior.

Children are generally expected to follow their parents' guidance without asking questions. In traditional Asian families, parents use punishment to gain compliance without much verbal communication. Researchers have found some differences among Asians who have been in the United States for a long time. These parents tend to use more verbal communication in the form of praise and small talk to their children than do recent immigrants or traditional Asian parents (Bond & Wang, 1983).

There is some evidence that teaching is an important aspect of parenting in the Asian culture. In general, teaching tends to be important in cultures where roles are fairly clear and the transition into adulthood is marked by a certain specified passage-way. Although Asian culture does not have rites of passage as some tribal cultures do, there are expectations and responsibilities that differ from mainstream American culture. For example, Asian parents place much emphasis on children being responsible for performing certain duties. Furthermore, children frequently work alongside parents in a family business. This tutelage of children is viewed as leading to a strong work ethic in children (Sigel, 1988; Stewart & Stewart, 1975).

Another factor in the parental emphasis on teaching is the strong attachment and affiliation that persons exhibit when undertaking a joint project (Sigel, 1988). One could argue that Asians lack creativity and initiative because they tend to value **conformity** to social expectations. Although this lack of aggression may be considered a liability in achieving some goals in American society, it may also be a tremendous advantage in group collaboration. This identity within the group, especially the family, increases stability and the commitment to carry out family roles and responsibilities.

Lin and Fu (1990) attempted to determine the differences and similarities in child-rearing practices in Chinese, immigrant Chinese, and Caucasian-Americans. Subjects included 138 parents of children in Taiwan and the United States. There were 44 Chinese children, 44 immigrant Chinese children, and 45 Caucasian-Americans. The average age of the children was between 6 and 7 years. The researchers instructed the parents of these children to complete four factors on the Child-Rearing Practices Report (CRPR) (Block, 1986, cited in Lin & Fu, 1990). The four factors were parental control, encouragement of independence, expression of affection, and emphasis on achievement.

This study revealed that Chinese and immigrant Chinese parents scored higher on parental control and emphasis on achievement. Contrary to expectations, Chinese and immigrant Chinese parents scored higher on encouraging independence than did Caucasian-American parents. No differences were found in any other groups on open expression of affection. Some **acculturation**—or taking on aspects of the majority culture—appears to be evident in findings such as the fact that Chinese mothers had the highest scores on parental control, Caucasian mothers had the lowest, and immigrant Chinese mothers were in the middle (Lin & Fu, 1990).

The finding that Chinese fathers have higher scores of promoting independence was surprising. The researchers concluded that it seems plausible that Chinese parents encourage cohesion to the family group while encouraging individual independence. In this way, Chinese offspring exhibit both family cohesion and success in the educational and occupational endeavors outside the family. Chinese view being successful in education and work as fulfilling one's obligation to the family (Lin & Fu, 1990).

One could interpret the finding of no difference on demonstration of parental affection as misunderstanding of the instrument because of inherent ethnic differ-

Table 10.2 ■ **Cultural and Racial Differences in IQ Scores**

• Blacks, Hispanics, and Native Americans tend to score lower on IQ tests than Anglo-Americans.

• Although test scores may to some degree reflect biases in test construction, researchers generally have found racial differences even in culture-fair tests.

• IQ tests predict future educational achievement for minorities as well as for whites.

• The testing situation may put minorities at a disadvantage. For example, they perform better when the examiner is warm and friendly.

• Minority children adopted in white middle-class homes have IQ scores 20 points higher than minority children reared in disadvantaged situations. The conclusion is that children tend to have higher IQs when they are reared in economically advantaged homes.

Source: Moore, 1986; Reynolds and Kaufman, 1985.

ences. On the other hand, this finding could be related to the slow acculturation into mainstream culture. As Chinese immigrants become acculturated, they probably will demonstrate less reserve and more emotion in parent/child relationships (Lin & Fu, 1990).

Asians-Americans and Education

Because Asian parents value education, there is a disproportionate number of Asians in colleges compared to the general population. Asian students tend to do well in the sciences, such as math, physics, and chemistry. Researchers have found that Asian students consistently perform better on standardized math tests at every socio-economic level than whites and blacks (Rogoff & Morelli, 1989).

Although Asian students score consistently higher on standardized math, science and IQ tests (see Table 10.2), there is some concern that some Asian students who appear very bright do poorly in school. Most of these students are from the lower socioeconomic class and are considered **dialect-speaking students,** speaking a non-English dialect at home and English at school. Although the typical pattern may represent students who are not successful, researchers have noted that some students from the same background have been successful and they have attempted to determine the differences in these students (Feldman, Stone, & Renderer, 1990).

Teacher and formal assessments have generally found that these dialect-speaking Asian students, particularly Hawaiian, are capable of doing very well in the use of formal operations. Researchers have suggested that these dialect-speaking students have some block that prevents them from being able to transfer their cognitive ability to perform successfully in school (Feldman, Stone, & Renderer, 1990).

Feldman, Stone, and Renderer (1990) conducted a study with dialect-speaking Hawaiian students from the tenth, eleventh, and twelfth grades in a school district in

■ *Asian parents value education and encourage their children to excel in school.*

Hawaii. They used the Colored Blocks Test (CBT), which duplicates Piaget's test of cognitive reasoning, as the measure to determine the level of cognitive functioning. In order to test for the transfer to a different circumstance, the researchers added a transfer section to the CBT, requiring students to apply the same abstract reasoning to a new pattern. The hypothesis was that students who did well on the transfer would do well in school achievement. In addition, students who did not do well in the transfer would be considered lacking the ability to use skills they possess in a new situation. This hypothesis was based on the fact that new input in the form of information must be presented in an appropriate symbolic form, occurring most often through the use of language.

Because these Hawaiian students used a different dialect at home and standard English at school, they had very little opportunity to practice using standard English. The researchers believed that the students' poor school performance occurred because they had to process material through essentially a different language.

Measures for the preceding research in addition to the CBT and transfer section were standardized reading and math tests and the Sentence Repetition Test. Results indicated that the ability to transfer is a powerful predictor of school success, especially at the highest levels of abstraction. A statistical procedure revealed that, as the subjects' cognitive level and the difficulty of the transfer items increased, school achievement could be predicted more reliably. The researchers found transfer ability to be related to and dependent on language (Feldman, Stone, & Renderer, 1990).

The implications of the results of this study suggest that when abstract concepts are taught to dialect-speaking children, teachers need to emphasize the connection to past learning. Children who don't like to express themselves in class need to be engaged in the learning dialogue. Teachers also need to help bidialectical children use their language to encode symbols for appropriate problem solving (Feldman, Stone, & Renderer, 1990).

Academic success has relied on standardized math tests as the measure of competency. Most studies to date have found only nominal differences among white, Asian, and black students when they enter school (Tizard, Blatchford, Burke, Farquhar, & Plewis, 1988). Differences tend to show up as students advance through the school years. These differences may characterize the variant influences that make up the students' total ecosystem.

A Systems Perspective of Parenting in Different Cultures

Both child psychologists and family experts generally accept the assertion that parental beliefs and values greatly influence the patterns by which particular children are reared. On the other hand, the extent to which these social or cultural patterns determine cognitive development in children is a debated issue.

American culture appears to be characterized by diversity of cultural ideals in child-rearing practices (Gutierrez & Sameroff, 1990). Many of these practices have been brought to the United States by different immigrant groups. Acculturation gradually takes place so that most immigrants incorporate values and behaviors from the larger culture. A **systems perspective of acculturation** broadens the concept so that acculturation includes the influence of immigrant beliefs and values on the larger culture. This perspective postulates that "culture" is changing and that new ideas of how children develop are emerging.

Immigrant parents who have a belief about development of children that is multi-dimensional and inclusive of various outcomes tend to adjust better to a larger culture (Gutierrez & Sameroff, 1990). The larger culture must also accommodate itself to the immigrant group and gradually change. When one views the process in this way, the rigid one-dimensional way of discussing acculturation is inadequate.

Immigrant parents must be members to some degree of two cultures at the same time. When they are able to accomplish this, they are referred to as **bicultural** (Szapocznik & Kurtines, 1980, cited in Gutierrez & Sameroff, 1990). Researchers have found bicultural individuals to be more flexible in parenting than individuals who hold on to the old culture.

Gutierrez and Sameroff (1990) attempted to determine the relation between acculturation, biculturalism, and concept of child development. Subjects for the study consisted of 60 middle-class Mexican-American and Anglo-American mothers divided into three categories: 20 moderately acculturated Mexican-American mothers, 20 highly acculturated Mexican-American mothers, and 20 Anglo-American mothers. All were matched on social class and age.

Measures consisted of the Concepts of Development Vignettes (CODV) to assess the level of complexity by which mothers understand child development. The vignettes depicted six developmental problems common to all cultures. Acculturation was determined by the Acculturation Rating Scale for Mexican-Americans (ARSMA) measuring such items as language familiarity and usage and ethnic identity. Biculturalism was determined by the Bicultural Involvement Questionnaire (BIQ), which measured the degree to which a person was comfortable in Hispanic and Anglo-American cultures independent of each other. Intelligence was determined by the vocabulary subtest of the Wechsler Adult Intelligence Scale (WAIS-R) or the equivalent test in Spanish. Traditionalism was determined by the Traditional Family Ideology Scale (TFIS). Such statements as "Some equality in the marriage is a good thing, but husbands should have more of the say-so in family matters" measure the degree of traditional values.

The findings on the acculturation analysis replicated earlier studies that highly acculturated Mexican-American mothers had a more **perspectivistic view of child development**—the dynamic interplay between the child's innate qualities and his/her environment—than their Anglo-American counterparts. In addition, bicultural Mexican-American mothers were the most perspectivistic when compared to the other two groups. Intelligence was not found to be related to the concept of development.

Gutierrez and Sameroff (1990) concluded that bicultural contexts are related to more perspectivistic concepts of development because biculturalism requires that persons appreciate the relativism of belief systems in each culture. The general outcome for parents who are bicultural is that they are more flexible in their views about child development and more encouraging of adaptive behavior in their children.

The preceding research is important because it underscores a systems perspective of the cultural influence on the parenting process. Views, or belief systems, about parenting are important because they tend to emerge within a particular changing context. Although intelligence and socioeconomic status are important factors, neither is the guiding factor in parental beliefs about parenting. Rather, each forms a context-specific position. An appreciation for biculturalism, for example, allows one to see the relativism of one's position and the ability to adapt to the changing context.

Transmission of culture whereby children are considered only as recipients is a static concept—and the usual way of understanding how children acquire certain ideas and values. Some theorists have suggested that, when children are considered as **co-transmitters of culture**, they transcend their culture by learning it. Although parents attempt to transmit their ideas and beliefs to their children, they never quite succeed. The input from the child and reciprocal interaction is sufficient to derail the best-laid plans for instilling certain beliefs and attitudes in the child (Valsiner, 1988).

As the child internalizes the values transmitted from the parent, the values are changed. The internal image of the social input only approximates the actual input.

The child is, therefore, an active partner in the socialization process. Children modify any input, including the cultural, in ways that create a "personal" experience of the world. Each one's personal culture is part of the personal ecosystem that may differ for various members of the family (Valsiner, 1988). The systems/dialectical process mentioned elsewhere provides the underlying framework for how the cultural input would be modified. For example, as parents "train" children to act in certain ways, this "official" way of viewing the world also implies its opposite, or its antithesis. **Internalization** is the process whereby the cultural input existing in creative tension with its opposite leads to a different perception. In this sense, culture can be viewed as something within the control of the person.

Family Portrait   ■ ■ ■ ■ ■ ■ ■ ■ ■ ■

Rasheed Taylor is a black 11-year-old fifth-grade student who has recently begun attending a private school that is 98% white. Prior to the fifth grade, he had been attending a school that was about 80% black. Although he displayed some disruptive behavior at times in his old school, he was considered no different from the majority of the other students. In his old school, there was a more relaxed attitude about assignments and complying with rules and regulations.

Rasheed is from a single-parent home, and his mother, Carolyn, has worked hard to give him opportunities to succeed. The change of schools was his mother's way of attempting to give him the best educational opportunity possible. She believes the new school has higher academic standards and will better prepare him for high school. The new school is some distance from her home, which means that she has to wake up earlier to get Rasheed to school and to get to her work on time. Sometimes there have been problems beyond her control, such as the car breaking down and not having a good backup way to get him to school. His mother's sometimes live-in boyfriend has been only marginally helpful in these emergencies because of his inconsistent work history and his drug and alcohol use.

Although Rasheed's father and his mother were never married, Rasheed knows his father but has infrequent contact with him. Rasheed's maternal uncle, who lived in the home when he was younger, served as a father role model. About a year ago Rasheed's mother began dating Robert, a younger man who seemed ambitious and on his way up. Shortly after meeting Robert, Carolyn believed that her search for an appropriate partner and role model for Rasheed had ended. Robert moved in and they began discussing future plans for marriage. Within a month of moving in Robert lost his job, because, he believed, of discrimination. When he was hired, he had some mixed feelings because most of the employees were white. He was quickly promoted to supervisor status, however. Then, as a result of some mismanagement, which involved Robert only marginally, he was fired. The company hired a white man as his replacement. Robert has consulted an attorney and has begun a discrimination case against the company.

Since he was fired, Robert has not handled his personal feelings very well. He had been a social drinker before losing his job, but to handle his loss of self-esteem and identity, he began frequenting bars and experimenting with drugs. Robert's father and two uncles were alcoholics. His father had instilled in him the value of hard work and the evils of racism and discrimination. Robert believed in hard work but also knew firsthand what can happen to a person who must experience daily the problems of racism and discrimination.

Rasheed looked up to Robert as the ideal black male who could withstand the threat of racism and succeed in the white society. When he began attending the private school, his goal was to be like Robert. It was shortly after Rasheed began attending the new school that Robert was fired from his job and began drinking. Rasheed's mother is split over the situation. She loves Robert and sees the potential in him, but she cannot fully support him in his efforts. She believes that Robert should take responsibility for his poor decision that cost him his job and look for another one based on his management experience. She has pointed out that Robert was not the only person fired from the company over the incident and that the others, who were all white, have already found employment elsewhere. Robert has been frustrated by Carolyn's reaction. He feels she is selling out and allowing herself to be duped by a system that is unresponsive to the needs of black people.

Rasheed had some of the typical adjustment problems one might expect from changing schools. He was worried that he was different and would have trouble making friends. His athletic ability, however, made him a popular student immediately. When Robert lost his job and began drinking, Rasheed soon began having problems in school. He is seen by his teachers as disruptive in class, and he only partially completes his homework. He and his mother generally got along well in the past, but now he talks back to her and refuses to cooperate around the house. He is beginning to "hang out" on the street, which he never did before. His mother sees all of her hopes and dreams for him dissipating. In her frustration, she has begun using physical punishment often. The outcome of such spankings has been a further deterioration of their relationship.

Compare and Contrast

None of the three parent-education approaches deals with the child in context, including the cultural context. The PET (Gordon, 1970) model would encourage Carolyn to listen to Rasheed's concerns and attempt to help him understand his behavior better so that he could then correct his behavior himself. If self-exploration was only marginally helpful, Carolyn might be encouraged to problem-solve using the no-lose method, by which she would help facilitate a solution that both she and Rasheed could accept. Other pertinent information, such as Robert losing his job or Rasheed's change of school, would be only of marginal importance according to the PET model.

A parent educator of the Adlerian approach would want Rasheed to learn responsibility for his behavior. Rasheed's mother would be encouraged to set consequences for his behavior at home. For example, when he failed to comply about turning down his music, she would set logical consequences for his behavior, such as removing his radio until he demonstrated that he could comply.

Dreikurs and Soltz (1964) would view school problems as external to the parent's control but within the child's control. As a result, the parent should remove him/herself from the crucial issue of taking over the school problem for the child. The child must handle the problem with the school without the parent's interference. Rasheed's school problem, therefore, would be left up to him to handle on his own.

Parent educators of a behavioral approach (Patterson, 1976) would direct Rasheed's mother toward an understanding of the type of reinforcement that was both causing and maintaining the problem. While behaviorists might view the broader social network as a reinforcer for Rasheed's behavior, they would not consider the reciprocal nature of interaction as very important. A behavioral approach would view Rasheed's behavior as being shaped by others in terms of a linear cause-and-effect paradigm. His contribution to other family members' behavior is not known, nor is it considered important since his behavior is the target of investigation.

Parent educators of a systems perspective would consider the total context as important in understanding Rasheed's behavior. They would see Rasheed's change in schools as a recent transition that he was still adjusting to. The loss of both the uncle and Robert as appropriate father figures and the parallel between his school change and Robert's job dismissal has resulted in an unbalancing of the family system. The mother's punitive response to Rasheed's behavior hinders his being able to make a better adjustment.

Coming into play at this time also are the two different strains of Rasheed's cultural heritage. His mother's views represent an adaptive response to minority survival in the majority culture. She believes in hard work and applying oneself in order to be ready when the right opportunity opens up. She views education as the vehicle to move out of poverty. Her style is to work with the majority culture rather than against it.

On the other hand, Robert's response to his situation represents a maladaptive pattern that pits minority and majority cultures as adversaries. This response is self-defeating in that Robert uses his disappointment to block further development of his potential.

Rasheed seems to be pulled between these two poles in his cultural background. His school problems represent this internal conflict and his inability to make a more adequate response. No doubt, Robert's modeling behavior is influential in his maladaptive response. Rasheed's increasing isolation in the white school is further evidence to him that blacks cannot succeed in a white environment. He sees his mother's frustration and punishment of him as justification for his resistive behavior.

From the preceding discussion, it would be necessary to intervene in Rasheed's total system. A systems specialist would encourage Carolyn to decrease her punitive behavior toward Rasheed while attempting to understand the conflicts he is feeling. It is also important to consider the role and impact of Robert's behavior on Rasheed's behavior. Robert should be encouraged to work through his anger and frustration in a context that does not interfere with other relationships. Counseling with Carolyn and Robert to help them come to a better understanding of their differences might be necessary to improve Rasheed's adjustment. Rasheed should be helped to separate his own situation from Robert's.

A systems specialist could point out how interrelated his behavior is with that of others; for example, when he refuses to do a school assignment, his teacher reacts negatively followed by more resistive behavior on his part, or when his mother spanks him for noncompliance, he becomes more noncompliant. It would be necessary to interrupt the negative feedback loop created by the current attempts to solve the problem. Second-order parenting, or changing the structure of the solutions to the problem, might help Carolyn become more supportive of Rasheed by taking a 180-degree turn from the punitive parenting pattern she has been using. She could be encouraged to treat him the same way she would treat him if he were behaving perfectly. Rasheed might respond to a more supportive and friendly attitude and be able to process his adjustment to the new school better.

■■■■■■■■■■

Parenting Proposition

Cultural patterns, one factor in parenting, change in reference to the interaction of the individual's relationships and exposure to majority culture.

Answers to "Test Your Knowledge"

1. T   4. T
2. F   5. T
3. F   6. T

Key Concept

systems/dialectical model

ecosystem

socialization in black families

racial socialization

white bias

black poverty

Moynihan's report

strengths in black families

the haves

the have nots

the underclass

educational deficits

enculturation

group affiliation

stoic emotional style

conformity

acculturation

dialectic-speaking students

systems perspective of acculturation

bicultural

perspectivistic view of child development

transmission of culture

co-transmission of culture

process of internalization

Study Questions

1 Discuss the concept of ecosystem. How does a systems/dialectical process model of child development support the ecosystem perspective?

2 Explore the meaning of socialization in black families. Explain the concept of racial socialization. Why do black children have a white bias?

3 Discuss differences in black and white children. How are these differences related to poverty and the experience of living as a member of the underclass? What was the Moynihan report, and is it still relevant to explaining the plight of the black family?

4 Discuss strengths in the black family.

5 Explain the concept of enculturation as it refers to the Hispanic family. What characteristics of the Hispanic family distinguish it from other families?

6 Discuss parenting in the Hispanic family. Compare and contrast parenting in Hispanic families with parenting in Asian, white, and black families.

7 Discuss parenting in the Asian family. Compare and contrast parenting in Asian families with parenting in black, white, and Hispanic families.

8 Discuss how the stoic emotional style and conformity are related to advantages in Asian families.

9 What are special problems of dialect-speaking people?

10 Discuss the concept of transmitting culture. Compare and contrast the concepts biculturalism, traditionalism, and perspectivism.

References

Aboud, F. (1987). The development of ethnic self-identification and attitudes. In J. Phinney & M. Rotheram (Eds.), *Children's ethnic socializations: Pluralism and development* (pp. 32–55). Beverly Hills, CA: Sage.

Allen, W. (1985). Race, income, and family dynamics: A study of adolescent male socialization processes and outcomes. In M. Spencer, G. Brookins, & W. Allen (Eds.), *Beginnings: The social and affective development of black children* (pp. 273–292). Hillsdale, NJ: Erlbaum.

Bartz, K. W., & Levine, E. S. (1978). Childrearing by black parents: A description and comparison to Anglo and Chicano parents. *Journal of Marriage and the Family, 40,* 709–719.

Belle, D. (1984). Inequity and mental health: Low income and minority women. In L. Walker (Ed.), *Women and mental health policy* (pp. 135–150). Beverly Hills, CA: Sage.

Billingsley, A. (1988). The impact of technology on American families. *Family Relations, 37,* 420–425.

Blau, Z. (1981). *Black children/white children: Competence, socialization, and social structure.* New York: Free Press.

Block, J. (1986). *The child-rearing practices report (CRPR): A set of Q items for the description of parental socialization attitudes and values.* Berkeley, CA: University of California Press.

Bond, M. H., & Wang, S. (1983). China: Aggressive behavior and the problems of maintaining order and harmony. In A. P. Goldstein & M. H. Segall (Eds.), *Aggression in global perspective* (pp. 58–74). New York: Pergamon.

Bowman, P. (1988). Postindustrial displacement and family role strains: Challenges to the black family. In P. Voydanoff & L. Majka (Eds.), *Families and economic distress* (pp. 75–101). Newbury Park, CA: Sage.

Buenning, M., & Tollefson, N. (1987). The culture gap hypothesis as an explanation for the achievement patterns of Mexican-American students. *Psychology in the Schools, 24,* 264–272.

Buriel, R., & Cardoza, D. (1988). Sociocultural correlates of achievement among three generations of Mexican-American high school seniors. *American Education Research Journal, 25,* 177–192.

Burrows, P. (1980). *Mexican parental roles: Differences between mothers' and fathers' behavior to children.* Paper presented at the annual meeting of the Society for Cross-Cultural Research, Philadelphia.

Children's Defense Fund. (1985). *Black and white children in America: Key facts.* Washington, DC: U.S. Government Printing Office.

Coalition of Advocates for Students. (1985). *Barriers to excellence: Our children at risk.* Boston: City Municipal Government.

Comer, J. P. (1985). Empowering black children's educational environments. In H. P. McAdoo & J. L. McAdoo (Eds.), *Black children: Social, educational, and parental environments.* Beverly Hills, CA: Sage.

Cotterell, J. L. (1986). Work and community influences on the quality of child rearing. *Child Development, 57,* 362–374.

Dreikurs, R., & Soltz, V. (1964). *Children: The challenge.* New York: Hawthorn/Dutton.

Durrett, M., O'Bryant, S., & Pennebaker, J. (1975). Child rearing reports of white, black, and Mexican American families. *Developmental Psychology, 11,* 871.

Education of Hispanics sets record. (1988, September). *Albuquerque Journal,* pp. A1, A3.

Feldman, C. F., Stone, A., & Renderer, B. (1990). Stage, transfer, and academic achievement in dialect-speaking Hawaiian adolescents. *Child Development, 61,* 472–484.

Fligstein, N., & Fernandez, R. M. (1982). *The causes of Hispanic educational attainment, patterns, and analyses.* Paper prepared for the National Commission on Employment Policy. Chicago: Opinion Research Center.

Gagnon, J. H. (1985). Attitudes and responses of parents to pre-adolescent masturbation. *Archives of Sexual Behavior, 14,* 451–466.

Gary, L., Beatty, L. A., Berry, G. L., & Price, M. D. (1986). Stable black families: Final report. In Institute for Urban Affairs and Research (Ed.), *Mental health research and development* (pp. 123–147). Washington, DC: Howard University.

Gibbs, J. T., & Huang, L. N. (1989). A conceptual framework for assessing and treating minority youth. In J. T. Gibbs & L. N. Huang (Eds.), *Children of color* (pp. 1–29). San Francisco: Jossey-Bass.

Gordon, T. (1970). *Parent effectiveness training.* New York: Peter H. Wyden.

Gottman, J., & Mettetal, G. (1986). Speculation about social and affective development: Friendships and acquaintances through adolescence. In J. M. Gottman & J. G. Parker (Eds.), *Conversations of friends* (pp. 139–161).

Gutierrez, J., & Sameroff, A. J. (1990). Determinants of complexity in Mexican-American and Anglo-American mothers' conceptions of child development. *Child Development, 61,* 384–394.

Hale-Benson, J. (1986). *Black children: Their roots, culture, and learning styles* (rev. ed.). Baltimore: Johns Hopkins University Press.

Hallinan, M. T., & Teixera, R. A. (1987). Opportunities and constraints: Afro-American, white differences in the formation of interracial friendships. *Child Development, 58,* 1358–1371.

Ho, M. (1987). *Family therapy with ethnic minorities.* Beverly Hills, CA: Sage.

Hoffer, K. R. (1983). Assessment and instruction of reading skills: Results with Mexican-American students. *Learning Disability Quarterly, 6,* 458–467.

Howe, C., & Wu, F. (1990). Peer interactions and friendships in an ethnically diverse setting. *Child Development, 61,* 537–541.

Kessler, R., & Neighbors, H. (1986). A new perspective on the relationship among race, social class, and psychological distress. *Journal of Health and Social Behavior, 27,* 107–115.

Kessler, R., Turner, J., & House, J. (1987). Intervention processes in the relationship between unemployment and health. *Psychological Medicine, 17,* 949–962.

Knight, G., & Kagan, S. (1977). Development of prosocial and competitive behavior in Anglo-American and Mexican-American children. *Child Development, 48,* 1385–1394.

Lai, H. (1980). *Chinese.* In S. Thernstrom et al. (Eds.), *Harvard encyclopedia of American ethnic groups* (pp. 217–234). Cambridge, MA: Harvard University Press.

Lin, C., & Fu, V. R. (1990). A comparison of child-rearing practices among Chinese, immigrant Chinese, and Caucasian-American parents. *Child Development, 61,* 429–433.

Lott, J. (1976). *Asian-American reference directory.* Washington, DC: U.S. Department of HEW, Office for Asian American Affairs.

McAdoo, H. P. (1982). Stress absorbing systems in black families. *Family Relations, 31,* 479–488.

McAdoo, H. P. (1986). Strategies used by black single mothers against stress. In E. M. Simms & J. Malveaux (Eds.), *Slipping through the cracks: The status of black women* (pp. 153–166). New Brunswick, NJ: Transaction Books.

McAdoo, J. L. (1988). The roles of black fathers in the socialization of black children. In H. P. McAdoo (Ed.), *Black families* (2nd ed.) (pp. 257–269). Newbury Park, CA: Sage.

Martinez, E. (1988). Child behavior in Mexican-American/Chicano families: Maternal teaching and childrearing practices. *Family Relations, 37,* 275–280.

Mirande, A. (1979). A reinterpretation of male dominance in the Chicano family. *Family Coordinator, 28,* 473–479.

Moore, E. G. J. (1986). Family socialization and the IQ test performance of traditionally and transactionally adopted black children. *Developmental Psychology, 22,* 317–326.

Moynihan, P. (1965). *The Negro family: The case for national alarm.* Washington, DC: U.S. Government Printing Office.

Norton, A. S. (1983). Family life cycle: 1983. *Journal of Marriage and the Family, 45,* 267–275.

Olvera-Ezzell, N., Power, T. G., & Cousins, J. H. (1990). Maternal socialization of children's eating habits: Strategies used by obese Mexican-American mothers. *Child Development, 61,* 395–400.

Patterson, G. R. (1988). Stress: A change agent for family process. In N. Garmezy & M. Rutter (Eds.), *Stress, coping, and development in children* (pp. 235–264). Baltimore: Johns Hopkins University Press.

Patterson, G. R. (1976). *Living with children* (rev. ed.) Champaign, IL: Research Press.

Patterson, G. R., DeBarsyshe, B., & Ramsey, E. (1989). A developmental perspective on antisocial behavior. *American Psychologist, 44,* 329–335.

Pearson, J. L., Hunter, A. G., Ensminger, M. E., & Kellam, S. G. (1990). Black grandmothers in multigenerational households: Diversity in family structure and parenting involvement in the Woodlawn community. *Child Development, 61,* 334–342.

Peters, M. F. (1988). Parenting in black families with young children. In H. P. McAdoo (Ed.), *Black families* (2nd ed.), (pp. 228–241). Newbury Park, CA: Sage.

Peters, M. F., & Massey, G. (1983). Chronic versus mundane stress in family stress theories: The case of black families in white America. *Marriage and Family Review, 6,* 193–218.

Peterson, G., & Peters, D. (1985). The socialization values of low-income Appalachian white and rural black mothers: A comparative study. *Journal of Comparative Family Studies, 16,* 75–91.

Phinney, J. S. (1989). Stages of ethnic identity development in minority group adolescents. *Journal of Early Adolescence, 9,* 34–49.

Ramirez, M., III, & Castaneda, A. (1974). *Cultural democracy, bicognitive development, and education.* New York: Academic Press.

Ramirez, M., III, & Price-Williams, D. (1974). Cognitive styles of children in three ethnic groups in the United States. *Journal of Cross-Cultural Psychology, 5,* 425–433.

Reynolds, C. R., & Kaufman, A. S. (1985). Clinical assessments of children's intelligence with the Wechsler Scales. In B. B. Wolman (Ed.), *Handbook of intelligence: Theories, measurements, and applications.* New York: Wiley.

Rogoff, B., & Morelli, G. (1989). Perspective on children's development from cultural psychology. *American Psychologist, 44,* 343–348.

Rotheram-Borus, M. J., & Phinney, J. S. (1990). Patterns of social expectations among black and Mexican-American children. *Child Development, 61,* 542–556.

Sherris, J. D., & Kahle, J. B. (1984). The effects of instructional organization and locus of control orientation on meaningful learning in high school biology students. *Journal of Research in Science Teaching, 21,* 83–99.

Sigel, I. E. (1988). Commentary: Cross-cultural studies of parental influence on children's achievement. *Human Development, 31,* 384–390.

Spencer, M. B., & Markstrom-Adams, C. (1990). Identity processes among racial and ethnic minority children in America. *Child Development, 61,* 290–310.

Staples, R. (1985). Changes in black family structure: The conflict between family ideology and structural conditions. *Journal of Marriage and the Family, 47,* 1005–1013.

Steckel, R. H. (1980). Slave marriage and the family. *Journal of Family History, 5,* 406–421.

Stewart, M., & Stewart, S. (1975). *Teaching-learning interactions in Chinese-American and Anglo-American families: Study in cognitive development and ethnicity.* Unpublished manuscript.

Szapocznik, J., & Kurtines, W. (1980). Acculturation, biculturation, and adjustment among Cuban Americans. In A. M. Padilla (Ed.), *Acculturation: Theory, models, and some new findings* (pp. 139–159). Boulder, CO: Westview.

Taylor, R. J. (1986). Receipt of support of black Americans: Demographic and familial differences. *Journal of Marriage and the Family, 48,* 67–77.

Thornton, M. C., Chatters, L. M., Taylor, R. J., & Allen, W. R. (1990). Sociodemographic and environmental correlates of racial socialization by black parents. *Child Development, 61,* 401–409.

Tizard, B., Blatchford, P., Burke, J., Farquhar, C., & Plewis, J. (1988). *Young children in the inner city.* Hillsdale, NJ: Erlbaum.

U.S. Bureau of the Census. (1983). *General population characteristics, United States summary* (1980 Census of the Population, PC801-1-1-B1). Washington, DC: U.S. Government Printing Office.

U.S. Bureau of the Census. (1986). *Statistical Abstracts of the United States* (106th ed.). Washington, DC: U.S. Government Printing Office.

U.S. Bureau of the Census. (1989). *Stepchildren and their families.* Washington, DC: U.S. Government Printing Office.

Valsiner, J. (1988). Epilogue: Ontogeny of co-construction of culture within socially organized environmental settings. In J. Valsiner (Ed.), *Child development within culturally structured environments* (Vol. 2, pp. 283–298). Norwood, NJ: Ablex.

Vega, W., Kolody, B., & Valle, R. (1986). The relationship of marital status, confident support, and depression among Mexican immigrant women. *Journal of Marriage and the Family, 48,* 597–605.

Weeks, J. R. (1989). *Population: An introduction to concepts and issues* (4th ed.). Belmont, CA: Wadsworth.

Willie, C. U. (1981). *A new look at black families.* Bayside, NY: General Hall.

Wilson, M. (1986). The black extended family: An analytical consideration. *Developmental Psychology, 22,* 241–258.

Chapter 11

Parenting the Exceptional Child

Parenting Myth ■ In parenting the exceptional child, the parent must consider the internal processes of the child's abilities or deficits rather than the contextual processes.

Text Your Knowledge ■ The following questions are designed to test your knowledge before reading the material in this chapter. Answers appear at the end of the chapter.

1 IQ is a good measure of giftedness. True or false?

2 The causes of Down's syndrome are not well known. True or false?

3 Children who are allowed freedom of choice tend to maximize their potential. True or false?

4 The gifted child is typically socially withdrawn. True or false?

5 Children diagnosed with attention-deficit hyperactivity disorder (ADHD) generally need no special attention in educational settings. True or false?

6. The gifted misfit may be bored with schoolwork that is not challenging. True or false?

T his chapter addresses parenting children whose development deviates from the expected norm. This deviation from the norm can be considered either "impaired" or "gifted" depending on the circumstances. **Impaired children** have a physical, psychological, mental, intellectual, or medical condition that prevents them from learning and behaving in the expected way. **Gifted children,** who may be extremely talented and bright, deviate from the norm in that they exceed expectations. Both impaired and gifted children need special attention from parents and educators to reach their full human potential. Parents need training, understanding, and patience to deal with exceptional children. Educators must develop unique programs that meet the specific needs of these students.

An in-depth examination of the topic of the needs of special children is beyond the scope of this chapter. Instead, the focus will be limited to a discussion of how physical, mental, and emotional disabilities affect parenting and child development. In addition, the special needs of gifted children and the strategies parents need to both encourage and structure gifted children will be discussed.

Children born with a disability may not be identified initially. Parents, lacking in knowledge of child development, may not recognize that their child has a learning disability, is deaf, or is hyperactive. Consequently, strategies parents use to change such behavior may be inappropriate, further hindering adequate development. For example, parents who mislabel a learning disorder as disobedience may punish the child rather than offer encouragement and support.

■ Parenting the Child with a Disability or Chronic Illness

The Developmentally Delayed or Mentally Retarded Child

Children who are **developmentally delayed,** or **mentally retarded,** occurring as the result of a number of factors including Down's syndrome, are viewed as having an IQ score lower than 70 (Grossman, 1983; Harris, 1986). The four levels of retardation—mild, moderate, severe, and profound—affect about 3% of the American society (Hallahan & Kauffman, 1982). Although most developmentally delayed children are educable and fall within the moderate level of retardation (IQ 50–69), they require more attention from parents and teachers than do normal children. Children with IQs lower than 20 are considered uneducable and need assistance from family or an institution throughout their lives.

Causes of Mental Retardation. Mental retardation occurs for a number of reasons. Sometimes retardation results from an organic cause in that the child was injured during the pregnancy or shortly after delivery. Other organic-type mental retardation may be caused by hereditary anomalies. For example, **Down's syndrome** is a hereditary disease that results in such characteristic physical features as short stubby limbs, sloping forehead, slanted eyes, a flat nose, and a protruding tongue. Other forms of retardation may be associated with prenatal and perinatal risk factors including poor nutrition and the use of drugs and alcohol (Grossman, 1983).

A new kind of impairment, referred to as occurring in **bio-underclass babies,** has been emerging in American society (Greer, 1991). The large number of inner-city babies born to drug-addicted mothers has frightening implications. The prognosis for future normal growth and development for these "drug babies" appears bleak. A whole new category of child impairments may need to be developed in order to explain the damage done to fetuses by drug-abusing mothers. In some geographic areas, such as the Watts area of Los Angeles and the inner city of New York, it has been estimated that 30% of pregnant women use illegal drugs regularly. Health officials do not know the extent of the problem, though it is believed that cocaine-addicted babies at birth will display chronic irritability and poor visual coordination and that they will need special education programs when they enter school.

Down's Syndrome.   Down's syndrome, occurring once in every 800 births as the result of an extra 21st chromosome, is the most common hereditary abnormality. Children with Down's syndrome have an average IQ of 50. Until recently children born with Down's syndrome were thought to be uneducable and were routinely placed in institutions for life (Pueschel, 1991). After the development of the procedure of **amniocentesis**—a surgical penetration of the abdomen to the uterus to obtain amniotic fluid—many experts felt that Down's syndrome could be eliminated through selective screening and abortion. Others point out the ethical implications and the right to life of all fetuses.

Recent research has concluded that children with Down's syndrome progress through similar developmental stages as normal children, but at a slower rate (Pueschel, 1991; Thompson, Cicchetti, Lamb, & Malkin, 1985). There tend to be differences in the intellectual functioning of children with Down's syndrome in that some can learn to read and function quite normally in many ways (Turkington, 1987). Furthermore, many in middle- and upper-middle-class homes may have happy and rewarding childhoods with family members who appreciate and understand them. On the other hand, some children with Down's syndrome may spend much of their lives in institutions and be considered quite abnormal by family members and relatives.

Although the cause of Down's syndrome is known, there is no definitive reason why it occurs. The occurrence increases profoundly as a woman ages. For example, a 25-year-old pregnant woman has a 1 in 600 chance of having a child with Down's syndrome. This possibility increases to 1 in 25 by age 45 (Pueschel & Goldstein, 1983). Although the possibility is much greater of having a child with Down's syndrome after age 35, about 80% of cases occur to mothers under 35 (Kolata, 1987). The reason for the high occurrence under 35 is because the vast majority of all children are born to mothers under 35.

A possible explanation for the increase in the occurrence of Down's syndrome as a woman ages is that as the ova age they become more susceptible to abnormality and degeneration. This explanation is not completely satisfactory because researchers have also found that about 25% of Down's syndrome children inherit it from the father rather than the mother (Magenis, Overton, Chamberlin, Brady, & Lorrien, 1977).

The answers are not as clear-cut as to how parents should deal with the knowledge that they are expecting a Down's syndrome baby. A number of options are available to them. They can terminate the pregnancy by abortion, carry to term and care for the child after birth, or carry to term and put the child up for adoption. Appropriate genetic counseling may help parents make informed and not emotional decisions (Pueschel, 1991).

Social, or Familial, Retardation. Another type of mental retardation in children is referred to as **social, or familial, retardation** (Grossman, 1983). This type of retardation is correlated with poverty, a poor family environment, and moderate retardation among other family members, and it plagues certain groups of people more than others, such as Appalachian mountain and inner-city black families. Social retardation is particularly troublesome because it could be prevented by more exposure to the larger culture and better medical and educational services.

When the mental retardation is mild, researchers suggest that these children are roughly in the same developmental stage as normal children in the Piagetian hierarchy of mental operations (McCormick, Campbell, Pasnak, & Perry, 1990). Teaching Piaget's concepts to developmentally delayed children has resulted in improved scores on IQ tests (Moreno & Sastre, 1971, cited in McCormick et al., 1990). A growing body of research supports the view that mildly retarded children can improve their overall aptitude through learning Piagetian concepts. In fact, some researchers have suggested that classification, seriation, and conservation concepts taught on a 30-minute remediation could drastically improve mildly retarded children's mastery of the curriculum in the early school grades.

Parents' Recognition of and Response to Down's Syndrome. When parents do not recognize the disability initially, as is usually the case, they may mislabel the child as fussy, disinterested, or unresponsive and respond to the child by being less spontaneous and even punitive. On the other hand, when the disability is known to parents from the beginning, as is the case with Down's syndrome, parents may have an advantage in that they may be more prepared to respond in appropriate ways. It is also true, however, that parents will have negative emotions about having a disabled child, ranging from feeling guilty to being resentful of the time and energy that caring for a disabled child requires. Not only do parents have to give more to a disabled child, they also receive less in return (Paul & Porter, 1982).

The birth of a developmentally disabled child may influence not only how parents respond but how siblings respond as well. Despite attempts to accept the disabled sibling, normal siblings are aware of differences and may feel a **loss of a playmate** because of the limitations of the disabled sibling. In addition, the frequent contact between the disabled sibling and normal siblings may affect the latter's view of themselves. Being the sibling of an impaired child may cause the normal child to feel a loss of identity and a loss of uniqueness of his/her own role in the family. The presence

Table 11.1 ■ Public Law 94–142

• Passed in 1975, this law guarantees access to education for all children.

• This law allows for handicapped students to be taught alongside other students.

• Although the intent was to reduce the stigma of the handicap, some researchers claim that regular classroom teachers may not be knowledgeable of the special needs of handicapped children.

• Process and outcome evaluations have been used to determine the effectiveness of this law.

• To date, studies have been inconclusive regarding the effectiveness of the law.

Source: Gallagher, 1989.

of a disabled sibling may mean reduction in the amount of time a normal child has for activities with friends (Crnic & Leconte, 1986; Stanhope & Bell, 1981).

Sibling relationships in families with an impaired child are, no doubt, marred by competition because one sibling is demonstrably lacking in at least one area of competition, such as academic performance. The family may function inadvertently to decrease competition. It could be that competition is decreased through various maneuvers, such as the impaired child being closer to one parent than the other or being "a good boy."

Researchers have found that normal siblings are more accepting of their developmentally disabled sibling when they are able to see similarities in their own behavior and the behavior of their disabled sibling (Bak & Siperstein, 1987; Grossman, 1972). For example, when normal siblings are able to view themselves as having an interest in the same activities as their disabled sibling, they can identify more with the sibling and see him/her as having strengths as well as weaknesses.

Children with a Learning Disability

The definition of a *learning disability* has been debated in the literature for some time. The major issue is that a thorough understanding of learning disability has not been devised (Kavale, Forness, & Lorsbach, 1991). The recent trend is to determine what the learning disability is in practical terms. Some researchers have suggested that definitions move away from semantics toward more concrete operational definitions. Learning disability can be defined operationally as part of a larger diagnosis of underachievement, which may represent a number of different areas including difficulty in perceiving, processing, storing, and understanding information. In addition, attention disorders, lack of motivation, and performance anxiety may account for other ways children can be defined as having a learning disability (Office of Education, 1976). Learning disorders typically refer to an impairment not accounted for by the child's IQ, family background, or age.

Learning disability, affecting roughly five times more boys than girls (Wojnilower & Gross, 1988), represents a number of different disorders that are determined by different diagnostic tests and procedures (Bryan, 1988). The classifications of a learning disability may vary among child psychologists and require subjective judgments by them. Although there may be many similarities between a learning disorder and a behavioral disorder, it is quite clear that these two phenomena are different. A learning disorder presupposes a neurological deficit, whereas a behavioral disorder presupposes an emotional disorder. The behavior alone may not be sufficient to distinguish it as a learning disorder or a behavioral disorder. For parents and schoolteachers, however, both types of disorders have similar effects on the child (Keogh,1986).

Learning-disabled students are more disliked by teachers, who regard their behavior as more disruptive than that of other children (Pullis, 1985, cited in White, Saudargas, & Zanolli, 1991). Generally, researchers have believed that disruptive behavior during independent seatwork by learning-disabled children preceded their being classified as having a learning disorder. Recently, researchers have concluded that direct observation of learning-disabled students and average and low-average students revealed no differences in their disruptive behavior before referral. Teachers' ratings were different for learning-disabled students both pre- and post-placement. After referral, learning-disabled students were much more likely to initiate questions with the teacher than were the other students. The researchers speculated that the more frequent contact between teacher and learning-disabled student after return to the classroom may be caused by the student's generalized response to the increased contact between teacher and student back in the classroom (White, Saudargas, & Zanolli, 1991). The attempt to treat learning-disabled students in the special resource room where the teacher–student ratio is very small may inadvertently contribute to the increase in disruptive behavior when students are placed back in the classroom.

Children who have a learning disability may have problems in relating with other children (Wiener, 1987). These poor peer relationships are generally related to increased social and psychological problems. Their behavior is inconsistent and generally hyperactive in that they respond at too great a rate for others to process and comfortably handle (Barkley, 1981). The inconsistent mood may vary from being depressed to being quite aggressive. Normal individuals are generally taken off balance by such behavior and, responding to it negatively, set in motion a scenario of negative outcomes. Once the negative feedback loop is set up with playmates, parents, and teachers it is extremely difficult to interrupt (Bryan, 1988).

A study by Wiener, Harris, and Shirer (1990) found that learning-disabled children are not as popular as their non-learning-disabled counterparts and are more likely to be both rejected and neglected by their peers. Although achievement and IQ are not predictors of peer status relationships, learning-disabled children are less likely to be considered leaders or as having a good sense of humor. Peer acceptance tends to decrease over time in the learning-disability group but not in the non-learning-disorder group. This latter finding suggests that over time children with learning disabilities tend to lose friendships, resulting in losing rather than gaining support over time.

It has been argued that the diagnosis of a learning disorder occurs too quickly, resulting in children being labeled as learning disabled only because they may be slower in developing certain skills (McGuinness, 1985). If children learn in different ways, they may also learn at different rates. Researchers have argued that if children were viewed as learning at different rates rather than being expected to display the same learning rates, fewer children would be classified as having a learning disability.

Because criteria for learning are socially defined, the arbitrariness of assigning certain values to learning ability must be kept in mind. Standards of performance vary according to the particular social setting in which the child participates. The context in which the child participates is an important factor in determining the label of a learning disability.

For the most part, the literature has ignored **familial learning problems,** or learning problems experienced by family members, and developmental factors as contributors to learning disability in children. A study by Oliver, Cole, and Hollingsworth (1991) explored the relationship between familial learning problems and developmental factors and the incidence of learning disability in children. Results indicated that familial learning problems, defined as the total severity of problems and the total number of problems experienced within a family, are a much greater predictor of learning disability in a family member than are developmental factors.

Other researchers have looked more at the bidirectional influences that affect persons within the family and social contexts. For example, Margalit and Heiman (1986) found that parents of children with learning disorders expressed more general dissatisfaction with their lives and more anxiety than parents of normal children. Families with a learning-disabled member tend to provide him/her with a more rigid and less supportive environment (Margalit, 1990). Furthermore, in comparing families with children who have attention-deficit hyperactivity disorder and families with learning-disabled children, researchers found that families with attention-deficit disorder were less supportive and more permissive. Families of learning-disabled children were found to have more dependent interpersonal relationships and more conflictual relationships and to demand more achievement and expect less personal growth (Margalit & Almougy, 1991).

Attention-Deficit Hyperactivity Disorder

In recent years, child psychologists have often used the diagnosis of **hyperactivity** or **attention-deficit hyperactivity disorder** (ADHD) (American Psychiatric Association, 1987) to describe the hyperactive behavior of certain children in the home and/or at school, particularly for boys. Generally, ADHD children are easily distracted and display impulsive behavior. They have difficulty waiting their turn when playing games with other children and begin but do not finish many activities. These children have much difficulty with school because in order to be successful there they must pay attention and follow rules.

Children with ADHD are generally placed in special education programs because they have much difficulty in the traditional classroom. Parents and teachers form patterns of relating to these children that tend to perpetuate the problem rather than solve it. The most typical response to an ADHD child is anger and frustration.

Recently, researchers have questioned the overuse of the hyperactive diagnosis for children who display boredom in learning and repetitive activities (McGuinness, 1985). Many children are believed to be very active and easily bored by repetitive activity. According to some child-development experts, the diagnosis of hyperactivity is made as a convenience to parents and teachers to make the child's behavior more acceptable and manageable. Studies of hyperactive children have not definitively determined either the cause or the most appropriate treatment for hyperactivity. Recently, some researchers have hypothesized that unusual and irregular brain growth during the prenatal period may be correlated with a high incidence of hyperactivity (Adler, 1989). Generally, the treatment for hyperactive children is to place them on medication. Although the medication may demonstrate a better control over certain behaviors than management techniques, it may have undesirable side effects and does not generally improve the child's ability to learn, the major objective.

The Physically Ill Child

A number of chronic diseases generally associated with children are: spina bifida, cystic fibrosis, and sickle-cell anemia. Children may also be born with, or develop shortly after birth, other diseases, such as leukemia, cancer, diabetes, kidney disease, and heart disease. In recent years, children born with fetal alcohol syndrome (FAS), addicted to drugs, and HIV-positive pose new and challenging problems for health-care personnel. The tragedy of the latter category of medical problems is that they could be prevented.

Chronically ill children require medical assistance outside the family. Although frequent hospitalization may be necessary to keep them alive, those who do survive reveal a similar developmental track as other children. The treatment and, perhaps, periods of recuperation in hospitals or other extrafamilial facilities are stressful on the parents as well as the ill child. How children react to the stress of chronic illness depends on a number of factors, not the least of which is the family environment (Hurley, 1987).

Both child and parent may experience much waiting and subsequent boredom during periods of hospitalization. Generally, recuperation or long hospital stays may be more difficult because of the lack of activity more than the physical or emotional pain. Resourceful parents can find many ways to get closer to their child during these periods.

The stress of a chronic illness in the child affects the parents and siblings equally. The length of time of the illness, the degree of medical involvement, and the interruption of family relationships are all important variables affecting the family with a

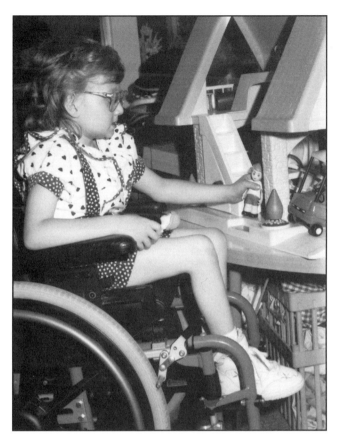

■ *Children with physical disabilities and those with medical problems require many resources in order to be able to participate equally with their peers.*

chronically ill child. Family members may have special needs as a result of having a member with a chronic illness and may need family therapy (Hurley, 1987).

Krulik (1980) has found that mothers of chronically ill children attempt to normalize the child's illness to improve the child's coping ability. Mothers also attempt to modify the surroundings to better accommodate the ill child. Researchers have noted that the major obstacle for parents with ill or physically disabled children is lack of community resources (Kornblatt & Heinrich, 1985).

Keeping lines of communication open is important for the family with a chronically ill child. Communication may be especially important for the marital bond. How the parents deal with a chronically ill child is no different from how parents handle other parent/child problems. If the mother and the father have vastly different methods of handling the child, it is likely that other problems will occur in addition to the expected stress in dealing with the chronic illness. For example, if the mother is overprotective and the father is withdrawn or peripheral, the mother may be prone to depression while the father may be unaffected by the chronic illness.

When parents do work together in dealing with this situation, they can be successful and may even feel that the illness brought them closer together (Hurley, 1987). This adjustment to a chronic illness may mean that the family is no longer focused on it in a negative way. Rather, the adjustment has been reframed as the family's adequate response to a challenge to the stability and the happiness of the family that the family successfully met. Many families feel that nothing could be as challenging as having to deal with the chronic illness of a child. It can be concluded that the family with a chronically ill child makes its own unique response to the illness based on the family ecological framework.

A Family Systems Model for Parenting the Impaired Child

A family systems model for understanding the parenting issues of impaired children is useful because it views the impairment relative to family relationships. According to this model, the process of how members relate to the impairment is more important than the actual impairment. A family systems approach implies that the total context, including extrafamilial relations such as the school and the family's socioeconomic status, predisposes families toward particular adjustments. For example, a single-parent mother whose income from two jobs barely supports her and her moderately mentally retarded child may have little time to spend helping the child to learn to read, whereas the upper-middle-income parents of a moderately retarded child may be able to hire a private tutor for the child.

Families with developmentally delayed or impaired children are frequently in contact with health-care, educational, and other systems. The interaction with these systems means that boundaries and roles are structured differently than in normal families. For example, the boundaries of a family with a chronically ill child must include doctors and other health-care personnel.

Family Structure and Communication Patterns.   First, a systems approach focuses on the family structure and communication patterns. According to a systems specialist, the family organization around the patterns of giving and receiving information is essential to the development of adequate functioning in a family with an impaired child. In addition, how the family adjusts to developmental changes as it moves through time is also an effective way for the systems specialist to understand the family environment of a family with an impaired child.

The **family life cycle** traces the family through stages relative to the birth and ages of children (Carter & McGoldrick, 1980). The birth of an impaired child would be expected to add new stresses to the expected ones. A significant issue after the birth of such a child would be that of parent/child bonding. Parents may find it more difficult to bond with an impaired child, affecting attachment and the emotional needs of the child. As mentioned earlier, the guilt and self-questioning that many parents of impaired children have may cause them to withhold the love and affection the child needs.

The birth of an impaired child may also affect the marital relationship. In the family life cycle, one of the most important stages is the beginning family, or the stage prior to the birth of a child. The marital bonding that takes place in this stage sets the pattern for the family (Carter & McGoldrick, 1980). A couple that has a child before marital bonding has taken place may have more difficulty making joint decisions after the child is born.

When the child is impaired, a weak bond between parents may become even weaker. The weak bond may also allow conflicts and dissatisfactions to emerge in the marital relationship. The degree of impairment in the child is another factor in marital conflict (Kazak, 1986). When the impairment is mild, the marital relationship suffers less than when the impairment is great.

As the family moves through the family life cycle, each stage is met with additional tasks as a result of the impaired child. For example, in the school-age stage the family must meet not only the challenges of having the child attend school, but also his/her special needs and the requirements of the school system. For example, if the child is chronically ill, the constant monitoring of the child's health may greatly increase family stress.

Siblings of the disabled or ill child may be neglected because their needs are less demanding on the parents. Older siblings of these children, especially girls, may be asked to perform certain tasks related to the care and support of the disabled or ill sibling. The progression through the adolescent years of the family life cycle, when the goal is to help the teenager differentiate from the family of origin, might be extremely difficult for a family with an impaired child. No doubt, this expectation to help take care of the disabled sibling is related to increased conflict between mothers and daughters (McHale & Gamble, 1989).

These adjustments are more difficult today because the nuclear family in American society is often cut off from the extended family. The nuclear family must either rely on outside help or make do with less help. Many sacrifices must be made to provide for the impaired child. It is not uncommon that careers suffer and social involvements are curtailed because of the demands in meeting the needs of this child.

Ecological Framework.   Second, a systems perspective of parenting the impaired child implies that it is essential to know the total ecological framework of the family in order to understand the outcome of these families (Bronfenbrenner, 1979). The family's ecosystem, as stated earlier, is an open system that changes and is changed by the same process. The individual, the family, and the social network, influenced by both biological and psychological factors, are constantly changing. A number of outcomes are available depending on the interaction of these factors. In some cases, an improvement in the impaired child occurs quickly, whereas in others the impairment becomes more severe. In still other families, the impairment may continue in a stable pattern indefinitely. According to the systems perspective, no single outcome is determined by the impairment itself; rather, an intricate interaction of the different factors involved determines the outcome.

Family Organization. Third, family structure is an important aspect of these families with impaired children. Family structure refers to the way the family is organized. As mentioned earlier, families are organized according to certain boundaries that determine the patterns of interaction. Two types of family structure, or organization, related to family functioning have been discussed: enmeshed and disengaged (Minuchin, 1974).

Enmeshed families are those that have rigid boundaries and in which members may intrude on each other's lives. It is characterized by lack of individuation and periods of extreme closeness and periods of extreme distance and conflict. Because family members are too closely connected, differentiation from the family is difficult for members to achieve. The overinvolvement may produce some periods during which members feel very close to each other. This sense of closeness may also be related to extreme hostility in that the way members attain individuality is through anger.

Parenting in an enmeshed family is characterized by assuming too much responsibility for the child's problem. For example, parents who are enmeshed with their child may force him/her to do activities, such as homework, without giving the child the opportunity to develop responsibility. These attempts to direct the child probably would be met with opposition and defiance.

A family with an impaired child might be especially prone to forming an enmeshed structure because parents and siblings are involved to some degree with the day-to-day care of this child. Typically, two patterns may emerge in an enmeshed family. First, the impaired child may react to the parental overinvolvement by doing even less for him/herself and being more helpless and dependent. Second, the parents may develop a style whereby one parent is overinvolved and the other parent is only marginally involved. This often leads to marital conflict, which is related to parenting ineffectiveness and family dissatisfaction.

When family structure is characterized as disengaged, a different but equally dysfunctional scenario emerges. Enmeshed families typically are characterized as having hierarchical imbalances (Haley, 1986). For example, parents may demand immediate compliance by the child through the use of force, intimidation, or threats. Children who are treated in such a disrespectful manner may openly resist the parents' efforts to both discipline and nurture them.

On the other hand, parents may abnegate their parental responsibility by deferring to the impaired child. They may feel too guilty to properly discipline or structure the impaired child. When this occurs, the family hierarchy develops with these children at the top of the hierarchy and the parents and other siblings farther down in the hierarchy.

Disengaged families have communication patterns that lack clarity and preciseness. Parents of impaired children may develop a communication style that either is too abrupt or does not provide enough clarity. Because of the poor communication patterns, small issues may escalate into unsolvable major problems. Discipline may be either nonexistent or inconsistent and punitive.

Reciprocal Interaction Between Family Members. The fourth aspect of a systems approach is an emphasis on the important reciprocal interaction among members that is related to the development and/or maintenance of an impairment. For example, when a child has a learning disability, the specific reciprocal interactions among family members would be expected to provide greater understanding of the disability. There is some evidence from the clinical literature which indicates that a learning disability may be a projection onto the child of a parent's own academic problems in school many years ago (Klein, Altman, Dreizen, Freidman, & Powers, 1981). The parent may stimulate a crippling paralysis in the child by projecting onto the child his/her own unrealized expectations. Unable to meet the parent's expectations, the child becomes discouraged and gives up.

A Homeostatic Function.   Fifth, the clinical literature suggests that the child's impairment may serve a homeostatic function in the family. The family becomes so preoccupied with the disability that the disability becomes the focal point for family stability. For example, the academic problems of a child diagnosed with a learning disability may keep the family organized and stable. If the child's school problems improve, the family would become unstable. Although the systems approach would not say that the homeostatic function of the family *caused* the learning disability, it would declare that there is an interplay of various factors including biological, social, and psychological. Researchers have concluded that children's feelings of failure at school are related to their parent's perceived helplessness (Campis, Lyman, & Prentice-Dunn, 1986). This perceived helplessness of the parent is interpreted as a demonstration of the child's own inability to achieve. The parent considers the child's academic failure to be caused by factors outside the control of the child.

The Total Family Context.   Sixth, the total family context is related to the impairment in any of its members. Researchers have found that academic achievement in school is related to a number of factors related to the family environment. For example, Klein and colleagues (1981) have found that children with a learning disability may have parents who had school-related problems or who blame the school inappropriately for the child's performance. Instead of working cooperatively with the school system, such parents pit themselves in opposition to the school. These children then act out their parents' frustrations and anger with the school system.

■   Parenting the Gifted Child

The **gifted child** is defined as having exceptional abilities and being capable of high performance (see Table 11.2). Initially, child development experts viewed gifted children as having a high IQ (Terman, 1954). Today, gifted children are viewed as representing a number of abilities. Their superior performance is demonstrated in such areas as general intellectual ability, specific academic aptitude, creative or productive thinking, leadership ability, and ability in visual and performing arts (Gardner & Wolf, 1988; Renzulli, 1979). Much of this giftedness appears to be present from birth and needs only to be given the opportunity to develop (Shaughnessy, 1988).

Table 11.2 ■ Giftedness

- Gifted children have IQs 130–140 and above.
- Gifted children weighed more at birth.
- They learned to walk and talk sooner than other toddlers.
- They reach puberty earlier and are healthier than non-gifted children.
- Gifted children who are placed in academically accelerated programs do not suffer from social maladjustment.
- Most gifted children continue to perform at a higher-than-average level in their careers as adults.

Source: Janos and Robinson, 1985.

Giftedness and Education

Gifted children need special educational programs designed to challenge them because the general topics relevant to their age are not interesting to them. Most states have adopted programs aimed specifically for the gifted child (Kitano & Kirby, 1986). These programs must also compete in priority with programs for the disadvantaged child. Because gifted children generally do well in school, the temptation in educational programs is to believe that the gifted child will do well regardless. Furthermore, programs for gifted children do not generally consider demographics, such as cultural, social, or racial differences (Patton, Prillaman, & VanTassel-Baska, 1990).

Determining whether a child is gifted requires a number of procedures. Researchers have found **IQ** scores to be a primary determinant of the gifted child. For example, IQ has been found to be highly related to school performance and graduation rates (Brody & Brody, 1976), and it is the major predictor of academic success in school (Minton & Schneider, 1980). IQ tests alone are not sufficient for determining giftedness, and some researchers view them as deficient (Sternberg & Davidson, 1986). The **triadic model,** first developed by child development expert Joseph Renzulli (1979), assesses the child's competence in aptitude (such as by an IQ test), creativity, and task commitment. IQ tests help determine the child's intellectual ability. **Creativity** and **reasoning ability** are difficult to assess by IQ tests. Current measures of creativity are limited as well (Hallahan & Kauffman, 1982). **Task commitment**—defined as high commitment to a task and commitment to complete a task—is also difficult to determine in children. Children who can become absorbed in a task and work on it for long periods of time would be considered gifted. Assessing this trait in children is not easy and teachers do not appear to be better at doing so than parents (Hallahan & Kauffman, 1982). Furthermore, teacher evaluations have been found to be of little value in assessing gifted children (Silverman, Chitwood, & Waters, 1986).

Characteristics of Gifted Children

Contrary to what might be expected, gifted children are not good at every task. They do share a number of characteristics, however, including perseverance in a task of

■ ■ ■ ■ ■ ■ ■ ■ ■ ■ ■

Box 11-1

Hints for Parenting the Gifted Child

Gifted children represent challenges for parents in a number of ways. Parents must change the way they parent to accommodate children whose intellect and behavior deviate from the norm. Parents have a tendency to fit in one of four patterns in parenting the gifted child (Hollingsworth 1990).

First, they tend to expect too much from the gifted child. The child may also come to expect too much from him/herself. Generally, parents may recognize the child's perfectionism, but not recognize how they reinforce it or contribute to its outcome. Instead of expecting perfection, parents need to recognize that despite the fact that their child is gifted he/she is not perfect and to recognize the effort put forth rather than simply the outcome. Gifted children must learn to deal with failure and learn from it rather than to expect to do a task right the first time.

Second, many parents of gifted children overindulge their child. They may be tempted to provide goods and services that have not been requested. Children must learn to

experience the consequences of their behavior for better or worse in order to grow up responsible.

Third, parents of gifted children may resort to overcoercion in order to maintain control. They may see themselves as the architects of their children's lives. Consequently, they must maintain control or fear that the child will not reach his/her full potential. Providing opportunities and listening to the child's feelings are necessary for the child's self-exploration.

Fourth, parents of gifted children may tend to give in to the child's wants and demands, on the basis that the child understands more than the average child and should be allowed more freedom. As a result, parents may not provide the guidelines and discipline the child needs to be able to act according to social expectations. Children respond to permissive parents with little respect and develop dysfunctional interactional patterns.

their interest, good problem-solving ability, good memory, sensitivity, and a wide range of interests. They have an advanced sense of humor for their age group and typically prefer older children as playmates (Silverman, Chitwood, & Waters, 1986). It has also been noted that gifted children have advantages in progressing through the developmental stages. They are typically more mature than their classmates (Janos & Robinson, 1985; Robinson & Janos, 1986).

Although the frail, emotionally immature, and socially inadequate child is sometimes depicted as the gifted child, the evidence seems to be quite the contrary (Montemayor, 1984). This developmental advantage appears to extend into adulthood. For example, gifted children appear to be quite successful in adult life when compared with the general population (Terman, 1954).

Cornell (1990) has pointed out the weaknesses of earlier research on the gifted child. Most early research did not distinguish between the popularity of a student and prejudicial attitudes toward gifted students. In some schools, gifted students may be unpopular because they are identified as gifted. In addition, most researchers have not compared within-group differences of high-ability students. In other words, most studies have not addressed the issue of the differences in gifted students—specifically, why some gifted students are popular and some are not liked by their peers.

In a study to correct these deficiencies in the literature on gifted children, Cornell (1990) studied a group of students in grades 5–11 who attended a gifted program sponsored by the University of Virginia Summer Enrichment Program. Students were admitted into the program on the basis of several independent evaluations including a teacher's evaluation, standardized test, school grades, and a series of questions regarding personal activities and interests. Families and students were asked to complete a questionnaire during the two-week program. The program consisted of a three-hour morning class on an academic subject, such as math or science.

Measures consisted of having students select the three same-sex best friends in the three-hour academic session, yielding a peer status measure. Peer rates were also measured by having students rate how much they liked each same-sex student on a five-point Likert-type scale ranging from (5) most liked to (1) least liked. Academic achievement was measured by school records on reading and math tests and by the Science Research and Associates achievement tests. Social status of the family was measured according to the educational and occupational status of the parents. Self-concept was assessed through Perceived Self-Competence Scale for Children. The Emotional Autonomy Scale measured the degree to which a student had become emotionally differentiated from his/her parents. The Child Manifest Anxiety Scale was used to assess the anxiety level of students.

The finding indicated that unpopular gifted children differed from popular gifted children on a number of factors. Specifically, the children differed on measures of social self-concept, the occupational status of the father, and academic self-esteem. No differences were found for academic scores and abilities (Cornell, 1990).

Unpopular gifted students typically had self-conceptions that did not significantly differ from those of other students in academic and physical abilities. Teacher ratings in academic self-esteem were lower, however, for unpopular students than for popular students. Unpopular students tended to lack initiative in working alone and in doing new or innovative tasks (Cornell, 1990).

Factors Related to Giftedness

A major factor that seems to be related to a child being gifted is the family background. Families with gifted children tend to place appropriate expectations on the child and provide an environment that is conducive to exploration (Scott, 1988). The

■ *Parental attention enhances a child's ability and may be a key factor in the child's being designated as gifted.*

degree of parental supportiveness and genuine caring for the child is highly related to competency in children. Contrary to expectation, these families tend to emphasize achievement per se less when compared with other families (Cornell & Grossberg, 1987). Instead, parents of gifted children spend more time just talking and reading to them than parents of average children spend (Karnes & Shwedel, 1987).

Bloom (1985) has found that **freedom of choice** is an important factor related to the presence of a gifted child. Although gifted children may decide what interests them, parents are extremely supportive and helpful to them in developing this area of interest. Fathers of gifted children believe in providing their children with more freedom and independence than do fathers of average students (Karnes & Shwedel, 1987).

Not only do parents of gifted children allow more independence than average students, they also teach their children persistence and patience. There is ample evidence that parents of gifted children have taught them how to be successful (Scott, 1988). Gifted children have the idea that to be successful one must be committed and resourceful. As long as 15 years may be required for the child to completely master an activity. The commitment to the developing of the talent or

---

Box 11-2

The Effects of Intergenerational Play on Creativity

Although **intergenerational play** has been ignored in the literature, presumably it would enhance the growth process in both children and parents (Bergen, 1989). Thinking patterns exhibited during play closely correspond to patterns used in creative thinking. While parents use pretend play with both disabled and normal children, with the former the type of play depends more on the child's physical condition than on any other factor. Play, humor, and cognitive development appear to involve similar intellectual and behavior patterns. The development of humor in children appears to be closely related to their interaction with parents and other adults. Creativity, like play, is enhanced by time, resources, and individual attention from adults. Play involving adults who allow freedom and flexibility in the play enhances the development of creative thinking in children. Creative play may generalize to other areas of life, including thinking logically and developing novel approaches to problems.

---

interest over years is what differentiates a gifted child from an average child (Bloom, 1985).

To some degree, discussing a gifted child and a gifted adult is mixing apples and oranges. The gifted second-grade child in math may or may not be a gifted mathematician at 25 years of age. Initially, children are motivated externally by parents and teachers, but in the course of receiving this positive feedback the motivation becomes internalized. Children then continue to be motivated because of the internal rewards and satisfaction they receive in performing the task.

Other factors of the parent/child relationship are related to the development of a gifted child. Gifted children generally come from families in which parents have higher than average IQs and value education. Greater opportunities are available to children from middle-class and upper-class backgrounds, not only for them to develop interest but also for them to be able to pursue it through the life course. Lower educational and occupational status of parents presumably is related to lower incidences of gifted children.

Some researchers suggest that parents of gifted children share certain characteristics in addition to social class and placing a high value on education. The total amount of time parents spend with their child, not just the quality of time, is extremely important. As one would expect, parents who spend more time with their children tend to have gifted children. Verbal activities, such as fathers reading to their children and playing word games with them, are highly correlated with having a gifted child (Karnes & Shwedel, 1987). Fathers who encourage independence were also more likely to have a gifted child.

The Gifted Misfit

Although many children labeled *gifted* generally become successful in grade school and carry this success over into adulthood, not all are successful as referred to earlier. In fact, the phenomenon of the **gifted misfit**—a bright child who does not perform as expected—has arisen in the literature. A number of factors have been associated with the gifted misfit. First, if parents expect too much from the child, they may not be supportive and nurturant of the child. Consequently, the child has the expectation to succeed without the parental support needed to succeed.

The converse of the preceding situation could also be true—parents may not expect enough from a highly capable child. The home environment may be one in which the child's real potential is not realized. When both parents are too busy to have much time for interaction with the child, they may not recognize the child's true potential. Another situation in which true potential goes unrecognized occurs when the gifted child who lacks adequate stimulation becomes bored with the subject matter in school and withdraws from competition. The child's teachers may not recognize that he/she is gifted.

Another factor in the gifted child performing below par is marital or family stress. As mentioned elsewhere, the marital relationship is extremely important for the child's success. If there is marital conflict, the child may act out the conflict by not performing at school. The nature of the child's school problem may be hidden to all, including the child. The poor performance eventually may convince even the child of his/her lack of competence.

In other cases, the parents may be supportive and loving of the gifted child, but the teacher and school situation may not be as supportive. In some cases where a child appears different from the other children, teachers misinterpret the child's efforts and classmates are critical and judgmental. This lack of support may cause the gifted child to dislike school.

There is some evidence that gifted misfits are not as socially or emotionally competent as other children. Despite having a high IQ, the average misfit has lower than average reading and spelling ability. The lack of social relations tends to become more problematic as the child nears adolescence because social competence is so integrated with other endeavors.

A Systems Perspective of Parenting the Gifted Child

As mentioned earlier, the family environment enhances or decreases a child's development. The ability to adjust to change and not get stuck in a stage of the family life cycle has been proposed as the difference between functional and dysfunctional families (Haley, 1986; Minuchin, 1974). Gifted children tend to come from families that are flexible and adapt well to change. As would be expected, family organization in families with gifted children reflects appropriate hierarchy and boundary alignments.

Families with gifted children appear to be very successful in other ways as well (Frey & Wendorf, 1985). They tend to be examples of stable families over a number of generations. These families may be the opposite of Bowen's fused or undifferentiated families who, over a number of generations, produced a schizophrenic member (Bowen, 1978). The dynamic operating in gifted families may be that flexible families over a number of generations produce a gifted child.

Gifted families tend to be organized hierarchically, but all members share in decision making (Cornell & Grossberg, 1987). Parents do not use their power to force compliance from children. This openness to change rules and share in power in these families tend to make them productive in the day-to-day activities of normal living (Minuchin, 1974).

Parent/Child Relationships in Families with Gifted Children

The literature indicates that parent/child relationships are good in gifted nonproblem families (Frey & Wendorf, 1985). Each family member tends to be valued equally. Parents are more authoritative in style than permissive. They tend to place a high value on teaching as opposed to punitive parenting behavior. Parents, especially fathers, tend to spend more time with gifted children than nongifted children (Karnes & Shwedel, 1987). This time together tends to be geared toward cultivating the child's talent or area of interest.

In families with a gifted child in which there is much conflict, more rigidity and lack of flexibility may be the rule. Parents who place too much pressure on their gifted child may influence him/her to give up to some degree. Furthermore, one parent may become more involved with the gifted child while the peripheral parent becomes less involved. This alignment between a parent and a child is related to an imbalance in family hierarchy.

Clear family roles have been viewed by family specialists as being related to having a healthy family (Minuchin, 1974). In gifted families, this possibility emerges because the gifted child may have a dual role of adult and child at the same time. When this occurs children may be confused and frustrated, and may miss out on many things related to childhood.

The presence of a gifted child in the family may increase family stress. In the same way that the birth of a child is seen as a crisis, the presence of a gifted child may require a period of adjustment. Siblings must adjust to having a gifted sibling. Initially, they may react with resentment or by negatively comparing themselves to the gifted sibling. Researchers have found that in comparison with gifted children, the nongifted siblings may appear to be less well adjusted (Cornell & Grossberg, 1987).

Family Portrait   ■■■■■■■■■■

Case 1

Billie and James, both 50 years old, have been married for 25 years. They have three children: Josh, 23 years old, attending law school; Ellen, a 14-year-old honor student in the eighth grade; and Paul, an 8-year-old second-grade student. Billie had been 42 years old when she unexpectedly became pregnant with Paul, and because of her age, she was at high risk for having a baby with Down's syndrome. When Billie and James found out before birth that Paul was diagnosed with Down's syndrome, they opted to have the child anyway because of their very strong religious beliefs. In Paul's early childhood, a number of operations were performed to change his appearance to near normal.

Billie and James planned for Paul's birth through reading about Down's syndrome and preparing for the worst. When he was born, however, they soon realized that he was capable of learning and accomplishing developmental landmarks, although at a relatively slow pace. Both parents made special attempts to work with him. Paul's older siblings, Ellen and Josh, were also helpful and showed no resentment or other negative feelings toward him. As time went by, Paul developed relatively normally until the past year, when a number of changes occurred. For one thing, Josh had attended college in the same town and was always in and out of the family home although he lived on campus. After graduating from college, Josh lived at home for a year before going to law school and was available to help take care of Paul. Soon after Josh left home James had a major heart attack and bypass surgery. Although James had partially recovered, his lifestyle changed in the ensuing months. James had worked for a newspaper prior to his heart attack and kept long work hours. He drank 5 to 10 cups of coffee a day and smoked at least two packs of cigarettes. He drank alcohol moderately and exercised several times a week by playing tennis or jogging.

After the heart attack, James gave up smoking, drinking, and strenuous exercise. He walked several miles a day and also rode a bicycle for exercise. He gave up his full-time job with the newspaper to write freelance. Family income drastically dropped. James continued to look for a full-time job that would be less demanding than the full-time newspaper job, but had not found a suitable one. Billie, who had not worked since the children had been born, was forced to find a job. She found a job as a legal secretary for a friend of the family. Billie was not satisfied with the job but felt she had no choice.

James's preoccupation with his health affected the family in that he cut back on the amount of time he had available for participating in activities with the family. His time with Paul was cut to a fraction of what it had been before the heart attack and subsequent surgery. On the other hand, Billie has tried to take up the slack not only in the loss of income but also in caring for Paul. Consequently, Billie has felt very dissatisfied and overburdened.

Ellen has always been an honor student and made straight A's throughout grade school. She never appeared bothered by her disabled brother in the past and often volunteered to help him with homework. She had been described by her parents as the ideal older sibling. Recently, she has begun to resent him somewhat and to feel neglected by both parents. When she attempted to discuss this problem with either parent, something would occur that would preempt the discussion.

Paul's development was normal except he was generally later than the other two children in walking and talking and had not showed as much curiosity. Because Paul functions as a borderline or mildly retarded person, he was allowed to enter a regular school. In the first grade he performed fairly well with the extra help of family members. During the second year, his performance dropped after his father's heart attack, his mother took a full-time job, and his older brother left home for law school. His academic problems also began to affect his social relationships. Some fellow students began to make fun of him on the playground. Because of his difficulty with mobility,

Paul was clumsy at walking and did not participate in physical activities. He began having some outbursts of temper at school when his frustration reached a certain level. These behavioral problems compounded his academic problems.

At home the same behavior began to appear, particularly aimed at his mother, whom he felt had abandoned him. Both parents felt more stressed about the family situation than they had ever felt in the past. In addition, Billie and James disagreed more about how to discipline Paul than ever before. Neither parent had used much punishment before, but James more than Billie was beginning to think that spanking might help. They were both very distraught and dissatisfied.

Case 2

Brenda and Richard have been married for 15 years, with two children: Sally, 13 years old, and LeRoy, 10 years old. They are both employed full-time, although Brenda did not work when the children were in preschool. Sally, a sixth-grade student, is not considered gifted in the school setting. LeRoy, on the other hand, is a very bright boy with many interests. He has always said that he wants to be an inventor. Many of his toys are self-selected because they were challenging to him, although some are too advanced for his age group. For example, when he was 5 years old he got a chemistry set designated for children 8 years of age and above. He sometimes works for hours making things in construction kits. He also designs his own games, magic tricks, and skits which he performs for his parents and extended kinfolk.

Brenda and Richard allow much flexibility in the family structure. At times, the family seems to be chaotic because it appears that no one is in charge. To complicate matters, both Richard and Brenda, especially Richard, occasionally travel out of town overnight on their jobs. This overnight travel is problematic because it means that both children must be left in an afterschool program until at least 5:30 and sometimes in the care of sitters until one parent arrives home. It is usually 7:30 before dinner is over. Bedtime routines are usually disrupted on these occasions. It is not infrequent for LeRoy to be past 11:00 P.M. getting to bed.

LeRoy is not always compliant at home and requires much coaxing to take his bath and get ready for bed. Sally, on the other hand, requires little attention at night and does her homework, takes her bath, and gets ready for bed without much fanfare. Brenda and Richard frequently disagree on how to handle LeRoy. In the bathtub, for example, LeRoy becomes preoccupied in some way with the water or the soap and forgets to take a bath. For example, one evening he carved a portrait of his pet dog out of the soap bar. Brenda has very little patience in dealing with LeRoy at these times, and her efforts to force him to be quicker or to keep his mind on the task at hand usually fail.

LeRoy was first described as gifted by his kindergarten teacher, who said that he had more art talent than any child she had ever worked with in her 25 years of teaching kindergarten, except one boy who was then in training at an art institute. Brenda was glad to hear this, but Richard preferred to think of him as just another boy who liked to draw and create things. Both parents, at times, attempted to motivate him to do his homework, which he always disliked and rebelled against. LeRoy claimed that doing homework was boring. Generally, he tried to complete it as quickly as possible so that he could get on to more interesting things.

LeRoy's first-grade teacher recognized his talents and his superior intellect. She frequently praised him for his creativity. His conduct at school generally was good but bordered at times on being problematic. His active mind sometimes wandered, or he created a new game or toy when he was supposed to be doing a specific assignment. Instead of giving him zeros for not turning in his work, his teacher would let him stay in the room during recess to complete the assignments.

In the second grade, LeRoy had a different type of teacher. She counted off for spelling because he failed to make the letters correctly, although she knew the words were spelled correctly. She counted off on his creative writing assignments because the letters were not made perfectly. When he daydreamed in class, she refused to tell him what he was supposed to be doing. Frequently, he had zeros because he did not hear the assignment. On his report card, he would have some subjects that needed improvement and some that were low passing. His math, science, and creative grades were always perfect. Although his report card did not reflect the extent of his gifted status, on the standardized tests at the end of the school year, his scores were among the top in the nation. In several areas, his scores were perfect. Despite his obvious gifted status, LeRoy did not think of himself as gifted and thought almost everyone in second grade was smarter than he was.

LeRoy believed that he should do everything perfectly. When he failed to do something perfectly after a few attempts, he would give up or not show as much interest in it. He was always comparing himself to his friends, and if the comparison was negative, he would not compete. This was especially true in sports or group games.

His parents frequently argued about the bedtime routine, which required both parents paying close attention to him in order for him to get his bath, have stories read to him, and get in bed. Brenda had very little patience with him and would frequently yell at him for dawdling. He responded to his mother's yelling in kind and by slamming doors, but not being more compliant. His father would withdraw from this mother/son confrontation until things were out of hand and would attempt to restore order. He would threaten to take away a favorite TV program or not allow LeRoy to play with a favorite friend on the weekend. LeRoy would then attempt to bargain with his mother or work out a "deal," such as getting his bath if she would read him a story while he was in the tub.

The main problem from the standpoint of the parents was getting LeRoy in bed at night, which they labeled as dawdling. Brenda particularly had difficulty with it and frequently negatively compared him with his older sibling. There would be some periods where LeRoy was quite compliant and helpful around the house in doing chores and completing his bedtime routine. Brenda and Richard were unable to determine why he was very cooperative at times and uncooperative at other times.

Compare and Contrast

None of the other three theories considers developmental issues or giftedness in discussing parenting strategies. This oversight in PET, Adlerian, and behavioral theories generally means that strategies are applied to all children regardless of special circumstances. It seems rather obvious in reading both of these cases that one must understand the familial context in order to suggest appropriate parenting.

It also seems that the behavioral approach would be more applicable than the Adlerian approach or PET for parenting Paul in the first case. Devising a token economy might be useful for helping Paul come to grips with his behavioral problems. In collaboration with his teachers, Paul's parents might develop a reward system for improving his work at school and controlling his temper tantrums at home (Patterson, 1975).

There is also the possibility that recent events in the family have changed the reinforcement schedule affecting Paul's behavior. Family members might be instructed to behave in certain ways to change the rewards so that Paul would behave more appropriately. When behaviorists do concern themselves with the specific context of a problem, as in this case, it is typically viewed as a cause-and-effect problem. For example, while behaviorists might consider the changes in the family as significant to Paul's behavioral and academic problems, they view the family relationships as one-dimensional rather than bidirectional. In other words, behaviorists see the family changes as affecting Paul's behavior, but not vice versa. The key from the behavioral point of view is for the family members to change their reinforcing behavior so that Paul will change his behavior (Patterson, 1975).

Adlerians and PET adherents would have little impact on improving Paul's behavior. The Adlerian approach would leave too much up to Paul's learning to take responsibility for his own behavior by suffering the consequences. Paul's ability to learn from his own experience would appear to need more structure than that provided in Adlerian parenting (Dreikurs & Soltz, 1964). Applying PET to Paul's problems would also not be structured enough to change his behavior. It seems plausible that giving Paul I-messages would fail to take adequate control of behavior that may escalate or be threatening to other members. In addition, the PET model would not consider bringing family pressure to bear on Paul's behavior. To focus the problem on either Paul or his mother would not seem consistent with the contextual information given in the case (Gordon & Sands, 1978).

In some ways, applying a systems approach to Paul's problem may seem even less specific than PET or Adlerian. Paul's problems seem more amenable to a direct specific approach as in behavioral theory. The total context must be understood and addressed, however, to effect real changes in such a system. In Paul's family, members have used personal resources to care for him and have felt burned out with it. Perhaps this family has attempted too much and had too great an expectation that Paul should be "normal." The effort the family places in helping Paul may signal that members have not accepted Paul's limited ability.

From a systems perspective, the disabled child is a member of a family that gives him/her a particular identity. Not only the child, but also the family, is labeled when a child has Down's syndrome. It would also be expected that Paul's behaviors are learned within the family context, and the change of those behaviors must be made within his family context.

A major area of concern in this family is the father's health. No doubt, his heart attack and subsequent restriction of activities may be a significant factor in Paul's problems with anger. Addressing the father's health issue may be essential to making changes in Paul's behavior. Although the other theories would not consider the father's health as much of a contributing factor, a systems perspective would view it as important because it contributed to the change in family roles and boundaries.

This change in roles and boundaries means that the family is thrown out of equilibrium, or homeostasis. Consequently, the family is attempting to reestablish homeostasis. A family systems specialist would see Paul's temper tantrums as an attempt to reorganize the family negatively around himself instead of the positive focus on himself in the past. Focusing on the family organization would be seen as more helpful to Paul and his family than focusing on his behavioral change.

The second case presents a family that apparently had little difficulty parenting the older daughter but has much difficulty parenting the gifted younger son, who appears to rule the home life by his dawdling in the evening routine. PET, Adlerian, and behavioral perspectives discuss dawdling behavior and strategies for changing it but not in the context in which it occurs. For example, from the PET perspective the dawdling behavior of the child needs to be viewed as either the parent's or the child's problem. In the case presented, the parents act as if the child's problem with the bedtime routine were their own problem. They have taken over the attempts to get LeRoy to take his bath, get his snack, and get in bed as their own problem. In a sense, one could reason that LeRoy does not have to worry about anything because his parents worry enough for him too (Gordon & Sands, 1978).

PET adherents would want the problem to rest on LeRoy's shoulders and the parents not to take responsibility for it (Gordon & Sands, 1978). In allowing LeRoy to assume responsibility for his own problems, the parents can act as consultants to him in solving it. For example, they may sit down with him and let him know what he must accomplish before he gets to bed. They could help him decide how he would accomplish these activities.

Adlerians discuss dawdling in terms of allowing the child to suffer the consequences of the behavior (Dreikurs & Soltz, 1964). For example, LeRoy would be expected to comply in the evening bedtime routines. Appropriate time frames for taking a bath, eating his snack, and having stories read to him would need to be determined. To improve his dawdling behavior, the parents may use a combination of natural or logical consequences. For example, the time frame may be set at 7:00 to get his bath, 7:30 to have his snack, and 7:45 to read stories, and 8:30 to be in bed. A natural consequence for not getting to the kitchen for snack time would be not getting a snack. The same would be true for not getting ready for his story to be read at 7:45. A natural consequence for not getting his bath may also be used in that he would have to go to school the next day dirty. A logical consequence for not getting a bath, which would seem to carry more weight, would be that he could not visit his friend's home dirty.

Behavioral theorists would begin by determining the frequency of the dawdling behavior (Patterson, 1975). The parents would be asked to determine what interactions were occurring before, during, and after the dawdling episode. They would also have to determine what behaviors to reward. The focus would be on decreasing the dawdling and reinforcing the desired behavior. LeRoy would be given certain rewards for complying with each aspect of the bedtime routine. To facilitate the compliance, each desired behavior would be addressed separately. For example, not taking a bath might be the first problem to be tackled. LeRoy might be given a certain reward for taking his bath during the time allowed. Once the bath problem was handled, the other problems might then be focused on.

A systems perspective applied to LeRoy's getting to bed problem would consider all of the information just given. One concern, not addressed in the other approaches, is the marital conflict. Richard and Brenda need to agree on the best way to handle LeRoy and to support each other's efforts. In one sense it appears that LeRoy knows how to get his parents angry at each other by manipulating their disagreement and controlling the family interactional patterns.

The fact that LeRoy is gifted is not taken into account by PET, Adlerian, or behavioral theories. A systems perspective, on the other hand, would consider the impact his gifted status makes on the family. A family systems specialist would view LeRoy's behavior as reflecting both internal and external motivations. Perhaps Brenda and Richard should think of unique ways of having the bedtime routine carried out. Rather than seeing his behavior as dawdling or misbehaving, they might reframe it in terms of his creative nature. LeRoy has problems getting in bed on time because of his active mind and imagination. Perhaps enlisting the same creative process to get him in bed at a more reasonable time not only would be a novel way of getting compliance but also might be more in tune with the circumstances. LeRoy is not so much misbehaving as he is being creative.

A family systems specialist might enlist LeRoy's creative endeavors by suggesting that he put his talents to use in devising a plan to get in bed at a reasonable time. Rather than seeing his behavior as needing discipline, his parents may see it as needing to be nurtured and guided. This nurturing and guiding of his behavior might also reduce his need to do things perfectly the first time. A more relaxed and flexible attitude toward LeRoy's behavior may in itself convey a more cooperative response from LeRoy.

■■■■■■■■■■

Parenting Proposition

Although some children by virtue of their individual characteristics are considered exceptional, the interaction with parents, siblings, and their social and cultural contexts are significant contributors to their behavior.

Answers to "Test Your Knowledge"

1. F   4. F
2. F   5. F
3. T   6. T

Key Concepts

impaired children   mentally retarded children
gifted children   Down's syndrome
developmentally delayed children   bio-underclass babies

amniocentesis

social, or familial, retardation

loss of a playmate

learning disability

familial learning problems

hyperactivity

attention-deficit hyperactivity disorder (ADHD)

chronically ill children

systems approach to parenting the impaired child

family life cycle

gifted child

IQ

triadic model

creativity

reasoning ability

task commitment

freedom of choice

intergenerational play

gifted misfit

systems perspective of parenting the gifted child

Study Questions

1. Discuss mental retardation and the developmentally delayed child.

2. What is Down's syndrome? What causes it, and how does it affect parenting? How does it affect sibling relationships?

3. Describe problems of drug babies and bio-underclass babies. How do their problems differ from those of other high-risk children?

4. What does social or familial retardation refer to? How would you describe it to someone who had never heard of the term?

5. Discuss a systems perspective of the impaired child. Compare and contrast it with other approaches.

6. Discuss the gifted child. How important is IQ in determining giftedness?

7. What is the triadic model? How is it used to assess giftedness?

8. Discuss the role of creativity and reasoning ability in the determination of giftedness.

9. Discuss the gifted misfit. How might parents and educators address the problems of gifted misfits?

10. Discuss a systems perspective of the gifted child.

References

Adler, T. (1989, November). Brain's language area is abnormal in disabled. *APA Monitor,* p. 7.

American Psychiatric Association. (1987). *Diagnostic and statistical manual of mental disorders* (3rd ed., rev.) DSM-III-R. Washington, DC: Author.

Bak, J., & Siperstein, K. (1987). Similarity as a factor affecting change in children's attitudes toward mentally retarded peers. *American Journal of Mental Deficiency, 91,* 524–531.

Barkley, R. H. (1981). *Hyperactive children: A handbook for diagnosis and treatment.* New York: Guilford Press.

Bergen, D. (1989). Intergenerational play: Influences on creativity throughout the life-span. *The Creative Child and Adult Quarterly, 14,* 230–238.

Bloom, B. S. (Ed.). (1985). *Developing talent in young people.* New York: Ballantine Books.

Bowen, M. (1978). *Family therapy in clinical practice.* New York: Jason Aronson.

Brody, E. B., & Brody, N. (1976). *Intelligence: Nature, determinance, and consequence.* Orlando, FL: Academic Press.

Bronfenbrenner, U. (1979). *The ecology of human development: Experiments by nature and design.* Cambridge, MA: Harvard University Press.

Bryan, T. (1988). Discussion: Social skills and learning disabilities. In J. K. Kavanagh & T. J. Truss (Eds.), *Learning disabilities: Proceedings of the national conference.* Parkton, MD: York Press.

Campis, L. K., Lyman, R. D., & Prentice-Dunn, S. (1986). The parental locus of control scales: Developmental and validation. *Journal of Clinical Child Psychology, 15,* 260–267.

Carter, E. A., & McGoldrick, M. (Eds.). (1980). *The family life cycle.* New York: Gardner Press.

Cornell, D. G. (1983). Gifted children: The impact of positive labeling on the family system. *American Journal of Orthopsychiatry, 53,* 322–344.

Cornell, D. G. (1990). High ability students who are unpopular with their peers. *Gifted Child Quarterly, 34,* 155–160.

Cornell, D. G., & Grossberg, I. (1987). Family environment and personality adjustment in gifted program children. *Gifted Child Quarterly, 31,* 59–64.

Crnic, K. A., & Leconte, J. (1986). Understanding sibling needs and influences. In R. R. Fewell & P. F. Vadasy (Eds.), *Families of handicapped children.* Austin, TX: Pro-Ed.

Dreikurs, R., & Soltz, V. (1964). *Children: The challenge.* New York: Hawthorn.

Frey, J., & Wendorf, D. J. (1985). Families of gifted children. In L. L'Abate (Ed.), *The handbook of family psychology and therapy* (pp. 781–809). Homewood, IL: Dorsey Press.

Gallagher, J. J. (1989). A new policy initiative: Infants and toddlers with handicapped conditions. *American Psychologist, 44,* 387–391.

Gardner, H., & Wolf, C. (1988). The fruits of asynchrony: A psychological examination of creativity. *Adolescent Psychiatry, 15,* 106–123.

Gordon, T., & Sands, J. (1978). *P.E.T. in action.* New York: Bantam.

Greer, J. V. (1991). The drug babies. *Exceptional Children, 56,* 382–384.

Grossman, F. (1972). *Brothers and sisters of retarded children.* Syracuse, NY: Syracuse University Press.

Grossman, H. J. (1983). *Classifications in mental retardation.* Washington, DC: American Association on Mental Deficiency.

Haley, J. (1986). *Problem-solving therapy.* San Francisco: Jossey-Bass.

Hallahan, D., & Kauffman, J. (1982). *Exceptional children: Introduction to special education* (2nd ed.). Englewood Cliffs, NJ: Prentice-Hall.

Harris, C. (1986). *Child development.* St. Paul, MN: West.

Hollingsworth, P. L. (1990 May/June). Making it through parenting. *Gifted Child Today,* pp. 2–7.

Hurley, D. (1987, August). A sound mind in an unsound body. *Psychology Today,* pp. 34–43.

Janos, P. M., & Robinson, N. M. (1985). Friendship patterns in highly intelligent children. Special Issue: Counseling gifted persons: A lifelong concern. *Roeper-Review, 8,* 46–49.

Karnes, M., & Shwedel, A. (1987). Differences in attitudes and practices between fathers of gifted and non-gifted children: A pilot study. *Gifted Child Quarterly, 31,* 79–82.

Kavale, K. A., Forness, S. R., & Lorsbach, T. C. (1991). Definitions or definitions of learning disabilities. *Learning Disability Quarterly, 14,* 257–267.

Kazak, A. E. (1986). Families with physically handicapped children: Social ecology and family systems. *Family Process, 25,* 265–281.

Keogh, B. (1986). Future of the learning disabilities field *Journal of Learning Disabilities, 18,* 455–460.

Kitano, M. K., & Kirby, D. F. (1986). *Gifted education: A comprehensive view.* Boston: Little, Brown.

Klein, R. S., Altman, S. D., Dreizen, K., Freidman, R., & Powers, L. (1981). Reconstructing dysfunctional parental attitudes toward children's learning and behavior in school: Family oriented psychological educational therapy (Part 1). *Journal of Learning Disabilities, 14,* 15–19.

Kolata, G. (1987, September 22). Tests of fetuses rise sharply amid doubts. *New York Times,* pp. 3,4, section F.

Kornblatt, E. S., & Heinrich, J. (1985). Needs and coping abilities in families of children with developmental disabilities. *Mental Retardation, 23,* 13–19.

Krulik, T. (1980). Successful normalizing tactics of parents of chronically ill children. *Journal of Advanced Nursing, 5,* 573–578.

McCormick, P. K., Campbell, J. W., Pasnak, R., & Perry, P. (1990). Instruction on Piagetian concepts for children with mental retardation. *Mental Retardation, 28,* 359–366.

McGuinness, D. (1985). *When children don't learn.* New York: Basic Books.

McHale, S. M., & Gamble, W. C. (1989). Sibling relationship of children with disabled and nondisabled brothers and sisters. *Developmental Psychology, 25,* 421–429.

Magenis, R. E., Overton, K. M., Chamberlin, J., Brady, T., & Lorrien, E. (1977). Parental origin of the extra chromosome in Down's syndrome. *Human Genetics, 37,* 7–16.

Margalit, M. (1990). *Effective technology integration: The family perspective.* New York: Springer-Verlag.

Margalit, M., & Almougy, K. (1991). Classroom behavior and family climate with students with learning disabilities and hyperactive behavior. *Journal of Learning Disabilities, 24,* 406–412.

Margalit, M., & Heiman, T. (1986). Family climate and anxiety in families with learning disabled boys. *Journal of the American Academy of Child Psychiatry, 25,* 841–846.

Minuchin, S. (1974). *Families and family therapy.* Cambridge, MA: Harvard University Press.

Minton, H. L., & Schneider, F. W. (1980). *Differential psychology.* Pacific Grove, CA: Brooks/Cole.

Montemayor, R. (1984). Changes in parent and peer relationships between childhood and adolescence: A research agenda for gifted adolescents. *Journal for the Education of the Gifted, 8,* 9–23.

Moreno, M., & Sastre, G. (1971). Evolution of subjective intellectual deficiencies in a learning operation. *Anuario de Psicologia, 4,* 71–146.

Office of Education. (1976). Assistance to states for education of handicapped children, notice of proposed rulemaking. *Federal Register, 41* (No. 230, 52404–52407). Washington, DC: U.S. Government Printing Office.

Oliver, J. M., Cole, N. H., & Hollingsworth, H. (1991). Learning disabilities as functions of familial learning problems and developmental problems. *Exceptional Children, 61,* 427–430.

Patterson, G. R. (1975). *Families: Application of social learning theory to family life* (rev. ed.). Champaign, IL: Research Press.

Patton, J. M., Prillaman, D., & VanTassel-Baska, J. (1990). The nature and extent of programs for the disadvantaged gifted in the United States and Territories. *Gifted Child Quarterly, 34,* 94–96.

Paul, J. L., & Porter, P. B. (1982). Parents of handicapped children. In J. L. Paul (Ed.), *Understanding and working with parents of children with special needs* (pp. 1–22). Holt, Rinehart & Winston.

Pueschel, S. M. (1991). Ethical considerations relating to prenatal diagnosis of fetuses with Down syndrome. *Mental Retardation, 29,* 185–190.

Pueschel, S. M., & Goldstein, A. (1983). Genetic counseling. In J. L. Matson & J. A. Mulick (Eds.), *Handbook of mental retardation.* Oxford: Pergamon Press.

Pullis, M. (1985). LD students' temperament characteristics and their impact on decisions by resource and mainstream teachers. *Learning Disability Quarterly, 8,* 109–122.

Renzulli, J. R. (1979). *What makes giftedness? Reexamining a definition.* Ventura, CA: National/State Leadership Training Institute on the Gifted and Talented.

Robinson, N. M., & Janos, P. M. (1986). Psychological adjustment in a college-level program of marked academic acceleration. *Journal of Youth and Adolescence, 15,* 51–60.

Scott, M. (1988). Gift-talented-creative children's development: Four parenting keys to help develop potential. *Creative Child and Adult Quarterly, 13,* 7–16.

Shaughnessy, M. F. (1988). Intra/interpersonal domains of creativity. *Creative Child and Adult Quarterly, 13,* 204–209.

Silverman, L., Chitwood, D., & Waters, J. (1986). Young Gifted children: Can parents identify giftedness? *Topics in Early Childhood Special Education, 6,* 23–33.

Stanhope, L., & Bell, R. (1981). Parents and families. In J. Kauffman & D. Hallahan (Eds.), *Handbook of special education* (pp. 688–713). Englewood Cliffs, NJ: Prentice-Hall.

Sternberg, R. J., & Davidson, J. E. (Eds.). (1986). *Conceptions of giftedness.* New York: Cambridge University Press.

Terman, L. M. (1954). The discovery and encouragement of exceptional talent. *American Psychologist, 9,* 221–230.

Thompson, R. A., Cicchetti, D., Lamb, M. E., & Malkin, C. (1985). Emotional responses of Down's syndrome and normal infants in the stranger situation: The organization of affective behavior in infants. *Developmental Psychology, 21,* 828–841.

Turkington, C. (1987, September). Special talents. *Psychology Today,* pp. 42–44.

White, D. F., Saudargas, R. A., & Zanolli, K. (1991). LD children's regular classroom behavior before and after identification and placement. *Learning Disability Quarterly, 13,* 196–204.

Wiener, J. (1987). Peer status of learning disabled children and adolescents: A review of the literature. *Learning Disabilities Research, 2,* 62–79.

Wiener, J., Harris, P. J., & Shirer, C. (1990). Achievement and social-behavioral correlates of peer status in LD children. *Learning Disability Quarterly, 13,* 114–127.

Wojnilower, D., & Gross, A. (1988). Knowledge, perception, and performance of assertive behavior in children with learning disabilities. *Journal of Learning Disabilities, 21,* 109–114.

Chapter 12

A Systems Perspective
of Family Violence

Parenting Myth ■ Parents who abuse their children are pathological or inadequate.

Test Your Knowledge ■ The following questions are designed to test your knowledge before reading the material in this chapter. Answers appear at the end of the chapter.

1 A systems approach to violence in the family suggests that the perpetrator of the violence should be punished. True or false?

2 A significant contribution to physical abuse of children is the parents' belief in the use of corporal punishment. True or false?

3 An increasing form of violence in American society is adolescent abuse of parents. True or false?

4 Violence seems to be passed from one generation to the next through an intricate network of socialization. True or false?

5 Researchers have found that women commit as many total acts of violence in the family as men do. True or false?

6 Although child abuse tends to be decreasing overall, it seems to be increasing in black families. True or false?

V iolence in American families is occurring at an alarming rate. Although the fact of violence in families is nothing new, the context in which violence is occurring is changing, and the models used to explain violence in families have lacked specificity. The context in which violence is most often examined is the sphere of individual maladjustment or personality disorder. Rarely has violence been viewed as an interactional component, or have relationship patterns been offered as a significant contribution to understanding the occurrence of violence. Likewise, models have been developed based on the belief that violence in families is an outcome of maladjusted persons. These models perpetrate a **victimization** approach to family violence and tend to not explain either the dynamics or the treatment of violence within the family. The victimization approach delineates a victim who in no way contributes to the violence and a perpetrator who is solely responsible.

This chapter develops an understanding of family violence from the context in which it occurs. It will be assumed that violence occurs within relationships relative to certain patterns and sequences that maintain the violence and prevent new patterns from occurring. It is hoped that this approach will be successful despite the tendency to discuss family violence in terms of victimization. Rather, a systems perspective of violence suggests that the individual, the family, and the social network are interdependent in explaining family violence. The psychological and interactional components of gender and parent/child relations are enacted in a particular sequence within a family to give a plausible explanation of why abuse occurs in one family but not another.

Family violence is physical or psychological aggression that is displayed through verbal and/or physical outbursts. Typically, the violence takes a repeatable pattern that may also escalate in intensity. Although most attention on family violence has focused on physical violence, such as wife battering or child abuse, it is obvious that other forms of violence may not only be as prevalent but also be as emotionally damaging as physical violence. This chapter gives a multilevel analysis of family violence from a systems perspective.

The Many Faces of Abuse

Although this book is about parenting, family systems specialists believe that spouse abuse and child abuse are interdependent and result from similar dynamics. Both child abuse and spouse abuse represent similar dysfunctional family behaviors with regard to expressing dissatisfaction and conflict. Typically, one family member is attempting to force compliance from another member, or there is a clash of wills whereby one member dominates.

Attitudes Toward Violence

Researchers have found that attitudes toward violence in general affect the likelihood of acting violent toward one's spouse or child (Scher & Stevens, 1987). For example,

■ *Boys are socialized to be more aggressive than girls even in their play.*

boys tend to be socialized to use and legitimize force in relationships more than girls are. This **socialization** toward more aggressive behavior begins at birth. A boy is heavily influenced by societal and cultural expectations to be masculine (Rice, 1989). Although these expectations have changed as more egalitarian marital roles emerge, traditional images of masculinity still reinforce the view that males should be dominant in interpersonal relationships.

Girls, on the other hand, are socialized to be more accepting of others, to be less dominant, and to show more nurturant behavior toward others. These differences, as mentioned in an earlier chapter, are characterized by different communication patterns between parent and child, different toys and clothes, and a different parental role model. Children who do not meet these societal expectations are generally thought of as different.

A contributing factor to child abuse is the acceptance of **corporal,** or physical, **punishment** as a means of parental discipline. There is a belief in American society that physical punishment is necessary for the child to comply with adult rules and restrictions at home or at school. When physical punishment is not used, it is believed that children will get completely out of control. This acceptance of the "belt" syndrome of parenting is but a small step to legitimizing child abuse.

Recently, a public outcry against wife battering and child abuse resulting in physical damage has occurred in the news media and among concerned organizations (Gross & Robinson, 1987; Hudson, 1986). This response is partially because of better reporting of abuse cases, which has brought the horrors of abuse to public attention. This attention on abuse has focused on the extremes of abuse rather than helping inform the public of all forms of family violence. For example, the implication is that as long as no one is physically damaged, abuse does not occur.

One of the most insidious beliefs that has influenced the direction of reporting both spouse and child abuse is that the victim deserved the abuse (Gelles, 1980). This line of reasoning concludes that the child deserved the "beating" because it was the last resort in controlling unwanted behavior. Likewise, the argument justifying spouse abuse suggests that when the wife stands in the husband's face and calls him names, he is justified in taking charge of the situation by hitting. Because this belief is shared by both the abuser and the spouse or child receiving the abuse, it has become firmly entrenched in the process of maintaining the abusive behavior.

Other Forms of Violence

Although most of the concern about family violence focuses on child abuse and spouse abuse, there is evidence that other forms of violence, such as **adolescent violence** toward parents, the abuse of elderly parents by adult children, and **sibling abuse** are increasing in American society. For example, the exact percent of the elderly who are abused, mistreated, exploited, or psychologically damaged is not known, but it is clear that the elderly stand a greater risk of receiving such treatment from caregivers and adult children (Hudson, 1986). There is some evidence to suggest that adult children who abuse their elderly parents are returning the harsh treatment they received as a child.

Adolescents who are violent toward parents typically have displayed problematic behavior in their families for years. A typical scenario is for the parent to have abused or severely punished the adolescent in early childhood and in adolescence the table is turned. Instead of the parent gaining respect from the child and developing a long-term bond with him/her, harsh parental punishment seems to be related to negative outcomes across the life span in interpersonal relationships.

Parent abuse by adolescents has been neglected in the literature, but it appears to be a common phenomenon (Gelles & Cornell, 1985). An estimated 10% of adolescents hit their parents in a year. Of the 10% about 3% are considered to have inflicted severe abuse. These incidences of severe parent abuse are as common as the incidences of severe child abuse (Charles, 1986).

Researchers have determined that parent abuse by an adolescent may result in very poor parent/child relations (Charles, 1986). Parents are reluctant to openly discuss the abuse or seek help from professionals because they are embarrassed and afraid that others will see them as ineffective parents. Family specialists view this secrecy surrounding the abuse by the adolescent as only symptomatic of the family's inability to relate in a functional pattern. The adolescent is viewed as acting out a pattern of abuse that makes sense within the family's relationship dynamics.

Parent abuse has intrigued researchers because it seems to involve the less powerful assaulting the more powerful (Gelles & Cornell, 1985). This pattern of abuse is a departure from the patterns of child abuse and spouse abuse, where the more powerful tend to abuse the less powerful. Whether this pattern represents a different set of factors or conforms to the same dynamics as child abuse and spouse abuse is only now being addressed by researchers.

Researchers have found that adolescent males are more likely to engage in parent abuse than are females (Peek, Fischer, & Kidman, 1985). Some researchers have found that fathers (Peek, Fischer, & Kidman, 1985) whereas others have found that mothers (Gelles & Cornell, 1985) were most often the target of abuse. A study by Agnew and Huguley (1989) concluded that males are more likely to hit fathers as they age, whereas females are more likely to hit both mothers and fathers as they age. In terms of racial background, whites are more likely to hit parents than are blacks, especially when the mother is the victim.

Agnew and Huguley (1989) developed a model for predicting adolescent abuse of parents based on models of child and spouse abuse. The typical adolescent abuser of parents is involved in other types of delinquent behavior. The researchers hypothesized that adolescents with certain internal controls would be less likely to commit abusive acts toward parents. Certain external means of controls, such as the commitment to conventional institutions and the probability the adolescent will be sanctioned by others for assault, were predicted to be negatively related to parent abuse. Association with others who were engaged in abusive or delinquent behavior was expected to be positively related to the incidence of parent abuse. In addition, the researchers expected that the level of strain or stress would be positively associated with the level of parent abuse.

Agnew and Huguley (1989) concluded that adolescents who assault their parents are similar in the following aspects: they have friends who assault their parents, approve of delinquency under certain circumstances, are white, and are weakly attached to parents. In addition, these researchers concluded that more traditional factors, such as drug use, social isolation, stress, and power differentials, are not related to parent abuse.

This research was a preliminary study that left important questions unanswered. For example, the relationship between parental assault and parental attachment was not determined from the linear model. Family systems specialists suspect that a recursive model in which factors are viewed from reciprocal influence would be better able to understand how the factors influence and are influenced by each other. In addition, the data for the Agnew and Huguley study were taken from the 1972 National Survey of Youth conducted by the University of Michigan. It is questionable that data this old accurately reflect adolescents who would be prone to attack parents in 1992. These data may not reflect the many changes that have occurred within families within the past 20 years.

■ Spouse Abuse

As inferred earlier, **spouse abuse** takes a number of forms including the following behaviors: grabbing, pushing, slapping, throwing things at the spouse, hitting with fist, yelling, threatening with an object or a gun, destroying furniture or other property, and intimidating through nonverbal behavior. Spouse abuse generally begins before the marriage takes place and continues in frequency and severity after marriage (Makepeace, 1987). Certain variables often related to this transmission of violence include: no religious affiliation, high or low income status, social isolation, minority racial status, poor social relationship skills, harsh parental treatment during childhood, and having been reared in single-parent or divorced families.

Table 12.1 gives the characteristics of abused women.

Intergenerational Transmission of Abuse

The preceding characteristics are sometimes referred to as **intergenerational transmission of violence.** Violence tends to be passed from one generation to the next via an intricate socialization process. There is ample evidence that children who received abusive treatment are more apt to grow up and be abusive themselves (O'Leary & Curley, 1986). The more children are exposed to violence through either being abused or witnessing the abuse of one parent by the other, the more likely they will complete the cycle and be abusive in their later adult relationships.

Although males are typically the perpetrators of violence, research evidence suggests that both males and females are more aggressive and accepting of violence when exposed to violence in their formative years (Kalmuss, 1984). This finding suggests that violence may be accepted more as an appropriate expression of intense feelings among some persons in society. Aggressive persons may be prone to gravitate toward each other in mate selection and participate unwittingly in the formation of abusive relationships.

Researchers in the area of the transmission of violence from the family of origin to the marital relationship generally focus on the dating relationship as the precursor of the marital bond. The evidence regarding violence in premarital relationships tends to suggest that the incidences of violence including both verbal threats and coercive acts are quite high (Thompson, 1987). Whereas some researchers have found that both males abused as children (Telch & Lindquist, 1984) and males who witnessed family violence as children (O'Leary & Curley, 1986) tended to be more violent in the

Table 12.1 ■ Characteristics of Abused Women

- Typically have low self-esteem
- Have traditional family beliefs
- Attempt to maintain peace in the family
- Appear to be the victims of psychological abuse
- Feel responsible for the abuse

Source: Walker, 1984.

marital relationship, others have found that females who were abused as children were more likely to engage in violence but that this was not true of males (Sigelman, Berry, & Wiles, 1984).

Studies on the transmission of violence in families have not delineated what is actually passed on to offspring. For example, the answer to the question of whether the transmission of violence is through influencing attitudes or acts is unclear. A study by Alexander, Moore, and Alexander (1991) attempted to determine the effect of witnessing or experiencing violence in the dating relationship, the effects of experiencing violence between parents in the family of origin, and the effects of one's attitudes toward women subsequent to violence in the dating relationship. In addition, the researchers found that males describe more witnessing abuse and receiving abuse in the family of origin than did females. Both males and females described the violence in the relationship as mutual or reciprocal, though it was not determined whether the violence was initiated or in self-defense. Neither witnessing the physical violence of one's parents nor receiving abuse from one's mother was predictive of marital abuse. On the other hand, physical abuse by the father was highly predictive of a male's both giving and receiving marital abuse.

Other findings of this study included a link between conservative attitudes toward women and males witnessing violence in the family of origin. Individuals with conservative views tended to be more violent toward their partners who held liberal views, but not toward partners who held conservative views. Men reported that their involvement in violence was unrelated to their attitudes toward women, while women tended to be both more abusive and abused when they described themselves as more liberal. Thus, it was the woman's attitude that was significantly related to abuse.

One inconsistent fact that puzzled the researchers was that whereas women in abusive relationships describe themselves as more liberal, men in abusive relationships describe their partners as more conservative. The researchers concluded that the woman in an abusive relationship may see herself as assertive in reaction to an abusive partner. This liberal view of herself may paradoxically help her justify maintaining a relationship in which she is the recipient of abuse. Men in abusive relationships apparently perceive their partners as conservative because they maintain the relationship despite the abuse.

One final conclusion drawn by Alexander and colleagues was that men and women in intimate relationships are influenced by their perceptions of the partner's attitudes, which are independent of the partner's intent or belief. In other words, what a man or a woman believes about the partner's attitude is a more important variable than what the partner's attitude actually is. Furthermore, the researchers concluded that partners should be treated within the relationship in a way that helps both partners to adjust their perceptions of the other's attitudes. When women are treated in consciousness-raising groups, they may not gain attitude changes that would insulate them from further abuse. Changes would take place in a relationship so that egalitarian roles would be established and attitudes of both spouses would be addressed. Consequently, the intergenerational transmission of abuse is understood more as a function of the interaction of attitudes than as a result of simply having witnessed marital violence.

In another study, researchers attempted to determine not only gender difference in the effects of family of origin aggression on spouse abuse, but also duration of effects. Most research on the effects of violence in the marriage is based on one assessment rather than several assessments across time. Malone, Tyree, and O'Leary (1989) found that physical aggression against parents, siblings, and spouses is similar regardless of gender.

While men tend to be more aggressive outside the family, it is easier to predict female aggression. The predictability of female aggression was found to increase across the course of early marriage as a consequence of family of origin violence. On the other hand, predictability of male violence as a consequence of family of origin violence was found to decrease across the course of early marriage. Findings indicated that by 18 months into the marriage husbands' physical aggression toward their wives was not a function of past experiences of aggression. Wives, on the other hand, did not show a decrease across time in the early marriage, and their experience of violence in past relationships extended to the marital relationship.

In addition, while physical aggression toward the spouse has not been easily predicted for husbands based on the family of origin, verbal abuse has been found to be predictive of later abuse toward the spouse. Malone and colleagues (1989) speculated that as marital discord becomes evident in the relationship, it will become more predictive of the relationship. This research supports the contention that abuse is a multidimensional problem that cannot be reduced to a simplistic linear cause-and-effect relationship.

Social Isolation

The relation between social isolation and dysfunctional family relationships is well delineated in the literature (House, Umberson, & Landis, 1988). The lack of social integration affects a couple because it limits the resources available for negotiating differences. It may also be related to less control of such impulses as violence or force.

Families that are well integrated in society tend to internalize the norms of conventional behavior. In contrast, families that do not integrate the norms of society tend to exhibit various problems related to poor social control, such as delinquency or alcoholism (Umberson, 1987). It is a reasonable assumption that socially isolated families would behave aggressively when tension or conflict arises (Stets, 1991).

Although violence occurs among marital couples and nonmarried or dating couples as mentioned elsewhere, there is some evidence that cohabitators experience more violence than married couples. A study by Stets (1991) attempted to determine the role of social isolation as a predictor of aggression in cohabitators compared with married couples. Two aspects of social isolation, social control and social support, were examined. Stets made a number of interesting conclusions. First, violence was found more frequently in cohabitators (14%) than married couples (5%) who reported an act of violence within the past year. Second, cohabitators tended to be less tied to groups than married couples, but they had more ties to family and friends. Contrary to expectations, it was married couples, rather than cohabitators, who were isolated from family and friends. However, because cohabitators are less tied to both their partners and social groups, they are not receiving certain normative expectations. Consequently, social isolation must be viewed as having multiple dimensions. Stets concluded that the difference in support from friends and family may only be a smoke screen. For example, to compensate for their isolation from groups, cohabitators may seek out the support of friends or family that is available to them. This support may actually be ineffective in providing resources that are needed when families are attached to society. As a result, cohabitators continue to live by rules that fall outside the norms of society

Stets concluded that social support, especially in the form of seeking help, has no direct effect on aggression. Indirectly, lack of social support influences aggression through depression. Persons without adequate social support may become depressed, influencing the onset of violence or aggression in the relationship. Furthermore, Stets suggested that since cohabitators are less tied to organizations and less committed to their partners, they are more likely to engage in non-normative behavior such as alcohol abuse, which is related to higher rates of couple violence.

Researchers have attempted to address the connection of courtship violence with later violence in marriage (Straus, Gelles, & Steinmetz, 1980). Studies of courtship violence generally have found that women who have been abused in the marriage were abused as children and were reared in a family where spouse abuse was common. In one study, 31% of the women in shelters for battered women were abused as children and 50% were reared in families where family violence was fairly common (Roscoe & Benaske, 1985). The training for violence in intimate relationships may also include the link between courtship and marriage (Flynn, 1987).

In one study, violence was present from the beginning of committed relationships in which moderate abuse and victimization took place. The peaks of violence occurred after the relationship had reached the commitment stage. The researchers concluded that violence may serve different purposes in different relationships. Some violence in relationships may develop to move the relationship into a more committed stance. Violence may have become accepted as a legitimate means of resolving conflicts between the spouses (Billingham, 1987). This research suggests that violence must be considered in terms other than merely one partner's attempt to be powerful or to dominate the other partner. In therapy, a technique that merely attempted to do away with the violence would be less desirable than a technique that viewed the violence as a disturbance in the patterns of achieving and accepting intimacy in the relationship. Treatment should be placed in the context of the particular relationship of the couple rather than in a generic context of treating the violent couple.

Factors Related to Spouse Abuse

A discussion on spouse abuse is somewhat problematic because not all is known about the rates of violence, the likelihood of occurrence, or whether the types of violence usually noted in research actually depict the types that are occurring in families (Straus & Gelles, 1986). In fact, a national survey of couples indicated that rates of spousal violence may have declined in the 1980s compared to the 1970s. It is not clear from the research data whether the decline was due to lower overall rates or reflected a reluctance to divulge violent behavior in a telephone interview.

Both spouses tend to be involved in about 50% of the reported cases of spouse abuse (Straus, Gelles, & Steinmetz, 1980). In total acts of violence, there is little difference in husbands and wives. In fact, wives tend to throw things, yell, slap their spouse, and threaten with a gun more often than husbands do (Straus, Gelles, & Steinmetz, 1980). This pattern of female violence has been explained in one of two ways. First, it is not known how much of the wife's violence may be in retaliation or self-defense. Second, wives inflict much less overall damage to the husband than vice versa. This focus on physical damage to the exclusion of emotional damage, however, may actually promote violence by the wife. If it is accepted that she cannot damage the husband as severely as he can damage her, it may be justified for her to hit him but not vice versa. A type of double standard exists when female violence is justified.

This pattern of **mutual violence** has generally been ignored in the literature. It is not known whether the abuse constitutes the same dynamics as when one partner is the abuser and the other the abused. More research is needed to determine the nature of various patterns of abuse. Mutual violence may be unique in many ways that remain unknown at present. It could be that certain ways of discussing wife battering, such as male dominance, do not fit with discussing mutual violence.

As mentioned earlier, spouse abuse takes many forms. Severe injury is not uncommon. In about 10% of cases, the husband may force himself on his wife sexually (Finkelhor & Yllo, 1985). The sexual assault may be accomplished though physical intimidation or physical battering. This type of abuse may be extremely damaging to a woman's emotional and psychological stability.

The occurrence of abuse has been referred to as the **cycle of violence** because it passes through a number of stages (O'Leary & Curley, 1986). The first time violence occurs may be shocking for the wife, who may feel that she did something to cause it. Generally, the husband may also express regrets to his wife and promise that the abuse will never happen again, fully believing that himself. After escalating tensions,

---

■ ■ ■ ■ ■ ■ ■ ■ ■ ■

**Box
12-1**

How Should We Intervene with Men Who Batter?

Interventions with wife abusers, taking the form of cognitive or attitudinal change, have not produced conclusive evidence of their effectiveness. Eisikovits, Edleson, Guttmann, and Sela-Amit (1991) attempted to determine the relation between cognitive styles and attitudes toward women and violent behavior toward women. Specifically, the researchers were attempting to determine the interplay between these variables and ecological conceptualizations of the family. Subjects consisted of 60 men who were violent toward their wives matched with 60 nonviolent men. In order to be considered violent, a man had to have exhibited at least one act of violence toward his partner in the last year. The men, all Jewish, were from 22 to 58 years of age. Measures included in the study included the Conflicts Tacits Scale, Rational Behavioral Inventory, Self-Control Scale, Internal Powerful Others and Chance Scale, and the Inventory about Wife Beating.

A statistical analysis found no significant differences between violent and nonviolent men on the cognitive variables. The only difference was that violent men held significantly less positive views toward the battering of women. When the data were analyzed, the researchers found that abusive and nonabusive men can be differentiated. This analysis revealed that the attitudes of these men distinguished between the violent and nonviolent groups.

This research supports the view that modifying the male abusers' attitudes about wife abuse would be a helpful technique in treatment. It also supports the view that wife abuse is multidimensional and cannot be reduced to single factors. Because attitudes are formed from the interaction of many factors, the researchers suggest intervention with the individual, family, social institutions, and the larger culture.

---

another episode may occur. The husband acts contrite and begs for forgiveness, once again promising that it will not happen in the future. This pattern becomes firmly entrenched as both partners become somewhat disenchanted with the prospect that they can relate without violence.

Spouse Abuse in Black Families

Spouse abuse in black families has been somewhat ignored in the literature. No doubt the nonrepresentative samples from shelters and clinical samples have contributed to the lack of data on black spouse abuse. Some researchers have concluded that black husbands have higher rates of violence toward their wives than white husbands do (Straus, 1980). The rate of severe violence of black husbands against their wives was found to be 113 per 1,000 compared to 30 per 1,000 for whites. Likewise, black wives were more likely to use violence toward their husbands than white wives were. The rate of violence of black husbands toward their wives remained the same during the decade 1975–1985, while the incidence of severe violence declined 43.4% (Hampton, Gelles, & Harrop, 1989). On the other hand, in 1985 the overall rates of black female violence toward their husbands increased by 33.3% and the severe violence rates increased by 41.2% to 108 per 1,000.

Compared to violence in white families, violence in black families still appears to be substantially greater overall. Although the rate of abuse of wives by husbands has declined among blacks, the rate for severe abuse of husbands by wives has increased. Perhaps the increase in violence of black wives toward their husbands can be explained by the increase in commitment of black women to the home, such as in single-parent families, and the concomitant decrease of commitment of black men to fulfill the role of provider (Hampton, Gelles, & Harrop, 1989). Black females' increase in power and status in the family has paralleled their achievements in education and work. Black males have not kept pace with black females in educational and occupational endeavors.

Models of Spouse Abuse

The early research on spouse abuse tended to focus on psychological factors of the abuser or the abused. For example, the abuser could be described as a person who had low self-esteem and low tolerance for frustration (Gelles, 1982). Abusive episodes frequently occur when the abuser is feeling depressed or when anxiety within the relationship has reached a certain level of intensity. The abuser may appear normal on the surface while concealing the maladaptive characteristics until abuse is triggered by certain circumstances (Bernard & Bernard, 1984).

Early researchers also found that the abused spouse may have some personality defects that contribute to his/her being victimized. For example, in a clinical study Snell, Rosenwald, and Robey (1964) found that abused women had disturbing personality traits that may have caused the husband to be abusive. The women were described as sexually unresponsive, domineering, and aggressive. The researchers implied that the wives may have deserved the abuse they received by such irritating personality traits.

Researchers, focusing on individual causes of abuse, have typically portrayed the husband as powerless in the relationship. In an attempt to maintain male superiority, husbands have resorted to their basic superiority of greater size and strength over women. Women who have more education than their husbands appear to be in great risk of abuse. To support these conclusions, researchers have found that women who attempt to leave their abusive husbands are in greater risk of being killed by their husbands than are any other group of women (de Santis, 1990).

It is not known whether the preceding descriptions were the result of researcher biases or were an adequate portrayal of the limited clinical cases surveyed. It is clear, however, that the focus on individual cases has not enhanced the understanding of family violence in the 1990s. Neither the wife nor the husband should be viewed as the cause of the abuse. Rather, the view should be that a number of interrelated factors lead to the outcome of a particular style of abuse in a particular family.

Not all models of family abuse have been based on individual dynamics. In an attempt to explain violence between spouses in relationship terms, a group of researchers developed a model for explaining marital violence labeled the **frustration/aggression model** (Dollard, Doob, Miller, Mowrer, & Sears, 1939). This hypothesis stated that under increasing frustration a person may resort to aggression or violence toward his/her spouse. Although the model was confirmed through a number of research projects and a relation between frustration and aggression has been clearly identified, the conditions under which frustration leads to aggression in marital relationships were not delineated. Consequently, other factors may link frustration and aggression together and determine how frustration may lead to violence in one marital relationship but not in another.

Another model of spouse abuse is **social learning theory,** or the belief that aggression is a learned response to a certain set of stimuli (Bandura, 1973). From the social learning model, aggression is viewed as stemming from some frustration that was reinforced and continued in a certain pattern. A family can be seen as a factory where abusive responses are learned and become second nature. The more children are exposed to violent parental models, the more likely they are to establish violent relationships in their family of marriage.

Husband Abuse

Although husband-initiated violence may decline with more egalitarian roles, the caveat might be an increase in wife-initiated violence. If, as some researchers have concluded (Kalmuss & Straus, 1982), spouse abuse is typically a way to maintain dominance, as wives become more dominant in the relationship they would initiate violence to maintain control of the spouse. Although no research data are available regarding increased power in the relationship and wife-initiated violence, it seems logical that as women gain more power in the relationship, they would be prone to initiate violence to protect or maintain their position. An increase in family power for the black female may be a plausible explanation for the increase in violence toward the husband.

Although some studies have found that women are as violent in the family as men are, little attention has been given to **husband abuse** (Straus & Gelles, 1986). Husband abuse is not defined as a problem by society because women inflict little physical damage on men and the violent acts are usually isolated incidents. In addition, researchers have found that women usually use force to break their husband's grasp (Walker, 1984). In a college sample of courtship violence, Makepeace (1986) found that men use violence to intimidate the partner and that women use violence to defend themselves.

Because of the small proportion of actual cases of battered husbands, some researchers have argued that it would be misleading to coin the phrase "battered husband syndrome" (Pagelow, 1984). One reason why the nomenclature of the battered husband syndrome may not catch on is that the economic resources available to husbands are greater. Consequently, some evidence also suggests that husbands do not tolerate abuse from wives and leave the relationship (Straus, Gelles, & Steinmetz, 1980). Husbands tend to remain in the relationship with an abusive wive if the abuse is minor and infrequent. In addition, husbands tend to stay in the relationship for many of the same reasons that women stay in an abusive relationship (Pagelow, 1984).

From a systems perspective, ignoring husband abuse means that a valuable piece of the information is missing in understanding the formation, maintenance, and treatment of family violence. Simply continuing to focus on the husband as the abuser and the wife as the abused fails to understand the recursive nature of relationship violence and the societal norms that influence violence. There is obviously a need to concentrate on the total picture of abuse including the communication and decision-making processes of the couple (Flynn, 1990).

A Systems Approach to Spouse Abuse

A **systems perspective of family violence** attempts to understand the pattern of spousal interaction that leads to and maintains violence in the relationship. Of primary interest is an understanding of how these patterns develop, escalate, and are maintained through the development of family rules and feedback loops. Theorists from a systems perspective assume that neither individual dynamics nor happenstance could adequately explain how violence becomes part of the ongoing interactional pattern of the couple.

When a couple marries, they begin an intricate system that is based on the weaving together of two persons from different systems. This weaving together of two persons into one system is accomplished through the development of rules that are constantly reinforced or challenged through feedback with the environment. When both spouses have been exposed to violence in their families of origin either through being abused by parents or through witnessing abusive acts of their parents, they may be more prone to establish a relationship that is abusive than are two persons from families that were not violent (Giles-Sims, 1983).

Although spouses may know that their partner was abused as a child or was in a previous relationship in which violence occurred, they often do not consider it an important variable before marrying. For example, wives typically give excuses for the husband's violent behavior before marriage and are generally not concerned about it. Likewise, violence that occurs before marriage is disregarded or explained away (Giles-Sims, 1983).

Members in a new system tend to bond together to form a sense of cohesion, which is necessary for adequate functioning (Olson, Russell, & Sprenkle, 1983). In terms of abuse, however, this natural bonding taking place between spouses may work to maintain violence because of the commitment to the relationship. The increasing commitment, resulting from a positive feedback loop, acts to prevent any acknowledgment of events that would change the overall structure of the relationship (Giles-Sims, 1983).

In stressful situations, spouses may react to each other as they do to family members in their families of origin or to other adults. Warning signals that violence might occur are ignored early in the relationship. This reaction to stress through violence becomes part of the patterned response of both spouses. In this sense it represents a negative feedback loop because no change is evident, and this pattern of violence will serve to reduce the stress in the relationship.

As the pattern is established in the relationship, the violence functions as a systems phenomenon to keep things the same. It operates to reinforce rules and maintain a steady state. This pattern may continue for years with no significant escalation. The family generally maintains a high level of privacy regarding family relationships. A characteristic of these families is social isolation, preventing and enabling new input that could create positive feedback. Family rules, such as "Father has a right to maintain control at all costs," are not challenged during this period.

Although family members may maintain violence by negative feedback for quite some time or indefinitely, it is not uncommon for violence to escalate out of control and challenge the family rules and homeostasis. For example, the wife may break the family privacy by telling others of the violence or by seeking help from social service agencies. This breaking of the silence could instigate a positive feedback loop that could move the system toward change.

The breaking of the rule that maintains the violence throws the family into crisis. This crisis may appear more threatening to the spouses than the continuation of the violence because it may signal the end of the relationship. Women have often endured violence for the sake of maintaining a home for their children (Straus & Gelles, 1986). Many times the incident that leads to change in the system is the fear that children will be abused, or the humiliation of the woman in front of the children.

This critical incident in the interruption of the violence means that new input into the system is likely. Over time the new input escalates and settles in new patterns of behavior that do not include abuse. When a positive feedback system begins, there is a fork in the road for the relationship in the sense that it can reorganize itself around another pattern that does not include violence, or it can dissolve.

One resource that has given women another option is the spouse abuse shelter. Shelters provide not only a place to go for shelter but also other services, such as job placement, family counseling, and support. Women who benefit most from the shelter also use a number of other services, such as calling the police, getting a restraining order, or contacting the mental-health center. When women use only the shelter without the other services, husbands change less and retaliate by continuing the violence (Berk, Newton, & Berk, 1986). From a systems perspective, the husband is resisting the new input and attempting to maintain patterns in the system. The more new input that comes into the system, such as mentioned previously, the more likely there will be sustained change.

Clinical studies are generally pessimistic about the prospects of change for wife abusers. Traditional psychotherapy has not been considered very successful in changing husbands who abuse their wives. Recently, research has shown that abusing husbands have received some help from group counseling with other abusers (Gelles & Maynard, 1987). Perhaps the group experience with other abusers provides a framework forcing the husband to look at his part of the responsibility for the violence.

As women gain more equality in society and obtain equal access to resources, the overall incidence of abuse should decline. Although husbands may resist giving up power and even increase violence toward women as retaliation, it is expected that egalitarian roles will decrease the amount of violence initiated by husbands.

Some researchers question the appropriateness of applying a systems paradigm to family violence because the focus on circularity may diminish the focus on an individual's experience of abuse (Dell, 1986). The reality of oppression within the family and the use of unilateral power by one member against other members may not be clearly addressed from a systems perspective (Imber-Black, 1986).

■ Child Abuse

Defining child abuse is difficult because practices for rearing children vary widely from culture to culture. Even within our own history the treatment of children has varied. In colonial America, for example, children were considered property and subject to the parents' control. It was not uncommon for parents to punish their children even after the children reached adulthood (Ariès, 1982). Infanticide, the practice of abandoning children after birth, has been a common practice in various societies of the world.

Although there is considerable agreement regarding the broad patterns of what constitutes child abuse today, there is not agreement about specific parental behaviors that might or might not be abusive. Generally, any behavior that is physically or psychologically harmful to a child under age 18 by a person or agent of that person in the care of said child is considered **child abuse.** The obvious acts of abuse include beating or other forms of physical violence, sexual abuse, overt neglect, and abusive language. Although most forms of abuse are generally thought to be aggressive acts toward the child, neglecting the physical or emotional needs of the child can have very detrimental effects (U.S. Department of Health, Education, and Welfare, 1975).

The number of cases of reported child abuse has risen about 10% a year since the mid-1970s (Straus & Gelles, 1986). This increase in reported cases of child abuse does not represent an increase in stranger-initiated abuse, but abuse within the household. Although these figures on abuse are staggering, researchers have warned that abuse of children may be actually decreasing rather than increasing. For example, reporting child abuse is now compulsory in all states, and some acts considered abusive now were not considered so in the past.

Child abuse occurs among persons of all socioeconomic backgrounds, although it is reported more often among minorities and low-income persons. Lack of economic

---

Box 12-2

■ ■ ■ ■ ■ ■ ■ ■ ■ ■ ■

Child Abuse and Neglect Among Migrant Farm Workers

A study by Tan, Ray, and Cate (1991) has documented the high risk factor for abuse of children of migrant farm workers, many of whom are Mexican-American. These families relocate often and live in overcrowded, unsanitary conditions. They also experience poor health, low educational attainment, and little or no job security. The children raised in these conditions are at high risk for developmental difficulties, which further lower their prospects for a normal life.

Children enter the family with developmental dispositions that predispose them toward certain behaviors. These factors are deeply entrenched in the social, cultural, and familial systems affecting migrant farm workers. Programs are needed that respond specifically to the deficits of these families. Typically, language barriers and cultural expectations reduce the support and involvement of the farm workers for programs that are available. Bilingual educational opportunities and sharing of the power and economic structure are among the suggestions made by Tan, Ray, and Cate (1991).

---

and social resources may be one of the major reasons for the higher incidence of child abuse among the disadvantaged. It is also possible that the reported cases are but the tip of the iceberg and that the actual number of abused children is much higher among all groups.

Factors Related to Child Abuse

A number of factors, sometimes referred to as **cycle of abuse,** are related to child abuse. First, parents who believe in corporal punishment are more prone to abuse their children. According to law, a parent must leave some physical damage to be guilty of abuse. This definition of abuse appears highly arbitrary because some parents are deemed abusers while other parents spank their child as hard but leave no bruises or noticeable injuries. Parents who do not spank their children, but scream and yell at them, may also be considered abusive.

Second, many parents who abuse their children were themselves abused as children (Egeland, Jacobvits, & Sroufe, 1988). The tendency, as mentioned earlier, is to transmit abuse through the generations. Parents tend to continue the same patterns of parenting they were exposed to as children. The converse is also true—children who are reared in accepting nonpunitive homes tend to produce children who mature into accepting and nurturant parents.

The route of transmission through the generations is not completely understood. For example, some children who are abused do not grow up to abuse their children. They have been able to make a decision that broke the cycle of abuse. Researchers have found that a number of factors are present when the cycle of abuse is broken (Kaufman & Zigler, 1987). A good relationship with one of the parents seems to be the most important factor in not repeating the abuse. Furthermore, these children were aware of the effects of abuse on their lives and were intent not to continue it with their children.

Third, parents are more likely to abuse their children when they lack basic knowledge of child development. These parents lack knowledge of the concept of developmental readiness and normal behaviors of children. These parents are more likely to interpret the discomforts of the child as the child being critical or nonaccepting of the parent (Trickett & Sussman, 1988). Children are unnecessarily frustrated by such parents, who often feel overwhelmed and discouraged. Consequently, many parents continue blindly the same type of parenting as their own parents even if those strategies were ineffective.

Finally, parents are affected by many stresses of living including how to survive financially. These problems are more severe in single-parent and remarried families in which child abuse is more frequent (Zigler, 1979). It is not uncommon that abuse occurs when stress is highest and when the parent is feeling extremely frustrated. Many parents guilty of abuse are attempting to do the best job they can do (Straus & Gelles, 1986).

Table 12.2 summarizes the risk factors for families of abused children.

Child Abuse in Black Families

Black family violence has been of recent concern in the literature. According to public reports, black children tend to have higher rates of neglect and abuse than white children. For example, in 1985 black children, comprising 15% of the population, accounted for 26.8% of the child-abuse reports (American Association for Protecting Children, 1987). To conclude that black children are at much greater risk for abuse may not be accurate because black children are more often labeled as abused than middle-class or majority children (Hampton, Gelles, & Harrop, 1989). In general, it appears that researchers have not found definite support in studies to corroborate the public reporting that black children are at greater risk for abuse.

A recent study, however, has shed new light on the question of abuse in black families. Using data from the national violence surveys, Hampton and colleagues (1989) concluded that between 1975 and 1985, the incidence of child abuse in black families increased. The rate of severe abuse increased by 48% during this decade. These changes, however, were not statistically significant.

The disturbing fact about the preceding research is that, although violence toward children was declining overall in society during this time period, it was increasing in black families. Hampton and colleagues (1989) also concluded that this increase

Table 12.2 ■ Risk Factors for Families of Abused Children

- The abusing parent was physically punished as a child.
- The abusing parent witnessed violence as a child.
- The abusing parent believes in corporal punishment.
- The father is the head of the family hierarchy.
- The abusing parent has low educational attainment.
- The abusing parent has low income.
- The marital relationship is conflictual.
- The abused child may have an unusual circumstance surrounding his/her birth.
- The abused child may be considered abnormal in some way.
- The abused child may be considered difficult.

Source: Steele, 1980; Straus, 1980.

was not due to a lack of education, prevention programs, or treatment facilities available to black families. They concluded that because in the black culture it is more acceptable to use an object to hit a child with during discipline, reports of severe child abuse in black families may be expected to differ from those in the majority culture.

Sexual Abuse of Children

Sexual abuse of children occurs more frequently than the number of reported cases indicates. Researchers have found that a number of factors, including the severity and duration of the sexual abuse, influence the effects on the victim (Kilpatrick, 1987). Depending on the factors, some sexually abused persons may have severe and long-lasting effects, whereas others may have only moderate effects. The inability to maintain long-term intimate heterosexual relationships is one of the consequences of having been abused sexually as a child (Lystad, 1982). Although the majority of cases of sexual abuse are male perpetrators and female victims, there is evidence that males may also be the target of sexual abuse (Burgess, 1985).

In child sexual abuse, the home situation tends to closely parallel the home environments of other types of abusive families. Contrary to popular belief, the sexual perpetrator tends to be known by the child and commonly lives in the same household. Biological fathers are much more likely to sexually abuse an offspring than are biological mothers, and stepfathers are six times as likely to abuse stepdaughters as are biological fathers (Hodson & Skeen, 1987).

Some researchers have noted that there is a substantial difference between abuse by a biological father and abuse by a stepfather, although these differences are rarely noted in studies (Giles-Sims & Finkelhor, 1984). Not only is the frequency of sexual abuse greater by stepfathers, but some researchers also have found that the severity of the abuse is greater (Russell, 1984). Other researchers have found that the severity of the abuse does not seem to be significantly related to the biological or nonbiological relationship. A boyfriend or live-in companion of the mother has been found to be more prone to abuse the mother's daughter than either a biological father or a stepfather is (Gordon & Creighton, 1988). Regardless of whether the perpetrator is the father, the stepfather, or the boyfriend of the mother, many cases of sexual abuse go unreported to authorities because the child is not believed by other family members, especially the mother.

Researchers have found that children who are sexually abused tend to share certain characteristics. Sexually abused girls are frequently placed in an adult role very early in their lives and consequently miss out on many normal activities of growing up. This adult role also redefines to some degree the relationship with the father or the stepfather, creating a more conducive atmosphere for sexual abuse. Early exposure to the adult role is correlated with early initiation into sexual promiscuity. These factors combined with the alcohol abuse of the father or the stepfather create a high risk potential for sexual abuse to occur (Hodson & Skeen, 1987; Martin & Walters, 1982).

Other factors are also related to the risk of sexual abuse of girls. The most common scenario occurs when girls are being reared in a home in which the mother either is a single parent or is remarried. Daughters of single dating mothers tend to be at greater risk, presumably because they are exposed to less supervision and encounter more contact with older, sexually active males. In fact, in one study researchers found that father–substitutes initiate more severe sexually exploitative relationships than either biological fathers or stepfathers do (Gordon & Creighton, 1988). These high-risk girls may also experience a greater sense of loss and low self-esteem, making them vulnerable to overt sexual overtures (Hodson & Skeen, 1987).

Researchers have also found that girls at high risk for sexual abuse tend to have emotional or psychological impairment. Other developmental difficulties may also be evident, such as intellectual inadequacies or physical disabilities. These developmental impairments of high-risk girls make them vulnerable to sexual abuse and other types of exploitation (Hodson & Skeen, 1987).

Nonparental Child Abuse

Some children are abused by baby sitters and in licensed day-care centers. In a recent survey, about 2% of parents said their child was abused and 14% said their child was neglected in a licensed day-care facility (Endsley & Bradbard, 1987). In a review of reported cases of sexual abuse in licensed day-care centers, researchers have found that the ratio of sexual abuse is 5.5 cases for every 10,000 children.

Children appear to be at greater risk for sexual abuse from adolescent male baby sitters (Margolin & Craft, 1989). Specifically, the risk factor has been found to be about four times higher for adolescent males as it is for adolescent females. Adolescents in general may be more prone to abuse children because of their maturity level and confused self-identity. In general, abuse of children is related to age of the caregiver. Researchers have found that as the age of the caregiver—maternal or nonmaternal—increases, abuse decreases (Daly & Wilson, 1988).

■ *Although celebrated court cases have given the general impression that sexual abuse is rampant in day-care centers, there is little evidence to support such impression.*

In a recent study, 13% of the mothers interviewed reported that their child had been abused by a caregiver (Margolin, 1991). Adolescent caregivers were involved in 83% of the sexual abuse and 47% of the physical abuse reported in the survey. Male caregivers accounted for 71% of the sexual abuse and 42% of the physical abuse. On the other hand, males and adolescents were responsible for only 8% and 18% of neglect, respectively. The most common place for the abuse was the home of the person providing the caregiving.

The findings in the preceding study suggest that males are much more prone to abuse children than are females. Although males accounted for only 6.1% of the child care, they were responsible for 40% of the abuse. Adolescents, who provided about 8.6% of the child care, were responsible for 25% of the abuse and neglect. In addition, most cases of abuse or neglect occurred in nonlicensed home-based day-care centers rather than in licensed day-care facilities. A child was about three times more likely to be abused in a home-based day-care center than in a licensed center.

The Effects of Child Abuse

Researchers have generally found that children who are victims of abuse tend to be depressed, angry, anxious, low in self-esteem, substance abusers, and socially inept. These effects tend to be pervasive and continue to be long-term into adulthood (Browne & Finkelhor, 1986). Throughout the school-age and adolescent periods, abused children tend to have many more problems with teachers and peers than their counterparts do.

Researchers have found that children who witness their parents fighting tend to have similar profiles as children who are abused (Jaffe, Wolfe, Wilson, & Zak, 1986). This finding implies that parent modeling may be an important influence on the development of patterns of relating intimately throughout one's life.

A systems perspective of parenting suggests that the interaction between parent and child must be considered in understanding child abuse. For example, some researchers have found that children who are the victims of abuse have similar characteristics just as parents who abuse their children have similar characteristics (Bugental, Blue, & Cruzcosa, 1989). Children who have special needs for attention and those who are considered temperamental, hyperactive, or unresponsive have a higher probability of being abused than other children do. In addition, low-birth-weight and premature babies are also more likely to be abused.

A Systems Perspective of Child Abuse

A **systems perspective of child abuse** is an attempt to understand the interlocking dynamics of child abuse that contribute to its formation and maintenance in the family. As indicated earlier, most incidences of abuse are part of an ongoing pattern of parent/child interaction that intensifies over time. Systems specialists believe that both child abuse and spouse abuse represent a patterned set of behaviors that stabilize family relationships.

A systems perspective of child abuse suggests that there is a "fit" among these family factors and the incidence of abuse: the cultural background, the parent's family of origin experiences, his/her ability to handle stress and knowledge of child development, and certain child characteristics. Although parents must be held accountable for their abusive acts in the same way that other deviant behavior within the family must be made accountable, child abuse can only be understood as a recursive feedback loop that includes both parent and child factors in the formation and maintenance of abuse.

Child abuse exists within a context where a cluster of factors tend to come together. First, the cultural experience of the family may contribute to the tendency of parents to physically abuse their children. This fact has been noted by researchers who have described communities where incidences of child abuse are high as being unattractive and isolated from the general population (Garbarino & Sherman, 1980). Persons who live in such environments are more likely to form attitudes and opinions about violence that contribute greatly to the occurrence of child abuse within society. For example, in societies where corporal punishment is nonexistent, there is very little child abuse. On the other hand, in societies where corporal punishment is accepted as a way to maintain control of the child, child abuse is high (Belsky, 1980).

Second, social factors such as poverty and marital problems contribute to child abuse. The issue of family income may be related to the increase in family stress that affects all aspects of the family's functioning. Marital problems have been associated with increased child abuse because parents are generally not cooperating in parenting and because of an energy drain related to the marital problems, making them less effective in parenting.

Third, parents who abuse their children tend to have been abused or neglected in their families of origin. Those dysfunctional patterns from the family of origin in negotiating differences and understanding the feelings of others contributed to the development of family violence. Family decisions tend to be made in an atmosphere of anger, hostility, and disregard for the feelings of others. The initial occurrence of child abuse may reflect an increase in stress in the family which is decreased by the act of abuse. As child abuse continues in the family, the pattern becomes well entrenched and governed by family rules. Family rules justify and make it difficult for the family to change.

Family members ritualize the continuing experience of abuse and cannot step outside this framework for a new experience. The rule that the parent must be in control at all costs seems to apply here. Even children come to believe that they deserve the beatings they receive. The family rule about abuse and the concomitant frame of reference that it is deserved by the child limits alternative interpretations and behavioral responses. The parent sees the child as "rotten," while the child acts in a way to promote this view. The frame of reference that both the parents and the child bring to the situation prevents alternate behavior.

This frame of reference is held together by a negative feedback loop—that is, neither parent nor child can introduce new input necessary to change the system. Any new input is quickly interpreted in light of the dominant frame of reference—that is, the child deserves the harsh treatment and must be controlled in this manner. Adding to this frame of reference is the fact that children who are abused by their parents tend to share certain characteristics that set them apart from others. These characteristics are justification for believing that the frame of reference is correct and serve to bolster the negative feedback loop.

In order to change this pattern, a new frame of reference must be found in which the abuse no longer makes sense. In other words, the negative feedback pattern must give way to a positive feedback loop in which child abuse no longer makes sense. Typically, a change in feedback loops takes place when the system has difficulty handling new input because of a crisis. The shaking up of the system may be necessary to produce a new patterned response.

Fourth, the pattern of child abuse continues because it is needed to stabilize relationships in the family. In the same way that some families stabilize around the use of alcohol and drug abuse, abusive families stabilize around the episodes of violence. When tension builds in the family over time and from different sources, the scapegoated child is the target for the release of the tension. The child readily accepts this role as congruent with his/her self-image.

Another way to discuss the homeostasis is that the abuse serves to replace the equilibrium when a parent is experiencing low self-esteem. From a systems perspective, the abuse is ritualistic behavior that serves the function of reducing stress and feelings of low self-esteem. Because of the ritual involved in the abuse cycle, changing the abuse is extremely difficult.

As referred to earlier, changing the pattern of abuse is very difficult and requires much effort (Katz, Hampton, Newberger, Bowles, & Snyder, 1986). The impetus for change most often must come from outside the system. Without some input from the outside, it is likely that child abuse will continue unabated until the child leaves the family. Intervention from the outside, however, must be directed toward new and functional patterns to replace the family's old style of relating.

Recently, researchers have suggested applying a mediation model to treating adolescent child abuse (Stahler, DuCette, & Povich, 1990). The idea of mediation is to help two parties negotiate in conflict resolution. Family systems specialists believe that this type of model in treating abuse not only would offer a vehicle for change but also would be the most appropriate way to prevent abuse from occurring in the future.

Family Portrait ■■■■■■■■■■

T he Brewer family consists of Will, the father, age 45; Susan, the mother, age 41; Willie, the symptomatic son, age 13; and Breda, a daughter, age 11. Will and Susan have been married for 15 stormy years. Will had been married briefly before marrying Susan. In fact, he was married when he met Susan, and his affair with Susan contributed to the dissolution of the first marriage. In arguments he sometimes has pointed out to Susan that she caused the breakup of his first marriage. She has flatly denied this and has accused him of lying to her about being "separated" and getting divorced when she met him. This marriage was the first for Susan, and she very much wanted to hold the family together.

Susan and Will had a short courtship period of about two months before moving in together. They were both finishing college and graduate school during this period. Will had some difficulty committing to the relationship and had a number of brief affairs during the period of cohabitation. Susan believed that getting married would help their relationship, and there was also pressure from both sides of the family to marry.

The family has had some very good years and some rough times. During the years when Will and Susan cohabited, there were a number of episodes in which Will had been moderately abusive to Susan. These episodes usually centered around her confronting him about seeing another woman. The argument would escalate to the point that Will would grab her by the arm and shake her, she would slap him, and he would follow by hitting her a few times with his fist. She believed he lacked sensitivity to her needs, and he thought of her as nagging and deserving to be hit. These episodes continued into the marriage and gradually became more severe. Susan left Will a number of times during the early years of the marriage, but each time they reconciled and agreed not to fight anymore.

Susan eventually stopped confronting Will about things that would upset him, and violence was less frequent and severe. Willie, as the oldest child, was exposed to the arguments when he was younger and as he developed. He was sometimes a referee to separate his parents in arguments, especially to protect Susan. His involvement was usually a signal that things had gotten out of hand, resulting in Will regaining control over his behavior.

As Willie approached puberty, he became more difficult to handle. In the school-age years and even younger, Susan and Will used spanking as the most frequent means of discipline, believing that a good "whipping" would make him behave. These spankings have gradually increased in frequency and intensity over the years. In the past few months, Susan has been having some problems getting Willie to comply with her wishes. He sometimes hits her when she attempts to gain control over his behavior.

Will lost his job of 14 years and was unemployed for about 8 months. During this time Susan went to work to support the family. When Will found another job, he put some pressure on Susan to quit her job or at least to cut back to part-time. Susan has been unwilling to do this. The frequent episodes with Willie's noncompliant behavior are also very exacerbating for Susan. Will is not involved in the ongoing events of the family and, consequently, Susan has most of the responsibilities of discipline. Breda is considered the perfect child, and Susan confides in her for support. Although just 11 years old, Breda is very helpful to her mother and exhibits a maturity beyond her years. Willie is frequently compared negatively with his younger sister. The incident that brought this family to the attention of authorities was Susan spanking Willie severely, leaving bruises on his legs and buttocks and a hand print on his face where she slapped him. Will was out of town on a business trip when the alleged incident occurred, but upon his return hs was verbally abusive to Susan about the incident.

Compare and Contrast

An explanation for abuse in families typically concludes that one member is the perpetrator and another is the victim. In this case, Susan is the perpetrator and Willie is the victim. Traditional treatment suggestions might include placing Willie in a foster home while Susan gets help with her lack of impulse control (Patterson, 1976). She would be referred to a parents group to discuss issues related to discipline of children (Dreikurs & Soltz, 1964). Willie may also be involved in some joint counseling with his mother. There may be an attempt to include Will and Breda, but because Will travels and has not been abusive to Willie himself, it would not be necessary for him to attend counseling.

The traditional focus of parent education would be to help Susan learn to control her impulse to strike out at Willie and be less punitive in her discipline strategies (Gordon & Sands, 1978). The family situation would come into play only to give some background to the problem that Susan was experiencing in parenting. In this traditional approach there would be little emphasis on the recursive nature of family violence.

Family experts working with Susan would offer alternative discipline approaches to help her master the ability to maintain control without resorting to punitive measures. Adlerian counselors (Dreikurs & Soltz, 1964), for example, would introduce

Susan to the use of natural and logical consequences. They might also introduce her to the behavioral technique of time-out and explain in a stepwise manner the appropriate way to use it.

A systems perspective would consider the functioning of family subsystems important in the formation and maintenance of family dysfunction. In the Brewer family, the boundaries between the subsystems, especially the parental and sibling subsystems, are unclear. It appears that Susan and Will do not function in the executive position in the family hierarchy. Will seems to be only marginally functional within the family, or underfunctioning, whereas Susan appears to be overfunctioning. There is some evidence that Breda, the perfect child, functions in the hierarchy with Susan.

In general, it appears that Susan and the children function in a coalition against Will, who early in the marriage abused Susan on a number of occasions. Susan became afraid that Will would also become abusive toward the children. As Willie grew up, however, his protectiveness of his mother decreased as he gradually began to exhibit poor impulse control when disciplined.

From a systems perspective, the transactional patterns that determined how this family performed functions are important. A typical transaction in this family is for Willie to be first confronted by Will and then for Susan to come to Willie's aid because she is afraid that Will might lose his temper and strike him as he often hit her early in the relationship. Although this transaction appears to prevent violence from Susan's perspective, the outcome is the increased likelihood that violence will occur. It would be more helpful for Susan to find ways to support Will's interventions than to step in to stop them. A systems perspective would focus on how Susan becomes overwhelmed in parenting Willie and spanks him in an unsuccessful attempt to make him behave. Her abuse of Willie was unintentional. Both Will and Susan need to understand how their relationship contributes to Susan's abuse of Willie. The hierarchical structure in the family needs to be restructured so that Will and Susan are equally involved in parenting. New transactions leading to more functional outcomes need to be developed.

Parenting Proposition

Child abuse can be understood in terms of the following correlates of abuse: the characteristics of the child and the parent, the social and contextual context, and the interactional patterns between parent and child.

Answers to Test Your Knowledge

1. F	4. T
2. T	5. T
3. T	6. T

Key Concepts

victimization

family violence

socialization

corporal punishment

adolescent violence

sibling abuse

spouse abuse

intergenerational transmission of abuse

mutual violence

cycle of violence

frustration/aggression model

social learning theory

husband abuse

systems perspective of child abuse

child abuse

cycle of abuse

black family violence

sexual abuse of children

systems perspective of family violence

Study Questions

1 Discuss the correlates of abuse. Are there personality "profiles" that explain the occurrence of abuse?

2 What is adolescent abuse of parents? What has led to the increase in reported cases?

3 What factors lead to abuse of one's spouse? Discuss wife abuse. What measures could help reduce the incidence of wife abuse?

4 Are shelters helpful in reducing wife abuse?

5 What factors contribute to husband abuse? Should social policy include protection for husbands who are abused by their wives?

6 Discuss the concept of mutual violence. Should an emphasis on mutual violence influence our conception of how violence occurs in our society?

7 Discuss a systems perspective of spouse abuse.

8 What are the correlates of child abuse? Should social policy be changed to eliminate corporal punishment of children?

9 Discuss factors that contribute to children at risk for sexual abuse.

10 How would a systems approach differ from other approaches in explaining child abuse?

References

Agnew, R., & Huguley, S. (1989). Adolescent violence toward parents. *Journal of Marital and Family Therapy, 51,* 699–711.

Alexander, P. C., Moore, S., & Alexander III, P. C. (1991). Intergenerational transmission of violence. *Journal of Marriage and the Family, 53,* 657–668.

American Association for Protecting Children. (1987). *Highlights of Official Child Neglect and Abuse Reports, 1985.* Denver: American Humane Association.

Ariès, P. (1982). The sentimental revolution. *Wilson Quarterly, 6,* 46–53.

Bandura, A. (1973). *Aggression: A social learning analysis.* Englewood Cliffs, NJ: Prentice-Hall.

Belsky, J. (1980). Child mistreatment: An ecological integration. *American Psychologist, 35,* 320–335.

Berk, R. A., Newton, P. J., & Berk, S. F. (1986). What difference a day makes: An empirical study of the impact of shelters for battered women. *Journal of Marriage and the Family, 48,* 481–490.

Bernard, J. L., & Bernard, M. L. (1984). The abusive male seeking treatment: Jekyll and Hyde. *Family Relations, 32,* 283–286.

Billingham, R. E. (1987). Courtship violence: The patterns of conflict resolution strategies across seven levels of emotional commitment. *Family Relations, 36,* 283–289.

Browne, A., & Finkelhor, D. (1986). Impact of child sexual abuse: A review of the research. *Psychological Bulletin, 99,* 100–117.

Bugental, D. B., Blue, J., & Cruzcosa, M. (1989). Perceived control over caregiving outcomes: Implications for child abuse. *Developmental Psychology, 25,* 532–539.

Burgess, A. W. (1985). *The social victimization of adolescents.* Rockville, MD: U.S. Department of Health and Human Services.

Charles, A. V. (1986). Physically abused parents. *Journal of Family Violence, 4,* 343–355.

Daly, M., & Wilson, M. (1988, October). Evolutionary social psychology and family homicide. *Science, 242,* 519–524.

Dell, P. (1986). In defense of "lineal causality." *Family Process, 25,* 513–521.

de Santis, M. (1990, June). Hate crime bill excludes women. *Off Our Backs,* p. 14.

Dollard, J., Doob, L. W., Miller, N. E., Mowrer, O. H., & Sears, R. R. (1939). *Frustration and aggression.* New Haven, CT: Yale University Press.

Dreikurs, R., & Soltz, V. (1964). *Children: The Challenge.* New York: Hawthorn.

Egeland, B., Jacobvits, D., & Sroufe, L. A. (1988). Breaking the silence of abuse. *Child Development, 59,* 1080–1088.

Eisikovits, Z. C., Edleson, J. L., Guttmann, E., & Sela-Amit, M. (1991). Cognitive styles and socialized attitudes of men who batter: Where should we intervene? *Family Relations, 40,* 72–77.

Endsley, R. C., & Bradbard, M. R. (1987). Dissatisfaction with previous child care among current users of proprietary center care. *Child and Youth Care Quarterly, 16,* 249–262.

Finkelhor, D., & Yllo, K. (1985). *License to rape: Sexual abuse of wives.* New York: Holt.

Flynn, C. P. (1987). Relationship violence: A model for family practitioners. *Family Relations, 36,* 295–299.

Flynn, C. P. (1990). Relationship violence by women: Issues and Implications. *Family Relations, 39,* 194–197.

Garbarino, J., & Sherman, D. (1980). High-risk neighborhoods and high-risk families: The human ecology of child maltreatment. *Child Development, 51,* 188–198.

Gelles, R. J. (1980). Violence in the family: A review of research in the seventies. *Journal of Marriage and the Family, 42,* 873–885.

Gelles, R. J. (1982). Applying research on family violence to clinical practice. *Journal of Marriage and the Family, 44,* 9–20.

Gelles, R. J., & Cornell, C. P. (1985). *Intimate violence in families.* Beverly Hills, CA: Sage.

Gelles, R. J., & Maynard, P. E. (1987). A structural family systems approach to intervention in cases of family violence. *Family Relations, 36,* 270–275.

Giles-Sims, J. (1983). *Wife battering: A systems theory approach.* New York: Guilford Press.

Giles-Sims, J., & Finkelhor, D. (1984). Child abuse in stepfamilies. *Family Relations, 33,* 407–413.

Gordon, M., & Creighton, S. J. (1988). Natal and non-natal fathers as sexual abusers in the United Kingdom: A comparative analysis. *Journal of Marriage and the Family, 50,* 99–105.

Gordon, T., & Sands, J. (1978). *P.E.T. in action.* New York: Bantam.

Gross, D. R., & Robinson, S. E. (1987). Ethics, violence and counseling: Hear no evil, see no evil, speak no evil? *Journal of Counseling and Development, 65,* 340–344.

Hampton, R. L., Gelles, R. J., & Harrop, J. W. (1989). Is violence in black families increasing? A comparison of 1975 and 1985 National Survey Rates. *Journal of Marriage and the Family, 51,* 969–980.

Hodson, D., & Skeen, P. (1987). Child sexual abuse: A review of the research and theory with implications for family life educators. *Family Relations, 36,* 215–221.

House, J. S., Umberson, D., & Landis, K. R. (1988). Structures and processes of social support. *Annual Review of Sociology, 14,* 293–318.

Hudson, M. F. (1986). Elder mistreatment: Current research. In K. A. Pillemer & R. S. Wolf (Eds.), *Elder Abuse: Conflict in the family.* Dover, MA: Auburn House.

Imber-Black, E. (1986). Maybe lineal causality needs another defense lawyer: A feminist response to Dell, *Family Process, 25,* 1–12.

Jaffe, P., Wolfe, D., Wilson, S., & Zak, L. (1986). Similarities in behavioral and social maladjustment among child victims and witnesses to family violence. *American Journal of Orthopsychiatry, 56,* 142–145.

Kalmuss, D. S. (1984). The intergenerational transmission of marital aggression. *Journal of Marriage and the Family, 46,* 11–19.

Kalmuss, D. S., & Straus, M. A. (1982). Wife's marital dependency and wife abuse. *Journal of Marriage and the Family, 44,* 277–286.

Katz, M. H., Hampton, R. L., Newberger, E. H., Bowles, R. T., & Snyder, J. C. (1986). Returning children home: Clinical decision making in child abuse and neglect. *American Journal of Orthopsychiatry, 56* 253–262.

Kaufman, J., & Zigler, E. (1987). Do abused children become abusive parents? *American Journal of Orthopsychiatry, 57,* 186–191.

Kilpatrick, A. C. (1987). Childhood sexual experiences: Problems and issues in studying long-range effects. *Journal of Sex Research, 22,* 221–242.

Lystad, M. (1982). Sexual abuse in the home: A review of the literature. *International Journal of Family Psychiatry, 3,* 13–31.

Makepeace, J. M. (1986). Gender differences in courtship violence victimization. *Family Relations, 35,* 383–388.

Makepeace, J. M. (1987). Social factors and victim–offender differences in courtship violence. *Family Relations, 36,* 87–91.

Malone, J., Tyree, A., & O'Leary, K. D. (1989). Generalization and containment: Different effects of past aggression for wives and husbands. *Journal of Marriage and the Family, 51,* 687–698.

Margolin, L. (1991). Abuse and neglect in nonparental child care. *Journal of Marriage and the Family, 53,* 694–704.

Margolin, L., & Craft, J. L. (1989). Child sexual abuse by caretakers. *Family Relations, 38,* 450–455.

Martin, M., & Walters, J. (1982). Familial correlates of selected types of child abuse and neglect. *Journal of Marriage and the Family, 44,* 267–276.

O'Leary, K. D., & Curley, A. D. (1986). Assertion and family violence: Correlates of spouse abuse. *Journal of Marital and Family Therapy, 12,* 281–289.

Olson, D. H., Russell, C. S., & Sprenkle, D. H. (1983). Circumplex model of marital and family systems: VI. Theoretical update. *Family Process, 22,* 69 83.

Pagelow, M. D. (1984). *Family violence.* New York: Praeger.

Patterson, G. R. (1975). *Families: Application of social learning theory to family life* (rev. ed.). Champaign, IL: Research Press.

Peek, C. W., Fischer, J. L., & Kidman, J. S. (1985). Teenage violence toward parents: A neglected dimension of family violence. *Journal of Marriage and the Family, 47,* 1051–1058.

Rice, F. P. (1989). *Human sexuality.* Dubuque, IA: William C. Brown.

Roscoe, B., & Benaske, N. (1985). Courtship violence experienced by abused wives: Similarities in patterns of abuse. *Family Relations, 34,* 419–424.

Russell, D. E. H. (1984). The prevalence and seriousness of incestuous abuse: Stepfathers vs. biological fathers. *Child Abuse and Neglect, 8,* 15–22.

Scher, M., & Stevens, M. (1987). Men and violence. *Journal of Counseling and Development, 65,* 351–355.

Sigelman, C. K., Berry, C. J., & Wiles, K. A. (1984). Violence in college students' relationships. *Journal of Applied Social Psychology, 5,* 530–548.

Snell, J. E., Rosenwald, R. J., & Robey, A. (1964). The wifebeater's wife: A study of family interaction. *Archives of General Psychiatry, 11,* 107–113.

Stahler, G. J., DuCette, J. P., & Povich, E. (1990). Using mediation to prevent child maltreatment: An exploratory study. *Family Relations, 39,* 317–322.

Steele, B. F. (1980). Psychodynamic factors in child abuse. In C. H. Kempe and R. Helfer (Eds.), *The battered child* (pp 235-257). Chicago: University of Chicago Press.

Stets, J. E. (1991). Role of social isolation in aggression among cohabitating partners. *Journal of Marriage and the Family, 53,* 669–680.

Straus, M. A. (1980). Victims and aggressors in marital violence. *American Behavioral Scientist, 23,* 681–704.

Straus, M. A., & Gelles, R. J. (1986). Sociological change and change in family violence from 1975 to 1985 as revealed by two national surveys. *Journal of Marriage and the Family, 48,* 465–479.

Straus, M. A., Gelles, R. J., & Steinmetz, S. K. (1980). *Behind closed doors: Violence in the American family.* Garden City, NY: Doubleday/Anchor.

Tan, G. G., Ray, M. P., & Cate, R. (1991). Migrant farm child abuse and neglect. *Family Relations, 40,* 84–90.

Telch, C. F., & Lindquist, C. U. (1984). Violent versus nonviolent couples: A comparison of patterns. *Psychotherapy, 21,* 242–248.

Thompson, W. E. (1987). Courtship violence: Toward a conceptual understanding. *Youth and Society, 18,* 162–176.

Trickett, P. K., & Sussman, E. J. (1988). Parental perceptions of child-rearing practices in physically abusive and nonabusive families. *Developmental Psychology, 24,* 270–276.

Umberson, D. (1987). Family status and health behavior: Social control as a dimension of social integration. *Journal of Health and Social Behavior, 28,* 306–319.

U.S. Department of Health, Education, and Welfare, Office of Human Development/Office of Child Development, Children's Bureau/National Center of Child Abuse and Neglect. (1975). *Child abuse and neglect: The problem and its management* (DHEW Publication No. OHD 75-30073).

Walker, L. E. (1984). *The battered woman syndrome.* New York: Springer.

Zigler, E. (1979). Controlling child abuse in America: An effort doomed to fail? In P. Bourne and E. Newberger (Eds.), *Critical Perspective on Child Abuse.* Lexington, MA: Lexington Books.

Credits

This page constitutes an extension of the copyright page. We have made every effort to trace the ownership of all copyrighted material and to secure permission from copyright holders. In the event of any question arising as to the use of any material, we will be pleased to make the necessary corrections in future printings. Thanks are due to the following authors, publishers, and agents for permission to use the material indicated.

8: Figure 1.1, adapted from *Families and Family Therapy*, by S. Minuchin. Copyright © 1974 by Harvard University Press. **14:** Figure 1.3, from *Living Systems*, by J. G. Miller, p. 36. Copyright © 1978 by McGraw-Hill. Reprinted by permission. **16:** Case of Mrs. Smith, from *Family Therapy and Beyond*, by S. Henggeler and C. Borduin, p. 14. Copyright © 1989 by Brooks/Cole Publishing Co. **19:** Figure 1.5, based on *Family Therapy in Clinical Practice*, by M. Bowen. Copyright © 1978 by Aronson. **79:** from "Client-Centered Skills-Training Programs for the Family: A Review of the Literature," by R. F. Levant. In *Counseling Psychologist*, 1983, p. 41. Reprinted by permission of Sage Publications, Inc. **83:** Summary, from *The Process of Parenting* (2nd ed.), by Jane Brooks, pp. 76–77. Copyright © 1987 by Mayfield Publishing Co. Reprinted by permission. **115:** Box 4.1, from "Child Development," by K. Lyons-Ruth, D. B. Connell, H. U. Grunebaum, and S. Botein, in *Child Development, 61,* 85–98. Copyright © 1990 by University of Chicago Press. Reprinted by permission. **121:** Box 4.2, from "Preventive Intervention and Outcome with Anxiously Attached Dyads," by A. F. Lieberman, D. R. Weston, and J. H. Pawl. In *Child Development, 62,* 199–209. Copyright © 1991 by the University of Chicago Press. Reprinted by permission. **147:** Box 5.1, from "Children's Language Acquisition," by M. L. Rice. In *American Psychologist, 44,* 149–156. Copyright © 1989 by the American Psychological Association. **155:** Table 5.2, adapted from "The Development of the Concept of Death in Childhood: A Review of the Literature," by M. Stambrook and K. C. H. Parker. In *Merrill-Palmer Quarterly,* 1989, *33,* 133–157. **156:** Box 5.2, from "Social Relationships and Their Developmental Significance," by W. W. Hartup. In *American Psychologist, 44,* 120–126. Copyright © 1989 by the American Psychological Association. **179:** Box 6.1, from "Young Children's Understanding of Changes in their Mental States," by A. Gopnik and V. Slaughter. In *Child Development, 62,* 98–110. Copyright © 1991 by the University of Chicago Press. Reprinted by permission. **188:** Excerpt, from *Path with a Heart: Ericksonian Utilization with Resistant and Chronic Clients,* by Y. M. Dolan. Copyright © 1985 by Brunner/Mazel. Reprinted by permission of the author. **189:** Excerpt, from *Therapeutic Communication with Children: The Mutual Storytelling Technique,* by R. A. Gardner. Copyright © 1971 by Science House. **194:** Story from *Two Trees in the Forest,* an unpublished manuscript by L. W. Crews, 1985. Reprinted by permission. **214:** Box 7.1, from "Linking Maternal Employment Patterns to Mother-Child Activities and Children Competencies," by M. J. Moorehouse. In *Developmental Psychology, 27,* 295–303. Copyright © 1989 by the University of Chicago Press. Reprinted by permission. **217:** Box 7.2, from "Child-Mother Attachment of Six-Year-Olds and the Social Competence at School," by D. A. Cohn. In *Child Development, 61,* 152–162. Copyright © 1990 by the University of Chicago Press. Reprinted by permission. **257:** Table 8.1, from U.S. Bureau of the Census: *Statistical Abstracts of the United States, 1989* (109th ed.), U.S. Government Printing Office. **262:** Box 8.1, from "Adolescent Separation-Individuation and Family Transitions," by

J. A. Daniels. In *Adolescence, 25,* 105–116. Copyright © 1990 by Libra Publication. Reprinted by permission. **264:** Table 8.2, from National Center for Health Statistics: *Vital Statistics of the United States, 1986: Vol. 2. Mortality, Part A* (DHHS Publication No. PHS 88-122) U.S. Government Printing Office. **281:** Table 9.1, adapted from "Growing Up a Little Faster: The Experience of Growing Up in a Single-Parent Household," by R. Weiss. In *Journal of Social Issues,* 1979, *35,* 97–111. **282:** Box 9.1, based on U.S. Census study: "Women Who Remain Above the Poverty Level in Divorce: Implications for Family Policy," by T. A. Mauldin. In *Family Relations,* 1990, *39,* 141–146. **289:** Table 9.2, adapted from *Intimate Relationships, Marriages, and Families,* by F. P. Rice. Copyright © 1990 by Mayfield Publishing Co. **309:** Table 10.1, from "Attitudes and Responses of Parents to Pre-adolescent Masturbation," by J. H. Gagnon. In *Archives of Sexual Behavior,* 1985, *14,* 451–466. **316:** Box 10.1, from "Black Grandmothers in Multigenerational Households: Diversity in Family Structure and Parenting Involvement in Woodlawn Community," by J. L. Pearson, A. G. Hunter, M. E. Ensinger, and S. G. Kellan. In *Child Development, 61,* 334–342. Copyright © 1990 by the University of Chicago Press. Reprinted by permission. **343:** Table 11.1, based on "A New Policy Initiative: Infants and Toddlers with Handicapped Conditions," by J. J. Gallagher. In *American Psychologist,* 1989, *44,* 387–391. **352:** Table 11.2, based on "Friendship Patterns in Highly Intelligent Children," by P. M. Janos and N. M. Robinson. In Special Issue: Counseling Gifted Persons: A Lifelong Concern, *Roeper-Review,* 1985, *8,* 46–49. **353:** Box 11.1, from "Making It Through Parenting," by P. L. Hollingsworth. In *Gifted Child Today,* May/June 1990, 2–7. Reprinted by permission. **356:** Box 11.2, adapted from "Intergenerational Play: Influences on Creativity Throughout the Lifespan," by D. Bergen. In *The Creative Child and Adult Quarterly,* 1989, *14,* 230–238. **377:** Table 12.1, from *The Battered Woman Syndrome,* by L. E. Walker. Copyright © 1984 by Springer Publishing Co., Inc. **391:** Box 12.1, from "Cognitive Styles and Socialized Attitudes of Men Who Batter: Where Should We Intervene?" by Z. C. Eisikovits, J. L. Edleson, E. Guttmann, and M. Sela-Amit. In *Family Relations,* 1991, *40,* 72–77. **387:** Box 12.2, based on "Migrant Farm Child Abuse and Neglect," by G. G. Tan, M. P. Ray, and R. Cote. In *Family Relations,* 1991, *40,* 84–90.

Photo Credits

Name Index